Narrative Criticism of the New Testament

An Introduction

James L. Resseguie

BakerAcademic
Grand Rapids, Michigan

Published by Baker Academic
a division of Baker Publishing Group
P.O. Box 6287, Grand Rapids, MI 49516-6287
www.bakeracademic.com

Printed in the United States of America

Library of Congress Cataloging-in-Publication Data
Resseguie, James L.
Narrative criticism of the New Testament : an introduction / James L. Resseguie.
p. cm.
Includes bibliographical references and index.
ISBN 0-8010-2789-6 (pbk.)
1. Bible. N.T.—Criticism, Narrative. I. Title.
BS2377.3.R47 2005
225.6′6—dc22 2005023440

Narrative Criticism of the New Testament

For my students and colleagues at
Winebrenner Theological Seminary

Contents

Illustrations

Preface

My first foray into literary criticism occurred in the summer of 1979 at a National Endowment for the Humanities Institute on the "Bible as Literature" at Indiana University. I remember being captivated by Kenneth R. R. Gros Louis's close readings of complex texts. His line-by-line, sometimes word-by-word analysis brought out the sublime beauty of John Donne's poem "Good Friday, 1613: Riding Westward," the artistry of George Herbert's "Easter Wings," and the complex nuances of James Joyce's *A Portrait of the Artist as a Young Man*. It was refreshing to study the works on their own terms as literature and to discover how the parts were connected, modifying and enriching one another to form a unified whole. At the time, I wondered why this method was not taught in departments of religion and at theological seminaries in this country. Part of the reason, I suppose, is that a whole generation of students and teachers has not been trained in doing close readings—a gap this book modestly aims to fill. Another reason is that close readings were waning in departments of literature at colleges and universities just as they were attracting attention among biblical scholars. This unfortunate confluence makes the method appear passé to some biblical scholars. This book attempts to show the merits of close readings for biblical studies and its applicability to New Testament exegesis.

Once I learned how to do close readings, I never turned back. Other methods of biblical interpretation could not offer the freshness and excitement of reading a New Testament narrative on its own terms. To discover the artistry of a New Testament narrative was like discovering a whole new world.

In chapter 1 of this book, narrative criticism is defined, the role of the reader is described, and the benefits of literary analysis are outlined. An analysis of Vincent van Gogh's painting *The Good Samaritan* shows that how we read a painting is similar to how we read a narrative text. Just as an analysis of a painting relies on close observation—attending to perspective, colors, characters, and more—so also narrative criticism relies on observation of what is in a text—its characters, rhetoric, and point of view.

Chapter 2 describes the rhetorical features of narratives. Specific rhetorical devices such as simile and metaphor and irony and double entendre delight the imagination and persuade us of the narrative's point of view. This chapter shows what to look for in reading the rhetoric of a narrative.

Chapter 3 turns to the role of setting in narrative analysis. Topographical, architectural, social-cultural, and religious settings are more than mere background for a narrative. Just as the arrangement of furniture in a classroom, for instance, suggests a relationship between student and teacher, so settings express a narrative point of view. We will look at the masterful way Ernest Hemingway uses setting to tell his story in "Hills Like White Elephants," and then we will apply the same technique of analysis to New Testament narratives.

Chapter 4 is about characters and characterization. What a character says or does reveals a character's traits. Narrative commentary such as asides to the reader and inside views into a character's thoughts and feelings also add to characterization. Frequently, the point of a narrative can be found in the changes a character undergoes in a narrative. We will look at Kate Chopin's "The Story of an Hour" to see how a protagonist's development clarifies and amplifies the point of the story. Then we will turn our attention to the way the development of characters in the New Testament reveals a narrative's theme or point of view.

Chapter 5 is devoted to point of view. This often used but little understood concept offers a glimpse into the narrator's worldview and ideological perspective. While some characters within the narrative support the narrative point of view, others represent a counter point of view. A reading of a short story by Kate Chopin, "Ripe Figs," shows the importance of point of view for narrative analysis and how it can help decipher the point of a story.

Chapter 6 explores the place of plot in narrative analysis. Plot is the narrative organization and structure that reveals the conflicts, themes, and point of view of a narrative. Generally speaking, New Testament plots are either U-shaped or inverted U-shaped structures. A U-shaped plot begins with a stable condition that moves downward towards disaster, but a reversal in the plot turns the direction upward to a new stable condition. In an inverted U-shape structure, the plot moves upward to prosperity, but a reversal in the character's condition turns the plot downward to adversity. We will look at a typical U-shaped plot that moves downward to disaster and then upward to a new stable condition: the book of Revelation. An analysis of the woodcuts by Albrecht Dürer accents the mystery, surprise, suspense, and characters' dilemmas within this plot.

Chapter 7 takes the reader on a concluding tour through the various steps of narrative criticism. Questions concerning rhetoric, setting, character, point of view, and plot are listed. Finally an analysis of the story of Nicodemus in the Gospel of John puts together all the steps of narrative criticism.

I owe a debt of gratitude to many who have made this book possible. Numerous grants from the National Endowment for the Humanities allowed me to study literary criticism and literary theory at some outstanding universities in this country. I am especially grateful to those seminar leaders who encouraged me to apply literary criticism and theory to the New Testament: James Ackerman, Calum Carmichael, David Daube, Kenneth R. R. Gros Louis, Giles Gunn, Herbert Lindenberger, and James Phelan. In 1990, the University of Iceland invited me to teach literary approaches to the New Testament as a Fulbright scholar. It was during that semester that the fundamentals of this book were formulated. I am grateful for the encouragement of my editor, James D. Ernest, and the other editors at Baker Academic Books to write this book. Dr. Ernest's numerous and helpful suggestions greatly improved the quality of this work. I thank my research assistant, Jeannine Grimm, whose enthusiasm for the project and helpful comments made this a more readable book, and the library staff at Winebrenner Theological Seminary and the University of Findlay, who helped make this book possible. I also thank my wife, Dianne, whose generosity of spirit is a constant source of encouragement. Finally, I dedicate this book to my students and colleagues at Winebrenner Theological Seminary, who make teaching at Winebrenner a delight.

Ash Wednesday, 2005
Findlay, Ohio

Abbreviations

AB	Anchor Bible
ABD	*Anchor Bible Dictionary*. Edited by D. N. Freedman. 6 vols. New York: Doubleday, 1992.
AnBib	Analecta Biblica
BDAG	*Greek-English Lexicon of the New Testament and Other Early Christian Literature*. 3rd ed. Edited by F. W. Danker. Chicago: University of Chicago Press, 1999.
BETL	Bibliotheca Ephemeridum Theologicarum Lovaniensium
BibInt	*Biblical Interpretation*
BIS	Biblical Interpretation Series
BS	Biblical Seminar
BTB	*Biblical Theology Bulletin*
CBQ	*Catholic Biblical Quarterly*
EDB	*Eerdmans Dictionary of the Bible*. Edited by David Noel Freedman. Grand Rapids: Eerdmans, 2000.
EDNT	*Exegetical Dictionary of the New Testament*. Edited by H. Balz, G. Schneider. ET. Grand Rapids: Eerdmans, 1990–1993.
EpCom	Epworth Commentaries
ETL	*Ephemerides theologicae lovanienses*
ExpT	*Expository Times*
FF	Foundations and Facets
HNTC	Harper's New Testament Commentaries
IDB	*The Interpreter's Dictionary of the Bible*. Edited by G. A. Buttrick. 4 vols. Nashville: Abingdon, 1962.
Int	*Interpretation*

ISBL	Indiana Studies in Biblical Literature
JAAR	*Journal of the American Academy of Religion*
JBL	*Journal of Biblical Literature*
JR	*Journal of Religion*
JSNT	*Journal for the Study of the New Testament*
JSNTSup	Journal for the Study of the New Testament: Supplement Series
JSOT	*Journal for the Study of the Old Testament*
JSOTSup	Journal for the Study of the Old Testament: Supplement Series
LCBI	Literary Currents in Biblical Interpretation
LCL	Loeb Classical Library
LitTh	*Literature and Theology: An Interdisciplinary Journal of Theory and Criticism*
MNTC	Moffatt New Testament Commentary
NIBCNT	New International Biblical Commentary on the New Testament
NICNT	New International Commentary on the New Testament
NLH	*New Literary History*
NovT	*Novum Testamentum*
NTS	*New Testament Studies*
NTT	New Testament Theology
OBT	Overtures to Biblical Theology
RNBC	Readings: A New Biblical Commentary
SBLDS	Society of Biblical Literature Dissertation Series
SBLMS	Society of Biblical Literature Monograph Series
SBT	Studies in Biblical Theology
SNTSMS	Society for New Testament Studies Monograph Series
ST	Studies and Texts
THL	Theory and History of Literature
TDNT	*Theological Dictionary of the New Testament*. Edited by G. Kittel and G. Friedrich. Translated by G. W. Bromiley. 10 vols. Grand Rapids: Eerdmans, 1964–1976.
TPINTC	Trinity Press International New Testament Commentaries
WBC	Word Biblical Commentary
ZNW	*Zeitschrift für die neutestamentliche Wissenschaft und die Kunde der älteren Kirche*
ZSNT	Zacchaeus Studies: New Testament

1

Introducing Narrative Criticism

1.1 Definition

Approaches to the study of the New Testament have greatly expanded over the past decade, providing an exciting but also bewildering array of methods. Newer methods—that is, newer than historical criticism—frame different questions and offer new ways of looking at familiar texts. Like the interloper at Simon the Pharisee's party in Luke 7:36–50, the newer approaches slip in unnoticed and upset the status quo with vexing indecorum. While everyone is enjoying the festivities of business as usual, these methods offer unsettling interpretive acts that infuse originality and excitement into biblical studies. As the interlopers proceed to make others uncomfortable with their out-of-the-ordinary textual moves, the party grinds to a halt. Some guests cast a scornful eye upon this affront to traditional, proven methodologies. Others sit at the table in stunned amazement, pretending not to notice what is happening. But others welcome the new approaches as creative and fresh ways of reviving scriptures that have long been domesticated by more staid techniques. One of the newer approaches, feminist criticism, turns a corrective eye to the subtle—and sometimes not so subtle—patriarchal readings of the New Testament.[1] It reminds us that gender is an important analytical

1. Sandra M. Schneiders, "Feminist Hermeneutics," in *Hearing the New Testament: Strategies for Interpretation*, ed. Joel B. Green (Grand Rapids: Eerdmans, 1995), 349–69; Danna Nolan Fewell, "Reading the Bible Ideologically: Feminist Criticism," in *To Each Its Own Meaning: An Introduction to Biblical Criticisms and Their Application*, ed. Stephen R. Haynes and Steven L. McKenzie (Louisville: Westminster John Knox, 1993), 237–51; Tina Pippin, "Ideological Criticisms, Liberation Criticisms, and Womanist and Feminist Criticisms," in *Handbook to Exegesis of the New Testament*, ed. Stanley E. Porter (Leiden:

category in the interpretation of the New Testament. Postcolonial biblical criticism unsettles the party with a reminder that the New Testament developed within—and at times in opposition to—the imperial domination of the Roman Empire in the first century. To the shock of those who expected the banquet to go on as usual, postcolonial approaches point out new forms of imperialism (even among the invited guests) and expose jaded Eurocentric perspectives that cloud the understanding of the New Testament.[2] Deconstructive criticism adds mischief to the festivities by reveling in language's inherent instability.[3] Wordplays and clever readings create a spectacle with stodgy traditionalists. Narrative criticism, which has been an interloper to the historical-critical party since the 1980s, adds to the confusion by welcoming the methods and techniques that secular literary critics apply to novels and short stories.

Narrative criticism[4] focuses on how biblical literature works as *literature*.[5] The "what" of a text (its content) and the "how" of a text (its

---

Brill, 1997), 267–76; Janice Capel Anderson, "Reading Tabitha: A Feminist Reception History," in *The New Literary Criticism and the New Testament*, ed. Edgar V. McKnight and Elizabeth Struthers Malbon (Valley Forge: Trinity, 1994), 108–44.

2. See, for example, R. S. Sugirtharajah, ed., *The Postcolonial Bible* (Sheffield: Sheffield Academic Press, 1998); J. R. Levison and P. Pope-Levison, *Jesus in Global Contexts* (Louisville: Westminster John Knox, 1992); R. S. Sugirtharajah, ed., *Voices from the Margins: Interpreting the Bible in the Third World* (Maryknoll, N.Y.: Orbis, 1991); Cain Hope Felder, ed., *Stony the Road We Trod: African American Biblical Interpretation* (Minneapolis: Augsburg Fortress, 1991).

3. Stephen D. Moore, *Poststructuralism and the New Testament: Derrida and Foucault at the Foot of the Cross* (Minneapolis: Fortress, 1994); idem, *Mark and Luke in Poststructuralist Perspectives: Jesus Begins to Write* (New Haven: Yale University Press, 1992); George Aichele et al., eds., *The Postmodern Bible: The Bible and Culture Collective* (New Haven: Yale University Press, 1995); David Seeley, *Deconstructing the New Testament*, BIS 5 (Leiden: Brill, 1994); Wallace W. Bubar, "Killing Two Birds with One Stone: The Utter De(con)struction of Matthew and His Church," *BibInt* 3 (1995): 144–57.

4. The term "narrative criticism" was used by David Rhoads in an article "Narrative Criticism and the Gospel of Mark," *JAAR* 50 (1982): 411–34; repr. in David Rhoads, *Reading Mark, Engaging the Gospel* (Minneapolis: Fortress, 2004), chapter 1. Narrative criticism and literary criticism are used interchangeably in this book since secular modern literary critics and theorists do not use the term "narrative criticism." For a general overview of literary approaches to the New Testament see David E. Aune, "Narrative Criticism," in *The Westminster Dictionary of New Testament and Early Christian Literature and Rhetoric* (Louisville: Westminster John Knox, 2003), 315–17; Stanley E. Porter, "Literary Approaches to the New Testament: From Formalism to Deconstruction and Back," in *Approaches to New Testament Study*, ed. Stanley E. Porter and David Tombs, JSNTSup 120 (Sheffield: Sheffield Academic Press, 1995), 77–128; Aichele et al., *The Postmodern Bible*, chapter 2; Petri Merenlahti and Raimo Hakola, "Reconceiving Narrative Criticism," in *Characterization in the Gospels: Reconceiving Narrative Criticism*," ed. David Rhoads and Kari Syreeni, JSNTSup 184 (Sheffield: Sheffield Academic Press, 1999), 13–48; Petri Merenlahti, *Poetics for the Gospels? Rethinking Narrative Criticism* (London: T. & T. Clark, 2002).

5. On introductions to narrative or literary criticism of the Bible see Elizabeth Struthers Malbon, "Narrative Criticism: How Does the Story Mean?" in *Mark & Method:*

rhetoric and structure) are analyzed as a complete tapestry, an organic whole. Narrative critics are primarily concerned with the literariness of biblical narratives—that is, the qualities that make them literature. Form and content are generally regarded as an indissoluble whole. Narrative criticism is a shift away from traditional historical-critical methods to the way a text communicates meaning as a self-contained unit, a literary artifact, an undivided whole. Historical, sociological, and anthropological approaches to the Bible seek to uncover the meaning of a text in its original context and for its original audience. What did the text mean to the hearers/readers in a Greco-Roman society, for instance? What is the repertoire of cultural, linguistic, and historical assumptions that shaped the text?[6] Although a biblical narrative critic also considers these questions important, the primary focus of a literary approach is on the formal features of a text in its finished form.

Literary criticism examines biblical narratives using the same methods and techniques that critics use to study the short stories of Kate Chopin and Ernest Hemingway, or the novels of Toni Morrison and the plays of William Shakespeare. It may seem strange to apply the techniques of modern literary criticism to a corpus of literature that for many is a religious foundation for beliefs, values, and norms. Yet biblical narrative literature exhibits literary characteristics that are also apparent in literature in general: characters, rhetoric, style, syntax, plot, imagery, setting, tone, point of view, narrators, and much more. Narrative critics recognize that the types of questions literary scholars ask of secular literature are also important to ask of biblical literature.

Some of these questions concern the shape and structure of a narrative. How does a narrative begin? How does it end? Matthew's Gospel, for instance, begins differently from that of Mark or Luke. Why does the

---

New Approaches in Biblical Studies, ed. Janice Capel Anderson and Stephen D. Moore (Minneapolis: Fortress, 1992), 23–49; Mark Allan Powell, *What Is Narrative Criticism?* (Minneapolis: Fortress, 1990); idem, *The Bible and Modern Literary Criticism: A Critical Assessment and Annotated Bibliography* (Westport, Conn.: Greenwood, 1992), 3–19; Daniel Marguerat and Yvan Bourquin, *How to Read Bible Stories: An Introduction to Narrative Criticism* (London: SCM, 1999); Robert Alter, *The Art of Biblical Narrative* (New York: Basic Books, 1981), 3–22; Michael Fishbane, *Text and Texture: Close Readings of Selected Biblical Texts* (New York: Schocken Books, 1979); Kenneth R. R. Gros Louis, *Literary Interpretations of Biblical Narratives*, 2 vols. (Nashville: Abingdon, 1974–1982); Wesley A. Kort, *Story, Text, and Scripture: Literary Interests in Biblical Narrative* (University Park, Pa.: Pennsylvania State University Press, 1988); David Rhoads, Joanna Dewey, and Donald Michie, *Mark as Story: An Introduction to the Narrative of a Gospel*, 2nd ed. (Minneapolis: Fortress, 1999).

6. "Repertoire" is Wolfgang Iser's term. See his *The Act of Reading: A Theory of Aesthetic Response* (Baltimore: Johns Hopkins, 1978), 69: "The repertoire consists of all the familiar territory within the text. This may be in the form of references to earlier works, or to social and historical norms, or to the whole culture from which the text has emerged."

narrator include a journey to Egypt rather than beginning his narrative some other way? And what does the beginning say about the overall point of view of the First Gospel? What patterns develop within a narrative? Are there repeated words or phrases that alert the reader to a narrative structure? Are repeated scenes used to develop a theme or motif? Why is Peter's vision, for instance, recorded three times in Acts, and why is Cornelius's vision repeated four times? And why are the visions sometimes recorded in great detail and other times in summary form?

A narrative critic is alert to rhetorical devices that may thicken and deepen the nuances of a text. Does the narrator use irony to emphasize a particular point of view, or to heighten a discrepancy between a familiar way and a new way of seeing the world? For instance, a mocking, satirical salute ("Hail, King of the Jews") turns upon itself and reveals the truth from an unlikely source. What images, symbols, paradoxes, or metaphors are present in the text? How do the ambiguities of words such as the Fourth Gospel's "born again/from above" complicate the nuances of a narrative? How can we know the narrative point of view and how is it expressed? Is there a point of view that the narrator wants the reader to adopt, and how does the narrator influence the reader to accept that perspective?

A narrative critic is attentive to the role of characters and their characterization. Characters, like us, reveal who they are in what they say and do. Their speech and actions are open windows to their biases, concerns, values, and worldview. A critic is also interested in the physical and spiritual changes, if any, that a character undergoes. What events, conflicts, and encounters contribute to the change? At what point in the narrative does a character develop? Is a recognition scene present in which a character awakens to his or her circumstances and averts disaster? In the parable of the Prodigal Son, for example, the younger son "came to himself" (Luke 15:17) and realized that home was better than a "distant country." What do characters say and do? And, just as important, how do they say it? The woman who anoints and washes Jesus' feet says nothing but her actions speak volumes. How do the characters speak about each other, or react to others? What tone is implied in their speech? Is it affirming or disparaging? Puzzled or amazed? Is the character lifelike, with several (perhaps conflicting) traits, or is the character one-dimensional, with few traits?

The narrator also provides important information for the reader, if only we know what to look for. What titles or epithets (descriptive phrases) does the narrator use for characters? The disciples may appear dense and the religious leaders disgruntled, but it is unlikely that we would know that without the narrator offering inside views or asides concerning the characters' thoughts and views toward Jesus. The narrator also provides an evaluative context to assess characters' actions and speech. What judgments or evaluations does the narrator make concerning characters and events? What beliefs, norms, values, and general worldview does the narrator want the reader to adopt? If the narrator writes to persuade the reader to view the world differently, how can we know what the narrator wants us to "see"? A narrator makes choices, provides options, and offers alternatives in the selection of scenes, in what characters say, in the settings elaborated, and in the interaction with other characters. A narrative critic is alert to the choices, options, and alternatives a narrator makes, and asks why a narrator chooses one scene over another, or develops one metaphor instead of another, or slows down or accelerates the narrative pace.

Narrative critics pay attention to the background or setting of narrative events. Are the settings symbolic? Do they recall events from Israel's past? A literary critic considers the importance of the place where events occur: on a mountain, in the desert, by the sea, on a housetop, in a synagogue, and so forth. A narrative critic is equally alert to temporal settings that may be significant for the interpretation of a narrative. Nicodemus comes to Jesus by night; Judas departs at night. Jesus heals on a Sabbath, makes epic pronouncements at the high point of a festival, and goes to the cross during Passover.

What conflicts develop in a narrative and how are they resolved? Conflicts may occur in several different arenas: battles with the supernatural forces of evil, conflicts within oneself or with society in general, conflicts with nature, conflicts between characters. The religious authorities and Jesus are at loggerheads over issues involving healing on the Sabbath and what is clean or unclean. Why is the point of view of the scribes and Pharisees at odds with that of Jesus? And why is rapprochement impossible? What is the outcome of the conflict? A narrative critic is aware of the conflict not only from Jesus' point of view but also from the point of view of the opposition. A more sympathetic and realistic reading of the religious authorities occurs when we understand their objection to Jesus' actions from their point of view.[7]

1.2 Narrative Criticism and New Criticism

One of the formative influences upon narrative criticism is New Criticism. Although New Criticism is now discredited for its excesses and considered passé among literary critics, including biblical literary

7. Rhoads, *Reading Mark*, chapter 6, does this very well in "Crossing Boundaries: Purity and Defilement in Mark."

critics,[8] two contributions of the New Critics significantly influenced the development of narrative criticism: (1) New Critics argue that the text is an organic whole, a unity that needs to be examined on its own terms, and (2) New Critics pay close attention to the words on a page, offering detailed and often painstaking analyses of texts called "analytical criticism," "*explication de texte*," or "close readings."[9]

Unity and Coherence of the Text

New Criticism is a theory and practice that developed between the two world wars and dominated literary criticism until the Vietnam War.[10] It opposed common literary practices of that era that focused upon biographies and psychological histories of authors—background information in general. It also opposed literary methods that focused upon the effects or results of a literary artifact on its readers. New Critics insisted that the proper concern of literary analysis was the text itself and not the external circumstances that gave rise to the text; similarly, the influence of the text upon readers was considered a distraction from the work itself. If a literary work is viewed as having three main components,

Author → Text → Reader

New Critics stressed the text over the role of the author and the reader. The concerns of the author ("intentional fallacy") and the effects upon

8. The New Critics are criticized for their attempts to focus on the text solely without reference to the author or to the readers of the text. They claimed that the background information about an author such as his or her designs and intentions for a work are irrelevant to the understanding of a text ("intentional fallacy"). Similarly, the effects or results of a poem on the reader are a distraction from the text itself ("affective fallacy"). New Critics also did not take into account factors of race, gender, politics, and sexuality in their readings. See William K. Wimsatt and Monroe C. Beardsley, "The Intentional Fallacy" and "The Affective Fallacy," in *The Verbal Icon: Studies in the Meaning of Poetry* (Lexington: University of Kentucky Press, 1954), 3–18, 21–39. For a critique of New Criticism see Lynn M. Poland, *Literary Criticism and Biblical Hermeneutics: A Critique of Formalist Approaches* (Chico, Calif.: Scholars Press, 1985); Gerald Graff, *Literature against Itself: Literary Ideas in Modern Society* (Chicago: University of Chicago Press, 1979), chapter 5; Frank Lentricchia, *After the New Criticism* (Chicago: University of Chicago Press, 1980), chapter 6.

9. For examples of close readings and an attempt to find common ground in formalist (New Critical) and postformalist readings in secular literature see Frank Lentricchia and Andrew DuBois, eds., *Close Reading: The Reader* (Durham and London: Duke University Press, 2003).

10. For overviews of New Criticism see M. H. Abrams, *A Glossary of Literary Terms*, 7th ed. (Fort Worth: Harcourt Brace College Publishers, 1999), s.v. "New Criticism"; David Robey, "Anglo-American New Criticism," in *Modern Literary Theory*, ed. Ann Jefferson and David Robey (Totowa, N.J.: Barnes & Noble, 1982), 65–83.

the reader ("affective fallacy") diverted attention from the most important element of analysis, the text, and thus the exploration of background information and reader-response could add little, if anything, to the understanding of a text. Despite the extreme position of the New Critics (i.e., bracketing the author and the reader from consideration), their emphasis upon the autonomous unity of the text remains immensely influential upon narrative criticism today.

Narrative critics embraced the central tenet of the New Critics, that the text is a world in itself and is the proper focus of analysis. Early biblical narrative critics focused upon the text as the proper area of concern for analysis. They bracketed out historical issues or the development of the text in its *Sitz im Leben*, or life situation, in order to focus on the text as a freestanding work in which form and content are inseparable. "Form was no longer to be seen merely as instrumental, the vehicle for an ideational or propositional content or a cultural or historical reality, separable from the literary organism and independent of it. Instead the meaning of the text was said to be indissolubly bonded with its form."[11] The New Critical influence on narrative critics can be seen in a statement by some of the earliest narrative critics:

> Our study reveals Mark's narrative to be of remarkably whole cloth. The narrator's point of view is consistent. The plot is coherent: Events that are anticipated come to pass; conflicts are resolved; prophecies are fulfilled. The characters are consistent from one scene to the next. Literary techniques of storytelling, recurring designs, overlapping patterns, and interwoven motifs interconnect the narrative throughout. . . . The unity of this Gospel is apparent in the integrity of the story it tells, which gives a powerful overall rhetorical impact. Mark's complex artistry has been compared to an intricately composed "fugue" or to an "interwoven tapestry."[12]

With the exception of the phrase "powerful overall rhetorical impact" (presumably upon the reader), this statement coincides remarkably with New Criticism in its holistic conception of the literary text.[13]

Close Reading

One of the enduring contributions of New Criticism to narrative criticism is the painstaking analysis of the nuances, ambiguities of

11. Aichele et al., eds., *The Postmodern Bible*, 86.
12. Rhoads, Dewey, and Michie, *Mark as Story*, 3.
13. It should be noted that nowhere do the authors mention New Criticism or their indebtedness to this form of criticism. The authors also refer to "gaps" in Mark's story and "rhetorical strategies" of the text, which are concerns of reader-response critics.

words, images, metaphors, and small units of a text. New Critics called such analysis "close reading" or "explication," from the French *explication de texte*.[14] Close reading is "the detailed analysis of the complex interrelations and *ambiguities* (multiple meanings) of the verbal and figurative components within a work."[15] It pays attention to the words on the page rather than to the contexts that produced those words. The earliest biblical literary critics relied on close readings to bring out the subtlety and interrelationships of a text. Robert Alter in *The Art of Biblical Narrative*, for instance, showed the importance of repetitions in biblical narratives and its affinity with repetitions in short stories, novels, and poems. His close analysis of similar and dissimilar repetitive scenes in the Old Testament demonstrated their similarity to Homeric type-scenes. In *Text and Texture*, Michael Fishbane offered close readings of narrative texts, prayers, and speeches in the Hebrew Bible.[16] In 1973, Jean Starobinski provided a literary analysis of the struggle with Legion in Mark 5:1–20 that appeared in *New Literary History*.[17] Phyllis Trible's reading of the book of Ruth is a classic close reading from a feminist perspective.[18] Other biblical critics applied New Critical methods to the sayings and parables of Jesus. Robert Tannehill brought out the metaphoric power, tensions, patterns, parallelisms, and paradoxes in the sayings of Jesus in his book, *The Sword of His Mouth*.[19] Dan Otto Via Jr. drew explicitly upon New Critical theory to show that the parables of Jesus are autonomous works in which form and content are inseparable.[20]

Biblical literary critics expanded their focus from close readings of smaller units such as sayings and parables to entire Gospels and other books of the New Testament. The Gospel of Mark was one of the earliest in which narrative critics described rhetoric, setting, character, plot, and point of view.[21] The

14. William Harmon and C. Hugh Holman, *A Handbook to Literature*, 8th ed. (Upper Saddle River, N.J.: Prentice Hall, 1999), 204.

15. Abrams, *Glossary*, 181.

16. For Alter and Fishbane, see n. 5 above.

17. J. Starobinski, "The Struggle with Legion: A Literary Analysis of Mark 5:1–20," *NLH* 4 (1972/1973): 331–56.

18. Phyllis Trible, *God and the Rhetoric of Sexuality* (OBT; Philadelphia: Fortress, 1978), chapter 6.

19. *The Sword of His Mouth: Forceful and Imaginative Language in Synoptic Sayings*, Semeia Supplements (Philadelphia: Fortress, 1975).

20. *The Parables: Their Literary and Existential Dimension* (Philadelphia: Fortress, 1967).

21. Rhoads, Dewey, and Michie, *Mark as Story*; Elizabeth Struthers Malbon, *In the Company of Jesus: Characters in Mark's Gospel* (Louisville: Westminster John Knox, 2000).

other Gospels,[22] Acts,[23] Paul,[24] and Revelation[25] also became fertile ground for narrative critical approaches. Narrative critics have come full circle and now are turning attention once again to individual narratives within the Gospels. David Rhoads, for example, examines the Syrophoenician woman in Mark in terms of rhetoric, characterization, settings, and plot.[26] Several of the readings in this book are studies of individual narratives in the Gospels and Revelation.

Although narrative critics today reject the extremes of New Criticism—for example, that a literary work is separable from the response of the reader—they are indebted to the New Critical emphasis upon the organic unity of a text and to their close, painstaking practice of analyzing texts. A reading of an unfamiliar visual text will allow us to see the potentialities and limitations of close readings.

22. On Matthew see David R. Bauer, *The Structure of Matthew's Gospel: A Study in Literary Design*, JSNTSup 31 (Sheffield: Almond, 1988); David B. Howell, *Matthew's Inclusive Story: A Study in the Narrative Rhetoric of the First Gospel*, JSNTSup 42 (Sheffield: JSOT, 1990); Jack Dean Kingsbury, *Matthew as Story*, 2nd ed. (Philadelphia: Fortress, 1988); Warren Carter, *Matthew: Storyteller, Interpreter, Evangelist*, rev. ed. (Peabody, Mass.: Hendrickson, 2004). On Luke see John A. Darr, *On Character Building: The Reader and the Rhetoric of Characterization in Luke-Acts* (Louisville: Westminster John Knox, 1992); Jack Dean Kingsbury, *Conflict in Luke: Jesus, Authorities, Disciples* (Minneapolis: Fortress, 1991); James L. Resseguie, *Spiritual Landscape: Images of the Spiritual Life in the Gospel of Luke* (Peabody, Mass.: Hendrickson, 2004); Robert C. Tannehill, *The Narrative Unity of Luke-Acts: A Literary Interpretation*, 2 vols., FF (Philadelphia/Minneapolis: Fortress, 1986–1990); Steven M. Sheeley, *Narrative Asides in Luke-Acts*, JSNTSup 72 (Sheffield: JSOT, 1992). On John see R. Alan Culpepper, *Anatomy of the Fourth Gospel: A Study in Literary Design*, FF (Philadelphia: Fortress, 1983); James L. Resseguie, *The Strange Gospel: Narrative Design and Point of View in John*, BIS 56 (Leiden: Brill, 2001); Jeffrey L. Staley, *The Print's First Kiss: A Rhetorical Investigation of the Implied Reader in the Fourth Gospel*, SBLDS 82 (Atlanta: Scholars Press, 1988); Mark W. G. Stibbe, *John as Storyteller: Narrative Criticism and the Fourth Gospel*, SNTSMS 73 (Cambridge: Cambridge University Press, 1992); Colleen M. Conway, *Men and Women in the Fourth Gospel: Gender and Johannine Characterization*, SBLDS 167 (Atlanta: Society of Biblical Literature, 1999); Gail O'Day, *Revelation in the Fourth Gospel: Narrative Mode and Theological Claim* (Philadelphia: Fortress, 1986).

23. Daniel Marguerat, *The First Christian Historian: Writing the "Acts of the Apostles,"* trans. Ken McKinney et. al., SNTSMS 121 (Cambridge: Cambridge University Press, 2002).

24. Norman Petersen, *Rediscovering Paul: Philemon and the Sociology of Paul's Narrative World* (Philadelphia: Fortress, 1985).

25. David Barr, *Tales of the End: A Narrative Commentary on the Book of Revelation* (Santa Rosa, Calif.: Polebridge Press, 1998); James L. Resseguie, *Revelation Unsealed: A Narrative Critical Approach to John's Apocalypse*, BIS 32 (Leiden: Brill, 1998).

26. David Rhoads, "The Syrophoenician Woman in Mark: A Narrative Critical Study," *JAAR* 62 (1992): 342–75; repr. in idem, *Reading Mark*, 63–94; also, Outi Lehtipuu, "Characterization and Persuasion: The Rich Man and the Poor Man in Luke 16,19–31," in *Characterization in the Gospels: Reconceiving Narrative Criticism*, ed. David Rhoads and Kari Syreeni, JSNTSup 184 (Sheffield: Sheffield Academic Press, 1999), 73–105.

A Close Reading of Vincent van Gogh's The Good Samaritan (after Delacroix)

Suppose that we have a work of art of which we know nothing. It is a self-contained artifact whose form and content is an organic unity. Furthermore, we know nothing of the author or painter of this work, and we do not have a history of reception—that is, how various "readers" or critics of the painting have interpreted this work. The artist may have painted himself as a character in the work and he may have lived a troubled life, but this information is not considered essential to the interpretation of the work. He may have relied on other painters for his work, such as Delacroix's *Good Samaritan*, but source criticism is also considered unimportant for the interpretation of the work. Further, the effect of the work on audiences, though interesting, is seen as incidental and irrelevant to the meaning of the work. In other words, all we have is the work itself, the bare text. What would a close reading of this work look like? What would we attend to? What nuances, ambiguities, and tensions in the text are noticeable? What patterns emerge? A painting tells a story in much the same way a literary text does. It has characters, setting, rhetoric, point of view, plot, tone, and so forth. It is also a self-contained artifact that can be interpreted on its own without regard to the details concerning the artist or the history of reception. What story does van Gogh's *The Good Samaritan* tell?

Van Gogh's painting of the Good Samaritan (see figure 1) uses shades of light and darkness, colors and contrasts, clothing and posture, space and distance to tell a story. There are four *characters* in this story: two fill the foreground while two recede into the distant background. As in a literary work, some characters are more developed than others, and, in this painting, the Samaritan and the wounded man command our attention and are fully delineated, while the priest and Levite are barely noticeable, cardboard characters in the background. The *setting* is a mountainous, serpentine path with a river on one side and a discarded chest on the other. The clothing, also part of the setting, changes from sepia tones for background characters to brilliant colors for foreground characters. Several props or details of the setting are important symbols for understanding the story: (1) a book, (2) a box or chest, (3) a river and waterfall, and (4) a garment shared by the Samaritan and the wounded man. The *rhetoric* or technique of persuasion is found in the colors and contrasts, posture of the characters, close-ups of expressions, the title of the painting, the overall tone or atmosphere, and metaphors. A *point of view* is expressed in the placement of characters in the painting as well as their size, color, posture, and demeanor. The *theme* of the visual narrative is found in the story it tells.

Figure 1. Vincent van Gogh (1853–90), *The Good Samaritan (after Delacroix)*, 1890. Oil on canvas. Rijksmuseum Kroller-Muller, Otterlo, Netherlands.

Two characters, barely visible, blend almost seamlessly into the background. In the far distance, the priest is dressed in a yellowish brown garment and is nearly indistinguishable from the bluish background. He walks away from disaster, down a narrow path through the mountain pass to Jericho. Not far behind is a second figure, the Levite, who is closer to the viewer's perspective, but like the priest he blends seamlessly into the background. He, too, is dressed in a brownish cloak, and, with his head lowered, he reads a book as he journeys through the mountainous path. A third and fourth figure, the Samaritan and the man in the ditch, fill the foreground of the painting, which bursts with vibrancy and pathos. The rhetoric of the narrative is expressed in the dimensions of the characters, the tones of the clothing, the facial expressions, and physical posture. The Samaritan and wounded man fill the foreground and command our attention by their prominence, while the priest and Levite fade into the distant landscape. The dull, muted colors of the characters—expressive of their inner character—change to the bright, vibrant colors of the Samaritan, suggesting hope and life. Two parts of the setting are metaphors for disaster and life. An open chest to the left, devoid of contents, is a reminder of disaster and tragedy on this road. The discarded chest is emblematic of the discarded man who is left for dead; it is also an apt metaphor for the Samaritan, who is a "discarded" person in Israelite society. On the right a stream and waterfall are metaphors of life. As the refreshing, nourishing water is nature's comforting presence in this harsh mountainous terrain, so the Samaritan is humanity's healing presence along the troubled road. The chest and waterfall underscore the themes of disaster and life.

Two props—a book and a garment—are metaphors for neglect and rescue, which represent also two opposing points of view within the painting. The Levite goes on his way reading a book, self-absorbed in a world of his own making and unconcerned for a world of pain and tragedy around him. The countermetaphor is a shared garment. The Samaritan's bright blue tunic matches exactly the blue garment placed around the wounded man to cover his nakedness. The book and garment underscore the themes of neglect, on the one hand, and rescue, on the other. The book—most likely the Torah—is a source of life just as the river and waterfalls are a life-giving source for a parched and thirsty land. But neither the priest nor Levite puts the commands and precepts of the Torah into action and stops to offer aid to the man in the ditch. Rescue or salvation instead comes through a stranger who shares his own garment with the discarded man and gives aid.

The characters' posture and clothing reinforce the themes of disaster and life and neglect and rescue. The Levite has his head down, attentive to the words on a page but not to the intent of those words. His demeanor contrasts with the Samaritan's posture. The priest and the Levite face away from us, but the Samaritan and the victim face toward us. The Samaritan's back is arched tightly like a bow and he struggles to lift the helpless man onto his donkey. He shares the man's pain and suffering. In contrast to the drab clothing of the priest and Levite, the Samaritan wears a bright golden cloak, a brilliant blue tunic, and red headgear. His vibrant appearance suggests life and hope in the midst of this tragedy. In contrast to the diminutive appearance of the priest and Levite, the Samaritan is painted larger-than-life, filling the foreground.

A spatial point of view is expressed in the placement of characters. The Samaritan travels in the opposite direction to the priest and Levite, thereby highlighting two divergent points of view. In the painting, the priest and Levite fade into the landscape and are barely distinguishable from the rugged terrain. The Samaritan travels in the opposite direction to the clerics; moving toward us and filling our field of vision, he represents a different response to the disaster and a different point of view. In the painting, the priest and Levite descend—figuratively as well as literally—while the Samaritan ascends. The lofty are brought down and the lowly are raised up. In addition to the characters' opposite directions, the travelers are placed in inverted order to their status in the socioreligious hierarchy of Israel. The priest and Levite are near the top of the status hierarchy. The Samaritan, on the other hand, falls off the scale of the status hierarchy and is somewhere near the bottom, along with the Gentiles.[27] Van Gogh, however, reverses this order. The priest and Levite are small, barely visible—much as Samaritans were barely visible to Israelites in New Testament times. (We need only to remember that Galilean Jews went out of their way to avoid traveling through Samaria on their way to Jerusalem.) By contrast, the person who is at the bottom of the status hierarchy looms larger than life in the painting. The striking differences in the characters' size and their colors and posture emphasize two divergent points of view. The point of view that prevails in the culture of that day—the perspective of the priest and Levite—is minimized; the point of view of the outsider—the Samaritan—is accentuated. In van Gogh's painting, the person who was invisible in Jewish society becomes highly visible, while society's highly visible representatives become nearly invisible.

Even the title of the painting expresses a point of view and reinforces the theme of rescue and life in the midst of disaster. Van Gogh entitled the painting *The Good Samaritan*, which is a paradox—for, in the cultural perspective of the New Testament era, the adjective does not belong with the noun. The Samaritans were despised renegades and synonymous with outsiders. Yet the one who proves to be the neighbor is the outsider. The title thus underscores the theme that rescue (salvation) comes not through the expected, familiar persons of society but through an unexpected foreigner.

What are the strengths and limitations of a close reading? Close readings attend to the words on a page or, in this case, the painting within the frame. It explores metaphors, develops contrasts, elaborates paradoxes, and attends to point of view. Yet a successful close reading cannot ignore background details. The reader of this painting must recognize that van Gogh's *Good Samaritan* refers to the biblical account found in the Gospel of Luke. Further, the critic must understand the diminished stature of the Samaritans in the first century and the prominent stature of the priests and Levites in the social and religious hierarchy within Israel. This is part of the repertoire of cultural and social expectations that the reader brings to the text. Although New Critics resisted bringing background

27. See Joachim Jeremias, *Jerusalem in the Time of Jesus: An Investigation into Economic and Social Conditions during the New Testament Period* (Philadelphia: Fortress, 1969), 352–58; Kenneth E. Bailey, *Through Peasant Eyes: More Lucan Parables, Their Culture and Style* (Grand Rapids: Eerdmans, 1980), 48. Bailey cites the Mishnah: "He that eats the bread of the Samaritans is like to one that eats the flesh of swine" (*m. Shevi'it.* 8.10).

information into the text, narrative critics recognize the importance of this information for interpretation. Nevertheless a close reading does not treat all background information equally. For instance, van Gogh places himself in the painting as the Samaritan. Although this is an interesting detail—and perhaps van Gogh is making the point that we, the viewer of the painting, should see ourselves as the Samaritan—it is not essential to the understanding of the painting, and narrative critics, like New Critics, consider this type of background information a diversion from the text itself.

1.3 Narrative Criticism and Reader-Response Criticism

New Critics also considered the effect of a work of art on its audience irrelevant to the interpretation of a work—a limitation of the New Critical method that narrative critics seek to overcome. The reader's response or the rhetorical effect of a work on an audience is now considered important to the understanding of a text.

The reader-response critic is concerned with what the text *does* to the reader. Reader-response criticism focuses on the reader's actions involved in responding to a text. Specifically, what change in outlook or worldview does the text effect in the reader and how does it bring about the change? In other words, reader-response criticism focuses on readers' reading and the dynamics involved in readers' assembling the meaning of a text. Literary critics use a bewildering array of terms to describe the reader of a text and the relationship of the reader to the text: an implied reader, informed reader, ideal reader, flesh-and-blood reader, super-reader, mock reader, extrafictional reader, and resisting reader, to name a few.[28] Generally speaking, the stance of the reader is one of three positions in relation to the text: (1) the reader can be *in the text*, i.e., a construct of the text; (2) the reader can be a real reader with complete dominance *over the text*; or (3) the reader can have a dialectical relationship *with the text*. [29] Some critics, for example, focus on the

28. See Wallace Martin, *Recent Theories of Narrative* (Ithaca: Cornell University Press, 1986), 154, for a listing of readers.

29. For what follows I rely, in part, on my article "Reader-Response Criticism and the Synoptic Gospels," *JAAR* 52 (1982): 307–24. This taxonomy was suggested to me by Steven Mailloux, "Learning to Read: Interpretation and Reader-Response Criticism," *Studies in the Literary Imagination* 12 (1979): 93–108, at 94. Both Powell, *What Is Narrative Criticism?* 16, and the editors of *The Postmodern Bible*, 27, adopt some form of this taxonomy. On reader-response criticism see the collection of essays in Jane P. Tompkins, ed., *Reader-Response Criticism: From Formalism to Post-Structuralism* (Baltimore: Johns Hopkins University Press, 1980); Susan R. Suleiman and Inge Crosman, eds., *The Reader in the Text: Essays on Audience and Interpretation* (Princeton: Princeton University Press, 1980).

reader *in the text* (e.g., Gérard Genette, Gerald Prince).[30] This reader is inscribed or encoded in the text and is a property of the text's meaning. The critics' function is to interpret the signals transmitted to the inscribed reader of the text. Other forms of reader-response criticism give the reader complete dominance *over the text* (e.g., Norman Holland, David Bleich).[31] This is a subjective form of reading that is freed from authorial intention or the literary dynamics of the text. The reader determines the meaning of the text. A third type of reader is neither inscribed within the text nor has complete dominance over the text; instead this reader interacts *with the text*. This "implied" reader (e.g., Wolfgang Iser) [32] or "informed" reader (e.g., early Stanley Fish)[33] interacts with the text in the production of meaning. For Wolfgang Iser, there are "gaps" or areas of "indeterminacy" in a literary text that must be filled in or "realized" by the reader. Guided by the text, the reader assembles the work through a process of "consistency building" that includes development of expectations followed by fulfillment or frustration of the expectations. Iser uses the analogy of two people gazing at the night sky to describe the interaction of text and reader:

> Both [may] be looking at the same collection of stars, but one will see the image of a plough, and the other will make out a dipper. The 'stars' in a literary text are fixed; the lines that join them are variable.[34]

Narrative critics do not agree on who is the reader of the text. Mark Allan Powell, for instance, speaks of an "implied reader who is presup-

---

On biblical reader-response criticism see "Reader-Response Criticism," in Aichele et al., *The Postmodern Bible*, 20–69.

30. Gérard Genette, *Narrative Discourse: An Essay in Method*, trans. Jane E. Lewin (Ithaca: Cornell University Press, 1980); Gerald Prince, "Introduction to the Study of the Narratee," *Poétique* 14 (1973): 177–96.

31. Norman N. Holland, *5 Readers Reading* (New Haven: Yale University Press, 1975); idem, "Unity Identity Text Self," *Publications of the Modern Language Association* 90 (1975): 813–22; David Bleich, *Readers and Feelings: An Introduction to Subjective Criticism* (Urbana, Ill.: National Council of Teachers of English, 1975).

32. Wolfgang Iser, "Indeterminacy and the Reader's Response in Prose Fiction," in *Aspects of Narrative*, ed. J. Hillis Miller (New York: Columbia University Press, 1971), 1–45; idem, "The Reading Process: A Phenomenological Approach," *NLH* 3 (1972), 279–99; idem, *The Implied Reader: Patterns of Communication in Prose Fiction from Bunyan to Beckett* (Baltimore: Johns Hopkins University Press, 1974); idem, *The Act of Reading: A Theory of Aesthetic Response* (Baltimore: Johns Hopkins University Press, 1978).

33. Stanley E. Fish, *Surprised by Sin: The Reader in "Paradise Lost"* (Berkeley: University of California Press, 1967); idem, *Self-Consuming Artifacts: The Experience of Seventeenth-Century Literature* (Berkeley: University of California Press, 1972).

34. Iser, *The Implied Reader*, 282.

posed by the text" and "distinct from any real, historical reader."[35] By "implied reader," Powell envisions "an ideal reader" who can read the text as an (implied) author intended the text to be read, i.e., transcribing all the clues within a text in the manner the author intended. Jack Dean Kingsbury also defines the implied reader as "no flesh-and-blood person of any century. Instead, it refers to an imaginary person who is to be envisaged . . . as responding to the text at every point with whatever emotion, understanding, or knowledge the text ideally calls for."[36] Other biblical critics refer to the "implied reader" in the Iseran sense as a hypothetical reader who, guided by clues in the text, fills in the gaps and indeterminacies of the text and assembles the work.[37] There is very little difference between Powell's "implied reader" and Iser's "implied reader" in the practice of biblical narrative criticism.[38] Both types are competent readers who are thoroughly familiar with the repertoire of literary, historical, social, linguistic, and cultural assumptions of the authorial audience—that is, the audience that the author has in mind when he or she writes the work. This reader is guided by the clues in the text and reads the text as the implied author[39] intended.

The importance of reader-response criticism for narrative criticism is the reemployment of the reader. The reader, who was abruptly fired by the New Critics as an irrelevant spectator in the production of the text's meaning, is now rehired. She or he is a full partner in the firm of Author, Text & Reader. No longer is the text the sole concern of investigation; the effects of the text upon the reader and how it transforms the reader's

35. Powell, *What Is Narrative Criticism?*, 19.

36. Kingsbury, *Matthew as Story*, 38; cf. also Malbon, "Narrative Criticism," 23–49 at 26–28. This concept of the "implied reader" is based on Seymour Chatman's communication model. See Seymour Chatman, *Story and Discourse: Narrative Structure in Fiction and Film* (Ithaca: Cornell University Press, 1978), 151.

37. Among critics who use Iser's concept of an implied reader are: James L. Resseguie, "Reader-Response Criticism and the Synoptic Gospels," *JAAR* 52 (1984): 307–24; Robert M. Fowler, "Reader-Response Criticism: Figuring Mark's Reader," in *Mark & Method*, ed. Anderson and Moore, 50–65; Bernard Brandon Scott, *Hear Then the Parable: A Commentary on the Parables of Jesus* (Minneapolis: Fortress, 1989); Richard A. Edwards, *Matthew's Story of Jesus* (Philadelphia: Fortress, 1985); Jouette M. Bassler, "The Parable of the Loaves," *JR* 66 (1986): 157–72; Howell, *Matthew's Inclusive Story*, chapter 5; and Mark Allan Powell, *Chasing the Eastern Star: Adventures in Biblical Reader-Response Criticism* (Louisville: Westminster John Knox, 2001), 16.

38. This is pointed out in Moore, *Literary Criticism and the Gospels*, chapter 6; Aichele et al., *The Postmodern Bible*, chapter 1.

39. See Wayne C. Booth, *The Rhetoric of Fiction*, 2nd ed. (Chicago: University of Chicago Press, 1983), 74–75: "The 'implied author' chooses, consciously or unconsciously, what we read; we infer him as an ideal, literary, created version of the real man; he is the sum of his own choices."

point of view is also important. Mark Allan Powell even "regard[s] narrative criticism as a subset or variety of reader-response criticism."[40]

But what specifically are the effects of the text upon the reader? And how does the text influence the reader's response? What moves does the reader go through in apprehending the text? Wolfgang Iser uses the term *defamiliarization* or *estrangement* to describe the effect a narrative text has on a reader. "The ultimate function of the [reading] strategies," Iser writes, "is to *defamiliarize* the familiar."[41] And in his book *The Implied Reader*, Iser says that "[the reading process] is steered by . . . techniques or strategies used to set the *familiar against the unfamiliar*."[42]

1.4 Defamiliarization of the New Testament

Ostranenie, which is the Russian term for defamiliarization, literally means "making strange."[43] The term was popularized by the Russian formalist Victor Shklovsky in 1917.[44] The Russian formalists believed that normal, everyday perception of the world becomes habitual and jaded. The routine numbs our senses to new perspectives and new ways of seeing the everyday and familiar. "Habitualization," Shklovsky writes, "devours works, clothes, furniture, one's wife, and the fear of war. . . . Art exists that one may recover a sensation of life; it exists to make one feel things, to make the stone *stony*."[45] The metaphor of making the stone *stony* is an accurate description for this reading process that allows us to see what is taken for granted and to see the everyday in a new, fresh way. Another analogy of the reading process is to consider the difference between walking and dancing. "Walking . . . is an activity which as we

40. Powell, *Chasing the Eastern Star*, 63. However, literary criticism, which is the broader category among secular literary critics, would not regard literary or narrative criticism as a subset of reader-response criticism.

41. Iser, *The Act of Reading*, 87 (emphasis Iser's).

42. Iser, *The Implied Reader*, 288 (emphasis mine).

43. Victor Shklovsky, "Art as Technique," in *Russian Formalist Criticism: Four Essays*, trans. Lee T. Lemon and Marion J. Reis (Lincoln: University of Nebraska Press, 1965), 3–24. On Russian formalism see Victor Erlich, *Russian Formalism: History, Doctrine*, rev. ed. (New Haven: Yale University Press, 1981); E. M. Thompson, *Russian Formalism and Anglo-American New Criticism: A Comparative Study* (The Hague: Mouton, 1971); Abrams, *Glossary*, 102–5; Ann Jefferson, "Russian Formalism," in *Modern Literary Theory: A Comparative Introduction*, ed. Ann Jefferson and David Robey (Totowa, N.J.: Barnes & Noble, 1982), 16–37.

44. On defamiliarization in the New Testament see Resseguie, *Strange Gospel*, 27–28; idem, "Defamiliarization and the Gospels," *BTB* 20 (1990): 147–53; idem, "Automatization and Defamiliarization in Luke 7:36–50," *LitTh* 5 (1991): 137–50; George W. Young, *Subversive Symmetry: Exploring the Fantastic in Mark 6:45–56*, BIS 41 (Brill: Leiden, 1999), 35–40.

45. Shklovsky, "Art as Technique," 12.

go about in everyday life we have ceased to be aware of; but when we dance, the automatically performed gestures of walking are perceived anew."[46] The automatic is foregrounded—disautomatized or separated from its routine background. Or another example: everyday language is made difficult in poetry so that we attend to the words and their sounds. In this way, poetry renews our perception of ordinary words. Words are deformed in poetry in the same way as commonplace points of view are deformed by the sayings of Jesus. Defamiliarization causes us to stumble, and as we stumble, we begin to take notice.

The formalists recognized that conventional norms and perspectives that are often thought to be obvious are made trivial, absurd, or seen as mistaken when viewed from a novel perspective. Staid, commonplace points of view, they contend, must be made odd to awaken the reader from the lethargy of the habitual; the familiar that clouds our ability to see things in a new, fresh perspective must be made strange. An anesthetized point of view, numbed by the routine and the formulaic, must be seen as tired and worn-out so that a new energized perspective replaces the old. By making the familiar seem strange, the strange becomes more familiar.

Deforming a Familiar Context

Defamiliarization suspends, twists, turns on its head the familiar or everyday way of looking at the world by substituting a new, unfamiliar frame of reference. Shklovsky cites an example from Tolstoy's work "Kholstomer" of a novel point of view that uproots the normal, everyday perspective concerning the ownership of private property.[47] The first-person narrator of "Kholstomer" is a horse that is a disinterested and impartial observer who finds the owning of personal property to be a befuddling, odd state of affairs. The novel frame of reference is intended to force the reader to see what is taken for granted or assumed to be obvious and to reexamine the assumptions behind the ownership of private property. In the New Testament, the point of view of the dominant culture—the religious authorities, the powerful, the wealthy, among others—shapes the norms and values of the society, and it is their ideological perspectives that Jesus and the narrator make strange. The actions and sayings of outsiders—for example, widows, Gentiles, Samaritans, sinners, tax collectors, and, in general, the marginalized of society—deform and make strange the commonplace point of view expressed by the religious leaders, wealthy landowners, and the powerful. An action, for instance,

46. Jefferson, "Russian Formalism," 19.
47. Shklovsky, "Art as Technique," 13–15.

may be viewed from two divergent perspectives—one familiar and habitual, the other unfamiliar and strange. Consider, for instance, the giving of gifts by the wealthy and the widow. A naturalized perspective expects that the giving of large gifts to the treasury is an accurate measurement of one's devotion to God or a display of spiritual fealty. The widow's gift, on the other hand, would go entirely unnoticed according to the norms of society. Yet Jesus' comment on her sacrificial gift displaces the ordinary way of judging the value of gifts from its familiar, habitual context, which in turn makes the naturalized method of evaluation seem arbitrary and strange. The wealthy give out of the poverty of their abundance while she gives out of the abundance of her poverty.

In Luke 7:36–50, a deformed context forces the implied reader to question the norms and values of the dominant culture.[48] The host, Simon the Pharisee, invites Jesus to a banquet, and all appears to proceed normally until a woman from the city enters and disrupts the banquet setting. Disruption is a hallmark of defamiliarization and nearly everything is disrupted in this story.[49] Both the narrator and the Pharisee label the woman a "sinner" (Luke 7:37, 39) and thus, according to conventional norms, she does not belong at this meal. Or does she? The narrator further deforms the context when she provides an effusive welcome while Simon, the reader learns later, did not offer water for the feet, a kiss for the cheek, or oil for the head. Simon treats Jesus as a stranger while the woman treats him as a welcomed guest. What assures the distortion of societal norms is the effective defamiliarizing device of withholding important information from the reader. The story, that is, the events in their chronological sequence, does not follow the plot, that is, the events as they unfold in the narrative world. The chronological sequence is as follows:

1. A Pharisee invites Jesus to dinner.
2. The host omits customary amenities for his guest.
3. A sinful woman enters and performs lavish acts of hospitality.
4. Simon objects.
5. Jesus confronts Simon.
6. Jesus pronounces the woman forgiven.

However, the narrative withholds the important information in #2 until Jesus confronts Simon in #5. Thus the plot of Luke 7 is 1, 3, 4, 5, 2, 6.

48. See Resseguie, "Automatization and Defamiliarization," 137–50.

49. This coincides with Peter J. Rabinowitz's "rules of undermining." The reader can expect situations of inertia to be upset. When Jesus is invited to a dinner party, for instance, the reader can expect that the state of affairs will not remain the same but will be dramatically reformulated. See *Before Reading: Narrative Conventions and the Politics of Interpretation* (Ithaca: Cornell University Press, 1987), 119–25.

By postponing damaging information, the context for evaluating the woman's actions and Simon's neglect is deformed. Simon is presented in a favorable light in the opening verses: he is the host, and the naïve reader, who has never read or heard this story before, is unaware that the Pharisee neglected to greet his guest properly. Simon's objections to the woman's presence at the meal and Jesus' failure to rebuke her appear valid to the reader who is aware of the dominant cultural expectations. In other words, the narrative invites stock responses from the reader only to overturn and dismantle those familiar expectations at the end. Further, familiar institutional labels are used to encourage habitual and automatized responses from the reader. The woman is "a sinner," and her violation of norms of decorum (she lets down her hair in public) reinforces that perception. But the stock responses are turned on their head and the norms of the dominant society are placed on shaky ground by Jesus' judicial parable (7:41–42) and startling confrontation of his host's egregious passivity. The defamiliarized plot allows a new set of norms and values to overturn the naturalized values of the dominant society. Jesus announces that the woman's "great love" is proof of her new status as a forgiven sinner, which impels the reader to reevaluate familiar institutional labels and the norms that support those labels. The deformed context has thus succeeded in making the strange behavior of the woman seem natural, and the familiar norms voiced by Simon seem strange.

Deforming Rhetorical Devices

Not only are contexts and plots estranged so that the reader pays attention, but also rhetorical devices may be used to make commonplace assumptions seem strange. In the following example, the hearer/reader is encouraged to make a premature conclusion that turns out to be wrong. When a dispute arose among the disciples as to which of them was to be considered the greatest, Jesus asks two rhetorical questions that the disciples cannot get wrong. "For who is greater, the one who sits at table or the one who serves?" To reinforce the obvious answer, Jesus rephrases the question in such a way as to require an affirmative reply: "Is it not the one at the table?" The questions encourage the reader to affirm an everyday perspective: "Of course, it is the one who is served who is greater." Yet Jesus surprises the reader when he turns the "correct" answer on its head: "But I am among you as one who serves" (Luke 22:24–27). Although Jesus has already said that the greatest must become like the youngest and the leader like one who serves, he elicits the disciples' acknowledgment of the common, accepted point of view within the dominant culture so that a new deformed perception can replace the old values.

An artistic turn of phrase is another defamiliarizing device that forces the reader/hearer to slow down and pay attention to the words on the page or the words spoken.

> The sabbath
> was made for humankind,
> and not humankind
> for the sabbath.
>
> (Mark 2:27)

This chiastic twist impedes the reading/hearing process and causes the reader/hearer to reconsider the commonplace societal norms that would turn this same saying around. Other artistic turns also impede the reading process and force the reader to evaluate everyday norms and values of society: first are last, last are first; exalted are humbled, humbled are exalted; whoever saves life will lose it, whoever loses life will save it.

Analogies that clash with the readers' expectations also cause the reader to slow down and reconsider what is being said—to see the *stony* stone. Consider, for instance, a saying about anxiety that uses a pedestrian analogy of birds and flowers to catch the reader's attention.

> Therefore I tell you, do not worry about your life, what you will eat, or about your body, what you will wear. . . . Consider the ravens: they neither sow nor reap, they have neither storehouse nor barn, and yet God feeds them. Of how much more value are you than the birds. . . . Consider the lilies, how they grow: they neither toil nor spin; yet I tell you, even Solomon in all his glory was not clothed like one of these. (Luke 12:22, 24, 27)

Do birds and flowers even know what it means to be anxious? Naturally, they are free from anxiety, which is the point of using an analogy that seems absurd. Birds should be among the most anxious of God's creation for they have neither storehouse nor barn, and flowers should be consumed with angst because their clothing is ephemeral, "alive today and tomorrow . . . thrown into the oven." Yet neither birds nor flowers experience worry, whereas humans, who do have storehouse and barn and clothing, are anxious. The analogy is disturbing because, curiously, those who are least able to take care of themselves are unaware of anxiety while those able to provide for themselves are filled with angst. This jarring analogy makes strange the readers' angst-driven lives, which Jesus appropriately labels as a sign of spiritual anxiety or "little faith."[50]

50. Tannehill, *Sword of His Mouth*, 60–67, also refers to the "strangeness" of this saying although he does not use the concept of defamiliarization.

A similar defamiliarizing twist occurs in Matt. 7:3: "Why do you see the speck in your neighbor's eye, but do not notice the log in your own eye?" Not only are the vehicles extreme ("speck" and "log"), but also the readers' expectations are turned upside down. The log—as anyone will readily admit—is in someone else's eye, and the speck—if it is possible to find it—is in our own eye. The reversal of contrasts causes readers to stumble into unfamiliar territory. They must reconsider "normal" ways of evaluating the actions of others and their own ability to evaluate what others do.

Defamiliarization works best when textual disruptions cause the reader to slow down and take notice, or when norms and values firmly held by an implied audience are developed and then dashed. An unusual context, a difficult saying, an unexpected twist, a puzzling response, a violation of readers' expectations, a shattering of commonplace assumptions—any of these disorients readers, forcing them to attend to something new. George Young notes that a defamiliarized experience of reading is "the point of commonality between the first century reader and the twentieth century reader."[51] A defamiliarized reading is one that is less automatic, less able to glide smoothly over the text; it is more aware of the bumps in the road and the disruptions in the text. It is a close reading that slows down and attends to the nuances of the text—aware, often for the first time, of the text's strangeness.

1.5 The Usefulness of Narrative Criticism

In sum, what can the reader of this book expect narrative criticism to do? What are the potentialities, strengths, and benefits of narrative criticism?[52] Why should narrative criticism be privileged over, say, the historical-critical method or other methods of interpretation?

1. Narrative criticism views the text as a whole. One of the acknowledged strengths of the narrative-critical method is that it avoids the fragmentation of the text associated with forms of historical criticism. Form criticism, for instance, divides narratives into smaller units and determines the life situation or *Sitz im Leben* of the text.[53] To take an example, the story of the bent woman in Luke 13:10–17 could be di-

51. Young, *Subversive Symmetry*, 37.

52. For a discussion of the benefits and limitations of narrative criticism see Powell, *What Is Narrative Criticism?* 85–98; Porter, "Literary Approaches to the New Testament," 112–20; Rhoads, *Reading Mark, Engaging the Gospel*, chapter 2. Howell, *Matthew's Inclusive Story*, 18–53, provides a lengthy discussion of the limitations of the historical-critical method and the benefits of narrative criticism.

53. For an overview of form criticism see Aune, *Literature and Rhetoric*, 187–90.

vided into two separate stories: a "healing story" that describes Jesus' healing of the woman (vv. 10–13) and a "controversy story" in which Jesus confronts the objections of the synagogue leader and ends with a pronouncement (vv. 14–17). A narrative-critical approach, on the other hand, views 13:10–17 as a unity, not two separate stories, and observes the connecting links that make the narrative a unified whole.[54] Redaction criticism is interested in the changes an evangelist makes in his sources to discover the evangelist's theology.[55] Why does Matthew, for instance, change the sequence of events in Mark's stilling of the storm? Instead of Jesus rebuking the storm and then the disciples (Mark 4:35–41), Matthew reverses the order and has Jesus rebuke the disciples and then the storm (Matt. 8:23–27). Narrative critics do not deny that form and redaction criticism are valid and helpful areas of inquiry, but they turn their focus instead to the text in its final form—with only an occasional glance at the various stages of transmission or emendations an evangelist makes in his sources. Narrative critics are interested in narratives as complete tapestries in which the parts fit together to form an organic whole.

2. *Narrative criticism examines the complexities and nuances of a text through close readings.* Literary critics read biblical literature as *literature*. The narrative critic attends to the nuances and interrelationships of texts: its structure, rhetorical strategies, character development, arresting imagery, setting, point of view, and symbolism, to name a few. A close reading, however, does not mean that the narrative critic is unaware of the social location, political environment, and other factors behind the text that influenced the reader—that is, the implied reader. The narrative critic joins this reader and has the cultural, linguistic, social, and historical competencies expected of the implied reader. The implied reader of New Testament narratives, for example, is competent in Greek and understands the socioreligious maps of first-century Palestinian society. The narrative critic joins the authorial audience[56]—that is, the audience envisioned by the implied author of a narrative—with the aim of reading the text as the author intended. But this intention is gleaned from the text itself—not primarily from information outside the text.

54. Joel Green, "Jesus and a Daughter of Abraham (Luke 13:10–17): Test Case for a Lucan Perspective on Jesus' Miracles," *CBQ* 51 (1989): 643–54, and Frances Taylor Gench, *Back to the Well: Women's Encounters with Jesus in the Gospels* (Louisville: Westminster John Knox, 2004), 84–85, argue for the unity of the narrative.

55. On redaction criticism see Aune, *Literature and Rhetoric*, 398–99.

56. The concept of an authorial audience is similar to implied reader and comes from Rabinowitz, *Before Reading*. Carter, *Matthew: Storyteller, Interpreter, Evangelist*, uses the concept of authorial audience.

3. Narrative criticism emphasizes the effects of a narrative on the reader. New Critics avoided the discussion of the effects of a poetic text[57] on its reader: a poem was not to be confused with its effects upon the reader ("the affective fallacy"). They reacted against impressionist readings that measured the value of a poem by its emotional effects upon the reader. Narrative critics, however, take into account the reader's response to the narrative. Since narrative criticism analyzes the narrative point of view, it can describe the text's effects upon a reader. "Point of view conditions and codetermines the reader's response to the text."[58] The narrative critic asks: What point of view does the narrative want the reader to adopt or to reject? Does the narrative want the reader to see reality differently? How does the narrative undermine or subvert the reader's accepted norms, values, and beliefs? What are the standards of judgment (ideological point of view) present in a narrative? Narrative point of view—especially ideological point of view—exists to persuade the reader to see the world in a different way, to adopt a new perspective, or to abandon an old point of view. By making strange our firmly held assumptions, values, norms, beliefs, and expectations, the text allows the reader to see a new self—indeed, to become someone else.

57. A poetic text is shorthand for any self-contained text.

58. Susan Sniader Lanser, *The Narrative Act: Point of View in Prose Fiction* (Princeton: Princeton University Press, 1981), 16.

2

Rhetoric

2.1 Definition

Rhetoric is the art of persuasion. It breathes life into a narrative and influences how we feel and think about what the author says. Rhetoric is sometimes thought to be a flourish of words or an imaginative turn of phrase that a speaker or writer uses to capture our attention. But it is not mere ornament or oratorical "emptiness."[1] Rhetoric delights while it persuades; it is an integral and indispensable part of every mode of discourse, whether written or spoken, for it is the means by which authors persuade us of their ideological point of view, norms, beliefs, and values. Rhetorical patterns such as repetitions may help identify the structure of a passage or the theme of a story. Irony may help us understand a writer's theology or the narrative dynamics of individual narratives. Similes and metaphors may slow down our reading so that we pause and puzzle over concepts that we thought we understood. The narrative

1. William Harmon and C. Hugh Holman, *A Handbook to Literature*, 8th ed. (Upper Saddle River, N.J.: Prentice Hall, 1999), 442. For definition of various rhetorical terms see M. H. Abrams, *A Glossary of Literary Terms*, 7th ed. (Fort Worth: Harcourt Brace College Publishers, 1999); Roger Fowler, ed., *A Dictionary of Modern Critical Terms*, rev. and enl. ed. (London: Routledge & Kegan Paul, 1987); Edward P. J. Corbett, *Classical Rhetoric for the Modern Student*, 3rd ed. (New York: Oxford University Press, 1990); Brian Vickers, *In Defence of Rhetoric* (Oxford: Clarendon, 1988); Heinrich Lausberg, *Handbook of Literary Rhetoric: A Foundation for Literary Study*, ed. David E. Orton and R. Dean Anderson, trans. Matthew T. Bliss et. al. (Leiden: Brill, 1998); David E. Aune, *The Westminster Dictionary of New Testament and Early Christian Literature and Rhetoric* (Louisville: Westminster John Knox, 2003).

critic is interested in the devices and techniques an author uses, such as figures of speech and figures of thought, that persuade the reader to make the proper interpretation of a work—that is, the interpretation the author wants the reader to make. The rhetorical devices or patterns discussed in this chapter are a sampling of the many rhetorical patterns found in biblical literature. These include (1) repetition, (2) framing narratives, (3) figures of speech or rhetorical figures, and (4) figures of thought (tropes).

2.2 Repetition

Repetition is a stylistic device that reiterates words, phrases, themes, patterns, situations, and actions for emphasis. When repetition is employed intentionally, it "adds force and clarity to a statement" or motif.[2] It is commonplace in biblical literature and helps identify the norms, values, beliefs, and point of view that the narrator considers important.[3] Repetition is also important for identifying narrative structure and design. A repeated word or thought may divide a narrative passage into smaller units. Repetition occurs in small units such as a repeated word at the beginning of consecutive phrases or sentences, or it occurs in very large units such as narrative type-scenes that have a set pattern of repeated events. Robert Alter suggests an ascending scale of repetitive devices in biblical narratives that runs from the smallest units to the largest, most composite units.[4]

Verbal Repetition

The smallest unit relies on reiteration of key words and phrases to tie together diverse narratives, to elaborate a theme, or to establish an ideological point of view. Verbal repetition thematically links narratives that on first glance appear to be unrelated. The temptation narrative in Matt. 4:1–11, for instance, seems to have little to do with Peter's rebuke of Jesus in Matt. 16:22–23, but a verbal thread ties the two together so

2. C. Hugh Holman, *Handbook to Literature*, 4th ed. (Indianapolis: ITT Bobbs-Merrill, 1980), 376.

3. On repetition in biblical literature see Janice Capel Anderson, *Matthew's Narrative Web: Over, and Over, and Over Again*, JSNTSup 91 (Sheffield: Sheffield Academic Press, 1994); Meir Sternberg, *The Poetics of Biblical Narrative: Ideological Literature and the Drama of Reading* (Bloomington: Indiana University Press, 1985), chapter 11.

4. Robert Alter, *The Art of Biblical Narrative* (New York: Basic Books, 1981), 95–96. The categories of verbal repetition, motif, theme, sequence of actions, and type-scenes are Alter's.

that the one illuminates the other. In Matt. 16:22–23, Peter takes Jesus aside and rebukes him for saying that he will suffer and die. Jesus, in turn, rebukes Peter: "Get behind me, Satan! You are a stumbling block to me; for you are setting your mind not on divine things but on human things." The phrase "Get behind me, Satan" echoes the third temptation of Jesus when the devil takes him to a high mountain and offers him all the world's kingdoms if he will worship him. Jesus' response is similar to his response to Peter: "Away with you, Satan! for it is written, 'Worship the Lord your God and serve only him'" (Matt. 4:10). Janice Capel Anderson notes that this is the only time in Matthew's temptation account that his adversary is called "Satan"; all other times he is called either the "tempter" (4:3) or the "devil" (4:5, 8, 11).[5] The verbal thread suggests that the two narratives are to be read in concert. Peter plays the role of Satan when he attempts to dissuade Jesus from completing his mission of going to the cross, and like Satan, he tempts Jesus to set his mind on the things of this world and not the things of God.

A "charcoal fire" is the verbal thread that links the actions of a principal character in the Gospel of John. The word for "charcoal fire" (*anthrakia*) occurs only twice in the New Testament—both times in the Gospel of John. When Peter enters the high priest's courtyard, he joins the posse that just arrested Jesus. He warms himself by the charcoal fire (John 18:18). This memorable setting is the backdrop for his denial of Christ; like the raging fire, Peter fiercely denies any association with Jesus. In John 21, Jesus invites the disciples to eat a breakfast of bread and fish, cooked on a charcoal fire (John 21:9). Shortly thereafter Peter professes his love for Jesus three times (John 21:15–17). The verbal thread of a "charcoal fire" ties the two antithetical events together: Peter's professed love for Jesus reverses his desertion. The verbal repetition clarifies for the reader that denial is not the end of the story.

Verbal repetition links similar stories, inviting comparison of the narratives. The repetition of the phrase "you of little faith" (*oligopistos*) in the stilling of the storm (Matt. 8:23–27) and in Peter's walking on the water (Matt. 14:22–33) provides a verbal thread that emphasizes "a faith that is too weak, that is paralysed in the storm."[6] Similarly, the repetition of "church" (*ekklēsia*) in Matt. 16:18 and in 18:17 (the only occurrences of the word "church" in the Gospels) draws the two episodes into a mutual commentary. In the one, Peter is given authority to "bind and loose" (Matt. 16:19); in the other, the members of the church are given that authority. Why is a power that is given to Peter alone also given

5. Noted by Anderson, *Matthew's Narrative Web*, 96.

6. Günther Bornkamm, "The Stilling of the Storm in Matthew," in *Tradition and Interpretation in Matthew*, ed. Günther Bornkamm, Gerhard Barth, and Heinz Joachim Held (Philadelphia: Westminster, 1963), 52–57 at 56.

to the group? Is Peter representative of the group? Or does Peter have unique powers in Matt. 16?[7]

Verbal repetition may also accent an author's theology. Matthew uses fulfillment citations to demonstrate that God is at work in the events and happenings of Jesus' life; what occurs does not happen by chance or apart from God's overall design. The stereotypical phrase—"All this took place to fulfill what had been spoken by the Lord through the prophet"—assures the reader that the event is part of God's plan (cf. Matt. 1:22; 2:15, 17, 23; 4:14; 8:17; 12:17; 13:35; 21:4; 27:9).

A famed repetition in the Gospel of Mark is found at the baptism of Jesus and at the tearing of the temple veil. At first there appears to be little relationship between the two events, but, unlike Matthew's account, Mark ties the events together with a verbal thread. He links the two episodes together with a word that is appropriate for the tearing of the temple veil but unusual for the opening of the heavens. At the baptism the heavens are ripped open (*schizō*, Mark 1:10) and at the crucifixion the temple veil is ripped (*schizō*, Mark 15:38) from top to bottom. Matthew uses a more natural verb for the opening of the heavens (*anoigō*, Matt 3:16), but in the process he destroys the verbal parallel between the two events. Mark's verbal thread forces the reader to search for parallels between the two. Rhoads, Dewey, and Michie note that the "'ripping' of the temple curtain just before the centurion recognizes Jesus as 'son of God' recalls by verbal association the 'ripping' of the heavens just before God pronounces Jesus to be 'my son.'"[8] Furthermore, the crucifixion is the first time in the Gospel that Jesus is called "son of God" by a human being, which establishes a correlation between Jesus' death on the cross and humanity's recognition that he is the Son of God. Although supernatural beings recognize Jesus as the "son of God" or "Son of the Most High God," (e.g., Mark 5:7), humans fail to make this association until the crucifixion. Verbal repetition highlights an important Markan theme: the cross is the decisive event that reveals Jesus as Son of God.

Verbal repetition may also clarify the structure of a gospel. Matthew repeatedly uses a stereotyped pattern that divides the Gospel into five major discourses with a prologue and epilogue.[9] The repeated phrase—at 7:28–29; 11:1; 13:53; 19:1; 26:1—is similar, though not identical, throughout: "and when Jesus finished these words"; "and when Jesus had finished instructing the twelve"; "and when Jesus had finished these parables." Jack Dean Kingsbury identifies another phrase that structures the Gospel differently: "from that time on Jesus began to proclaim . . ." and "from

7. These are questions raised by Anderson, *Matthew's Narrative Web*, 94.

8. David Rhoads, Joanna Dewey, and Donald Michie, *Mark as Story: An Introduction to the Narrative of a Gospel*, 2nd ed. (Minneapolis: Fortress, 1999), 48.

9. B. W. Bacon, *Studies in Matthew* (New York: H. Holt, 1930).

that time on, Jesus began . . ." (Matt. 4:17; 16:21).[10] The repetition breaks the Gospel into three sections: (1) the person of Jesus Messiah (1:1–4:16); (2) the proclamation of Jesus Messiah (4:17–16:20); and (3) the suffering, death, and resurrection of Jesus Messiah (16:21–28:20).[11]

Motif

A motif occurs when "a concrete image, sensory quality, action, or object recurs through a particular narrative."[12] A motif may be a way of organizing a narrative, giving it formal coherence, or it may be symbolic. It may rely on key words, and it may not be meaningful in itself outside the context of the narrative. The narrative is the defining context for a motif. Alter cites the usage of "fire" in the Samson narrative as an example of a motif. Samson snaps cords with his strength, which are likened to flax dissolved in fire (Judg. 15:14); the Philistines threaten Samson's first wife with death by fire (Judg. 14:15); Samson sets the Philistines' fields on fire (Judg. 15:4–5); and the Philistines make a bonfire out of Samson's household (Judg. 15:6). The recurrent imagery of fire is a metonymic image for Samson's uncontrollable rage. He is "a blind, uncontrolled force, leaving a terrible swath of destruction" consuming everything that stands in his way, including himself.[13]

An inside/outside motif is prominent in Pilate's to-ing and fro-ing during Jesus' trial (John 18:28–19:16a). In itself, going in and out of a building would not be significant, but Pilate's shuttling back and forth qualifies as a motif because of the narrative context. The recurrent pattern of going inside the praetorium and then outside to the crowd occurs in a context of indecisiveness. The procurator is like a revolving door, torn between two choices.[14]

Inside: Jesus enters the praetorium (18:28).
Outside: Pilate goes outside (18:29).
Inside: Pilate returns inside (18:33).
Outside: Pilate goes back outside (18:38b).

10. Jack Dean Kingsbury, *Matthew: Structure, Christology, Kingdom* (Philadelphia: Fortress, 1975), 7–25.

11. For an evaluation of Bacon and Kingsbury, see Anderson, *Matthew's Narrative Web*, 134–38, and David R. Bauer, *The Structure of Matthew's Gospel: A Study in Literary Design*, JSNTSup 31 (Sheffield: Almond, 1988), chapter 2.

12. Alter, *Art of Biblical Narrative*, 95.

13. Ibid.

14. For a character study of Pilate that underscores his reluctant participation in Jesus' trial and crucifixion, see Martinus C. de Boer, "The Narrative Function of Pilate in John," in *Narrativity in Biblical and Related Texts*, ed. G. J. Brooke and J.-D. Kaestli, BETL 149 (Leuven: Leuven University Press, 2000), 141–58.

Inside: Jesus is scourged (19:1–3).
Outside: Pilate and Jesus go outside (19:4–5).
Inside: Pilate and Jesus go back inside (19:9).
Outside: Pilate takes Jesus outside again (19:13).

Inside Pilate speaks privately to Jesus (John 18:33; 19:9) while outside he speaks to the authorities and the crowd (18:29; 18:38b). Pilate's movements underscore his equivocation and the impossibility of remaining neutral in a face-to-face encounter with Jesus. He wants to be both inside and outside; to listen both to the voice of Jesus inside and to the dissonant, unappeasable voices outside. His shuttling back and forth parallels his desire to compromise truth and falsehood, light and darkness, Jesus' innocence and the strident crowd's desire to have him crucified.

Theme

A theme is an idea that is part of the value system of the narrative and may be associated with key words and motif. It may be a moral, theological, or political theme that is evident from a recurrent pattern. The motif of literally following Jesus on the road, up a mountain, or into a boat may not in itself be significant; but as a recurring pattern it elaborates and develops a theme such as discipleship. Günther Bornkamm argues convincingly that the figurative and literal merge in Matthew's repetition of the key word, "to follow."[15] In Matt. 8:18–22, two sayings on discipleship use the verb "follow." A scribe comes to Jesus and says, "I will follow you wherever you go." Jesus says to another potential disciple, "Follow me." The literal merges with the figurative: to follow Jesus means also to follow him in a deeper sense as his disciple. In the following narrative, the stilling of the storm (Matt. 8:23–27), the narrator records that Jesus got into the boat and "his disciples followed him" (8:23). Although the narrator intends the literal usage, the deeper significance of the word has not "suddenly . . . lost its significance" in 8:23.[16] They are to follow Jesus in times of trouble, especially when they are about to sink (Matt. 8:25).[17]

Luke does not repeat the word "follow" in his account of Jesus praying on the Mount of Olives, but he does reiterate the key words "pray" or "prayer," which influence how we understand the word "follow." Jesus

15. Bornkamm, "The Stilling of the Storm," 52–57.

16. Ibid., 55.

17. Bornkamm sees the stilling of the storm in Matthew as a warning against anyone who "over-thoughtlessly presses to become a disciple" (p. 57), whereas I see the story as encouraging those who are in trouble to follow Jesus, who stills the inner storms as well as the outer storm.

went up to the Mount of Olives "as was his custom" and the disciples "followed him" (Luke 22:39). Luke intends that they literally followed him. Or does he? Jesus commands the disciples to "pray that [they] may not enter into temptation" at the beginning and at the end of the narrative (Luke 22:40, 46). In between this framing device, Jesus prays. Luke not only repeats the word "pray/prayer" several times (Luke 22:41, 44 [?], 45) but also cites Jesus' actual prayer. Jesus prays earnestly that the Father's will be done while the disciples, who are to pray that they not succumb to temptation, fall fast asleep. The word repetition and word association suggest that both meanings of "follow" are present in this account. The disciples are not only to follow Jesus up the mountain; they are to follow his example of earnest prayer.

In Mark "bread" is a key word that links two feeding miracles: (1) an encounter with a Gentile woman, and (2) a discussion with the disciples in a boat on the sea. In Mark 6:30–44 "bread" and "loaves" are repeated several times. The disciples wonder whether they should buy bread for the five thousand; Jesus asks them how many loaves they have; he multiplies the loaves, and twelve baskets of broken pieces [of bread] are gathered. The second narrative dealing with bread is found in Mark 7:24–30. A Syrophoenician woman asks Jesus to cast the demon out of her daughter, but he refuses, saying that the "children" need to be fed first, for it is not right to give their "bread" to the "dogs" ("food" in the NRSV obscures the connection). She replies that even the dogs under the table eat the children's crumbs, recognizing that the bread Jesus offers is sufficient for both the children (Jews) and the dogs (Gentiles). Jesus then heals her daughter.

The third narrative is the feeding of the four thousand in Mark 8:1–9. Again, the disciples wonder, "how can one feed these people with bread here in the desert?" (Mark 8:4). Seven loaves are multiplied and seven baskets of broken pieces are gathered. The last bread narrative in this sequence occurs in a boat on the sea with Jesus and his disciples (Mark 8:14–21). The disciples have forgotten to bring bread for the trip and they have only "one loaf" with them in the boat. When they say they have no bread, Jesus asks why they are talking about the lack of bread. "Do you still not perceive or understand? Are your hearts hardened? Do you have eyes, and fail to see? Do you have ears, and fail to hear? And do you not remember?" (Mark 8:17–18). By reiterating the key words "bread," "loaves," or "crumbs" in these narratives in Mark 6–8, the evangelist suggests that the "one loaf" sufficient for their needs is Jesus himself. The Gentile woman recognized that Jesus could supply her needs; the disciples apparently needed more time to come to this conclusion. Although Mark lacks John's "I am the bread of life" discourse after the feeding of the five thousand (John 6:35–51), he does not need that lengthy discourse. Instead he has tied together separate narratives with the key word "bread" to form a theme similar to that of the Fourth Gospel: Jesus is sufficient for every need.

In Paul, key words not only develop and elaborate themes but also provide important clues as to the nature of the problems that occasion Paul's letters. In Galatians, for example, the key word "flesh" (*sarx*) suggests that the problem at Galatia has something to do with issues involving the "flesh." Paul's opponents at Galatia claim to have the perfect solution to the dilemma created by the liberating freedom of the gospel, on the one hand, and the desires of the flesh, on the other.[18] In 3:3 Paul chides the Galatians: "Having started with the Spirit, are you now ending with the flesh?" In 5:13 he encourages the Galatians not to use their freedom as an opportunity for "self-indulgence" (Greek = *sarx*, "flesh"), and in 5:16 he warns them not to "gratify the desires of the flesh." In 5:17 he bluntly states that what the flesh desires is opposed to the Spirit and what the Spirit desires is opposed to the flesh. In 5:19–21 Paul lists the works of the flesh. In 5:24 he says, "those who belong to Christ Jesus have crucified the flesh with its passions and desires." Flesh is the topic of 6:8, and Paul's opponents want "to make a good showing in the flesh" by compelling the Galatians to be circumcised (Gal. 6:12, 13). The reiteration of "flesh" establishes an underlying theme that Paul addresses. According to Hans Dieter Betz, the Galatians departed from the gospel so quickly after Paul's departure because adversaries—Jewish-Christian missionaries—offered an attractive solution to keep the desires of the flesh in check. The Galatians could pummel the desires of the flesh by supplementing Paul's deficient gospel with the law.

> When "transgressions" had occurred in their community [the Galatians] found themselves unprepared to deal with them. Paul's opponents, however, had the means which seemed to be adequate and effective: Torah and circumcision. The Christian faith coupled with the safeguards provided by the Jewish religion appeared to be a better way to protect the new Christian life from deterioration and destruction than Paul's concept of "freedom."[19]

18. See Hans Dieter Betz, *Galatians: A Commentary on Paul's Letter to the Churches in Galatia*, Hermeneia (Philadelphia: Fortress, 1979), 5–9; Richard N. Longenecker, *Galatians*, WBC 41 (Dallas: Word, 1990), xcvi–c.

19. Betz, *Galatians*, 29. Robert Jewett uses the popular movie *Groundhog Day* as a lens through which to view the Galatian problem. See Robert Jewett, "Stuck in Time: *Kairos*, *Chronos*, and the Flesh in *Groundhog Day*," in *Explorations in Theology and Film: Movies and Meaning*, ed. Clive Marsh and Gaye Ortiz (Oxford: Blackwell, 1998), 155–65.

Sequence of Actions

This form of repetition relies on actions in numerical series (twos, threes, fours, and so forth) to create emphasis. Mark, for instance, uses *two-step progressions* for emphasis.[20] The second step clarifies, elaborates, or amplifies the first step. "That evening, at sundown" in Mark 1:32 appears to be merely repetitious, but "at sundown" adds important information to "that evening." The second step clarifies that the Sabbath was over and people could travel to Jesus for healing without violating the Sabbath laws.[21] The poor widow who put two copper coins in the treasury "put in everything she had, all she had to live on" (Mark 12:44). The second step, "all she had to live on," clarifies the first step. The widow did not merely put in everything she had with her on that day; she put in everything she had to live on, her whole living. Other two-step progressions in Mark include the opening of the Gospel in 1:1 ("the beginning of the good news of Jesus Christ, the Son of God");[22] Jesus' proclamation of the good news ("the time is fulfilled, and the kingdom of God has come near," Mark 1:15); the designation of the woman whose daughter is healed as a "Gentile, of Syrophoenician origin" (Mark 7:26); the clarification of an unfamiliar custom ("on the first day of Unleavened Bread, when the Passover lamb is sacrificed," Mark 14:12).[23] In the book of Revelation, John also uses two-step progressions for emphasis. In Rev. 5:2, for instance, a mighty angel asks, "Who is worthy to open the scroll and break its seals?" The first part in itself would seem to be adequate, for the scroll is described as "written on the inside and on the back, sealed with seven seals" (Rev. 5:1). But the second part adds important information. Not only does the Lamb open the scroll; he also inaugurates the content of the scroll by breaking each of the seven seals.

A series of three may indicate that an action is complete, finished.[24] There may be an intensification of an action from one occurrence to the next, with the third in the series representing a climax. In Matthew's account of Peter's denial each occurrence is progressively intensified. Initially, Peter denies knowing what the maid is talking about when he is questioned (Matt. 26:70). In the second denial, he ups the ante by

20. See Rhoads, Dewey, and Michie, *Mark as Story*, 49–51, for a more complete discussion.

21. Ibid., 49.

22. Some important manuscripts lack the second step, "the Son of God." See Bruce Metzger, *A Textual Commentary on the Greek New Testament*, 2d. ed. (New York: United Bible Societies, 1971), 62.

23. See Frans Neirynck, *Duality in Mark: Contributions to the Study of the Markan Redaction*, rev. ed., BETL (Leuven: Leuven University Press, 1988), for a complete discussion of two-step patterns.

24. Gerhard Delling, "τρεῖς, τρίς, τρίτος," *TDNT* 8:216–25 at 222.

taking an oath when he says, "I do not know the man" (Matt. 26:72). The third denial is intensified further: not only does he take an oath but he even invokes a curse on himself (Matt. 26:74). The repetition and intensification of each occurrence in the series underscores Peter's total abandonment of Jesus.

At the garden of Gethsemane, Mark's series of three emphasizes the disciples' complete failure to stay awake in a time of trial. At first, the narrator's comment is unremarkable: Jesus "came and found them sleeping" (Mark 14:37). His comments, however, are greatly expanded in the second occurrence, and the word "once more" emphasizes the disciples' failure (Mark 14:40). The narrator also uses three finite verbs to highlight the actions: Jesus *"came"* and *"found* them sleeping, for their eyes were very heavy," and "they *did not know* what to say to him." The final occurrence is heightened with the annotation "the third time" (Mark 14:41). "The third time" accentuates their total resistance to Jesus' request. Their physical drowsiness is symbolic of their spiritual drowsiness or lethargy in this time of trial.

In John 21:15–17, Jesus asks Peter three times if he loves him. Each occurrence has three parts (question, response, command) that are either intensified or elaborated in some way as the series progresses. The first time Jesus says, "Simon son of John, do you love me more than these?" Peter responds, "Yes, Lord; you know that I love you." And Jesus commands, "Feed my lambs." The narrator enumerates the second occurrence, "Simon son of John, do you love me?" "Yes, Lord; you know that I love you." "Tend my sheep." Finally the narrator enumerates the third occurrence twice and includes a commentary on Peter's bruised ego: "He said to him *the third time,* 'Simon son of John, do you love me?' Peter felt hurt because he said to him *the third time,* 'Do you love me?' And he said to him, 'Lord, you know everything; you know that I love you.' Jesus said to him, 'Feed my sheep.'" The similarities and differences in the three occurrences are the subject of doubtful conjecture.[25] One similarity that is important, however, is the patronymic that Jesus uses for Peter. Jesus calls him "Simon son of John," Peter's pre-discipleship name, suggesting that Peter needs to start over again as a disciple. Further, each occurrence is progressively intensified, with the third focusing on Peter's disconsolation. The narrator also frames Jesus' question with the repetition of "the third time." The scene in John 21 invites comparison with Peter's denial of Jesus. A threefold denial requires a threefold restoration. Just as the third denial is made more dramatic

25. It is often noted that the verbs for love are different. In the first two occurrences Jesus uses *agapaō* while Peter responds with *phileō*; in the third occurrence both Jesus and Peter use *phileō*. Raymond E. Brown, *The Gospel according to John* (New York: Doubleday, 1966–70), 1:497–99, has shown that the two verbs are used interchangeably in the Gospel.

with the cock crowing, the third restoration is dramatized with Peter's emotional response to Jesus' question. The disciple "became distressed" (John 21:17).[26] As the threefold denial underscores the completeness of Peter's abandonment, so also the threefold question and affirmation in John 21 underscore his readiness to follow Jesus not on his own terms, as in his first call, but on the risen Lord's terms. The narrator then highlights Simon's complete restoration by using his discipleship name, "Peter" (21:17).[27]

Other occurrences of threes are important.[28] There are three temptations in Matthew and Luke, stressing the completeness and finality of Jesus' triumph over his adversary. The temptations in Matthew build to a climax from lesser to greater with the last representing the gravest of all temptations: the worship of a false god (Matt. 4:9). There are also three predictions of the passion in each of the Synoptic Gospels (Mark 8:31–33; 9:30–32; 10:32–34 and parallels). The series of three emphasizes Jesus' resolve to go to Jerusalem and to fulfill God's plan. Also the crucifixion is marked by three-hour intervals (nine o'clock, noon, and three o'clock); the resurrection occurs on the third day; and Pilate declares three times that he finds "no case against [Jesus]" (John 18:38b; 19:4, 6).

In Acts, a voice commands Peter to eat three times. A sheet descends from heaven with all kinds of four-footed creatures and reptiles and birds, and Peter is commanded to kill and eat. But he refuses: "I have never eaten anything that is profane or unclean" (Acts 10:14). A second time the voice says that what God has made clean must not be called profane (Acts 10:15). This happens a third time and then the sheet is taken up to heaven. The threefold repetition underscores the theological point of view of the narrative: what God makes clean must not be treated as profane. Similarly, Peter's meeting with Cornelius is repeated three times with variations (Acts 10:9–48; 11:5–18; 15:7–11).[29] And the conversion

26. BDAG, s.v. λυπέω, 2a.

27. The normal procedure for the narrator is to introduce Peter into a narrative with his full name, Simon Peter, and then return to the shortened form, Peter. In John 21, for instance, the narrator calls him "Simon Peter" in 21:2, 3, 7, 11, 15. After Peter's restoration, he is called simply "Peter" (21:17, 20, 21). The one exception is 21:7a where he is called by the shortened name. On Peter's name in John see James L. Resseguie, *The Strange Gospel: Narrative Design and Point of View in John*, BIS 56 (Leiden: Brill, 2001), 150–55, and J. K. Elliott, "Κηφᾶς: Σίμων Πέτρος: ὁ Πέτρος: An Examination of New Testament Usage," *NovT* 14 (1972): 241–56.

28. Mark 2:1–12 is replete with threes. See Petri Merenlahti, *Poetics for the Gospels? Rethinking Narrative Criticism* (London: T. & T. Clark, 2002), 90. The Letter of Jude contains 20 sets of threes. See J. D. Charles, "Literary Artifice in the Epistle of Jude," *ZNW* 82 (1991): 106–24, and the discussion of threes in Aune, *Literature and Rhetoric*, 473.

29. See Ronald D. Witherup, "Cornelius Over and Over and Over Again: 'Functional Redundancy' in the Acts of the Apostles," *JSNT* 49 (1993): 45–66, for repetitions or "functional redundancy."

of Paul is recorded three times with variations in each occurrence (Acts 9:1–25; 22:1–21; 26:1–23).[30] A close reading will identify not only what is present in each account but also what is absent; what is repeated and what is elaborated; what is eliminated and what is developed; and what theological point of view is shared and what point of view is unique to each narrative. In Revelation, sequences of threes describe God's action and being. In Rev. 1:4 God's eternity is underscored with threes: "who is and who was and who is to come." And in Rev. 10:6, threes describe God's work as Creator: "who created heaven and what is in it, the earth and what is in it, and the sea and what is in it." Similarly, threes are associated with the counterfeit god, Satan, and his emissaries: "And I saw three foul spirits like frogs coming from the mouth of the dragon, from the mouth of the beast, and from the mouth of the false prophet" (Rev. 16:13).

In Revelation, fours are associated with creation or the earth.[31] There are four corners to the earth (Rev. 7:1; 20:8), and four winds that blow from the corners (Rev. 7:1). When John uses sequences of four in the Apocalypse, he emphasizes creation's full and complete participation in an event. Saints are ransomed "from every tribe and language and people and nation" (Rev. 5:9), and "every creature in heaven and on earth and under the earth and in the sea" sing "blessing and honor and glory and might" to God and the Lamb (Rev. 5:13). In Rev. 18:11–13 the list of cargo that Babylon imports from the merchants of the earth consists of twenty-eight items, or four times seven. The cargo represents all the products (seven = completeness) of the whole earth (four = earth).[32]

Type-Scenes

The largest units of repetition are the type-scenes, which are "dependent on the manipulation of a fixed constellation of predetermined motifs."[33] Type-scenes are narratives that have recurrent motifs that the reader recognizes as conventional. Just as we recognize Westerns or detective novels by their fixed constellation of patterns, type-scenes in ancient literature have a fixed pattern of events. Alter refers to the betrothal scenes in the Old Testament as one such type-scene: a future bridegroom

30. See Ronald D. Witherup, "Functional Redundacy in the Acts of the Apostles: A Case Study," *JSNT* 48 (1992): 67–86.

31. Actions in Revelation also involve sevens, tens, twelves, and other patterns. See James L. Resseguie, *Revelation Unsealed: A Narrative Critical Approach to John's Apocalypse*, BIS 32 (Leiden: Brill, 1998), 48–69.

32. Noted by Richard Bauckham, *The Climax of Prophecy: Studies on the Book of Revelation* (Edinburgh: T. & T. Clark, 1993), 31.

33. Alter, *Art of Biblical Narrative*, 51. Alter takes his clue from Homeric type-scenes.

travels to a foreign land; he encounters a girl or girls at a well; the girl or girls rush home to bring news of the stranger's arrival; a betrothal is concluded between the stranger and the girl, often involving a meal.[34] The variations in the different betrothal type-scenes not only add to the artistry of individual scenes but also draw attention to important words, motifs, themes, and personages of each narrative. Indeed the variations to a convention may be the most interesting aspect of type-scene analysis. Examples of betrothal type-scenes are: the encounter between Abraham's servant and Rebekah (Gen. 24:10–61); Jacob's encounter at the well with Rachel (Gen. 29:1–20); Moses and Zipporah (Exod. 2:15b–21); and the book of Ruth. In the New Testament, Jesus' encounter with the woman at the well in John 4 is a betrothal type-scene, though a betrothal of a very different kind—"not in marriage but in worship (4:21–24) and in mission (4:35–42)."[35] Other type-scenes include the annunciation of a hero's birth,[36] trial/temptation in the wilderness, danger and rescue on the sea, healing miracles, exorcisms, meal scenes, and recognition type-scenes.[37] Trial in the wilderness has a fixed constellation of motifs and actions: a large group follows a leader into the desert; the group becomes hungry; a test occurs; a source of sustenance is supernaturally provided; all are sated; an abundance of leftovers are gathered up. One such type-scene is the feeding of the multitudes in the Gospels, and its Old Testament counterpart is the feeding of Israel in the wilderness. There are artful variations on the feeding type-scene. Jesus' temptation in the desert includes a feeding test that he rejects (Matt. 4:2–4; Luke 4:2–4). Matthew and Mark include two feeding miracles—the feeding of the five thousand (Mark 6:32–44; Matt. 14:13–21) and the feeding of the four thousand (Mark 8:1–10; Matt. 15:32–39)—that exhibit similarities and differences. John places the feeding miracle on a mountain and follows it with a "bread of life" discourse (John 6:1–15, 26–59). A variation of the

34. Ibid., 52.

35. C. Clifton Black, *The Rhetoric of the Gospel: Theological Artistry in the Gospels and Acts* (St. Louis: Chalice, 2001), 17. See also L. Eslinger, "The Wooing of the Woman at the Well: Jesus, the Reader, and Reader-Response Criticism," *LitTh* 1 (1987): 167–83; Jo-Ann A. Brant, "Husband Hunting: Characterization and Narrative Art in the Gospel of John," *BibInt* 4 (1996): 205–23. The connections between John 4 and OT betrothal scenes, however, are doubtful. See Resseguie, *Strange Gospel*, 75n45, and Teresa Okure, *The Johannine Approach to Mission: A Contextual Study of John 4:1–42*, WUNT, 2nd series, 31 (Tübingen: J. C. B. Mohr [Paul Siebeck], 1988), 88–89.

36. Alter, *Art of Biblical Narrative*, 51; idem, "How Convention Helps Us Read: The Case of the Bible's Annunciation Type-Scenes," *Prooftexts* 3 (1983): 115–30.

37. A detailed analysis of the barren wife type-scenes in the Old Testament can be found in John Petersen, *Reading Women's Stories: Female Characters in the Hebrew Bible* (Minneapolis: Fortress, 2004), 30–69. On healing type-scenes see David Rhoads, *Reading Mark: Engaging the Gospel* (Minneapolis: Fortress, 2004), 69–73.

type-scene also occurs in the book of Revelation. The dragon or Satan pursues a woman, who is an image of the church, into the wilderness; there she is given sanctuary and provided with divine sustenance for "a time, and times, and half a time" (Rev. 12:13–17).

The sea narratives in the Gospels are type-scenes with a fixed sequence of motifs and actions: there is danger on the sea; Jesus is distant, on the shore or asleep in the boat; the disciples are afraid; Jesus calms the sea; the disciples are amazed. In the stilling-of-the-storm narrative, Jesus is present with the disciples in the boat and he rebukes them for their lack of faith (Mark 4:35–41; Matt. 8:23–27; Luke 8:22–25). In the walking-on-the-water narrative, Jesus is not present in the boat but appears later to the disciples by walking on the sea (Mark 6:45–52; Matt. 14:22–33; John 6:16–21). Variations occur: in Matthew and Mark, Jesus calms the sea, whereas John omits the taming of the sea but narrates another miracle, the disciples' sudden arrival at their destination the moment Jesus boards the boat (John 6:21). In Matthew, Peter ventures out into the water and sinks. By comparing similarities and differences between specific type-scenes, the reader can see more clearly the narrator's theological emphases and point of view.

2.3 Framing Narratives

A framing narrative is an envelope for another narrative, thus forming an A B A′ pattern. The embedded narrative (B) interrupts the framing narrative (A, A′), which is resumed after the embedded narrative ends. New Testament critics also call this rhetorical pattern *intercalation* or *sandwiching*. Mark, for example, splits a narrative in half to nestle a second narrative within the frame.[38] The framing narrative may comment on the embedded narrative by either comparison or contrast, or the embedded narrative may comment on the framing narrative.[39]

A famed example of a framing narrative and its embedded narrative is the cursing and withering of the fig tree and the cleansing of the temple in Mark. Whereas Matthew has the cursing and withering as a single event that happens after the cleansing of the temple (Matt. 21:18–19),

38. On intercalations in Mark see Tom Shepherd, "The Narrative Function of Markan Intercalation," *NTS* 41 (1995): 522–40; James R. Edwards, "Markan Sandwiches: The Significance of Interpolations in Markan Narratives," *NovT* 31 (1989): 193–216; Rhoads, Dewey, and Michie, *Mark as Story*, 51–52; Frank Kermode, *The Genesis of Secrecy: On the Interpretation of Narrative* (Cambridge: Harvard University Press, 1979), 128–34.

39. Edward's thesis that the "*middle story nearly always provides the key to the theological purpose* of the sandwich" is too restrictive (italics Edwards). He acknowledges that the outer frame also comments on the inner. See Edwards, *Markan Sandwiches*, 196, 208.

Mark splits the cursing and withering so that it frames the cleansing of the temple (Mark 11:12–14 [A]; 11:15–19 [B]; 11:20–21[A′]). The withering and cursing of the fig tree thus serves as a commentary on the future of the temple. Other Markan framing narratives include: (1) a narrative about Jesus' family (3:20–21, 3:31–35) frames an accusation that he is demon-possessed (3:22–30); (2) a story about Jairus and his daughter (5:21–24, 5:35–43) frames the narrative of a woman with a hemorrhage (5:25–34); (3) a story about the sending and return of the Twelve (6:7–13, 6:30–32) frames the narrative of the death of John the Baptist (6:14–29); (4) a story of conspiracy and intrigue (14:1–2, 14:10–11) frames a story of the anointing of Jesus at Bethany (14:3–9); and (5) the story of Peter's denial (14:53–54, 14:66–72) frames Jesus' trial before the Sanhedrin (14:55–65).

On a larger scale, Mark frames an entire section of his Gospel with two healing miracles. The framing narrative forms a commentary on the embedded narratives. Mark's healing miracles of the blind (Mark 8:22–26; 10:46–52) are a metonymic image for the disciples' own blindness. Mark has only two narratives that have as their subject matter the healing of the blind, and both are strategically placed to illustrate the inner material. By themselves the miracles would not be an annotation on the disciples' opacity, but the Markan framing turns the narratives into a commentary on their imperceptiveness. The healing of the blind man at Bethsaida (Mark 8:22–26), which occurs only in Mark's Gospel, requires two steps. After Jesus spits on the man's eyes and lays his hands upon him, his vision is cloudy. "I can see people; but they look like trees, walking" (Mark 8:24). A second time Jesus lays his hands on his eyes and he "saw everything clearly" (Mark 8:25). The two-stage process is puzzling but takes on meaning when we see the disciples stumble in their understanding of Jesus' words and actions. The second healing miracle at Jericho (Mark 10:46–52) brackets the disciples' opacity. In between the healing of the blind men are instances of the disciples' spiritual blindness: (1) After Peter confesses Jesus as the Christ, he rebukes him for predicting that he will be killed (Mark 8:32). (2) At the transfiguration the disciples puzzle over the meaning of "rising from the dead" (Mark 9:10). (3) When Jesus foretells his passion a second time, the disciples fail to understand (Mark 9:32). (4) The disciples rebuke the people who bring the children to Jesus (Mark 10:13). (5) And conflict occurs among them when James and John ask to have the places of honor next to Jesus (Mark 10:35–45). The recurrent pattern of the disciples' failure to see, sandwiched between two stories of men who are unable to see, suggests that the disciples also need healing. Like the man who could see partially but not fully, the disciples have merely partial vision concerning Jesus' identity and thus need a second touch.

In Revelation, embedded narratives disrupt the opening of the seals and the blowing of the trumpets and provide close-ups of the events.[40] The opening of the seals (6:1–8:1) is halted after the sixth seal (6:12–17), while a story about the 144,000 and the countless multitude is inserted (7:1–17). At the conclusion of the embedded narrative the seventh seal is opened (8:1). Similarly, the trumpets (8:2–11:18) are interrupted after the sixth is blown (9:13–21) so that 10:1–11:14 can be inserted before the blowing of the seventh trumpet (11:15).

2.4 Rhetorical Figures

Rhetorical figures or *figures of speech* depart from customary or standard usage of language by the order and pattern of words and phrases. They use words and phrases in their customary or literal manner, but they achieve special effects by the arrangement of words, phrases, clauses, and syntactical forms. Rhetorical figures include but are not limited to rhetorical questions, antithesis, parallelism, chiasmus, inclusions, and anaphora.

Parallelism is the similarity in structure of a pair of words, phrases, clauses, or syntactical arrangements. For example, in Rev. 22:11,

A Let the evildoer still do evil,
  A′ and the filthy still be filthy,
B and the righteous still do right,
  B′ and the holy still be holy.

The first two clauses (A, A′) are a *synonymous parallelism*, as are the last two (B, B′). The parallel clauses reiterate the same concept but use different words. Notice also that the two parts are marked off by the same adverb and verb combination: "still do"/"still be"//"still do"/"still be." And, finally, the last two clauses contrast with the first two. *Antithesis* is also a form of parallelism in which the second line or couplet contrasts with the first. John 9:39—as well as the above example—demonstrates antithesis:

I came into this world for judgment so that
  those who do not see may see,
  and those who do see may become blind.

Some of the rhetorical devices discussed in this section are forms of repetitions (e.g., chiasm, inclusion, anaphora, parallelism) that could

40. Aune, *Literature and Rhetoric*, 231.

be part of the section on repetitions. But they are placed here for convenience because they are common rhetorical figures. Four rhetorical figures are discussed in detail: (1) anaphora, (2) inclusion, (3) chiasm, and (4) rhetorical question.

Anaphora

Anaphora (sometimes called *epanaphora*) is the repetition of the same expression at the beginning of two or more successive clauses or sentences to add force to an argument. In 1 Cor. 3:9 Paul uses anaphora to hammer into the Corinthians' heads the role of the apostles: "For we are God's servants, working together; you are God's field, God's building." In Phil. 2:1-2 Paul's repetition of "any" builds to a forceful climax. "If then there is any encouragement in Christ, any consolation from love, any sharing in the Spirit, any compassion and sympathy, make my joy complete." In chapter 11 the writer to the Hebrews summarizes his theological point of view with two words: "by faith."[41] "By faith we understand . . ."// "by faith Abel . . ."// "by faith Noah . . ."// "by faith Abraham . . ." // "by faith Isaac . . ."// "by faith Jacob . . ." // "by faith Joseph . . ." // "by faith Moses . . ."// "by faith the people passed through the Red Sea . . ."// "by faith the walls of Jericho fell . . ."// "by faith Rahab. . . ." The entire sweep of Jewish history is summed up in the anaphora.

An interesting combination of anaphora and antithesis for theological emphasis is found in 1 Cor. 12:4–6:

> Now there are varieties of gifts,
>   but the same Spirit;
> and there are varieties of services,
>   but the same Lord;
> and there are varieties of activities,
>   but it is the same God who activates all of them in everyone.

The form corresponds to the content, underscoring both unity and diversity, both sameness and difference.

Inclusion (Inclusio)

Inclusions are words, phrases, or concepts that bracket narratives or larger units such as a section of a book or even an entire book. Inclusions are framing devices that identify beginnings and endings of narratives, or underscore prominent themes and concepts of a story. Matthew, for

41. In the Greek there is one word, but, as in English, two syllables: *pis-tei*.

instance, opens and closes his Gospel with the repetition of "God with us." In Matt. 1:23 Jesus is "Emmanuel," which means "God is with us"; the Gospel comes full circle with the same concept on the mountain: "I am with you always" (Matt. 28:20). The temple is the thematic bracket of Luke's Gospel. Luke opens with Zechariah in the temple (Luke 1:8–23) and closes with the disciples "continually in the temple blessing God" (Luke 24:53). In the book of Revelation, God's speech brackets the narrative: "I am the Alpha and Omega" (Rev. 1:8) and "It is done! I am the Alpha and Omega, the beginning and the end" (Rev. 21:6). John's artistry is on display here: not only does God's speech bracket the narrative but also the content of God's discourse emphasizes beginnings and endings. The theological point of view is thus reinforced by literary artistry. Similarly, Jesus' speech brackets the narrative with words nearly identical to those of God: "I am the first and the last" (Rev. 1:17) and "I am the Alpha and Omega, the first and the last, the beginning and the end" (Rev. 22:13).

Individual narratives are also bracketed with words, phrases, and concepts that help identify the themes of the narratives as well as beginnings and endings. Matthew's genealogy, for instance, is bracketed by references to Jesus as the Messiah, the son of David, and the son of Abraham. He opens with "an account of the genealogy of Jesus the Messiah, the son of David, the son of Abraham" (1:1), and closes the genealogy in reverse order: Abraham, David, and the Messiah (Matt. 1:17). Within the inclusion are additional brackets that divide the genealogy into three sections of fourteen generations. The Matthean inclusio places Jesus' birth within the entire sweep of Israel's history while accenting key christological titles of the Gospel. The inclusion also provides a glimpse into the narrator's ideological perspective. The neatly structured patterns of Matthew's genealogy suggest that he views God as bringing order into this world. In 1 Cor. 13 Paul wraps his encomium with the word "love": "If I speak in the tongues of mortals and of angels, but do not have love . . ." // "the greatest of these is love" (1 Cor. 13:1, 13). In Phil. 2:6–11 the word "God" forms an inclusion that brackets the second half of the hymn, identifying a new section with a change in subject. "Therefore God also highly exalted him"// "and every tongue should confess that Jesus Christ is Lord to the glory of God the Father" (Phil. 2:9, 11).

Chiasm (Chiasmus)

The word chiasm is derived from the Greek letter chi (written X), which symbolizes the crossover pattern of words, phrases, clauses, or ideas that are repeated in reverse order.[42] The simplest type of chiasm is A B B′ A′—a structure that comes full circle by highlighting key concepts in reverse order. A chiastic pattern in Mark 2:27, for instance, keeps the reader's or hearer's attention focused on the main concepts.

A The *sabbath* was made
  B for *humankind*
  B′ not *humankind*
A′ for the *sabbath*.

Chiasms may draw attention to a theological or ideological perspective. Jesus' prayer in the garden of Gethsemane is an example of literary artistry at its best. The literary form reinforces the theological perspective. In Luke 22:42, for example:

A Father, if *you* are willing.
  B remove this cup from *me*;
  B′ yet, not *my* will
A′ but *yours* be done.

The first person singular (me, my) is placed within the second person singular (you, yours), which visually underscores that Jesus' will is completely enclosed within the will of the Father. This becomes a model prayer for all: our will needs to be conformed to God's will, not the other way around.

Paul uses chiasms to wrap together an entire book with key theological concepts. In the Letter to the Ephesians he brackets his correspondence with the words "grace" and "peace" (also in 2 Thess. 1:2 and 3:16, 18).

A *Grace* to you
  B and *peace*. . . .
  B′ *Peace* be to the whole community. . . .
A′ *Grace* be with all who have an undying love for our Lord Jesus Christ.
(Eph. 1:2; 6:23, 24)

42. Narrative critics usually do not distinguish between chiasmus and antimetabole, which is the repetition of two or more words in inverted order. For a more complete discussion of chiasmus see Aune, *Literature and Rhetoric*, 93–96; J. Breck, "Biblical Chiasmus: Exploring Structure for Meaning," *BTB* 17 (1987): 70–74; J. P. Heil, "The Chiastic Structure and Meaning of Paul's Letter to Philemon," *CBQ* 82 (2001): 178–206; A. Boyd Luter and Michelle V. Lee, "Philippians as Chiasmus: Key to the Structure, Unity, and Theme Question," *NTS* 41 (1995): 89–101; I. H. Thomson, *Chiasmus in the Pauline Letters*, JSNTSup 111 (Sheffield: Sheffield Academic Press, 1995); Augustine Stock, "Chiastic Awareness and Education in Antiquity," *BTB* 17 (1984): 70–74.

Paul comes full circle, underscoring an important theological perspective: where there is grace, there is peace, and where there is peace, there is evidence of God's grace. Paul also uses interlocking chiasms to highlight the mystery of the Christian faith. In 1 Tim. 3:16, for example, an interlocking pattern explains "the mystery of our religion."

> [Jesus] was revealed in *flesh,*
> vindicated in *spirit,*
> seen by *angels,*
> proclaimed among *Gentiles,*
> believed in throughout the *world,*
> taken up in *glory.*

Two sets of overlapping chiasms bring two separate worlds together—this world and the world above. One set—flesh (A), spirit (B), angels (B′), Gentiles (A′)—is joined by a second set—angels (A), Gentiles (B), world (B′), glory (A′). The interlocking pattern suggests that Jesus brings together in balanced harmony two worlds that were separated or at odds with each other.[43]

Some narrative critics find chiasms or *ring compositions* in a series of episodes or narratives. Joanna Dewey, for example, identifies an A, B, C, B′, and A′ pattern in the five episodes of Mark 2:1–3:6.[44] A and A′ are healing stories: one about a paralytic and the other about a man with a withered hand. B and B′ are stories about eating: eating with tax collectors and sinners on the one hand, and eating plucked grain on the other. In the center of this concentric pattern (C) is Jesus' teaching about fasting, which illuminates all the other scenes.

Rhetorical Question

A rhetorical question is a statement in the form of a question that does not expect a reply but is stated to achieve greater persuasive power than a direct statement. The answer to a rhetorical question is usually obvious and is the only one available. In the New Testament, Paul uses rhetorical questions to enliven and embolden his argument, and Jesus uses rhetorical questions to reveal the disciples' dull-wittedness, lack of faith, or some other gap in their understanding or beliefs. Jesus also uses rhetorical questions to expose gaps in an adversary's point of view

43. See James L. Resseguie, "New Testament as Literature," *EDB*, 815–17 at 817.

44. See Joanna Dewey, *Markan Public Debate: Literary Technique, Concentric Structure, and Theology in Mark 2:1 to 3:6*, SBLDS 48 (Chico, Calif.: Scholars Press, 1980); see also John Dart, *Decoding Mark* (Harrisburg, Pa.: Trinity Press International, 2003); Rhoads, Dewey, and Michie, *Mark as Story*, 52–54.

as well as to state the obvious. When the Pharisees, for instance, point out the unlawfulness of the disciples' plucking of grain on the Sabbath, Jesus dismantles their objection with two rhetorical questions.

> Have you not read what David did when he and his companions were hungry? He entered the house of God and ate the bread of the Presence, which it was not lawful for him or his companions to eat, but only for the priests. Or have you not read in the law that on the sabbath the priests in the temple break the sabbath and yet are guiltless? (Matt. 12:3–5)

This shows the forceful impact that rhetorical questions can have in a narrative. Jesus uses rhetorical questions from two portions of the Torah to refute those who are defenders of the law. "Have you not read" is a withering critique of his audience's objection. To the Corinthians, Paul states the obvious, using a series of rhetorical questions. "Am I not free? Am I not an apostle? Have I not see Jesus our Lord? Are you not my work in the Lord?" (1 Cor. 9:1).

2.5 Figures of Thought (Tropes)

Figures of thought or tropes use words and phrases that depart from customary or standard ways of using the language. This device is different from rhetorical figures. Rhetorical figures use language in the customary, standard, or literal way but depart from standard usage by the syntactical order or pattern of words. Parallelism, for instance, uses language in its customary way but departs from standard usage by placing words, phrases, concepts, and syntax in parallel arrangement. Coordinate ideas are represented by coordinate constructions.[45] Similarly, anaphora is a rhetorical figure in which the same expression is repeated at the beginning of two or more sentences.

Figures of thought, on the other hand, use words and phrases in a nonliteral way. Some figures of thought are hyperbole, paradox, simile, synecdoche, metonymy, metaphor, understatement, double entendre, misunderstanding, and carnivalesque. *Metonymy* (Greek for "change of name") substitutes one term for another concept with which it is closely associated. "The White House" is metonymic for the president of the United States; "the crown" for a king, and so forth. "Fire" in the Samson narrative, as Alter has shown, is a metonymic image for Samson's rage. In 1 Cor. 12:30 "tongues" stands for languages. And when Jesus says that Lazarus is asleep, he is substituting sleep for death (John 11:11).

45. Harmon and Holman, *Handbook*, 373–74.

Paradox is a figure of speech that seems absurd or contradictory yet upon closer reflection is true. It demands attention and causes us to slow down and think. Mark 8:35 is a paradox: "For those who want to save their life will lose it, and those who lose their life for my sake, and for the sake of the gospel, will save it." *Synecdoche* is a metaphor in which the part signifies the whole or, more rarely, the whole signifies the part. "All hands on deck" is a synecdoche for all sailors on deck. When Paul refers to the Jews and Greeks as "circumcised" and "uncircumcised," he is using synecdoche. *Understatement* (Greek *meiōsis*, "lessening") is a form of irony in which something is intentionally represented as less than it is. The most common form of understatement in the New Testament is *litotes*, which asserts an affirmative by negating the opposite. In Acts 12:18, for instance, Luke says there was "no small commotion" among the soldiers over Peter's absence from prison. *Hyperbole* (Greek for "overshooting") is the opposite of understatement. It is an exaggeration or bold overstatement to heighten an effect, to call attention to a norm or value, to shock the reader into seeing something that could not readily be seen. When Jesus says, "If your right eye causes you to sin, tear it out and throw it away" (Matt. 5:29), we get the point without taking it literally. Or, when he says that it is easier for a camel to enter the eye of a needle than for a rich person to enter the kingdom of God (Mark 10:25), we recognize that he is using hyperbole to make a point that could not be made effectively with standard or literal language. The search for a literal meaning of Jesus' saying—for example, a low gate named Eye of a Needle—obscures the hyperbole and its intended effect.

The figures discussed in detail here are (1) simile and metaphor, (2) double entendre and misunderstanding, (3) irony, and (4) carnivalesque.

Simile and Metaphor

A *simile* compares two distinctly different things with the use of "like" or "as."[46] The parable of the Leaven in Matt. 13:33 is a simile that compares the kingdom of heaven to leaven: "The kingdom of heaven is *like* yeast that a woman took and mixed in with three measures of flour, till all of it was leavened." The kingdom of heaven does not look like leaven and it is not a yeastlike substance, but it works in the same way as leaven works in flour. A *metaphor*, on the other hand, does not state explicitly a comparison between two distinctly different things. Instead, a metaphor ascribes an action or quality of one thing to a second by way of identity. For example, Jesus' statements "I am the bread of life" and "I am the light

46. On simile and metaphor see G. B. Caird, *The Language and Imagery of the Bible* (Philadelphia: Westminster, 1980), 144–59.

of the world" are metaphors, for two different qualities or objects—bread and light—are applied to Jesus by way of identity. Bread in its literal usage denotes one kind of thing that is applied figuratively to Jesus to assert something important about him. As Craig Koester aptly notes, "Jesus was not claiming to be a baked mixture of flour and water in a physical sense." Instead the incongruity between the literal or standard usage of bread and the way Jesus uses the concept forces people "to understand the meaning in another way, asking in what sense Jesus *is* claiming to be bread."[47]

I. A. Richards's concepts of *tenor* and *vehicle* are helpful terms for the analysis of metaphors and similes.[48] A tenor is the subject of the comparison and the vehicle is the metaphorical term itself. Or, to phrase it differently, the vehicle is the image that illumines the tenor or subject of the metaphor. The vehicle and tenor together make up the metaphor, and the reader must discover the implied analogy or implicit comparison that exists between the two parts. Although Richards used these terms for metaphors, they could also be applied to similes and parables with equal success. Many parables are extended similes or metaphors, so identifying the vehicle, tenor, and point of comparison may be important to understanding a parable's meaning.[49] The parable of the children playing in the marketplace illustrates Richards's concepts:

> To what then will I compare the people of this generation, and what are they like? They are like children sitting in the marketplace and calling to one another,
>
> "We played the flute for you, and
> you did not dance;
> we wailed, and
> you did not weep."
>
> (Luke 7:31–32)

In this example "like" is used to make a comparison. The tenor is the "people of this generation" and the vehicle is the analogy of children playing in the marketplace. But even this analogy requires close attention and analysis. We are to imagine two groups of children playing a game in the marketplace with each group shouting back and forth. One group

47. Craig R. Koester, *Symbolism in the Fourth Gospel: Meaning, Mystery, Community* (Minneapolis: Fortress, 1995), 96.

48. I. A. Richards, *The Philosophy of Rhetoric* (New York: Oxford University Press, 1936), 119–27.

49. Adolf Jülicher, *Die Gleichnisreden Jesu*, 2nd ed. (Tübingen: J. C. B. Mohr, 1910), analyzed *similitudes*, i.e., parables that are extended metaphors, in a similar way. He identified a "picture part" or *Bildhälfte* ("vehicle" in Richards's terms), a "reality part" or *Sachhälfte* ("tenor" in Richards's terms), and a point of comparison or *tertium comparationis* between the picture part and the reality part.

wants to celebrate (i.e., play wedding), but the second group does not want to play this game. The first group then calls back and suggests that they mourn (play funeral), but again the second group refuses to play. The point of the comparison between the children and this generation is that no matter what is offered—and notice that two opposite games are suggested, celebration and mourning—"this generation" does not want to participate. Luke explains the analogy further with a reference to John the Baptist and the Son of Man. "For John the Baptist has come eating no bread and drinking no wine, and you say 'He has a demon'; the Son of Man has come eating and drinking, and you say, 'Look, a glutton and a drunkard, a friend of tax collectors and sinners!" (Luke 7:33–34).

More difficult is the following metaphor: "Wherever the corpse is, there the vultures will gather" (Matt. 24:28). The tenor can only be gleaned from the context. Nevertheless, the vehicle should be analyzed on its own terms before identifying the tenor. The part that bears the weight of the comparison (vehicle) is an analogy involving vultures and a corpse. When one sees vultures circling above, it is obvious that a carcass is nearby. But the metaphor is obscure until the tenor is identified from the surrounding context. In the end times false messiahs and false prophets will appear that will "produce great signs and omens, to lead [people] astray" (Matt. 24:24). Some will be swayed by their appearance and announce that the Messiah has appeared in the desert or in inner rooms—in other words, in secret (Matt. 24:26). The metaphor of vultures and corpses applies to the appearance of the Messiah at the second coming, which is the tenor.[50] Will it be obvious to all? Or will the Messiah appear in secret to some? The point of comparison between the vehicle (vultures and corpse) and the tenor (appearance of Messiah) is that the coming of the Son of Man will be as unmistakable as the presence of vultures indicates a carcass nearby. Matthew reinforces the comparison with a simile: "For as the lightning comes from the east and flashes as far as the west, so will be the coming of the Son of Man" (Matt. 24:27).

Double Entendre and Misunderstanding

A *double entendre* or double meaning (also called a *double entente*) is a word that has two meanings and both meanings are intended. An example of a double entendre is the word *katalambanein* ("overcome"

50. See Warren Carter, "Are There Imperial Texts in the Class? Intertextual Eagles and Matthean Eschatology as 'Lights Out' Time for Imperial Rome (Matthew 24:27–31)," *JBL* 122 (2003): 467–87, for a different interpretation. Carter argues that the eagles (vultures) represent the defeated Roman imperial order and share the same eschatological fate as the corpse.

or "understand") in the prologue of John's Gospel (John 1:5). The verb means "seize" in the sense of "grasp," which passes over to the sense "comprehend." It can also mean "seize with a hostile intent, overcome."[51] Does the narrator say, "the light shines in the darkness, and the darkness did not comprehend it"? Or does he say, "the light shines in the darkness, and the darkness did not overcome it"? Or does he intend both senses of *katalambanein*? Commentators are divided. Rudolf Bultmann understands it in the first sense: the darkness does not comprehend the light.[52] Francis J. Moloney argues for the second meaning: the darkness does not overcome the light, which is also the translation in the NRSV.[53] C. K. Barrett avers that both meanings are intended.[54] Darkness is both uncomprehending of the light and hostile to the light.

A *misunderstanding* uses double entendres, ambiguous statements, or metaphors to create bewilderment or misunderstanding in the hearer, which is then resolved either by Jesus or the narrator. J. H. Bernard offers a deceptively simple definition of misunderstanding: "A saying of deep import is uttered by Jesus; His hearers misunderstand it, after a fashion that seems stupid; and then He repeats the saying in a slightly different form before He explains it and draws out its lesson."[55] Misunderstandings occur when a hearer selects one meaning for a word that has more than one meaning, and believes that the meaning he or she has selected exhausts the range of meanings. According to Rudolf Bultmann, "the misunderstanding comes when someone sees the right meaning of the word but mistakenly imagines that its meaning is exhausted by the reference to earthly matters."[56] R. Alan Culpepper identifies three parts to Johannine misunderstandings:[57] (1) Jesus makes a claim using a double entendre or metaphor that is ambiguous. (2) The hearer selects one meaning for the statement over another possible meaning. Usually the hearer selects a literal meaning when Jesus intends a figurative meaning. (3) Jesus or the narrator clarifies the misunderstanding with an explanation.

51. BDAG, s.v. καταλαμβάνω.

52. Rudolf Bultmann, *The Gospel of John: A Commentary*, trans. G. R. Beasley-Murray (Philadelphia: Westminster, 1971), 47–48.

53. Francis J. Moloney, *Belief in the Word: Reading the Fourth Gospel, John 1–4* (Minneapolis: Fortress, 1993), 33.

54. C. K. Barrett, *The Gospel according to St. John: An Introduction with Commentary and Notes on the Greek Text*, 2nd ed. (Philadelphia: Westminster, 1978), 158–59. See also Resseguie, *Strange Gospel*, 51–52.

55. J. H. Bernard, *A Critical and Exegetical Commentary on the Gospel according to St. John*, 2 vols. (New York: Scribner's, 1929), 1:cxi.

56. Bultmann, *John*, 135n1.

57. R. Alan Culpepper, *Anatomy of the Fourth Gospel: A Study in Literary Design* (Philadelphia: Fortress, 1983), 152.

The stories of the woman at the well and of Nicodemus provide two fine examples of Johannine misunderstandings that rely on ambiguity and double entendres. In John 4, the woman stumbles over the meaning of "living water" (*hydōr zōn*). In part 1 of the misunderstanding, Jesus asks a Samaritan woman for a drink of water. When she wonders why a Jew is asking a Samaritan for a drink, Jesus responds with an ambiguous statement: "If you knew the gift of God, and who it is that is saying to you, 'Give me a drink,' you would have asked him, and he would have given you living water" (John 4:10). In part 2, the woman assumes that Jesus knows about a flowing stream ("living water") somewhere that will make her job of fetching water easier: "Sir, you have no bucket, and the well is deep. Where do you get that living water?" (John 4:11). In part 3, Jesus explains that the living water he provides is unlike everyday, mundane water: "Everyone who drinks of this water [from the well] will be thirsty again, but those who drink of the water that I will give them will never be thirsty" (John 4:13–14). The misunderstanding is an effective literary device not only because of the ambiguity inherent in the meaning of living water but also because of the appropriateness of water as an analogy. Living water may be a flowing stream, as the woman thinks, or "a spring of water gushing up to eternal life" in the believer, as Jesus intends. The desire to quench thirst sharpens the misunderstanding and drives home the point of the narrative. The drive to slake thirst at the physical level is a desire for satisfaction—to quench our thirst—and this innate drive at the mundane level is a common expression of a more profound desire to quench our thirst at the spiritual level, once and for all.

In John 3, Nicodemus stumbles over Jesus' words. In part 1 of the misunderstanding, Jesus makes an ambiguous claim: "Very truly I tell you, no one can see the kingdom of God without being born *from above*." Or should it be "born *again*"? Translators do their share of stumbling over the double entendre, *anōthen*, because both meanings are intended, and translators naturally have to choose one meaning over another. The problem is not that Nicodemus chose the wrong meaning for the word; the problem is that he adopted a crassly material understanding of the word when Jesus intended a spiritual understanding. In part 2, Nicodemus states his misunderstanding: "How can anyone be born after having grown old? Can one enter a second time into the mother's womb and be born?" (John 3:4). Nicodemus understands *anōthen* in terms of "born *again*" to mean a second physical birth. In part 3, Jesus explains what he means, although Nicodemus is still befuddled: "Very truly, I tell you, no one can enter the kingdom of God without being born of water and Spirit. What is born of the flesh is flesh, and what is born of the Spirit is spirit. Do not be astonished that I said to you, 'You must be born *from above*'" (John 3:5–7). The narrator intends both meanings of the word. Nicodemus must be born *again, from above*. Nicodemus assumes that salvation is a work of humankind, an act of self-improvement, while for Jesus rebirth is entirely an act of God. Nicodemus, however, was not entirely wrong: a person must be born again, but it is a spiritual second birth, from above.

These examples illustrate the value of understanding an author's rhetorical devices. They allow us to read at a deeper level. Misunderstanding and double entendres are not simply clever rhetorical devices to keep the reader's attention. They are profound ways of communicating the depth of the writer's theology. In the two examples cited above there is a clash between the material and the spiritual, the everyday and the eternal, the mundane and the supramundane. The misunderstanding allows one to move from a reading at the surface level to a deeper reading. A surface reading sees only the everyday, the quotidian, the ordinary—just as the woman at the well understands water at a physical, mundane level. Yet to read and to understand at this level is not sufficient. John wants the reader to move from the surface to a deeper, spiritual understanding—just as the woman comes to see that Jesus is talking about spiritual matters, not mundane water.

Irony

Roger Fowler defines irony as "a mode of discourse for conveying meanings different from—and usually opposite to—the professed or ostensible ones."[58] Irony's effectiveness relies on exploitation of the distance between words and events and their contexts. D. C. Muecke identifies three basic features of all irony. First, irony depends on a double-layered or two-story phenomenon for success. "At the lower level is the situation either as it appears to the victim of irony (where there is a victim) or as it is deceptively presented by the ironist."[59] The upper level is the situation as it appears to the reader or the ironist. Second, the ironist exploits a contradiction, incongruity, or incompatibility between the two levels. Third, irony plays upon the innocence of a character or victim. "Either a victim is confidently unaware of the very possibility of there

58. Fowler, *Modern Critical Terms*, 128. On irony in the New Testament see Jerry Camery-Hoggatt, *Irony in Mark's Gospel: Text and Subtext*, SNTSMS 72 (Cambridge: Cambridge University Press, 1992); Paul Duke, *Irony in the Fourth Gospel* (Atlanta: John Knox, 1985); Resseguie, *Strange Gospel*, 28–41; Stephen H. Smith, *A Lion with Wings: A Narrative-Critical Approach to Mark's Gospel*, The Biblical Seminar 38 (Sheffield: Sheffield Academic Press, 1996), chapter 6.

59. D. C. Muecke, *The Compass of Irony* (London: Methuen, 1969), 19.

being an upper level or point of view that invalidates his own, or an ironist pretends not to be aware of it."[60]

All irony falls into two major categories: verbal, which applies to a statement, and situational, which applies to an event.[61] In verbal irony a contradiction occurs between what is expressed and what is implied. The writer or speaker makes explicit one attitude or evaluation but implies a different attitude or evaluation that is often the opposite of what is expressed.[62] Appreciation of verbal irony depends upon recognizing a sharp disparity between what a writer says and what a writer means. In everyday speech, tone of voice and context provide clues that the speaker is ironical; with tongue-in-cheek the ironist indicates a double significance through intonation. But in written discourse irony relies upon techniques of indirection such as understatement, pun, paradox, hyperbole, sarcasm, or other forms of incongruities and reversals for its success.[63] Jane Austin, for example, opens her novel *Pride and Prejudice* with a famous ironical statement that highlights the nineteenth-century assumption that a single woman must be in search of a wealthy husband: "It is a truth universally acknowledged, that a single man in possession of a good fortune, must be in want of a wife."[64]

Situational irony depends for its success on an incongruity or contradiction between what a speaker says and what the author intends. Whereas in verbal irony a contradiction or incongruity—shared by both speaker and reader—exists between what is said and what is intended, in situational irony the speaker is naïve about the irony and unaware that he or she is being ironical. Only the author and reader share insight into the irony. In Muecke's two-story phenomenon, the author and reader are in a superior position upstairs while the victim of the irony, the character or speaker, is downstairs unaware of the second level. In Sophocles' *Oedipus*, for instance, the audience knows something that Oedipus does not. Oedipus hunts for the person whose actions have caused a plague upon Thebes. Although the audience knows that Oedipus caused the plague by committing incest and parricide, Oedipus himself is unaware that the hunter is the hunted. This form of irony is also called *dramatic irony* because the audience or reader shares knowledge with the author about present or future circumstances of which the character is ignorant.

60. Ibid., 20.

61. Fowler, *Modern Critical Terms*, 128.

62. Abrams, *Glossary*, 135.

63. Fowler, *Modern Critical Terms*, 129.

64. Jane Austin, *Pride and Prejudice*, ed. Donald Gray, 3rd ed. (New York: W. W. Norton, 2001), 3.

Another form of situational irony is *structural irony*, in which the author uses a structural feature "to sustain a duplex of meaning and evaluation throughout the work."[65] The writer sometimes uses a naïve hero, naïve narrator, or naïve spokesperson as a literary device to sustain the irony. The naïve speaker puts an interpretation on events and words that the perceptive reader knows must be altered or reinterpreted.

Verbal Irony

Verbal irony can be very subtle and requires close attention to clues. When Jesus says to the Pharisees, "You have a fine way of rejecting the commandment of God in order to keep your tradition!" (Mark 7:9), the clue to Jesus' ironic tone is conveyed in the word "fine." In the crucifixion scenes verbal irony relies on verbal clues such as "Aha," and expressive actions such as wagging the head.[66] The context also intensifies the irony. In Mark 15:29–32a the irony is heavy among passersby, chief priests, and scribes, who join in hurling taunts at Jesus on the cross:

> Those who passed by derided him, shaking their heads and saying, "Aha! You who would destroy the temple and build it in three days, save yourself, and come down from the cross!" In the same way the chief priests, along with the scribes, were also mocking him among themselves and saying, "He saved others; he cannot save himself. Let the Messiah, the King of Israel, come down from the cross now, so that we may see and believe."

The irony works on two levels. On one level the speakers do not mean what they say. When the chief priests and scribes refer to Jesus as "Messiah, the King of Israel," they say this with tongue in cheek, for it is inconceivable that the long-awaited Messiah would be rejected and killed. The chief priests and scribes believe they are upstairs in Muecke's diagram, and from their superior vantage point Jesus' claims are fraudulent. But in an ironic twist the verbal irony becomes dramatic irony, and suddenly the ironists are downstairs, unaware of a second level to their own words. When, for example, the passersby hurl at Jesus his claim that he would destroy the temple and rebuild it in three days, little do they realize that what they say as a taunt might be the truth. Jesus' claim that "in three days I will build another [temple], not made with hands" (Mark 14:58b) alludes to his resurrection. Since these are the words of his accusers and not Jesus' actual words, they may not be an accurate reflection of what he said; nevertheless, Mark's readers are well aware of claims and counterclaims and the ironical situation created by the

65. Abrams, *Glossary of Literary Terms*, 135.

66. See Robert M. Fowler, *Let the Reader Understand: Reader-Response Criticism and the Gospel of Mark* (Minneapolis: Fortress, 1991), 156–63.

words of the passersby. And when the ironists taunt, "Save yourself, and come down from the cross," little do they realize that Jesus' mission is to suffer and die (Mark 8:31; 9:31; 10:33–34). Similarly, the chief priests and scribes are unaware of a second layer of irony in their jeer, "he saved others, he cannot save himself" (Mark 15:31). As verbal irony it ridicules the absurdness of a crucified Messiah; as dramatic irony it voices "one of the supreme ironies of history," which eludes the religious leaders.[67] Mark thus uses irony to speak the truth and Jesus' adversaries to proclaim the gospel.

Situational Irony

A classic example of situational or dramatic irony is Nathanael's overconfidence concerning Jesus' origin: "Can anything good come out of Nazareth?" (John 1:46). Nathanael does not believe anything good can come out of Nazareth, but John exploits his overconfidence and turns it into dramatic irony. Muecke's three features of irony are present. First, the reader and the author are upstairs with the knowledge that Jesus is the Messiah while Nathanael, who is downstairs, lacks this information. Second, the distance between what the reader and author know and what Nathanael says is exploited. An incongruity occurs between what Nathanael believes to be certain and what the reader and author know to be true. Third, Nathanael is an innocent victim, unaware of a second level of meaning. This irony of mistaken assumption is exploited by John to show how God acts in this world. Nathanael's words are intended to dismiss Philip's assertion that they have found the Messiah: certainly nothing good can come out of such an insignificant place as Nazareth. But the evangelist uses Nathanael's quip to unveil a new perspective: God does not work in this world according to commonplace expectations but in new and surprising ways. "God's action is surprising and incredible; and the offence of the Messiah's coming from Nazareth belongs . . . to the offence of the incarnation of the Logos."[68]

A famed case of dramatic irony occurs in Caiaphas's remark to the chief priests and Pharisees: "You know nothing at all! You do not understand that it is better for you to have one man die for the people than to have the whole nation destroyed" (John 11:49–50). Caiaphas intends no irony, but nevertheless his statement is ironical because the choice of words is ambiguous. In Muecke's diagram, he is downstairs, unaware of a second level of meaning to his words, which John exploits with wonderful success. The high priest's solution is merely a practi-

67. Vincent Taylor, *The Gospel according to St. Mark*, 2nd ed. (London: Macmillan, 1960), 592.

68. Bultmann, *John*, 103–4.

cal response to a troublemaker: Jesus' preaching and healing pose a threat to the safety of Israel; it is better to sacrifice one person to spare the nation than to have the Romans come and destroy the temple and the nation. Caiaphas says more than he intends but not less than what the narrator intends. A second level of meaning of which Caiaphas is unaware turns his straightforward statement into dramatic irony. The preposition "for" or "in place of" (*hyper*) can also have the meaning "on behalf of." Caiaphas intends "in place of." Jesus must die in place of Israel to spare the people. But the narrator intends "on behalf of." Jesus must die on behalf of the people. Jesus' death spares the people but not in the way Caiaphas thinks, and the narrator clarifies this upstairs meaning for the reader: "He did not say this on his own, but being high priest that year he prophesied that Jesus was about to die for [*hyper*] the nation, and not for the nation only, but to gather into one the dispersed children of God" (John 11:51–52). The high priest "could not suspect that Jesus would die, not in place of Israel but on behalf of the true Israel."[69]

A subtle form of irony relies upon paradox to bring out seeming contradictions in the nature of Jesus' mission. At one point in the Gospel of John, Jesus says, "I came into this world for judgment so that those who do not see may see, and those who do see may become blind" (John 9:39). At another point, however, he says, "I judge no one" (John 8:15) and "I came not to judge the world, but to save the world" (John 12:47). How is it that Jesus comes to judge but not to judge? Does he judge some and not others? The paradox captures the situational irony of Jesus' ministry and mission. He comes both to judge and not to judge, but he does not need to judge because people bring about judgment on themselves by their response to Jesus' words and deeds. The ones who receive sight (insight), such as the blind man in John 9, are at the upper level and understand the meaning of Jesus' words and deeds, while those who think they see but are actually blind are at the lower level. The authorities in John 9 persist in seeing when in reality they are unseeing. They remain imperceptive because they refuse the insight that Jesus brings, so that by their response to Jesus they bring judgment on themselves. Gail O'Day explains the paradox:

> Those who encounter Jesus' revealing words will either become "blind" to them and be unable to move beyond the literal level or will "receive sight" and be able to make the necessary judgments and movement to comprehend both levels of his statements. The responsibility for the interpretation of

69. Brown, *John*, 1:442.

> Jesus' words is placed on each individual, which is why Jesus is able to say that he comes both to judge and not to judge.[70]

In some forms of situational irony an *eiron* brings into focus two contrasting views. The opposite of the eiron, who feigns ignorance, is an *alazon,* or braggart who pretends to know more than he actually knows. In John 9, the blind man is an eiron who deflates the overconfident claims of the alazon or religious leaders. The irony is delicious, for example, when the authorities want to hear a second time how the man was healed. "Why do you want to hear it again," he says. "Do you also want to become his disciples?" (John 9:27). And when the authorities say, "We know that God has spoken to Moses, but as for this man [Jesus], we do not know where he comes from," the man punctures their braggadocio: "Here is an astonishing thing! You do not know where he comes from, and yet he opened my eyes" (John 9:29–30).

A different sort of duel takes place in the parable of the Tax Collector and the Pharisee (Luke 18:9–14). There is no verbal exchange between the characters, but the posture and words of the tax collector serve to deflate the braggart's claims. The tax collector knows his status before God: he is a sinner and cannot look up to heaven. Instead he beats his breast in contrition and prays for mercy. The Pharisee, however, reveals his alazony in a prayer that drips with self-congratulatory confidence. "God, I thank you that I am not like other people: thieves, rogues, adulterers, or even like this tax collector. I fast twice a week; I give a tenth of all my income" (Luke 18:11–12). This is also an instance of tragic irony, for one of the main characters brings about his downfall with his own words. The person justified is not the person who thinks he is justified.

The trial of Jesus in Mark is an instance of structural irony that relies on naïve spokespersons and the readers' awareness of events that elude the characters. Before Jesus is put on trial at the high priest's residence, he predicts that Peter will deny him: "This day, this very night, before the cock crows twice, you will deny me three times" (Mark 14:30). Although the reader and narrator are aware of Jesus' prediction, the high priest's guards are obtuse, persisting in the belief that Jesus is a false prophet. They spit on him, blindfold him, and strike him. Then they beat him and demand, "Prophesy!" (Mark 14:65). A second level of irony builds upon their verbal irony. They are the naïve spokesmen who persist in knowing when, in fact, they are unknowing. Although they believe he is not a prophet, the reader and narrator who are upstairs have knowledge that those downstairs cannot possibly know. In the very next scene

70. Gail R. O'Day, *Revelation in the Fourth Gospel: Narrative Mode and Theological Claim* (Philadelphia: Fortress, 1986), 9.

(Mark 14:66–72) Peter is asked three times if he was with Jesus, and three times he denies it. Peter's actions unwittingly confirm Jesus as a prophet (Mark 14:30). At the very moment the guards blindly mock Jesus' prophetic ability, Jesus' prophesy of Peter's denial comes true. The reader will also recognize in the irony the incongruity of a blindfolded Jesus who is knowing while the seeing guards are blind.

This narrative also develops another aspect of structural irony. When narratives are placed side by side, they may mutually illumine each other, creating an ironical situation. This happens in the trial of Jesus before the Sanhedrin (Mark 14:53–65) and the informal trial of Peter that occurs in the courtyard of the high priest's residence (Mark 14: 66–72). The two trials illumine each other, reinforcing Jesus' innocence and identity and Peter's guilt and frail loyalty. In Jesus' trial the testimony against him is false and the accusers cannot even agree on their testimony. He remains silent and offers no defense against the false charges (Mark 14:61). Yet when he speaks, he speaks truthfully. The high priest asks him, "Are you the Messiah, the Son of the Blessed One," and Jesus does not deny it. Jesus vindicates himself because he speaks truthfully and refuses to defend himself against false accusations. He is innocent and loses his life. By contrast, Peter's trial is one of true accusations and false denials. His guilt spares his life but only at the cost of his identity as a disciple of Jesus. The servant-girl accuses him, "You also were with Jesus, the man from Nazareth" (Mark 14:67), but Peter denies it saying, "I do not know or understand what you are talking about" (Mark 14:68). A second time the servant-girl says that he is one of the disciples of Jesus, but Peter again denies it. Finally some bystanders say to him, "Certainly you are one of them; for you are a Galilean" (Mark 14:70). This time Peter curses and swears an oath in a desperate act of self-preservation, "I do not know this man you are talking about." Ironically his denial is true: he does *not* know Jesus. His estrangement is complete and the cock crows twice. The situational irony highlights the innocence of Jesus and the truthfulness of his claims while accentuating Peter's alienation and shame. The narrative began with Peter following "at a distance" (Mark 14:54) and ends with Peter distant in another sense.

The Value of Irony

The narrative function of irony is (1) to convince the reader of the narrator's point of view, (2) to build a community of believers, (3) to heighten narrative claims in ways that straightforward discourse cannot achieve. Irony is used to persuade the reader of the narrator's beliefs, norms, values, and point of view.[71] Since irony functions on two levels at the same time—upstairs and downstairs—the reader moves from downstairs, or a naïve form of reading, to upstairs, or a mature form of reading. An upstairs reading is deeper, thicker, and more in line with the author's worldview. When Jesus, for example, claims to judge but not to judge, the incongruity forces the reader to gain a deeper understanding into the nature and purpose of Jesus' mission.

Irony also functions to build community. The community-building nature of irony results from the superior position of the reader, who sees and understands what escapes the characters. Their obtuseness is a reminder that the reader could also, in similar circumstances, be as dense. Peter's Panglossian outlook—"even though all become deserters, I will not" (Mark 14:29)—builds sympathy among readers who know that they would act the same way in a similar situation. Or the reader may smile when James and John ask Jesus if they can sit at his right and left when he enters his glory, not realizing that his glory is the cross (Mark 10:35–40). The sympathetic reader knows that he or she may be just as unknowing in a similar situation. The irony accents for the reader that God's ways do not conform to our expectations. For Wayne Booth irony builds community in ways that straightforward discourse is powerless to achieve:

> It seems clear that Mark's irony builds a larger community of readers than any possible literal statement of his beliefs could have done. If he had said simply, "Those who gathered to mock Jesus did not know that he was in fact King, king not only of the Jews but of all mankind, quite literally the Son of God," a host of unbelievers would draw back, at least slightly. But the ironic form can be shared by everyone who has any sympathy for Jesus at all, man or God; even the reader who sees him as a self-deluded fanatic is likely to join Mark in his reading of the irony, and thus to have his sympathy for the crucified man somewhat increased.[72]

A third function of irony is to heighten narrative claims in ways that straightforward discourse cannot accomplish. There is no finer example of this function of irony than the soldiers' salute, "Hail, King of the Jews!" (Matt. 27:29; Mark 15:18; John 19:3). With verbal irony they mock Jesus as a dismal failure and a pretend king, while dramatic irony accents the truth. The narrator and reader who are upstairs know that the acclamation rings true in ways that the soldiers could not possibly understand.

71. Camery-Hoggatt, *Irony in Mark's Gospel*, 180, also concludes that irony functions on the level of ideological point of view.

72. Wayne C. Booth, *A Rhetoric of Irony* (Chicago: University of Chicago Press, 1974), 29.

Not only is Jesus King of the Jews, but also the soldiers' actions strangely confirm the nature of his rule: he is a suffering and rejected Messiah. Straightforward discourse could not convey the ambiguity and paradox of Jesus' mission as effectively as the acerbic irony of the Roman soldiers. The dramatic irony of the Pharisee in the temple who thinks he is righteous but is not drives home the peril of a self-congratulatory spiritual life in ways that standard discourse fails to do.

Carnivalesque

Carnivalesque relies heavily on satire and parody to question, ridicule, and invert commonplace norms, values, and beliefs of the dominant culture.

Bakhtin and the World of Carnival

Carnivalesque is a concept, popularized by Mikhail Bakhtin, that highlights the upside down, inside out, top to bottom, inverted world of carnival. Carnival predates Christianity and expresses "life drawn out of its *usual* rut" and "the reverse side of the world (*'monde à l'envers'*)" in which everyday social hierarchies are turned upside down and mocked by normally suppressed voices of the culture.[73] Carnivalesque is prominent in the passion scenes of the Gospels, where symbols and actions mock a staid, authoritarian society and provide the transforming regenerative power for an alternative society. Opposites that underscore the relativity of all structure and order are paired in carnival: king with slave, crowning with de-crowning, exaltation with debasement, and sacred with profane. Similar opposites are paired at the crucifixion: an innocent man dies while an outlaw goes free (Barabbas); the sun fails at noon; the temple veil is torn from top to bottom; a carnival procession mocks the king, which, in turn, mocks the triumphal processions of conquering heroes; a cross serves as a throne; jeers (carnivalistic laughter) deride while ironically affirming truth. The images of carnival are linked to the paradox of death and rebirth. Carnivalesque is never simple negation but has a

73. Mikhail Bakhtin, *Problems of Dostoevsky's Poetics*, ed. and trans. Caryl Emerson, THL (Minneapolis: University of Minnesota Press, 1984), 122. See also Mikhail Bakhtin, *Rabelais and His World*, trans. Hèléne Iswolsky (Bloomington: Indiana University Press, 1984), 5–12. On the carnivalesque in biblical literature see Kenneth M. Craig, *Reading Esther: A Case for the Literary Carnivalesque*, LCBI (Louisville: Westminster John Knox, 1995); Robert L. Brawley, *Text to Text Pours Forth Speech: Voices of Scripture in Luke-Acts*, ISBL (Bloomington: Indiana University Press, 1995), chapters 4 and 5. On Bakhtin's theory of aesthetics and Matthew's Gospel see John A. Barnet, *Not the Righteous but Sinners: M. M. Bakhtin's Theory of Aesthetics and the Problem of Reader-Character Interaction in Matthew's Gospel*, JSNTSup 246 (London; T. & T. Clark International, 2003).

second, positive level of meaning. The downward, negative movement that characterizes the crucifixion world of abuse, curse, debasing, profanation, mockery, and death contains within it the regenerative power of an upward, positive movement of rejuvenation, renewal of life, and transformed symbols of power. In this sense, carnivalesque is like a U-shaped plot with a downward turn that moves upward to a new stable condition.[74] Bakhtin identifies four basic categories that distinguish this alternative world.

First, the laws, prohibitions, restrictions, and hierarchical structures that are associated with the structure and order of everyday life are suspended in carnival. "All the forms of terror, reverence, piety, and etiquette" that support existing hierarchical structures are destabilized. As a result, distance between people is suspended and "a special carnival category goes into effect: *free and familiar contact among people*."[75] Second, a new mode of interrelationship between individuals occurs. "The behavior, gesture, and discourse of a person are freed from the authority of all hierarchical positions (social estate, rank, age, property) defining them totally in noncarnival life."[76] In carnival the latent sides of human nature reveal and express themselves.

Third, carnival combines "the sacred with the profane, the lofty with the low, the great with the insignificant, the wise with the stupid."[77] A free and familiar attitude spreads over values, thoughts, and phenomena. Fourth, carnival is characterized by profanation or "carnivalistic blasphemies, a whole system of carnivalistic debasings and bringings down to earth, carnivalistic obscenities."[78] Spitting, cursing, mocking, deriding are part of the profanation in carnival.

For Bakhtin, the primary carnivalistic act is the mock crowning and subsequent de-crowning of a carnival king. Crowning and de-crowning is a "dualistic ambivalent ritual" that typifies the inside-out world of carnival and the *"joyful relativity* of all structure and order, of all authority and all (hierarchical) position."[79] In carnival, the one who is crowned is the antipode of a real king, thereby subverting and inverting normal concepts of kingship. The symbols of crown, scepter, and robe that symbolize structures of authority in the ordinary world take on new meanings in this mock ritual. Serious symbols become mere stage props to undermine the "heavy," "serious" structures of the everyday world. Coronation is incomplete without de-coronation: regal vestments

74. See 6.3 below on plot.
75. Bakhtin, *Dostoevsky's Poetics*, 123.
76. Ibid.
77. Ibid.
78. Ibid.
79. Ibid., 124.

are stripped off, the crown and scepter are removed, and the mock king is beaten. The de-crowning, however, is "not naked, absolute negation and destruction," but rather it expresses "the carnival pathos of shifts and renewals, the image of constructive death."[80] The old symbols die so that a new concept of kingship is born.

The Crowning and De-crowning of Jesus

In Matthew's account of the crowning/de-crowning narrative (Matt. 27:27–31), Gentile soldiers lead Jesus to the praetorium, place a scarlet cloak on his shoulders, a mock crown on his head, and a reed as a scepter in his right hand. Then they kneel and ridicule him. De-crowning completes the act of crowning: the royal cloak and scepter are stripped away and Jesus' own clothes are put on him again. Carnivalesque heightens the hidden contradictions in Jesus' reign. In the noncarnival world, i.e., in the noncrucifixion world, the religious establishment or prophets enthrone kings within Israel in a solemn ceremony that usually includes anointing with oil. The priest Zadok anointed Solomon in the presence of the prophet Nathan (1 Kings 1:39), and Samuel anointed Saul and David.[81] In Matthew and Mark the carnivalistic anointing is a complete profanation of this solemn ceremony in ancient Israel. The soldiers anoint Jesus with spittle—an act that demonstrates contempt not only for Jesus but for all structures of authority. The investiture is also a total debasing of coronation in the noncarnival world. It is not performed by representatives at the top of the status hierarchy—the religious establishment—but by complete outsiders, members of the lowest stratum, Gentile soldiers. The hierarchical world is turned inside out in the coronation. The soldiers' coronation sneers at the suggestion that Jesus is King of the Jews. Yet carnivalistic acts are always dualistic, ambivalent symbols with a positive as well as negative connotation. The coronation by complete outsiders heightens, intensifies, and even celebrates in a strange sort of way the different type of kingship Jesus inaugurates. This ambivalence is underscored also in the soldiers' speech. Their acclamation, "Hail, King of the Jews," is a carnivalistic debasing, a form of carnival laughter that ridicules Jesus as a messianic pretender (Matt. 27:29). Yet their insincere, hollow words are ironic testimony—by outsiders no less—that Jesus is "King of the Jews." Carnival also "brings together, unifies, weds, and combines the sacred with the profane, the lofty with the low, the

80. Ibid., 125.

81. Marc Zvi Brettler, *God Is King: Understanding an Israelite Metaphor*, JSOTSup 76 (Sheffield: Sheffield Academic Press, 1989), describes the coronation process in ancient Israel.

great with the insignificant."[82] This wedding of the lofty with the low (*carnivalistic mésalliances*) happens when a slave becomes a mock king, another debasing of normal hierarchical structures. The soldiers are unaware of what Jesus has said about the exercise of authority, but the reader is aware. The disciples are not to "lord" over others; instead they are to be slaves just as Jesus came "not to be served but to serve" (Mark 10:42–45; Matt. 20:25–28). Jesus combines these opposites; he is the antipode of everyday kings—a king who is slave.

The investiture emphasizes the "joyful relativity" of all structure and order. "Heavy" symbols of robe and crown are mocked as they are reduced to mere stage props that ridicule the mock king. The symbols of power—scarlet robe, crown, and scepter (reed)—are given to Jesus only to be taken away once they have served to debase. In Matthew, the soldiers place a mock scepter in his right hand and kneel before him. A golden scepter in the ancient world is a symbol of power and sovereignty. It is also an instrument of protection. Only those who are summoned with the scepter could approach the throne (Esther 5:2; 8:4).[83] Jesus' scepter is a complete inversion of the golden scepter of kings. His scepter is a reed, which is not a symbol of dignity but of degradation, and to add to Christ's indignity, the soldiers take the reed out of his hand and strike him on the head with it. In both Matthew and Mark the royal cloak is stripped away. The ritual of changing clothes is an important carnivalistic act. Royal robes that are put on and then stripped away say something about the relativity of structures of power and authority. It is a role reversal: Jesus is at once king but not king. Or, more precisely, Jesus is king, but not the type of king who wears the garments of everyday kings and rulers. His rule is of a different order, and therefore, everyday symbols of power and authority must be stripped away to make way for a new kind of king. One vestige of authority remains in the Gospel accounts, although even this symbol is ambivalent, pointing to a new kind of rule. The crown is left on Jesus' head as a sign that he is a ruler of a different order. But this crown is ambivalent. It is not made of gold or laurel; instead it is a wreath of indignity, a crown of thorns.

The carnival scene of the crowning and de-crowning of Jesus appears on the surface to be absolute negation: jeering, abuse, spitting, and mockery of a pretend king. But within the ludic celebration of negativity is a positive side. Jesus inaugurates a new kind of order, a different type of kingdom. He came not to be served but to serve, not to "lord it over others" but to be a slave. By unraveling rigid and dogmatic structures of authority, carnivalesque suggests new ways of structuring this world.

82. Bakhtin, *Dostoevsky's Poetics*, 123.
83. Craig, *Reading Esther*, 101.

2.6 A Reading of Rhetoric in Luke 24:13–35

This reading examines the literary devices of a sample narrative to demonstrate the integral and indispensable part that rhetoric plays in narrative analysis. Since character, plot, setting, point of view, and other aspects of narrative are not fully developed, the reading is necessarily partial and incomplete. Nevertheless, it illustrates how one aspect of narrative analysis can contribute to our understanding of a narrative. Among the literary devices elaborated are repetition, inclusion, chiasm, irony, metaphor, two-step progression, and rhetorical question.

The Emmaus narrative is a *recognition type-scene,* or a recognition plot that has a set configuration of events. A mysterious stranger happens to come upon a traveler on a journey. The traveler does not recognize the stranger or in some other way lacks sight or insight, and he invites the stranger to join him or to stay for a meal. The stranger interprets Scripture or reveals himself. The traveler then recognizes Jesus or understands scripture in a new way. The stranger then mysteriously disappears.

Philip's encounter with the Ethopian eunuch (Acts 8:26–40) is in various ways both similar and dissimilar to the Emmaus account.[84] Philip comes upon a traveler who is reading a passage from Isaiah. Prompted by the Holy Spirit, he goes over and joins the Ethopian, who then invites him into his chariot. The Ethopian does not understand about whom Isaiah speaks. Philip metaphorically opens his eyes by interpreting the Scriptures, and when they come upon some water, the Ethopian is baptized. Philip then mysteriously disappears: "the Spirit of the Lord snatched Philip away; the eunuch saw him no more, and went on his way rejoicing" (Acts 8:39). Other recognition type-scenes include Mary Magdalene's encounter with Jesus in John 20:11–18 and the seven disciples' recognition of Jesus in John 21:1–14. Although each account varies slightly, the common thread is an awakening to a risen Lord.

13. And behold two of them on that same day were going to a village about a hundred and sixty stadia from Jerusalem, named Emmaus.[85]

The narrative exposition identifies the characters ("two of them"), the day ("that same day"), their city of departure ("from Jerusalem"), their destination ("Emmaus"), and the distance ("one hundred and sixty stadia," or seven miles). Lukan artistry is apparent at every turn. The references to time and place are *inclusions* that frame the narrative and introduce important themes.

84. See Joseph A. Grassi, "Emmaus Revisited (Luke 24,13–35 and Acts 8,26–40)," *CBQ* 26 (1964): 463–67, for a development of the similarities.

85. The translation of Luke 24:13–35 is the author's.

Time:

on that same day (v. 13)
and that same hour (v. 33)

Place:

from Jerusalem (v. 13)
to Jerusalem (v. 33)

The temporal notation in verse 13 places the conversation on the road to Emmaus on "that same day," which is the first of three references to the resurrection day (vv. 13, 21, 33). The second temporal setting, at the end of the narrative, adds a note of urgency concerning the disciples' discovery (v. 33). After the travelers recognize that Jesus is the mysterious stranger, they get up from the table "that same hour" and return to Jerusalem. Since a *two-step progression* emphasizes that the day is already spent ("stay with us because it is towards evening and the day is far spent," v. 29), the return to Jerusalem "that same hour" is important. The urgency of their seven-mile journey corresponds to the urgency of their discovery (cf. v. 35).

The second inclusion hints at the point of the story. They travel from Jerusalem (v. 13) and return to Jerusalem (v. 33), which is emblematic of the many reversals or changes in perspective, expectation, and mood in the narrative. This is a story about shattered expectations that are reformulated; closed eyes that are opened; nonrecognition that turns to recognition; disconsolation that becomes a burning heart.

14. and they were talking with each other about all these things that had happened.

"These things" is a *verbal thread* that runs throughout the narrative. The repetition accents not only the importance of the events of that day but also highlights the characters' divergent interpretation of those same events. Jesus approaches the two and asks them "what are these words" they are talking about (v. 17). Cleopas wonders if Jesus is the only stranger in Jerusalem who does not know "the things that have taken place there in these days" (v. 18). Jesus asks them, "what things?" and they respond, "the things concerning Jesus of Nazareth" (v. 19). In recounting their story they say, "it is the third day since these things happened" (v. 21), and Jesus chides the two with a *rhetorical question*: "Was it not necessary that the Messiah should suffer these things and to enter into his glory?" (v. 26). He then interprets "the things concerning himself in all the scriptures" (v. 27). When the two return to Jerusalem, they tell the others "the things that happened on the road" (v. 35). Just as the characters undergo a transformation in the narrative, "these things" undergo a transformation. At first, "these things" are the events of the past few days—the suffering and death of Jesus—that the two recount with remarkable detail. In one sense they know "these things," yet in another sense they do not know "these things." Their understanding lacks insight. Their perspective is clouded by false expectations of the way God works in this world. At the conclusion of the narrative "these things," (*tauta*) or "the things" (*ta*) takes on a new meaning; the phrase no longer represents their failed insight but summarizes their new understanding.

The inclusion—"were talking with each other" and "they said to one another"—is the frame for their awakening. It brackets both Jesus' surprising appearance and his sudden disappearance.

> And they *were talking with each other* about these things. (v. 14)
>
> *And they said to one another,* "Were not our hearts on fire within us while he was talking to us on the road, while he opened to us the scriptures?" (v. 32)

15–16. *And it happened while they were talking and discussing Jesus himself drew near and went with them. But their eyes were kept from recognizing him.*

"Eyes" are one of two *metaphors* of the human anatomy for their altered point of view and their new insight. Closed eyes represent nonrecognition while opened eyes symbolize recognition. The other metaphor is "heart." In verse 25, the two have a slow heart, and in verse 32, they have a burning heart. A slow heart is a metaphor for dullness while a burning heart represents renewed perception. By pairing the metaphors with their opposites, Luke underscores the reversal of the old and the start of the new—an artistic way to underscore the multiple ways resurrection day shatters old perceptions and creates new ones.

A *chiasm* also brackets the disciples' nonrecognition and its reversal. A chiasm itself is a reversal of form (A, B, B′, A′) that, at least in this instance, corresponds to its content. The opening of blocked eyes parallels their awakening to a new understanding.

> A But *their eyes*
>   B *were kept* from recognizing him (v. 16).
>   B′ Then *they were opened,*
> A′ *the eyes,* and they recognized him (v. 31).

Other references to the travelers' blocked vision are sandwiched between this chiasm. Some of the disciples went to the tomb, "but they did not see" Jesus (v. 24). The Scriptures are also closed to the disciples' understanding until Jesus opens (i.e., interprets) them (vv. 26, 27, 32).

Situational or dramatic irony underscores the travelers' lack of insight, which the emphatic pronoun heightens: "*Jesus himself* drew near and went with them" (v. 15). The one whom they are discussing becomes their traveling companion. The passive voice adds suspense and mystery to the recognition plot. "Their eyes were kept from recognizing him." Who or what keeps their eyes from recognizing Jesus? The reader must read on, but the grammar and irony suggest a barrier to recognition. How is it possible to recognize Jesus when he appears as a stranger, God incognito? What is needed to see him?

17–18. And he said to them, "What are these words that you discuss with one another while walking? And they stood still looking sad. Then one by the name of Cleopas answered and said to him, "Are you the only stranger in Jerusalem who does not know the things that have taken place there in these days?"

Cleopas's question amplifies the irony. "Stranger" is a possible interpretation of the Greek and adds to the irony. Indeed Jesus is a stranger until their eyes are opened. It is curiously ironical that Jesus is asked if he is the only one who does not know the things that have taken place in Jerusalem. The irony underscores that the disciples cannot possibly know the events of resurrection day unless Jesus himself reveals those things. An inclusion of references to their inner disposition frames and heightens their awakening:

> They stood still, *looking sad.* (v. 17)
>
> "Were not our *hearts burning* within us?" (v. 32)

19–21. And he said to them, "What things?" And they said to him, "The things concerning Jesus of Nazareth who was a prophet mighty in word and deed before God and all the people, and how our chief priests and leaders handed him over to be condemned to death and crucified him. And we were hoping that he is the one about to redeem Israel. Indeed, besides all this, this day is the third day since these things happened.

Dramatic irony heightens the narrative tension and underscores the narrator's ideological point of view. Cleopas says that "we were hoping that he is the one about to redeem Israel," not realizing that the person before them is Israel's hope for redemption. The irony accents the misunderstanding and, more important, their limited point of view. Their hope for redemption was dashed with Jesus' death and crucifixion—for they were expecting a Messiah to deliver them from political oppression by the Romans.[86] But it is precisely his death and crucifixion that make possible redemption, and not until they see this point of view will their eyes be opened. Two divergent points of view are thus represented in the phrase "the third day." For Cleopas and his friend, who are downstairs in Muecke's two-story house, the arrival of "the third day" merely confirms their shattered expectations. Their expectations were crushed on crucifixion day. For the readers, who are upstairs in a superior position, "the third day" is the fulfillment of what Jesus had prophesied all along (9:22; 13:32; 18:33).

22–24. "Moreover, some of the women from our group amazed us. They were at the tomb early this morning, and they did not find his body, and they came saying that they had even seen a vision of angels who said that he was alive. And some of those who were with us went to the tomb and found it just as the women said; but him they did not see."

Once more "seeing" is a key verbal thread. The "seeing" recognize that Jesus is alive; the "unseeing" fail to see him. The women "had seen a vision of angels" who said that Jesus was alive, but those who went to the tomb "did not see him." Sight, whether literal or figurative, is essential in this narrative. Those who are seeing find Jesus alive; those who are unseeing do not find him. Appropriately, this key theme is placed at the center of the narrative.

25–27. And he said to them, "You foolish ones, and slow of heart to believe in all that the prophets have spoken! Was it not necessary that the Messiah should suffer these things and enter into his glory?" And beginning with Moses and all the prophets he interpreted to them the things concerning himself in all the scriptures.

A two-step progression emphasizes the disciples' failure. The phrase "you foolish ones, and slow of heart" seems to suggest the same failure of dull-wittedness, but the second step augments the first. Their failure is not merely cognitive; it is also affective. The heart (*kardia*) is the "seat of physical, spiritual and mental life;" it is the "center and source of the whole inner life,"[87] and thus, the metaphor refers to their inner dispositions, attitudes, and commitments.[88] The second step of the progression emphasizes that the disciples need an inner awareness, a whole new way of seeing, a new orientation, a change of direction. Although they knew the events of the past three days, their interpretation of the events

86. Joseph A. Fitzmyer, *The Gospel according to Luke: Introduction, Translation, and Notes*, 2 vols., AB 28–28A (Garden City, N.Y.: Doubleday, 1981–1985), 2:1564.

87. BDAG, s.v. καρδία 1b, although BDAG translates it as "slow of comprehension."

88. Joel B. Green, *The Gospel of Luke*, NICNT (Grand Rapids: Eerdmans, 1997), 848.

was skewed because they assumed that God would work according to their expectations. While they expected God to redeem Israel from its alien occupiers, God chose to redeem Israel in a completely different way: through the death and resurrection of the Messiah. Thus they are foolish and slow of heart.

A rhetorical question underscores the obvious: "Was it not necessary that the Messiah should suffer these things and enter into his glory?" The negative, *ouchi*, expects an affirmative answer: "Yes, of course, it was necessary."[89] In other words, their lack of comprehension is derived from their failure to grasp the obvious. Yet, a suffering Messiah is by no means obvious until Jesus, the master exegete, reveals what was in Scripture all along. "All the scriptures" may be a *hyperbole*—an exaggeration or bold overstatement of a fact or possibility for emphasis—but the narrator may intend that Scripture as a whole testifies to Christ. In either case, what was supposedly obvious was clearly unseen by the two disciples.

28–31. And they drew near to the village to which they were going, and he appeared to be going further. But they urged him strongly saying, "Stay with us because it is towards evening and the day is already far spent." And he went in to stay with them. And it happened when he reclined with them, he took bread, blessed, and broke and gave to them. And their eyes were opened and they recognized him. And he vanished from their sight.

The situational irony of the invited guest who becomes the host accents the ideological point of view of the narrative. When Jesus is invited "to stay," he becomes the host.

Verbal threads link the Emmaus meal with feeding narratives in Luke's Gospel. "The day is already far spent," or "the day is already declining," recalls the narrative introduction to the feeding of the five thousand: "the day was drawing to a close" (9:12). Several other verbal threads link the two narratives. In both, the groups recline and Jesus takes bread, blesses, breaks, and gives it to the disciples (9:15, 16; 24:30). In the five thousand, loaves and fish are multiplied; in the Emmaus account, the disciples' insight is multiplied. Two of the words—"take" and "break"—also occur in the Last Supper account in Luke 22:19, and two other words—"having given thanks" and "gave"—are similar. With the opening of their eyes the narrative has come full circle (cf. 24:16). The clarifying moment in the breaking of bread reveals that Jesus is present with his disciples in a different way. This is the final irony of the narrative. When Jesus is present, he is unseen; when he is seen, he vanishes. Or, to put it differ-

89. BDAG, s.v. οὐχί 3. This is a strengthened form of the negative *ou*.

ently, when Jesus is not recognized, he needs to be present, but when he is recognized, he no longer needs to be present.

32–35. And they said to one another, "Were not our hearts on fire within us while he was talking to us on the road, while he opened to us the scriptures?" And that same hour they got up and returned to Jerusalem and they found the eleven and those with them gathered together. They were saying, "The Lord has risen indeed, and he appeared to Simon." And they told the things that happened on the road, and how he had been made known to them in the breaking of the bread.

The rhetorical question summarizes their changed orientation more forcefully than a declarative statement of what had happened. While at the beginning of the journey they were sullen, now they have a heart that rages like a fire within them. What are the *vehicle* and the *tenor* of the metaphor? The vehicle is the burning heart, while the tenor is an inner attitude or orientation to life that is altered in their encounter with the divine. Their awakening to Jesus' resurrection has changed more than their lack of understanding; it has changed their emotional and spiritual state, their inner disposition. No longer are they melancholy or slow of heart. The fire within is uncontrollable, and therefore, "at that very hour" they returned to Jerusalem to announce the good news.

A verbal thread summarizes the disciples' awakening. That Jesus "had been made known to them" recalls the imagery of eyes (vv. 16, 31) and the related threads of recognition (vv. 16, 31) and seeing (vv. 23, 24, 34). Their awakening reinforces a main theme of the narrative: Jesus is seen in a new way.

The return to Jerusalem brings the narrative full circle. The recognition type-scene has a U-shaped plot. The narrative begins with the disciples going in the wrong direction. They leave Jerusalem, the place of the resurrection, and set out on a journey away from the place of revelation. This downward turn in the U-shaped plot parallels their characterization. They are bewildered, saddened, and downcast by the events of the past three days. Their hopes for redemption are dashed. Yet a reversal takes place in the plot when a stranger joins them and their eyes are opened. A recognition scene occurs when they invite the stranger to stay with them. The guest then becomes their host and their eyes are opened, and Jesus vanishes. Their awakening signals the upward turn of the U, as they now return to Jerusalem to share their new discovery with the other disciples.

What is the point of the narrative? It is found in the disciples' characterization and the development of the plot. They awaken not merely to Jesus as their traveling companion; more important, they see him in a new way. The Jesus of their expectations had hindered them from seeing this new Jesus. But when their expectations were shattered, they were able to see the new Jesus. The same point applies to the reader of the narrative: only when our expectations of who Jesus should be are dashed are we able to see the Jesus who reveals himself to us.

3

Setting

3.1 Definition

Setting is the background against which the narrative action takes place.[1] It may be the physical, social-cultural, temporal, or religious environment. A setting may be geographical (Jerusalem, Jericho, Judea, Samaria, Galilee), topographical (mountain, sea, desert, river), religious (Sabbath, festival), or architectural (house, pool, synagogue, temple, tomb). It may be social or cultural (Jew, Gentile, Samaritan, clean, unclean),[2] political (Rome, Pharaoh, kingdom of God), temporal (night, day, forty days, millennium), or spatial (heaven, earth, abyss). Minor characters—what

1. William Harmon and C. Hugh Holman, *A Handbook to Literature*, 8th ed. (Upper Saddle River, N.J.: Prentice Hall, 1999), 417. On setting in the New Testament see Elizabeth Struthers Malbon, *Narrative Space and Mythic Meaning in Mark*, New Voices in Biblical Studies (San Francisco: Harper & Row, 1986); David Rhoads, Joanna Dewey, and Donald Michie, *Mark as Story: An Introduction to the Narrative of a Gospel*, 2nd ed. (Minneapolis: Fortress, 1999), chapter 3; Mark Allan Powell, *What Is Narrative Criticism?* (Minneapolis: Fortress, 1990), chapter 6; James L. Resseguie, *Revelation Unsealed: A Narrative Critical Approach to John's Apocalypse*, BIS 32 (Leiden: Brill, 1998), 15–19, 70–102; idem, *The Strange Gospel: Narrative Design and Point of View in John*, BIS 56 (Leiden: Brill, 2001), chapter 2; idem, *Spiritual Landscape: Images of the Spiritual Life in the Gospel of Luke* (Peabody, Mass.: Hendrickson, 2004), chapters 1 and 2.

2. See Bruce J. Malina, *The New Testament World: Insights from Cultural Anthropology*, 3rd ed. (Louisville: Westminster John Knox, 2001); *Reading Mark: Engaging the Gospel* (Minneapolis: Fortress, 2004), chapter 6.

Seymour Chatman calls "walk-ons"[3]—may also be part of the setting (crowd, soldiers, passersby).

Props are part of the setting. For example, the Samaritan woman's water jar that is left at the well is a prop, a puzzle to be solved. Why does the narrator mention the jar? Is it symbolic? Is it important for the interpretation of the story? Some props are crucial to the plot. Alfred Hitchcock calls them *MacGuffins*.[4] The camera pans to a coffee cup laced with poison, for instance, and the viewer knows that it is an important device of the plot. Similarly, the narrator of John pans to focus on a head wrapping that is "rolled up in a place by itself" (John 20:7). The mention of this seemingly insignificant prop is an important device.

Setting contributes to the mood of the narrative,[5] or delineates the traits of a character, or contributes to the development of plot conflicts. Settings may highlight the religious, moral, social, emotional, and spiritual values of the characters. When Jesus heals on the Sabbath, for instance, the highly charged religious setting is essential to the plot and point of view. Conflict between Jesus and the authorities occurs because of divergent points of view. Although not all settings are pregnant with meaning, seldom do they merely fill in background detail. Setting may develop a character's mental, emotional, or spiritual landscape; it may be symbolic of choices to be made; it provides structure to the story and may develop the central conflict in a narrative.[6]

3.2 A Reading of Setting in Hemingway's "Hills Like White Elephants"

In Ernest Hemingway's "Hills Like White Elephants," setting is used extensively to develop character and theme. Hemingway relies on topography to reflect the inner terrain of the two main characters and architectural space to elaborate their emotional setting. The story is about a couple's reflections on the unusual landscape while they wait for an express train from Barcelona. Hemingway uses topographical (hills, parched land, Ebro valley, trees, river, mountains), architectural (train station, rails, barroom), geographical (Barcelona, Madrid), and temporal (forty minutes, two minutes) settings to develop and elaborate the point of the story. He also uses props (bead curtain, luggage, drinks) as MacGuffins to suggest the central conflict. The full text of

3. See Seymour Chatman, *Story and Discourse: Narrative Structure in Fiction and Film* (Ithaca: Cornell University Press, 1978), 138–39.

4. See Chatman, *Story and Discourse*, 140.

5. Ibid., 141.

6. Rhoads, Dewey, and Michie, *Mark as Story*, 63.

Hemingway's short story is presented with a commentary on the meaning of its settings.

Hills Like White Elephants

The hills across the valley of the Ebro were long and white. On this side there was no shade and no trees and the station was between two lines of rails in the sun. Close against the side of the station there was the warm shadow of the building and a curtain, made of strings of bamboo beads, hung across the open door into the bar, to keep out flies. The American and the girl with him sat at a table in the shade, outside the building. It was very hot and the express from Barcelona would come in forty minutes. It stopped at this junction for two minutes and went on to Madrid.

"What should we drink?" the girl asked. She had taken off her hat and put it on the table.

"It's pretty hot," the man said.

"Let's drink beer."

"Dos cervezas," the man said into the curtain.

"Big ones?" a woman asked from the doorway.

"Yes. Two big ones."

The woman brought two glasses of beer and two felt pads. She put the felt pads and the beer glasses on the table and looked at the man and the girl. The girl was looking off at the line of hills. They were white in the sun and the country was brown and dry.

"They look like white elephants," she said.

"I've never seen one," the man drank his beer.

"No, you wouldn't have."

"I might have," the man said. "Just because you say I wouldn't have doesn't prove anything."

The girl looked at the bead curtain. "They've painted something on it," she said. "What does it say?"

"Anis del Toro. It's a drink."

"Could we try it?"

The man called "Listen" through the curtain. The woman came out from the bar.

"Four reales."

"We want two Anis del Toro."

"With water?"

"Do you want it with water?"

"I don't know," the girl said. "Is it good with water?"

"It's all right."

"You want them with water?" asked the woman.

"Yes, with water."

"It tastes like licorice," the girl said and put the glass down.

"That's the way with everything."

"Yes," said the girl. "Everything tastes of licorice. Especially all the things you've waited so long for, like absinthe."

"Oh, cut it out."

"You started it," the girl said. "I was being amused. I was having a fine time."

"Well, let's try and have a fine time."

"All right. I was trying. I said the mountains looked like white elephants. Wasn't that bright?"

"That was bright."

"I wanted to try this new drink. That's all we do, isn't it—look at things and try new drinks?"

"I guess so."

The girl looked across at the hills.

"They're lovely hills," she said. "They don't really look like white elephants. I just meant the coloring of their skin through the trees."

"Should we have another drink?"

"All right."

The warm wind blew the bead curtain against the table.

"The beer's nice and cool," the man said.

"It's lovely," the girl said.

"It's really an awfully simple operation, Jig," the man said. "It's not really an operation at all."

The girl looked at the ground the table legs rested on.

"I know you wouldn't mind it, Jig. It's really not anything. It's just to let the air in."

The girl did not say anything.

"I'll go with you and I'll stay with you all the time. They just let the air in and then it's all perfectly natural."

"Then what will we do afterward?"

We'll be fine afterward. Just like we were before."

"What makes you think so?"

"That's the only thing that bothers us. It's the only thing that's made us unhappy."

The girl looked at the bead curtain, put her hand out and took hold of two of the strings of beads.

"And you think then we'll be all right and be happy."

"I know we will. You don't have to be afraid. I've known lots of people that have done it."

"So have I," said the girl. "And afterward they were all so happy."

"Well," the man said, "if you don't want to you don't have to. I wouldn't have you do it if you didn't want to. But I know it's perfectly simple."

"And you really want to?"

"I think it's the best thing to do. But I don't want you to do it if you don't really want to."

"And if I do it you'll be happy and things will be like they were and you'll love me?"

"I love you now. You know I love you."

"I know. But if I do it, then it will be nice again if I say things are like white elephants, and you'll like it?"

"I love it. I love it now but I just can't think about it. You know how I get when I worry."

"If I do it you won't ever worry?"

"I won't worry about that because it's perfectly simply."

"Then I'll do it. Because I don't care about me."

"What do you mean?"

"I don't care about me."

"Well, I care about you."

"Oh, yes. But I don't care about me. And I'll do it and then everything will be fine."

"I don't want you to do it if you feel that way."

The girl stood up and walked to the end of the station. Across, on the other side, were fields of grain and trees along the banks of the Ebro. Far away, beyond the river, were mountains. The shadow of a cloud moved across the field of grain and she saw the river through the trees.

"And we could have all this," she said. "And we could have everything and every day we make it more impossible."

"What did you say?"

"I said we could have everything."

"We can have everything."

"No, we can't."

"We can have the whole world."

"No, we can't."

"We can go everywhere."

"No, we can't. It isn't ours any more."

"It's ours."

"No, it isn't. And once they take it away, you never get it back."

"But they haven't taken it away."

"We'll wait and see."

"Come on back in the shade," he said. "You mustn't feel that way."

"I don't feel any way," the girl said. "I just know things."

"I don't want you do anything that you don't want to do—"

"Nor that isn't good for me," she said. "I know. Could we have another beer?"

"All right. But you've got to realize—"

"I realize," the girl said. "Can't we maybe stop talking?"

They sat down at the table and the girl looked across at the hills on the dry side of the valley and the man looked at her and at the table.

"You've got to realize," he said, "that I don't want you to do it if you don't want to. I'm perfectly willing to go through with it if it means anything to you."

"Doesn't it mean anything to you? We could get along."

"Of course it does. But I don't want anybody but you. I don't want anyone else. And I know it's perfectly simple."

"Yes, you know it's perfectly simple."

"It's all right for you to say that, but I do know it."

"Would you do something for me now?"

"I'd do anything for you."

"Would you please please please please please please please stop talking?"

He did not say anything but looked at the bags against the wall of the station. There were labels on them from all the hotels where they had spent nights.

"But I don't want you to," he said. "I don't care anything about it."

"I'll scream," said the girl.

The woman came out through the curtains with two glasses of beer and put them down on the damp felt pads. "The train comes in five minutes," she said.

"What did she say?" asked the girl.

"That the train is coming in five minutes."

The girl smiled brightly at the woman, to thank her.

"I'd better take the bags over to the other side of the station," the man said. She smiled at him.

"All right. Then come back and we'll finish the beer."

He picked up the two heavy bags and carried them around the station to the other tracks. He looked up the tracks but could not see the train. Coming back, he walked through the barroom, where people waiting for the train were drinking. He drank an Anis at the bar and looked at the people. They were all waiting reasonably for the train. He went out through the bead curtain. She was sitting at the table and smiled at him.

"Do you feel better?" he asked.

"I feel fine," she said. "There's nothing wrong with me. I feel fine."

Hemingway highlights the importance of the setting in the title. "Hills like white elephants" or a similar phrase occurs four times in the story itself. The topography on one side of the railroad station resembles a white elephant—a symbolic setting that suggests that the topic of discussion is something that is of little or no value to one person but is of value to someone else.[7] The landscape is brown and dry and the hills look white in the sun. On the other side of the railroad station, however, the landscape, is different—almost the opposite. A river flows on that side and there is a field of grain with trees along the banks and mountains in the distance. A "shadow of a cloud" moves across the field of grain, and through the trees the girl can see the river.

The other prominent setting is architectural. The story takes place at a railroad junction sitting between two lines of rails. The station has a bar with tables outside. Three props are used to develop characterization and plot. (1) The drinks, beer and Anis del Toro, elaborate the characters' emotional landscape. The Anis is a green, bitter-tasting liqueur that is flavored with wormwood or a substitute such as anise. (2) The luggage, decorated with labels from several hotels, leans against the wall. (3) A bead curtain separates the barroom from the tables outside. The temporal setting of a two-minute stop contributes a note of urgency to their decision.

The settings and dialogue mutually complement each other. Outer landscape reflects inner landscape of the characters; physical terrain corresponds to their emotional terrain. Architectural space and props elaborate the characters' dilemma. Although the operation is unnamed, the reader understands that the two discuss whether to abort a fetus or to keep the unborn child. The topography reflects not only their dilemma but also their diverse points of view. On one side, the landscape is desiccated, barren, and dead; on the opposite side, the landscape is fertile, pregnant with river, trees, and a grain field bursting with its fruit.

The hills are a metaphor for the abortion and the couple's relationship. For the man, the unborn child is unwanted—a white elephant that complicates their relationship and places a burden on their unencumbered lifestyle. "That's the only thing that bothers us. It's the only thing that's made us unhappy," he says. "I don't want anybody but you. I don't want anyone else." The girl, however, has a different point of view, which the fecund landscape amplifies. After she crosses to the other side of the depot, she says: "And we could have all this. And we could have everything and every day we make it more impossible." For her, the white elephant is their relationship, which, like the bitter drinks, has a dispiriting sameness. "Everything tastes of licorice. Especially all the things you've waited so long for, like absinthe." The repetitive dialogue—going over and over the same topic—parallels the monotony of their relationship. Their life together reverberates with the sameness of the everyday, and her comment sums up her ennui. "That's all we do, isn't it—look at things and try new drinks?"

The bead curtain, a MacGuffin mentioned eight times in the story, is made of hollow bamboo and, like the hollowness of their relationship, is

7. *Merriam-Webster's Collegiate Dictionary*, 11th ed., s.v. "white elephant."

blown about by the wind. The curtain is a barrier between the barroom inside and the tables outside—a threshold or liminal space one passes through to get to the other side. It divides inner space from outer space. When the man picks up the bags and takes them to the other side of the station, he stops in the bar for another Anis del Toro. Looking around, he sees all the people "waiting reasonably for the train" in the bar. Then he passes through the bead curtain to where Jig is sitting outside. The curtain separates reasonable space from unreasonable space. The man believes that his point of view is reasonable, similar to the people who wait reasonably inside. Jig's point of view, on the other hand, represents an unreasonable perspective to the American. In addition to the bead curtain that separates inside from outside, a second threshold or liminal space is described. As the curtain separates reasonable from unreasonable space, the train station separates two kinds of landscapes. It is a barrier that the girl must go around in order to see the fertile landscape of the Ebro Valley. This is the threshold she desires to cross, but every day it becomes more impossible.

A train junction is a place to change directions. The train stops for two minutes and the couple must decide which direction they will go: to Madrid or Barcelona. Or will one go to Barcelona and the other to Madrid? The brief span of time heightens the urgency of their decision. Although the story is about whether to abort the fetus, it is also a story about important decisions in general. The contrasting landscapes and the railroad junction with its two choices suggest that the story is about critical decisions in life and how they are made. Some of life's most important decisions—life-altering, life-determining decisions—are made in a fleeting moment, and there is, as the girl says, no turning back: "And once they take it away, you never get it back." Just as there are two landscapes, two rails of track, two destinations, two drinks, two monotonous activities, and two strands of beads, there are two options for the American and Jig: life or death, fulfillment or emptiness. The couple must resolve this crisis in a brief span of time and their choices are limited. It is either on to Madrid or back to Barcelona.

3.3 Setting in the New Testament

A close reading of setting adds to the interpretation of characterization, plot, theme, and point of view. In the following we will look at how six different types of settings contribute to our understanding of narrative: (1) topographical; (2) architectural; (3) props; (4) temporal; (5) social and cultural; and (6) religious. A close reading of these settings in Mark 5:1–20 will illustrate the way setting influences interpretation.

Topographical Settings

Rivers are boundaries that separate one side from another, and thus are thresholds from one place to another. They may also represent metaphorical thresholds such as the abandonment of a past life and the beginning of a new life. The Israelites, for instance, crossed a threshold at the Jordan River. Their old life of desert wandering lay in the past while a new life in a new land lay ahead. The Synoptic Gospels recall the Jordan crossing in their account of the baptism by John at the river, a threshold that marks the abandonment of past ways and the acceptance of a new future. The Gospel of Mark uses hyperbole ("all") and synecdoche ("Jerusalem" = Israel) to accent the importance of this crossing: "*all* the country of Judea, and *all* the people of Jerusalem" went out to the Jordan and were baptized in the river, "confessing their sins" (Mark 1:5, RSV). Like the Israelites of old, the new Israel figuratively crosses over to another side through baptism. Luke's Gospel amplifies the threshold experience at the Jordan. Some ask, "What then should we do?" And John replies, "Whoever has two coats must share with anyone who has none; and whoever who has food must do likewise" (Luke 3:11). Baptized tax collectors are to "collect no more than the amount prescribed for [them]," and soldiers are to refrain from extortion and violence and be satisfied with their wages (Luke 3:13–14). Their crossing at the Jordan—that is, their baptism—symbolizes that past ways are abandoned and new ways adopted. The river as a symbolic threshold reappears at the end of the New Testament. In Rev. 16, the river of Babylon, the Euphrates, restrains the kings of the east from crossing to the battlefield of Armageddon. The sixth angel of the Apocalypse, however, pours his bowl on the river and dries it up, allowing the kings to cross over the river for the battle "on the great day of God the Almighty" (Rev. 16:12–16; cf. 9:14).

The desert or wilderness is in-between space.[8] It is neither here nor there, neither Egypt nor the promised land.[9] It is space between captivity and freedom, between past oppression and future freedom. Like a haunting landscape in an Ingmar Bergman film, the desert is life at the edges, distant from the security of human structures. There are no houses

8. On the desert in biblical literature see G. Kittel, "ἔρημος κτλ," *TDNT* 2:657–60; W. Radl, "ἔρημος," *EDNT* 2:51–52; Ulrich W. Mauser, *Christ in the Wilderness: The Wilderness Theme in the Second Gospel and Its Basis in the Biblical Tradition*, SBT 39 (Naperville, Ill.: Allenson, 1963); Malbon, *Narrative Space*, 72–75; Shemaryahu Talmon, "The 'Desert Motif' in the Bible and in Qumran Literature," in *Biblical Motifs: Origins and Transformations*, ed. A. Altmann, ST 3 (Cambridge: Harvard University Press, 1966), 31–63; Belden C. Lane, *The Solace of Fierce Landscapes: Exploring Desert and Mountain Spirituality* (New York: Oxford University Press, 1998); Resseguie, *Spiritual Landscape*, 12–16; idem, *Revelation Unsealed*, 80–81.

9. Robert L. Cohn, *The Shape of Sacred Space: Four Biblical Studies* (Chico, Calif.: Scholars Press, 1981), 14.

in the desert, only temporary dwelling places, and there are no marketplaces, only divine sustenance. It is a nomadic, unsettled, and rootless existence. It is also threatening space, a dwelling place for the satanic and demonic and every foul creature. The desert is where the Israelites were tested concerning their fealty to Yahweh. Will they rely on divine grace or return to the fleshpots of Egypt? Desires, commitments, and loyalties are laid bare in the harsh, feral landscape of the desert. Yet it is also a place of divine succor. The Israelites received divine favor with a cloud to lead them by day, fire to guide them by night, and manna to sustain them each day.

Like the Israelites, Jesus' loyalties are tested in the unreceptive terrain of desert landscape. Temptation determines resolve and resolve determines future direction. Will Jesus follow a false god and receive now the "kingdoms of the world and [their] splendor" (Matt. 4:8; Luke 4:5–6)? Or will he remain faithful to the Lord God? And like the Israelites, Jesus is not only tested but also receives divine succor in the wilderness. Mark simply says that "the angels waited on him" (Mark 1:13; cf. Matt. 4:11), but the point is unmistakable: divine compassion is present in the harsh desert spaces. The disciples also are tested in the desert and receive divine comfort. The feeding narratives take place in the wilderness, although our translations do not always make explicit this allusion to Israel's wandering in the desert. In Matthew, Mark, and Luke the RSV translates *erēmos* as "lonely place"; the NRSV recalls the Old Testament setting by calling it "a deserted place" (Matt. 14:13; Mark 6:32; Luke 9:12). In the feeding of the four thousand, the setting is "the desert" in both the RSV and NRSV (*erēmia*, Matt. 15:33; Mark 8:4). For the disciples, the wilderness test is to provide food for the multitudes. But how is it possible to feed a great crowd in the inhospitable terrain of uninhabitable places? "Where are [they] to get enough bread in the desert to feed so great a crowd?" (Matt. 15:33; cf. Mark 8:4). Should they send the multitude away to inhabited places to buy something to eat? Or should they go and buy two hundred denarii worth of bread? Their test clarifies their resolve. Will they rely upon human resources to solve a problem that can only be solved preternaturally? Or will they rely upon divine solace? The desert is where life's choices are clarified: will one count on human resources alone or rely upon God's uncommon grace?

The desert reappears as a place of testing and divine grace in Paul's writing and in the book of Revelation. The Israelites' temptation to idolatry in the wilderness is a type (*typos*) or example for the Corinthians. The desert test of the Corinthians is to shun eating idol meat in temples to pagan gods and not succumb to idolatry (1 Cor. 8–10). In Rev. 12 the woman flees to the wilderness where she receives a place of divine nourishment for 1,260 days (Rev. 12:6; cf. 12:14). Like the Israelites, God's people are protected and given sanctuary in times of distress.

The lake or sea is uncontrollable space, a place of chaos or an impassable barrier.[10] Humans can tame the land by tilling it into symmetrical furrows or building towering cities, but they are powerless to calm the sea. God alone tames the restless waters, which in Ps. 65:7 is also a metaphor for disquieted peoples: "You silence the roaring of the seas, the roaring of their waves, the tumult of the peoples." The sea is also the habitat of the terrifying monsters, Leviathan and Rahab (Ps. 74:13–14; 89:10; Job 9:13; Isa. 27:1). Figuratively, the sea is a place of raging chaos that God alone tames.

In the New Testament, the sea or lake is the setting for several narratives. It is a place of spiritual awakening to Jesus' transcendence and to the disciples' own fragile faith. During an entire night of fishing, Simon Peter, James, and John catch nothing, but Jesus tames the recalcitrant lake and they catch a large shoal of fish (Luke 5:1–11). Jesus' mastery over the lake of Gennesaret awakens Peter to the presence of the numinous, and he leaves everything to follow Jesus (5:11).[11] The other disciples also awaken to a transcendent Jesus on the sea. They leave Jesus behind and cross to the other side of the Sea of Galilee. John notes that it was dark (John 6:17) while the others say it was evening (Matt. 14:23; Mark 6:47). The sea was restless and the wind was strong, and the disciples were "battered by the waves" (Matt. 14:24), and they were "straining at the oars" (Mark 6:48). But like Moses at the Red Sea, Jesus tames the turbulent water and walks on it as if it were dry land. His *egō eimi* ("I am") startles them into recognition, and in Matthew they worship and confess that he is "truly . . . the Son of God" (Matt. 14:33). In Matthew's account, Peter also wants to tame the sea, but his faith is too fragile in the presence of disquieting winds (Matt. 14:30–31).

The most famous sea narrative—a subject of numerous paintings—tells the story of Jesus asleep in the boat on the Sea of Galilee (Matt. 8:23–27; Mark 4:35–41; Luke 8:22–25). Rembrandt's *Christ in the Storm on the Sea of Galilee* at the Isabella Stewart Gardner Museum in Boston is a contrast in light and dark that accentuates the threatening sea in contrast to divine calm.[12] The raging sea is the outer landscape; the inner landscape is the "tumult of the peoples" (Ps. 65:7) or the troubled disciples, whose

10. On the sea in biblical literature see Elizabeth Struthers Malbon, "The Jesus of Mark and the Sea of Galilee," *JBL* 103 (1984): 363–77; idem, *Narrative Space*, 76–79; Reinhard Kratz, "θάλασσα," *EDNT* 2:137–28; John Paul Heil, *Jesus Walking on the Sea: Meaning and Gospel Functions of Matt 14:22–33, Mark 6:45–52, and John 6:15b–21*, AnBib 87 (Rome: Biblical Institute, 1981).

11. Luke prefers the technically correct "lake" to "sea."

12. This painting was stolen in 1990 and has not yet been recovered.

frail faith is disquieted by the raging sea. As they cross the lake, a gust of wind sweeps down the Galilean hillside awakening the resting waters. The disturbed lake beats against the vessel, filling it with water, while the captain of this boat sleeps on a cushion in the stern (Mark 4:38). In the Old Testament, a sleeping God is a metaphor for God's absence in times of distress. The Psalmist, for instance, says, "Rouse yourself! Why do you sleep, O Lord? Awake, do not cast us off forever" (Ps. 44:23). Deep in sleep, the seemingly absent Jesus is awakened. In Mark, the disciples are frantic: "Teacher, do you not care that we are perishing?" (Mark 4:38; cf. Matt. 8:25; Luke 8:24). But the problem is not an absent God who needs to be awakened; rather, it is an absent faith that needs to be aroused. Jesus stills the roiling waters with a simple command, exorcising the sea of its chaotic turbulence: "Peace! Be still!" (Mark 4:39). The external threat is calmed. The internal threat of failing faith is then quieted. In this narrative, outer distress corresponds to inner turbulence.

In some instances, the sea is an impassible barrier that is miraculously turned into safe passage for God's people (e.g., 1 Cor. 10:1–2; Heb. 11:29; and Rev. 12:15–16; 15:2). The author of Hebrews emphasizes that "by faith" the Israelites "passed through the Red Sea as if it were dry land, but when the Egyptians attempted to do so they were drowned" (Heb. 11:29). In Rev. 12:15 a flood pours forth from the mouth of the dragon to sweep away the woman, but the earth opens its mouth and swallows the torrent (12:16). As the earth swallowed Egyptians at the Red Sea (Exod. 15:12), the earth swallows the dragon's flood, allowing the woman to gain safe passage to the wilderness. Later, those who conquer a new pharaoh, the beast from the sea, stand beside a "sea of glass mixed with fire" (a red sea) and sing the song of Moses and of the Lamb (15:2–3) for their safe passage to the other side.

The mountain is literally the earth reaching to the heavens and is thus an appropriate place for divine/human encounters.[13] Ascending the mountain can be an act of defiance against God—an attempt to mock God or to be like God. In Isa. 37:24, Sennachrib, King of Assyria, takes chariots "up the heights of the mountains" in order to mock God.[14] It can also be a place of prayer where God's clarifying word is heard. Jesus ascends the mountain to pray and to listen to God. In Luke 6:12, he prays all night and then selects the Twelve. In Luke 9:28–29, he ascends the Mount of Transfiguration to pray, and in Luke 22:39–46, he goes up the

13. On the mountain as setting see Malbon, *Narrative Space*, 84–89; Cohn, *Shape of Sacred Space*, 38–41; Werner Foerster, "ὄρος," *TDNT* 5:475–87; Terence L. Donaldson, *Jesus on the Mountain: A Study in Matthean Theology*, JSNTSup 8 (Sheffield: JSOT Press, 1985); Willard M. Swartley, *Israel's Scripture Traditions and the Synoptic Gospels: Story Shaping Story* (Peabody, Mass.: Hendrickson, 1994).

14. See Cohn, *Shape of Sacred Space*, 33.

Mount of Olives seeking to change God's will. In this last instance, the mountain is a place of spiritual struggle.

The mountain is also a place of epiphany or theophany. Jesus reveals his divine glory on a "high mountain" (Matt. 17:1; Mark 9:2). The great sermon in Matthew occurs on the mountain (Matt. 5:1). As God gives the law to Moses on Mount Sinai, Jesus gives a new teaching to the disciples. On a mountain, Jesus teaches about future things in Matthew and Mark (Matt. 24:3; Mark 13:3). The mountain is also a place of divine refuge where God provides a sanctuary in times of distress. At the end times when the desolating sacrilege is set up where it ought not to be, those in Judea are to flee to the mountains (Matt. 24:15–16; Mark 13:14; Luke 21:20–21). In Rev. 14:1 Mount Zion is a spiritual refuge where all God's people—symbolically represented by the 144,000—are gathered together.

The way or road is a common symbolic reference in the New Testament as well as in secular literature.[15] Some of the classics of Western literature use a journey as a setting for understanding and discovery: Homer's *Odyssey*, Chaucer's *Canterbury Tales*, and Dante's *Divine Comedy*, for instance. In the New Testament, "the way" is a metaphor for a spiritual journey with a well-defined goal such as the kingdom of God, heaven, or the new Jerusalem. In Acts, the Christian community is called "the Way" (Acts 9:2, 19:9, 23; 22:4; 24:14, 22), and in the Gospel of John, Jesus calls himself "the way" (John 14:6). Mark's Gospel opens with a reference to the way (*hodos*, Mark 1:2; cf. Isa. 40:3; Mal. 3:1).

> See, I am sending my messenger
> ahead of you,
> who will prepare your *way*;
> the voice of one crying out in the
> wilderness:
> "Prepare the *way* of the Lord,
> make his paths straight."
> (1:2–3)

John the baptizer prepares "the way of the Lord," and Jesus prepares the way to the new promised land, the kingdom of God. The itinerary of this exodus (*exodos* in Luke 9:31) is suffering and death in Jerusalem (Mark 8:31–33; 9:31–32; 10:33–34 and parallels). Jesus' journey is described in

15. *Hodos* occurs 101 times in the New Testament: 22 times in Matthew; 16 times in Mark; 20 times in Luke; and 4 times in John. On the "way" in biblical literature see Wilhelm Michaelis, "ὁδός," *TDNT* 5:65–91; Ernest Best, *Following Jesus: Discipleship in the Gospel of Mark*, JSNTSup 4 (Sheffield: JSOT Press, 1981); Resseguie, *Spiritual Landscape*, chapter 2; J. R. Donahue, *Theology and Setting of Discipleship in the Gospel of Mark* (Milwaukee: Marquette University Press, 1983).

terms of resolute determination and divine necessity: he "set[s] his face" (Luke 9:51) to go to Jerusalem, which is a route he "must" (*dei*) travel (Luke 13:33). His journey is a "well-mapped plan of salvation."[16]

The journey is also a time of community formation. The Israelites formed a community in the wilderness, which Robert Cohn describes as follows: "Through the hardships they endure, the Israelites are purged of their pride, thrown on the mercy of God. They are taught that passivity and humility are the qualities needed to survive in the wilderness. For example, despite human competitiveness, all who collect manna find that in the end they have the same amount, neither too much nor too little."[17] Community formation occurs *on the way* in the Gospels. In Mark 10:32, the disciples follow Jesus literally, but the figurative understanding is just beneath the surface. "They were *on the road*, going up to Jerusalem, and Jesus *was walking ahead of them*." Jesus leads, the disciples follow, discipling occurs. The journey of community formation is surprising: the least are the greatest, the last are first, and the humble are exalted. In the formation of a new community, competitiveness and one-upmanship are noticeably lacking. James and John, for instance, want the places of honor and privilege when Jesus comes into his glory; but their request is turned on its head: the only places available on Jesus' right and left side are places of suffering and death (Matt 20:20–23; Mark 10:35–40).

The journey is also a metaphor for understanding and spiritual awakening. The prodigal son "came to himself" and journeyed back to his father's house (Luke 15:11–24). On the road to Emmaus the two disciples' eyes are closed to the way God works in this world (Luke 24:13–35). When their eyes are opened, they change direction (Luke 24:33).

Architectural Settings

Architectural settings are human-made structures such as a house, synagogue, temple, pool, tomb, garden, courtyard, sheepfold, praetorium, door, or housetop.[18] In architectural structures, characters go in and out of buildings, travel to and from places, open and close doors, and so forth. Some architectural settings are symbolic. For example, Mieke Bal suggests that inside and outside space is significant:

> A contrast between *inside* and *outside* is often relevant, where inside may carry the suggestion of protection, and outside that of danger. These mean-

16. John Nolland, *Luke*, 3 vols., WBC 35A–C (Dallas: Word, 1993), 2:465.
17. Cohn, *Shape of Sacred Space*, 15–16.
18. On architectural settings see Malbon, *Narrative Space*, chapter 4; Resseguie, *Revelation Unsealed*, 91–95; idem, *The Strange Gospel*, 63–95.

> ings are not indissolubly tied to these oppositions; it is equally possible that *inside* suggests close confinement, and *outside* freedom, or that we see a combination of these meanings, or a development from one to the other.[19]

In the Gospel of John several architectural spaces are symbolic. Inside space may be safe and protective space while outside space is threatening. The sheepfold (*aulē*) and the garden (*kēpos*) are places of safety in John.[20] In John 10:1–18, the sheep pen is an open-air enclosed structure that is either freestanding or attached to a building. It protects the sheep from thieves and bandits who lurk outside the pen (John 10:1). Although inside space is secure, the pasture lies outside the sheep pen. Thus a good shepherd—one who does not flee or leave the sheep unprotected when danger approaches—is needed to lead the sheep to pasture where there is life (John 10:4, 12). The good shepherd also lays down his life for the sheep (John 10:11–18).

Similar to the sheepfold, the garden (*kēpos*) is protective or safe space. The garden in John is an enclosed open-air structure located across the Kidron valley from Jerusalem (18:1–11, 26). Jesus and the disciples enter the garden and the arresting party comes to raid the pen. Like the bandits and thieves of John 10, the menacing posse approaches the garden and attempts to arrest Jesus and the disciples. Jesus, however, protects his own by going out (*exēlthen*) to the arresting party (18:4). In terms of the architectural setting, he protects those in the garden. "So if you are looking for me, let these men go," he says in 18:8. Once the disciples are safe, Jesus goes with the arresting party to lay down his life for the sheep (cf. John 10:11, 15, 17–18).

Going in and out of architectural structures may symbolize a wavering, indecisive point of view. In John 18:28b–19:16a, Pilate goes in and out of the praetorium or his residence eight times. Four times he enters the praetorium and an equal number of times he goes outside to the crowd. As he shuttles back and forth, he listens to Jesus (inside) on the one hand, and to the crowd (outside) on the other. His to-ing and fro-ing, back and forth, in-and-out movements represent his wavering position between two divergent points of view. As Raymond Brown concludes, "Pilate's constant passing from one setting to the other gives external expression to the struggle taking place within his soul, for his certainty

19. Mieke Bal, *Narratology: Introduction to the Theory of Narrative*, trans. Christine van Boheemen (Toronto: University of Toronto Press, 1988), 44. Italics are Bal's.

20. M. W. G. Stibbe, *John as Storyteller: Narrative Criticism and the Fourth Gospel* (Cambridge: Cambridge University Press, 1992), 102–3; cf. also Resseguie, *The Strange Gospel*, 64–67.

of Jesus' innocence increases at the same rate as does the political pressure forcing him to condemn Jesus."[21]

Inside space may represent confined space that needs to be opened up. The tomb (*mnēmeion*) is an obvious example. The demoniac lives in tombs (Matt. 8:28; Mark 5:2–3; Luke 8:27). He is in between life and death: socially and spiritually dead, barely alive physically. Lazarus's tomb is also inside space that is opened up. The stone is rolled away, the binding cloth removed, and the *sudarium* unwrapped. The tomb no longer is inside, confining space, but is a threshold to outside, freeing space (John 11:1–44). For Jesus, the tomb is a threshold to a new existence, freeing him from the confines of this life. The inside space of the holy of holies in the temple is opened up with the rending of the curtain to the temple. It no longer confines the deity, so to speak. In John, the disciples are behind locked doors after the resurrection. While the closed door keeps them safe from those whom they fear, it also keeps them from accomplishing a mission. Jesus comes and breathes on them the Holy Spirit, empowering them to move beyond the confines of locked doors (John 20:19–29).

The opening and closing of doors symbolizes accessibility or denial of accessibility. In Rev. 4:1 a door in heaven is swung open and the mysteries of heaven are opened up. In Rev. 9:1 a door to the bottomless pit is opened and locusts are released to wreak havoc on the earth. On the other hand, a door is closed in Rev. 20:2–3. Satan is locked up for a thousand years. He is denied accessibility to the nations, no longer able to deceive them. In Mark, Jesus teaches in a house so crowded that there is "no longer room for [the people], not even in front of the door" (Mark 2:2). Because the door is blocked, Jesus is inaccessible; but the roof, instead, is converted into a door for the paralyzed man. Jesus is accessible even when he seems inaccessible. The closed door at Laodicea keeps Jesus out of the church. He stands at the door knocking, waiting for the church to let him in (Rev. 3:20). The Laodicean door contrasts with the locked and shut doors of John 20:19, 26 and with the sealed tomb. While those doors are unable to keep Jesus either in or out, it appears that some doors can keep Jesus out.

A shut door denies access to the kingdom of God. Some stand at the door knocking but are stunned by the unexpected reply: "I do not know where you come from" (Luke 13:25). The five bridesmaids who are late for the wedding banquet find the door shut and are likewise surprised by the response: "Truly I tell you, I do not know you" (Matt. 25:12). In these instances, a closed door is equivalent to nonrecognition, and the

21. Raymond E. Brown, *The Gospel according to John*, 2 vols. (New York: Doubleday, 1966–1970), 2:858.

hearers who thought they were insiders learn that they are outsiders. An open door represents an opportunity that is opened up. When Paul went to Troas to proclaim the gospel, a door was opened for him (2 Cor. 2:12), and he asks the Colossians to pray that "God will open to us a door for the word" (Col. 4:3).

Some familiar settings are made to seem strange so that they are viewed in different ways. Or they are made strange so that a new kind of setting replaces the old, familiar setting. The temple and well, for instance, are the background for a different type of temple and well. In John, a discussion about tearing down and rebuilding the temple is the backdrop for a new kind of temple (John 2:13–22). The rhetoric of misunderstanding makes strange the familiar setting. (1) Jesus makes a statement that is ambiguous; (2) the hearers—quite naturally—think he is speaking of the physical temple, and (3) the narrator intervenes to explain a new kind of temple.

When those who witness the cleansing of the temple ask for a sign, Jesus says, "Destroy this temple [*naos*], and in three days I will raise it up" (John 2:19). The hearers are bewildered: "This temple [*naos*] has been under construction for forty-six years, and will you raise it up in three days?" (2:20). Adding to the hearers' confusion is the usage of *naos* instead of *hieron*.[22] The word for the temple building and its outer court is *hieron*, which is used in 2:14, 15. *Naos*, on the other hand, is the dwelling place of the deity. It can refer either to the temple building or, in a more restricted sense, to the inner sanctuary or shrine where the deity dwells.[23] But Jesus makes strange the familiar and uses the temple in a figurative sense. The narrator clarifies the misunderstanding for the readers: "But he was speaking of the temple [*naos*] of his body" (2:21). Architectural space is also redefined in Heb. 9:11 where Christ is "the greater and perfect tent (not made with hands, that is, not of this creation)." In Rev. 21:22 the temple as architectural space is useless, for God and the Lamb are the eternal city's temple. In Paul, the temple refers to the Christian congregation or the human body. The Corinthians are "God's temple" and "God's Spirit dwells in [them]" (1 Cor. 3:16; cf. 1 Cor. 3:17; 2 Cor. 6:16; Eph. 2:21). In 1 Cor. 6:19 the human body of the individual believer is the temple of the Holy Spirit.

The well (*pēgē; phrear*) in John is the setting for a different type of fount. Jacob's well at the foot of Mount Gerizim near the village of Sychar sustained life for generations (John 4:1–42). Yet human-made wells, though essential for life, have several limitations. Jacob's well is "deep"

22. M. W. G. Stibbe, *John*, RNBC (Sheffield: JSOT Press, 1993), 52, develops the opposition between outer and inner space in this passage.

23. BDAG, s.v. ναός; O. Michel, "ναός," *TDNT* 4:880–89; cf. G. Shrenk, "ἱερός, ἱερόν," *TDNT* 3:232–47, esp. 232–33.

and requires a special container, a bucket or water jar, to retrieve its thirst-quenching water (4:11). In addition, well water slakes thirst only for a short period of time, and it requires daily treks to the immobile source to get more water. The well thus is an appropriate setting for the discussion of another type of well and another kind of water—one without these limitations.

The rhetorical device of misunderstanding and double entendre highlights the differences between the kinds of water. (1) The first part of the misunderstanding occurs because of the ambiguity of the word "living water" (*hydōr zōn*, 4:10), which can mean literally spring water or figuratively transcendent life-giving water.[24] (2) The woman responds in a literal way, assuming that Jesus knows of a flowing stream that will make her job easier. She unwittingly reveals the limitations of a human well, which requires a bucket to get water from its depths (4:11). Jesus also points out the limitations of Jacob's well water. Those who drink water from his well will be thirsty again, whereas the water Jesus offers quenches thirst once and for all. And whereas Jacob's well is deep and requires a bucket to draw water, the water he provides is "a spring of water gushing up to eternal life." The vocabulary used for Jesus' well and Jacob's well also accentuates the differences between the water and its sources. One word is dynamic while the other describes a cistern, although both are used for Jacob's well.

Narrator:	"Jacob's well [*pēgē*] was there, and Jesus . . . was sitting by the well [*pēgē*]" (4:6).
Woman:	"The well [*phrear*] is deep" (4:11).
Woman:	"Are you greater than our ancestor Jacob, who gave us the well [*phrear*]?" (4:12).
Jesus:	"The water that I will give will become in them a spring [*pēgē*] of water" (4:14).

A *pēgē* is a spring of water that supplies a well, whereas a *phrear* is a well or cistern or shaft.[25] Either word can be used for a well, but only one word is appropriate for the type of water Jesus provides. The woman uses the less dynamic word twice to describe Jacob's well (*phrear*). Jesus, on the other hand, uses the dynamic word (*pēgē*) to describe a well that springs up in the believer. The contrast appears intentional. Jacob's well is no better than a cistern[26]—troublesome to get to and only temporally

24. BDAG, s.v. ὕδωρ.

25. BDAG, s.vv. πηγή; φρέαρ.

26. R. H. Lightfoot, *St. John's Gospel: A Commentary* (Oxford: Clarendon, 1956), 121; BDAG, s.v. φρέαρ, notes the play on words with the contrast between *pēgē* and *phrear*; Brown, *John*, 1:170.

satisfying—whereas the water Jesus gives "wells up"[27] to eternal life. Just as the wells are different, so also the type of water is different. The water that Jesus provides not only eliminates repeated trips to a human-made well but also slakes thirst completely.

Props

Props are the type of detail that could easily be omitted and no one would notice. A water jar (*hydria*), which the Samaritan woman left at Jacob's well, is the type of detail that seems to be merely background information. Yet it is a puzzle to be solved, an enigma that the reader easily glosses over. "Then the woman left her water jar and went back to the city" (John 4:28): could it be that she left the jar for Jesus to draw water? Or did she leave the bucket behind because she intended to return to the well with the villagers?[28] Or perhaps she was in such a hurry to tell the villagers about Jesus that she simply forgot the jar? Or does the abandonment of the jar have symbolic value? Luise Schottroff suggests that the jar symbolizes the woman's freedom from "her entire oppression."[29] She is no longer in bondage to the man she is living with and no longer bound by the tasks that women normally do in that society, such as fetching water. Or is the abandoned water jar the equivalent of the male disciples' leaving their fishing nets behind?[30] Like the disciples, she abandons her past to follow Jesus; water jars and fishing nets are no longer needed. Or perhaps she leaves her water jar behind because it is worthless for the type of water she has found. Raymond Brown adopts this view: "This detail seems to be John's way of emphasizing that such a jar would be useless for the type of living water that Jesus has interested her in."[31] Whatever the explanation for the abandoned water jar, the small

27. BDAG, s.v. ἅλλομαι 2.

28. So G. R. Beasley-Murray, *John*, WBC 36 (Waco: Word, 1987), 63; Gail O'Day, *Revelation in the Fourth Gospel: Narrative Mode and Theological Claim* (Philadelphia: Fortress, 1986), 75; Barnabas Lindars, *The Gospel of John*, NCB (London: Oliphants, 1972), 193.

29. Luise Schottroff, "The Samaritan Woman and the Notion of Sexuality in the Fourth Gospel," in *What Is John?*, vol. 2, *Literary and Social Readings of the Fourth Gospel*, ed. Fernando Segovia (Atlanta: Scholars Press, 1998), 157–81 at 166 and 174.

30. Sandra Schneiders, *The Revelatory Text: Interpreting the New Testament as Sacred Scripture* (San Francisco: HarperSanFrancisco, 1991), 192. Robert Gordon Maccini, *Her Testimony is True: Women as Witnesses according to John* (Sheffield: Sheffield Academic Press, 1996), 141, offers a critique of Schneiders and others who hold this view.

31. Brown, *John*, 1:173; also Dorothy A. Lee, *The Symbolic Narratives of the Fourth Gospel: The Interplay of Form and Meaning* (Sheffield: JSOT Press, 1994), 84–85; Craig R. Koester, *Symbolism in the Fourth Gospel: Meaning, Mystery, Community*, 2nd ed. (Minneapolis: Fortress, 2003), 190–91; R. Alan Culpepper, *Anatomy of the Fourth Gospel:*

detail is offered so that the reader ponders the questions: Why did she leave it there? And why did the narrator bother to mention it?

Clothing seems like an incidental item, of little relevance to narrative analysis. Yet it may symbolize new stages in a character's development, or reveal the inner landscape of a character—his or her values and commitments—or it may accent a character's social and spiritual status. For example, the parable of the Wedding Feast in Matt. 22:1–14 tells the story of a man who arrives at the banquet with no wedding garment. The king is incredulous that the man comes to the party without the proper garment. "Friend, how did you get in here without a wedding robe?" (Matt. 22:12). The man is speechless and offers no explanation because any excuse would be unacceptable. By arriving in his work clothes rather than a wedding garment, in jeans rather than a tux, he has flouted convention. The king has him bound hand and foot and thrown into outer darkness—that noisy, annoying place where there is weeping and gnashing of teeth (Matt. 22:13). The missing wedding robe is a prop—a MacGuffin to use Hitchcock's term—that is essential to the point of the parable. Clothing is the outward sign of his inner disposition and character. A festal occasion requires a festal garment. But this man shows up in soiled, everyday work clothes.[32] "For any such occasion guests would be expected to wear clothes that were both longer than those worn by ordinary working people on working days and also newly washed."[33] Although he accepted the invitation to join the party, he does not really want to be there. His clothes announce his desires. The invitation is to rejoice in the marriage of the king's son, which requires a festive garment at the very least.[34] He is like the guests who reject the invitation and refuse to attend. Although he shows up, he does not want to participate in the festivities. He is present, yet absent. This is not the party for him, so the king fulfills his wishes—symbolized by clothing—and sends him away. "Those who are unworthy of entering the kingdom of God are not only those who spurn the Gospel invitation but also those who ostensibly accept it while rejecting what it really represents."[35]

A Study in Literary Design (Philadelphia: Fortress, 1983), 194; Hendrikus Boers, *Neither on This Mountain nor in Jerusalem: A Study of John 4*, SBLMS 35 (Atlanta: Scholars Press, 1988), 182–83.

32. Richard Bauckham, "The Parable of the Royal Wedding Feast (Matthew 22:1–14) and the Parable of the Lame Man and the Blind Man (*Apocryphon of Ezekiel*)," *JBL* 115 (1996): 471–88 at 485. See also Wesley G. Olmstead, *Matthew's Trilogy of Parables: The Nation, the Nations, and the Reader in Matthew 21:28–22:14*, SNTSMS 127 (Cambridge: Cambridge University Press, 2003), 126.

33. Bauckham, "Wedding Feast," 485.

34. Ibid., 487.

35. Ibid., 488

Clothing represents transitions in the spiritual or social life. The prodigal son departs home, squanders his inheritance, and descends into a social and spiritual abyss. But he arises to new life; when he returns home, he receives the best robe, sandals for his feet, and a ring (Luke 15:22). His festive clothing represents his transition from death to life, from spiritual and social alienation to reconciliation and new life. Clothing also symbolizes the demoniac's transition from death to life. Before the exorcism the man is stark naked like an animal; afterward he rejoins the human race, putting on clothes.

> For a long time he had worn *no clothes.* (Luke 8:27)

> They found the man from whom the demons had gone sitting at the feet of Jesus, *clothed* and in his right mind. (Luke 8:35)

Discarded clothing can mark a threshold experience from this life to eternal life. Lazarus comes out of the tomb with his grave clothes on; he will return to the tomb at some other time. Jesus, on the other hand, leaves his grave clothes in the tomb, a useless relic of a past age. His transformed body can no longer fit into death's clothing.

The disciples receive a new garment to mark their transition to a new age. In Luke 24:49, the disciples are to remain in Jerusalem until they are "clothed" (*endyō*) with power from on high. This new garment is the Spirit that empowers them to proclaim the gospel (Acts 1:8).

Clothing reveals the inner character or spiritual state of a person. In Zech. 3:1–5 Joshua's dirty clothing is a sign of his guilt, and his festal apparel represents a removal of his guilt. On the Mount of Transfiguration Jesus' clothing is altered, revealing who he is. In Matt. 17:2 and Luke 9:29 his clothes became "dazzling white" and in Mark 9:3 "glistening, intensively white, as no fuller on earth could bleach them" (RSV). This garment reveals his transcendent glory, his otherness. God's clothing also accentuates God's mysterious, transcendent nature. At the transfiguration God's garment is a cloud, which reveals and conceals at the same time. In Rev. 4:3 God's clothing is equally mysterious—precious gems and an emerald rainbow.

Bright, pure linen, which represents "the righteous deeds of the saints," is mandatory dress at the marriage feast of the Lamb (Rev. 19:8). The 144,000 wear white robes (Rev. 7:14); the armies of heaven are clothed with "fine linen, white and pure" (19:14). The Laodiceans' character, however, is unworthy and shameful; they need to purchase white robes "to keep the shame of [their] nakedness from being seen" (Rev. 3:18). At Sardis the garments of some are dirty, a sign of their unworthiness (Rev. 3:4). Blood is the bleach used to make these garments white. The multitude of Rev. 7:14 is dressed in white robes washed in the blood of the Lamb. Jesus appears in a robe dipped in blood in Rev. 19:13, which is not the blood of others as sometimes thought,[36] but his own blood shed on the cross.[37]

Garments of wealth not only announce a high social status but also may reveal a self-absorbed and parsimonious spirituality. The quality of fabric, the condition of the clothing, the length of the garment, the color, and the type of ornamentation are markers of social status.[38] Purple dye, linen, and fine silk, for instance, were very expensive dyes and fabrics that were available only to the wealthy and those of high social rank. Long cloaks and tunics were the garb of the rich and dignitaries, whereas the poor and slaves dressed in short tunics and cloaks.[39] The scribes loved to walk around in "long robes," to be greeted in the marketplaces, and to have the "best seats" in the synagogues. They also devoured widows' houses and said long prayers for the sake of appearance (Luke 20:46–47). Their outward lavishness and craving for public approbation testify to an unctuous spiritual life of self-promotion. The rich man in Luke's parable "was dressed in purple and fine linen" whereas Lazarus was clothed with "sores" (Luke 16:19, 20). Their respective clothing testifies to their social and spiritual condition. The rich man needs no consolation; just as he gave none, he receives none. His well-stocked material life leaves him spiritually impoverished. Lazarus, on the other hand, is materially indigent and in great need. He receives consolation. The whore of Babylon is dressed "in purple and scarlet, and adorned with gold and jewels and pearls" (Rev. 17:4). Her conspicuous wealth is a product of economic and religious fornication with the kings and merchants of the world (Rev. 18). But her garment is of little value because it is the product of an age that is passing away.

Temporal Settings

Mark Allan Powell identifies two types of temporal settings: chronological and typological.[40] Chronological references refer to the time an

36. *Pace* Robert H. Mounce, *The Book of Revelation*, NICMT, rev. ed. (Grand Rapids: Eerdmans, 1998), 345. The blood cannot be from the battle of Rev. 19 for the battle occurs after the description of Jesus' blood.

37. See Resseguie, *Revelation Unsealed*, 116; O. Michel, "κόκκος, κόκκινος," *TDNT* 3:810–14 at 813; David L. Barr, "The Apocalypse as a Symbolic Transformation of the World: A Literary Analysis," *Int* 38 (1984): 39–50 at 42; Richard Bauckham, *The Theology of the Book of Revelation*, NTT (Cambridge: Cambridge University Press, 1993), 106.

38. See Gildas Hamel, *Poverty and Charity in Roman Palestine, First Three Centuries C.E.* (Berkeley: University of California Press, 1990), chapter 2.

39. Ibid.

40. Powell, *What Is Narrative Criticism?*, 72–74. Powell also uses Paul Ricoeur's distinction between mortal time and monumental time to describe temporal settings. "Mortal time

action takes place. The Jerusalem temple, for instance, was built over a forty-six-year span, which merely indicates the length of time it took to build the temple (John 2:20); it is not a symbolic notation. A temporal setting like Mark's "immediately" or "at once" (*euthys*) is not symbolic either, but it adds a note of urgency that signals the importance of an event: "Immediately [the disciples] left their nets and followed [Jesus]" (Mark 1:18); "Immediately he called them" (Mark 1:20). Each event is so compelling that the characters respond without hesitation. Some chronological references accent the rhythms of life. What characters do on a daily basis highlights what is important or what they value. The rich man of Luke 16, for instance, feasts sumptuously "every day" (*kath' hēmeran*, 16:19). The disciples are commanded to take up their cross "daily" (Luke 9:23).[41] In Acts, the disciples are in the temple and break bread "day by day" (2:46); the churches are strengthened in the faith and increase in numbers "daily" (16:5); and the Beroeans examine the Scriptures "every day" (17:11). In Hebrews, Jesus has no need to offer sacrifices like other priests "day after day," for his sacrifice was once for all (7:27, cf. 10:11). The demoniac howls "night and day" (Mark 5:5); the four living creatures of the Apocalypse sing praises "day and night" (Rev. 4:8).

Typological references indicate the "kind of time" in which an action takes place, and may be symbolic.[42] When Judas leaves the Last Supper to hand Jesus over to the authorities, "it was night" (John 13:30). Night represents a kind of time; Judas goes out into the darkness to join the powers of darkness. "Early on the first day of the week, while it was still dark," Mary Magdalene came to the tomb (John 20:1). Mary, who is "in the dark" about the risen Jesus, arrives at the tomb while it is still dark. The contrast between night and day is the setting for Jesus' appearance to the seven disciples in John 21. They fished all night but caught nothing; just after daybreak Jesus appears and their haul is so great that their nets are threatened (John 21:3–6). Jesus' temptation in the wilderness for forty days is an allusion to the Israelites' wandering and testing in the desert for forty years. Luke uses the temporal setting "today" (*sēmeron*) to mark the dawning of a new day: "To you is born *this day* in the city of David a Savior, who is the Messiah" (Luke 2:11). "*Today* this scripture has been fulfilled in your hearing" (4:21). "Zacchaeus, hurry and come

---

is measured by calendars, watches, clocks, and sundials. Monumental time, on the other hand, refers to the broad sweep of time that includes but also transcends history," 74.

41. These examples come from Outi Lehtipuu, "Characterization and Persuasion: The Rich Man and the Poor Man in Luke 16:19–31," in *Characterization in the Gospels: Reconceiving Narrative Criticism*, ed. David Rhoads and Kari Syreeni, JSNTSup 184 (Sheffield: Sheffield Academic Press, 1999), 73–105 at 86.

42. Ibid., 73.

down; for I must stay at your house *today*" (19:5). "*Today* salvation has come to this house" (19:9). "Truly I tell you, *today* you will be with me in Paradise" (23:43). The Gospel of John uses "hour" (*hōra*) to "designate a particular and significant period in Jesus' life."[43] The hour is the time of Jesus' return to the Father—the time of his death, resurrection, and glorification. "Jesus knew that *his hour* had come to depart from this world and go to the Father" (John 13:1).

Revelation is filled with symbolic temporal notations. Time, times, and half a time; forty-two months; 1,260 days; and three and a half years are all the same interval of time and refer to a period of intense persecution and divine protection. The millennium refers to a kind of time, not to a length of time; it is a Satan-free period in which the saints reign.

Some temporal settings develop and elaborate a social setting. In Mark 13:18 the disciples are to pray that the end-time tribulation "not be in winter." It is understandable why one would not want to flee to the mountains during winter. Matthew, however, has an additional reference to the time: "Pray that your flight may not be in winter or *on a sabbath*" (Matt. 24:20). The added detail provides a glimpse into Matthew's social setting. Other temporal settings having to do with religious observance, such as Sabbaths, Passover, and Tabernacles, are considered in the section under religious settings.

Social Settings

Social settings develop and elaborate class structures, cultural and social customs, and economic and political structures.[44] The meal is one of the most common and significant social settings in the New Testament: Jesus eats at the table of Pharisees, tax collectors, and sinners; Peter refuses to eat at the table of Gentiles at Antioch (Gal. 2:11–14), and the Corinthians eat at the table of pagan gods (1 Cor. 8–10).[45] Table fellowship shapes community identity and creates social boundaries.[46] Meals reflect the cultural and societal norms and values of a first-century Mediterranean society. The social maps of the Pharisees, for instance,

43. Brown, *John*, 1:517.

44. Powell, *What Is Narrative Criticism?*, 74–75. On social settings in the New Testament see David Rhoads, "Social Criticism: Crossing Boundaries," in *Mark and Method: New Approaches in Biblical Studies*, ed. Janice Capel Anderson and Stephen D. Moore (Minneapolis: Fortress, 1992), 135–61; idem, *Reading Mark, Engaging the Gospel* (Minneapolis: Fortress, 2004), chapter 6.

45. On meals see Dennis E. Smith, *From Symposium to Eucharist: The Banquet in the Early Christian World* (Minneapolis: Fortress, 2003); Resseguie, *Spiritual Landscape*, chapter 4.

46. D. E. Smith, *From Symposium to Eucharist*, 175.

establish firm boundaries that outline what can be eaten, where one can sit at a banquet, with whom one can eat, and proper preparation for meals (e.g., washing of hands). Peter's social map prevented him from associating or eating with non-Jews. But a MacGuffin in the form of a sheet lowered from heaven with all kinds of four-footed creatures and reptiles and birds of heaven convinces him to alter his social and religious boundaries (Acts 10:1–11:18). The command to kill and eat the animals offends his sensibilities: "By no means, Lord; for I have never eaten anything that is profane or unclean" (Acts 10:14). Peter is "greatly puzzled about what to make of the vision that he had seen," and he is still pondering the vision when the Spirit instructs him to greet the men who were sent by the Gentile centurion, Cornelius (Acts 10:17–21).

The distinction between clean and unclean arises in Mark 7:1–13. The Pharisees and some of the scribes notice that some of Jesus' disciples eat with defiled hands. Contrary to a common perception among some of the religious authorities, the things outside the body do not pollute. Rather, things inside pollute the body: "Do you not see that whatever goes into a person from outside cannot defile, since it enters, not the heart but the stomach, and goes into the sewer? (Thus he declared all foods clean)" (Mark 7:18–19). Table talk was an occasion for redefining social and religious boundaries. David Rhoads notes that personal, bodily boundaries replicate social boundaries. "As anyone may enter the network without making the group unclean, so anything may go into the body without making it unclean. There is no need to guard the boundaries from what is outside the person or the group."[47] When social boundaries are altered, the religious landscape changes. The distinctions between unclean and clean are eliminated; instead, one's moral and ethical behavior defines the new religious landscape.

Table fellowship implies acceptance of the social values and status of others. Jesus is criticized for eating with tax collectors and sinners. His acceptance of meals with the "other" threatens the social and religious boundaries put in place by the religious establishment of the day. Paul also is keenly aware of table fellowship with the "other." In his discussion of food sacrificed to idols, he urges the Corinthians not to seek their own advantage but "that of the other," that is, the person whose conscience will not allow him or her to eat meat sacrificed to idols (1 Cor. 10:24).[48] At Galatia, Paul addressed the social issue of two separate tables for one community of believers—one table for Jewish Christians and another

47. Rhoads, *Reading Mark*, 170.

48. On this see D. E. Smith, *From Symposium to Eucharist*, chapter 7.

table for Gentiles.[49] Separate tables, however, nullify the truth of the gospel (Gal. 2:14). As there is one gospel, there is also one table.

Social ranking at tables is turned upside down in a Lukan parable (Luke 14:7–11). When Jesus saw that the guests were jockeying for the places of honor at a meal, he told them a parable. Instead of seeking the places of honor at a wedding banquet, one should take the lowest place at the feast. A more eminent late-comer may arrive, and the person in the place of honor will be shamed when asked to go lower. On the other hand, when the host invites the person to go to a higher position, he or she will be honored in the presence of the other guests. This new table ranking redefines the social and spiritual landscape. In this scenario, it is impossible to bestow honor on the self because no one can possibly know whether a late-arriver of a higher rank will join the feast. Jockeying for position and engaging in self-promotion is thus pointless. In fact, it may result in being shamed in the presence of others. The social ranking that Jesus suggests radically alters the social and religious landscape—for it makes little sense to choose the place of honor unless one wants to be shamed. But if everyone chooses the lowest place, all are on an equal plane. Self-promotion and self-serving behaviors are of little value when one is powerless to influence the outcome.

Table fellowship in the Gospels redefines boundaries between social and economic groups. Jesus cites the customary practice of inviting "friends," "brothers," "relatives," or "rich neighbors" to a banquet in a parable. Instead, "the poor, the crippled, the lame, and the blind" are to be invited (Luke 14:12–14). One group can repay the invitation; the other group cannot. The type of banquet Jesus envisions overturns balanced reciprocity. If a person is invited to a meal, the expectation is that the invitation will be repaid. This is balanced reciprocity. Jesus, however, advocates generalized reciprocity in which no repayment is expected. Indeed, the recipients of generalized reciprocity are incapable of returning the invitation.[50] Not only is the social and economic landscape radically altered in a shift from balanced to generalized reciprocity, but the spiritual landscape looks different as "outsiders" are treated as "insiders."

Like clothing, meals mark transitions in the spiritual life. The messianic banquet signals the transition from this age to the new age; those who hunger now will be filled and those who are full now will be hungry (Luke 6:21, 25). The prodigal son is hungry, longing for the pods that the pigs eat, but when welcomed back into the father's house, he feasts.

49. Ibid., 175.

50. On forms of reciprocity in the ancient world see Halvor Moxnes, *The Economy of the Kingdom: Social Conflict and Economic Relations in Luke's Gospel* (Philadelphia: Fortress, 1988), 34–35, 129–34, 174.

His redemption is the occasion for a banquet. The Last Supper marks the transition from an older covenant to a new covenant: "This cup that is poured out for you is the new covenant in my blood" (Luke 22:20). Two separate banquets mark spiritual transitions in John's Apocalypse. The "marriage supper of the Lamb" is a time of rejoicing and exulting for all the saints (19:7, 9), while the "great supper of God" is a ghoulish feast—an ironic parody of the marriage feast of the Lamb—where the unrepentant gather to be eaten (19:17). The scavenging birds in mid-heaven devour "the flesh of kings, the flesh of captains, the flesh of the mighty, the flesh of horses and their riders—flesh of all, both free and slave, both small and great" (19:18).

Religious Settings

Religious days and feasts (Sabbath, Passover, Tabernacles) are settings for healings and for conflicts between Jesus and the authorities. In John, Jesus heals on the Sabbath because the "Father is still working, and [Jesus] also [is] working" (John 5:17). In Luke, he heals a crippled woman on the Sabbath because the Sabbath day is an opportune time to set her free from bondage (Luke 13:10–17). In Mark, the disciples work on the Sabbath by plucking grain, because the Sabbath is made for humankind, not humankind for the Sabbath (Mark 2:23–28; cf. Matt. 12:1–8; Luke 6:1–5).

The work Jesus does on the Sabbath, however, causes conflict with the religious leaders, which crystallizes the divergent points of view of Jesus and the authorities. A synagogue leader objects to Jesus' healing of the crippled woman because "there are six days on which work ought to be done" (Luke 13:14). Holiness is a core value of the Jewish religious leaders as stated in the law: "You shall be holy, for I the Lord your God am holy" (Lev. 19:2).[51] The Sabbath laws thus help define the appropriate boundaries that keep the Sabbath a holy day and honor God's holiness. Yet boundaries can also be stifling and subjugate a person to bondage. While oxen can be untied and donkeys led to water on the Sabbath, a woman who was crippled for eighteen years cannot be healed on the Sabbath. Religious settings are important in plot and characterization, for they accent the differing perspectives of protagonist and antagonist.

Religious festivals such as Passover and Tabernacles amplify important events in Jesus' ministry and times for solemn pronouncements. Passover celebrates God's deliverance of the Israelites from bondage in Egypt. In John, Jesus is the "Lamb of God" (1:29, 36) who is sacrificed at the time the Passover lamb is slaughtered, the day of Preparation (19:14, 31). In case

51. Rhoads, *Reading Mark*, 154.

the reader should miss the importance of this religious setting, the narrator slows the narration down. Whereas John 1–12 covers the first two and a half years of Jesus' ministry, John 13–19 encompasses a mere twenty-four hours. Luke uses repetition to hammer into the reader's head the importance of the Passover and Unleavened Bread (Luke 22:1, 7, 8, 11, 13, 15).

The Feast of Tabernacles[52] is an important festival that becomes the setting for one of Jesus' solemn pronouncements. Tabernacles is an autumn harvest festival associated with the triumphant "day of the Lord." During the feast, texts from Zech. 9–14 were read, including the prophecy that the messianic king would come to Jerusalem on a donkey (Zech. 9:9) and that living waters would flow out of Jerusalem, one half to the eastern sea (the Dead Sea) and one half to the western sea (the Mediterranean Sea) (Zech. 14:8). The climax of the festival included a solemn ceremony in which water was poured out onto the altar. A procession would go down the hill from the temple to the fountain of Gihon that supplied the water to the pool of Siloam. A priest would fill a golden pitcher with water, which he would then carry back up the hill through the Water Gate to the altar of holocausts in front of the temple. After the procession circumambulated the altar waving *lulabs* (myrtle and willow twigs tied with palm) and singing Ps. 118, the priest poured the water into a funnel, which then flowed to the ground. This is the religious setting for Jesus' climactic pronouncement "on the last day of the festival, the great day" (John 7:37): "Let anyone who is thirsty come to me, and let the one who believes in me drink. As the scripture has said, 'Out of the believer's heart[53] shall flow rivers of living water'" (John 7:37–8). The religious festival interprets the significance of the event and the event reinterprets the religious setting.

3.4 A Reading of Setting in Mark 5:1–20

The settings of Mark 5:1–20 are numerous and diverse, and many are symbolic. The following are especially important for understanding the story:

52. This account of Tabernacles relies on Brown, *John*, 1:326–29; see also J. C. Rylaarsdam, "Booths, Feast of," *IDB* 1:455–58.

53. Whether the water flows out of the believer or out of Jesus is debated. For a discussion see Margaret Davies, *Rhetoric and Reference in the Fourth Gospel*, JSNTSup 69 (Sheffield: JSOT Press, 1992), 144–45; Rudolf Schnackenburg, *The Gospel according to St. John*, 3 vols. (New York: Crossroad, 1980–1990), 2:152–55; C. K. Barrett, *The Gospel according to St. John: An Introduction and Commentary and Notes on the Greek Text*, 2nd ed. (Philadelphia: Westminster, 1978), 326–29; Brown, *John*, 320–23; Joel Marcus, "Rivers of Living Waters from Jesus' Belly (John 7:38)," *JBL* 117 (1998): 328–30.

geographical (country of the Gerasenes)
topographical (mountains, sea, country)
architectural (tombs, city, house)
temporal (night and day, immediately)
props (clothing, swine, walk-ons [swine herders, neighbors, and disciples], chains and fetters, stones)
social (Gentile territory, unclean/clean, naming)

After the stilling of the tempestuous storm on the Sea of Galilee (Mark 4:35–41), Jesus and the disciples arrive at the country of the Gerasenes.[54] A two-step progression places the story in the *geographical* locale of Gerasa and highlights the social-ethnic nature of this territory: "They came to the other side of the sea, to the country of the Gerasenes" (5:1). Geographically it is the other side of the shore, and socially and ethnically it is a foreign region, the country of Gerasa. The otherness of this side is alluded to in the narrator's opening description: "they came to the *other* side of the sea." This side, as Ched Myers notes, is the other side of humanity, "a journey to the unknown, the foreign."[55] By crossing to the other side, Jesus makes a voyage to the beyond. Jean Starobinski notes that the crossing entails "the confrontation with a diabolical world; it is the equivalent of a descent into hell, of a *katabasis*. . . . The other shore becomes the homologue of another diabolical world, and the voyage of Christ symbolizes a crossing of the universe to its darkest depths."[56] That side is an "antishore," a world turned inside out and upside down.

> It is the other, the inverse, not only in its quality of place opposite but also in its quality of opposing power. The shore beyond is an antishore; the day beyond is an antiday; the tombs, abode of the dead, are an antilife; the demons are rebels.[57]

As soon as Jesus steps out of the boat, a man with an unclean spirit who lives in tombs "immediately" meets him. That favorite Markan term[58] increases the urgency of the inevitable battle. The man does not *have* an

54. The precise location is debated. The better and more difficult reading is "Gerasenes." Gerasa is located some thirty miles southeast of the Sea of Galilee. Some manuscripts have "Gadarenes" and others "Gergesenes." See Metzger, *A Textual Commentary on the Greek New Testament*, 2nd. ed. (New York: United Bible Societies, 1971), 18–19 and 72.

55. Ched Myers, *Binding the Strong Man: A Political Reading of Mark's Story of Jesus* (Maryknoll, N.Y.: Orbis Books, 1988), 195.

56. Jean Starobinski, "The Struggle with Legion: A Literary Analysis of Mark 5:1–20," *NLH* 4 (1973): 331–56 at 337.

57. Ibid.

58. "Immediately" (*euthys*) occurs more than forty times in Mark.

unclean spirit; literarily, he is *"in* an unclean spirit." He is captive to an alien, occupying force, "swallowed up by his possessing spirit,"[59] and the opposition (i.e., the legion of demons) does not wait to be vanquished but comes out to negotiate favorable terms with the superior power. The singular and plural pronouns underscore the man's divided, confused identity. The demon-possessed man is singular yet multiple. In the initial encounter with Jesus he speaks in the singular: "What have you to do with *me,* Jesus, Son of the Most High God? *I* adjure you by God, do not torment *me"* (Mark 5:7). But the singular is ambiguous, for the demons and the man speak with one voice.[60] In other words, the individualized nature of the man is taken over by a plural enemy. When Jesus asks for the demon's name, the confusion of identity is apparent. *"My* name is Legion; for *we* are many" (Mark 5:9). The singular and plural are used together. The name Legion is a collective singular, which the second half clarifies: "we are many." By naming, the plural is separated from the singular, and when Jesus banishes the invading army to its proper place in the sea or the abyss, the man's singular identity is restored.

The *props*—chains and fetters—are humanity's attempt at binding Satan, but their ineffectiveness demonstrates the overwhelmingly destructive energy of the possessing power. A string of negatives reinforces the terrifying might of this occupying force: *"No one* could restrain him *no longer, not even* with a chain" (Mark 5:3, author's translation). He is thus bound twice: once by Satan, which is a spiritual binding, and a second time by his fellow townspeople, which is a social and physical binding. The Gospel of Luke amplifies his alienation from other human beings: "for a long time he had worn no clothes" (Luke 8:27). Having left his humanity behind, he is stark naked like an animal. A *temporal setting* (night and day) underscores his relentless, unceasing torment while a topographical setting (a mountain) is the battleground for a supernatural confrontation: night and day among the tombs and on the mountains he shrieked and mutilated himself with stones (Mark 5:5). The battle, however, is one-sided, for the demoniac bows down before the superior power.

A great herd of pigs, unclean animals that are essential props (MacGuffins), are feeding nearby. They become the new host for the demons, but not before Jesus learns the demons' identity. Their name is Legion. A legion is a Roman division of approximately six thousand soldiers at full strength.[61] The spirits plead with Jesus "not to send them out of the country [or region]," the territory they control, which Jesus

59. Joel Marcus, *Mark 1–8: A New Translation with Introduction and Commentary,* AB 27A (New York: Doubleday, 2000), 342.

60. Noted by Starobinski, "The Struggle with Legion," 341–42.

61. BDAG, s.v. λεγιών.

grants by sending them into a herd of swine. The herd then stampedes down a cliff and drowns in the sea. Although some commentators assume that Jesus tricked the demons,[62] he does not actually send them out of the country or region. Instead he grants their request, but in so doing he sends them to their proper place, the abyss. (In Luke 8:31, they plead not to be sent into the abyss, i.e., the sea.)

The *topographical setting* of mountains is a natural place for a battle between opposing supernatural powers. Similar to the supernatural battle that takes place at Harmagedon—the mountain of Meggido—the mountains at Gerasa are a symbolic battleground; there God routs Satan, and Jesus vanquishes the demonic army. Elizabeth Struthers Malbon also suggests that the mountain setting recalls another mountain scene in the Old Testament where divine rescue is the prominent theme.[63] In the land of Moriah God provides a sacrifice on a mountain. As Abraham readies his only son, Isaac, for a burnt offering, the angel of the Lord forbids the sacrifice of Isaac, and a ram is offered on the altar instead (Gen. 22). Similarly, Jesus rescues the demoniac from a legion of demons on another mountain. A last-minute substitute—a herd of pigs—is found, and the man is set free from the torment of the unclean spirits. The pigs, now the sole possessors of the unclean spirits, are sacrificed, plunged into the suffocating sea. The drowning in the sea recalls Pharaoh's armies that were entombed in a watery grave. Appropriately, unclean spirits enter unclean animals and rush to their death in the realm of chaos. "The plunge of the pigs into the sea is a figure of the fall of the rebellious spirits into the abyss."[64]

The foreign possessing power, "Legion," is used figuratively to refer to the destructive nature and overwhelming magnitude of the demonic army. Like the overpowering, brutal force of the Romans in Palestine, the unclean spirits are a foreign, destructive force in the man. At six thousand in full strength, this alien power cannot be subdued by human means. Chains and fetters are of little use in binding Satan; only the "stronger one" can bind the "strong one" and plunder his property, liberating the singular identity of the bound person (Mark 3:27).

The *architectural* change in setting from tomb to house parallels the restoration of the man's identity. Tombs are places of the dead while the house is the place of human socialization. The man possessed by an alien, destructive power is figuratively dead. His self-mutilation leaves him near death, and he dwells in the farthest outreaches of "the other." After the demons are exorcised, he is no longer naked but clothed, no

62. E.g., J. Marcus, *Mark*, 345.
63. Malbon, *Narrative Space*, 84–85.
64. Starobinski, "The Struggle with Legion," 339.

longer shrieking but sitting, no longer mad but in his right mind. He is then sent back to the place of normalcy, the home. Restored to life, he is given back his singular identity.

The swine herders are walk-ons who tell the people in the city and the country what has happened, and the townspeople come out to see for themselves. What they see is a man "clothed and in his right mind" (Mark 5:15). Clothing marks the man's transition from a feral, mad state to a human, rational state. The townspeople, also walk-ons, are afraid and beg Jesus to leave their neighborhood. The demonic opposition now takes a new form: human opposition to Jesus' presence in their territory. The man, on the other hand, begs to remain with Jesus, but Jesus refuses and sends him to his house to tell his friends of the good news (5:19).

With the expulsion of Legion everything is returned to its proper order. As Starobinski notes, at the beginning everything is out of order, and at the end everything or nearly everything is returned to order.[65] The demons "have ventured out of their proper place," the abyss, and entered a man who is then evicted from his proper place, his house and community.[66] He shrieks like a wounded animal day and night and dwells with the dead. But Jesus intervenes and puts all back in its place. The demons are sent back to the abyss; the man is restored to his humanness and puts on clothes once again. He is then returned to the community that banished him, where he proclaims to his "friends" the good news.

The restoration of order, however, has an unseen result. Some, it seems, prefer everything as it was before Jesus intervened. Opposition to Jesus at the supernatural level has a disturbing parallel at the human level.[67] The verbal thread, "beg" (*parakaleō*), links the requests of the demons and the townspeople, and clarifies the parallel between the supernatural and the human. The demons "beg" Jesus not to send them out of the territory, which he grants (5:10), and the townspeople "beg" him to leave their neighborhood, which he also grants (5:17). Evil's banishment to the sea, it appears, resurfaces in a "residue of opposition"[68] when the townspeople ask Jesus to leave their neighborhood. While Jesus is triumphant over demonic opposition, he allows "human opposition to reappear and persist." [69] Did the demons gain the upper hand by having human representatives evict Jesus from their territory? Or is there some other design to Jesus' rejection? The verbal thread, "beg," reappears one more time to demonstrate the way Jesus deals with the "residue of

65. Ibid., 343.
66. Ibid.
67. Marcus, *Mark*, 352.
68. Starobinski, "The Struggle with Legion," 345–46.
69. Ibid., 346.

opposition."[70] "As [Jesus] was getting into the boat, the man who had been possessed by demons begged [*parakaleō*] him that he might be with him" (Mark 5:18). While he granted the requests of the demons and the townspeople, he refuses the request of the man. Instead he sends him back to his village to face on the human level what Jesus encountered at the supernatural level.

What is the point of this story? Richard Horsley and Ched Myers suggest that the settings allude to Roman imperialism. Myers concludes that we are "encountering imagery meant to call to mind the Roman military occupation of Palestine."[71] Richard Horsley concurs: "The struggle between transcendent *spiritual* forces, between God and Satan, between Jesus and the demons is also a this-worldly *political* struggle."[72] The key to this political interpretation is the name Legion, which is a Latin loanword for a division of Roman troops. "The identity of the demon is *Roman army*," says Horsley.[73] Military terms are used to describe the confrontation. Legion begged Jesus not "to send" (*apostellō*) them out of the country—a military term that refers to an officer dispatching a troop or other military force.[74] The word for "herd" (*agelē*) is used for a band of military recruits. And the pigs line up in tight formation like a military unit. This is unpiglike behavior, according to J. Duncan M. Derrett. Pigs do not move in herds like sheep, horses, and cattle, and they do not line up in close formation. When they panic, they tend to scatter. "Pigs exist in families like human beings (whom they very much resemble in many ways); they are un-herdlike: and here they became a military unit . . . and went over the cliff once the Legion entered into them."[75] Furthermore, the word for "permit" is a double entendre for "order" (*epitrepō*). "He gave them permission" to enter the swine is appropriate here; but the other meaning—"order"—is just beneath the surface. Like a commanding officer, Jesus "orders" the unclean spirits into the swine. Then they "rush" (*hormaō*) to the sea—a term that also describes troops charging into battle.[76] The unpiglike behavior of the possessed animals constitutes an allusion to a Roman regiment in military formation.

The topographical setting of the sea also supports a political interpretation of Mark 5. As Pharaoh's army is drowned in the Red Sea in their

70. Ibid., 345–46.

71. Myers, *Binding the Strong Man*, 191.

72. Richard A. Horsley, *Hearing the Whole Story: The Politics of Plot in Mark's Gospel* (Louisville: Westminster John Knox, 2001), 141 (italics are Horsley's).

73. Ibid. (italics are Horsley's).

74. J. Duncan M. Derrett, "Contributions to the Study of the Gerasene Demoniac," *JSNT* 3 (1979): 2–17.

75. Ibid., 5–6.

76. Ibid., 5.

pursuit of the fleeing Israelites, the legion of demons rushes over the cliff and drowns in the sea. Horsley develops the connection:

> When Jesus casts out "Legion," which is then destroyed by charging into the Sea, he brings the political conflict to the fore, at least in a symbolic way. Once Jesus has ordered the demon to come out of the man and elicits its name, it is evident that the struggle is really against Roman imperial rule—and by implication when Legion enters the swine who charge to their death in the Sea, that the struggle promises to result in the people's liberation from Legion.[77]

A narrative-critical approach looks at all the settings, the development of characters, the rhetoric, and the plot to find the point of a narrative. Horsley's and Myers' interpretations are less convincing when all the aspects of narrative analysis are considered. To be sure, Legion is a reference to the Roman army; but it is also an appropriate term to illustrate the strength of the foreign occupying force within the demon-possessed man. Similarly, the drowning of the pigs in the sea does recall Pharaoh's troops suffocating in the Red Sea, but this imagery need not refer to the defeat of Roman imperialism in Palestine; rather it can refer to the deliverance of a new Israel from a new pharaoh—in this case, the subjugating forces of Satan and his emissaries. A political interpretation of Mark 5 is certainly correct, but the political battle is a spiritual warfare between two powerful kingdoms—the kingdom of God and Satan's realm. The man is representative of a lost, alienated, and subjugated humanity. He is "the other."

77. Horsley, *Hearing the Story*, 147.

4

Character

4.1 Definition

Characters are the *dramatis personae*, the persons in the story. Like the Lord God, who takes dust from the earth and breathes life into Adam, the author of a narrative breathes life into a character that is realized in the reader's imagination. This does not imply that biblical characters are fictional any more than Mary of Magdala or Jesus would be considered fictional characters. Rather it implies that an author is selective in what he or she writes in a narrative, for only some events and speeches can be narrated. No author can give a complete record of everything that happens in a person's life, and no autobiographer can record everything about himself or herself. Thus, to a certain extent, literary characters, whether real life or fictional, are given life by an author and re-created in the reader's imagination. How can we realize the character that the author intended us to see? What should we look for?

Characters reveal themselves in their speech (what they say and how they say it), in their actions (what they do), by their clothing (what they wear), in their gestures and posture (how they present themselves). Characters are known by what others say about them. What do the disciples or authorities say about Jesus, for instance? Or what does the narrator say about him? Characters are also known by the environment or setting in which they work and play. Does the setting provide more than a backdrop for their speech or actions? Is it symbolic? Are the settings highly charged with meaning: the temple or synagogue, a Sabbath or feast day, for instance?

Characters are also known by their position within society. Are they part of the structures of power and domination? Or are they at the margins of society—unseen and invisible? Characters may develop within a narrative and undergo an important change either for the better or for the worse. These are dynamic characters. Or characters may be static: the same at the end of the narrative as at the beginning. Some of the most interesting character stories in American literature are about individuals who have risen from relative obscurity and poverty to positions of immense wealth and power. The Horatio Alger story—a tale of a character born into poverty who rises to a position of power and often wealth by his or her hard work—captivates the American imagination.[1] It is the narrative of Andrew Carnegie and Abraham Lincoln—a rags-to-riches story of individuals who overcame great odds to move from the margins of society to the center, from the lowest rungs of the status ladder to the highest levels. What traits or events enable them to rise above dismal circumstances? How do they deal with roadblocks to success? Equally as fascinating are stories about characters who move from the centers of influence to the margins of society, from honor to dishonor, from glory to shame. What trait or error of judgment contributed to the downfall of such powerful and well-known individuals? What is the character flaw that leads to disaster? And how can their error of judgment be avoided?

Many biblical characters are either at the margins of society or at the centers of power and influence, either rising to prominence or falling to oblivion. Because we learn from the success and failure of others, the study of character and characterization can be a fascinating part of narrative analysis.[2] The enjoyment of a narrative lies in the discovery

1. Horatio Alger was a popular nineteenth-century novelist who wrote over a hundred stories featuring a youth born into poverty who rises by his own hard work to the highest levels of society. See H. Porter Abbott, *The Cambridge Introduction to Narrative* (Cambridge: Cambridge University Press, 2002), 43–44.

2. On characterization in literature see Baruch Hochman, *Character in Literature* (Ithaca: Cornell University Press, 1985); Thomas Docherty, *Reading (Absent) Character: Towards a Theory of Characterization in Fiction* (Oxford: Clarendon, 1983); Seymour Chatman, *Story and Discourse: Narrative Structure in Fiction and Film* (Ithaca: Cornell University Press, 1978); James Phelan, *Reading People, Reading Plots: Character, Progression, and the Interpretation of Narrative* (Chicago: University of Chicago Press, 1989); Mary Doyle Springer, *A Rhetoric of Literary Character: Some Women of Henry James* (Chicago: University of Chicago Press, 1978); Walter J. Harvey, *Character and the Novel* (Ithaca: Cornell University Press, 1965); Mieke Bal, *Narratology: Introduction to the Theory of Narrative* (Toronto: University of TorontoPress, 1985), 79–93; Shlomith Rimmon-Kenan, *Narrative Fiction: Contemporary Poetics* (London: Routledge, 1983). On characterization in biblical literature see Mark Allan Powell, *What Is Narrative Criticism?* (Minneapolis: Fortress, 1990), chapter 5; Daniel Marguerat and Yvan Bourquin, *How to Read Bible Stories: An Introduction to Narrative Criticism*, trans. John Bowden (London: SCM, 1999), chapter 5; Elizabeth

of complex, developing characters that help define or redefine our own quests.

4.2 Round and Flat Characters

E. M. Forster distinguished character types as either *round* or *flat*.[3] A round character is three-dimensional, possessing several complex traits. He or she is unpredictable and shows depth that "cannot be summed up in a single phrase."[4] This character type is lifelike and capable of surprising the reader in a convincing way. "If [the character] never surprises, it is flat. If it does not convince, it is a flat pretending to be round."[5] Jesus and the disciples are round characters with complex and, in the case of the disciples, conflicting traits.[6] Flat characters, on the other hand, are two-dimensional, constructed around a single idea or quality; they can be summed up in a single phrase or sentence. A flat character lacks hidden complexity or depth and is incapable of surprising the reader. "When there is more than one factor [in a flat character], we get the beginning of the curve towards the round."[7] Major characters are generally round and minor characters are generally flat, but not always. Religious leaders in the Gospels, for instance, are major characters, but they lack complexity. They are flat, exhibiting various forms of a single root trait of duplicity and destructiveness.[8] By contrast, minor characters, such as the Syrophoenician woman, can be surprising. Her wit and refusal to take no for an answer surprise the reader, and even though she is a

---

Struthers Malbon and Adele Berlin, eds., "Characterization in Biblical Literature," *Semeia* 63 (1993); John A. Darr, *On Character Building: The Reader and the Rhetoric of Characterization in Luke-Acts*, LCBI (Louisville: Westminster John Knox, 1992); Elizabeth Struthers Malbon, *In the Company of Jesus: Characters in Mark's Gospel* (Louisville: Westminster John Knox, 2000); David Rhoads, Joanna Dewey, and Donald Michie, *Mark as Story: An Introduction to the Narrative of a Gospel*, 2nd ed. (Minneapolis: Fortress, 1999), chapters 5 and 6; Wesley A. Kort, *Story, Text, and Scripture: Literary Interests in Biblical Narrative* (University Park, Pa.: Pennsylvania State University, 1988), chapter 2; David Rhoads and Kari Syreeni, eds., *Characterization in the Gospels: Reconceiving Narrative Criticism*, JSNTSup 184 (Sheffield: Sheffield Academic Press, 1999).

3. E. M. Forster, *Aspects of the Novel* (New York: Harcourt, Brace, 1927), 78.

4. Ibid., 69.

5. Ibid., 78.

6. Black, *Rhetoric of the Gospel*, 36–37, argues that Jesus is a *flat* character in Matthew "because the many traits ascribed to him are manifestations of a single, 'root trait,' which is diversely identified as 'righteousness,' 'obedience,' 'faithfulness,' or simply 'goodness.'" Jesus, however, is more complex than Black allows. He is capable of expressing anger and vituperation.

7. Forster, *Aspects of the Novel*, 67.

8. Black, *Rhetoric of the Gospel*, 38.

minor character, her traits of perseverance, faith, and humor make her a round character.

In addition to round and flat characters, three other character types are helpful for apprehending biblical characters: *stock*, *foil*, and *walk-on*. A stock character is a type that appears repeatedly in narratives and is recognizable as part of the conventions of a literary genre.[9] In fairy tales, the cruel stepmother and the charming prince are stock characters. In Westerns, the hombre with a dark hat is the villain while the mysterious stranger with a white hat is the hero. Film noir relies on stock characters of a malevolent type in a sleazy setting: the charming and mysterious femme fatale, for instance, is a stock character of film noir. Abrams lists as stock characters the *eiron* (from which we get irony), or self-derogatory character, and the *alazon*, or self-deceiving braggart, whose perspective the eiron unravels. The fool in Shakespeare's play, for instance, is an eiron who pretends to know less than he knows. In John 9, the man born blind is an eiron who feigns ignorance yet knows more than the self-deceived braggarts of the narrative. Other stock characters include the demons in the Gospels and an antichrist type that makes several appearances in apocalyptic literature: counterfeit christs in Mark 13, the lawless one of 2 Thess. 2:3–10, and the beast from the sea of Rev. 13:1–10. This stock character masks evil by appearing good.

A *foil* is literally a contrasting background, such as a sheet of shiny metal that is placed under jewels to increase their brilliance. "In literature, the term is applied to any person who through contrast underscores the distinctive characteristics of another."[10] The foil provides what Walter J. Harvey calls "perspectives of depth." He or she "may focus the protagonist's dilemma more clearly" or may "illuminate the protagonist's blindness and folly."[11] A foil may also illuminate the deficient qualities of groups of characters. The poor widow is a foil for those who put far more in the treasury but give far less. Her self-giving shames the self-protective giving of the rich. A Gentile who demonstrates great faith illuminates the lack of faith of some within Israel. The women's appearance at the cross casts a glaring spotlight on the male disciples' defection.

9. M. H. Abrams, *A Glossary of Literary Terms*, 7th ed. (Forth Worth: Harcourt Brace College Publishers, 1999), s.v. "Stock Characters." Some narrative critics define a "stock" character as having only one trait. For example, David Rhoads, *Reading Mark, Engaging the Gospel* (Minneapolis: Fortress, 2004), 11. This definition, however, is too broad. M. H. Abrams's definition is more precise: "Stock characters are character types that occur repeatedly in a particular literary genre, and so are recognizable as part of the *conventions* of the form."

10. William Harmon and C. Hugh Holman, *A Handbook to Literature*, 8th ed. (Upper Saddle River, N.J.: Prentice Hall, 1999), 216.

11. Harvey, *Character and the Novel*, 63. Although Harvey uses the term "ficelle," he applies the functions of a foil to this character type.

The Gentile centurion who sees Jesus as the Son of God contrasts with those in Israel who see him merely as a messianic pretender.

Walk-on is a term used by Seymour Chatman for characters that are not fully delineated and individualized; rather they are part of the background or setting of the narrative.[12] Roman soldiers, for instance, are walk-ons—faceless and nameless characters that function as an essential part of the crucifixion plot. The crowds in the Gospels are also undifferentiated characters that may be considered part of the setting rather than characters in their own right.[13] Despite walk-ons' lack of telling details, they have an important function in the plot design. The crowd in the Zacchaeus story makes his quest more difficult by blocking both physically and socially his access to Jesus (Luke 19:3). They are one of many barriers he must overcome for a successful quest. The crowd also acts like an ancient Greek chorus, voicing complaints about Jesus' association with sinners (Luke 19:7).

4.3 Dynamic and Static Characters

Characters are either *dynamic* (*developing*) or *static*.[14] A dynamic character undergoes a radical change throughout the course of a narrative, displaying new behaviors and changed outlooks. The change can be for better or for worse, and may be large or small. But the change is not minor or insignificant: it is a basic and important change in the character.[15] A dynamic—or what Thomas Docherty calls a *kinetic* character—is capable of being absent from the text. "This character's motivation extends beyond that which is merely necessary for the accomplishment of the design of the plot, and he or she 'moves' in other spheres than the one we are engaged in reading."[16] Zacchaeus, for example, is a dynamic character whose change of attitude to wealth and the poor marks an important development in his characterization. A *static* character, however, does not develop or change; he or she remains stable in outlook and disposition throughout the story. According to Docherty, a static character is unable to step outside the bounds of the narrative, a cardboard character completely accounted for in the narrative and simply a function of the plot.[17]

12. Chatman, *Story and Discourse*, 139.

13. Some narrative critics, however, treat the crowd as a unified character. See Malbon, *In the Company of Jesus*, chapter 3.

14. These terms and definitions are taken from Thomas R. Arp, *Perrine's Story and Structure*, 9th ed. (Fort Worth: Harcourt Brace College Publishers, 1998), 79–80.

15. Ibid.

16. Docherty, *Reading (Absent) Character*, 224.

17. Ibid.

The rich young ruler, for example, undergoes no fundamental change in the narrative—a static character who could be Everyman. When faced with a crisis of decision, he favors wealth over discipleship. Generally speaking, a round character is dynamic and a flat character is static.[18]

One of the more promising aspects of narrative criticism is its focus on character development and spiritual growth—its ability to identify positive traits that promote faith or negative traits that resist grace. How does the character develop and what traits or activities contribute to success or failure? How does the character overcome obstacles, either within the environment or within the self? Does the character change inwardly? Inward change is a Christian contribution to the understanding of modern narratives. According to Robert Scholes and Robert Kellogg, "the character whose inward development is of crucial importance is primarily a Christian element in our narrative literature."[19] In Jesus' saying on adultery in Matt. 5:27–28, for instance, the inner life attains equal footing with outward action.[20]

Changes in characters elaborate and develop a narrative's meaning. Since character and plot are intricately bound, a change or development in a character often provides a clue to the direction and meaning of the plot and theme. As Laurence Perrine says, the way a protagonist responds to a crucial situation in his or her life will "likely be the surest clue to the story's meaning." [21] And "to state and explain the change [in a character] will be the best way to get at the point of the story." [22]

4.4 Showing and Telling

Two generally recognized narrative techniques of characterization are *showing* and *telling*. In showing, which is also called the *dramatic method*

18. One of the criticisms Rimmon-Kenan, *Narrative Fiction*, 40–41, has of Forster's classification is that complex (i.e., round) characters can be undeveloping (static) and simple (i.e., flat) characters can be developing (dynamic).

19. Robert Scholes and Robert Kellogg, *The Nature of Narrative* (New York: Oxford University Press, 1966), 165.

20. This example is taken from Scholes and Kellogg, *Nature of Narrative*, 167–68.

21. Arp, *Perrine's Story and Structure*, 80. This represents a departure from some narrative critics who believe that most New Testament characters show little change or development. See, for example, Rhoads, Dewey, and Michie, *Mark as Story*, 100. Character development, however, can be one of the more promising contributions of narrative criticism. See Resseguie, *Spiritual Landscape: Images of the Spiritual Life in the Gospel of Luke* (Peabody, Mass.: Hendrickson, 2004), chapter 3, and idem, *The Strange Gospel: Narrative Design and Point of View in John* (Leiden: Brill, 2001), chapter 3, for character development from a narrative-critical perspective.

22. Arp, *Perrine's Story and Structure*, 80.

or *indirect presentation*, "the author simply presents the characters talking and acting and leaves the reader to infer the motives and dispositions that lie behind what they say and do."[23] The narrator can use a setting, such as a lame man on a mat at a pool (John 5), to show us not only his physical attributes but also his social ranking in first-century Palestinian society. Or the narrator can rely upon what a character says and does, or what other characters say, to show his or her traits. A narrator can even reveal the inner thoughts and feelings of a character through *interior monologues* and *inside views*.[24] This narrator—called an *omniscient narrator*—exercises the freedom to move at will from the external world to the inner world of characters and knows everything connected with the story. This separates literary characters from real-life characters, for we cannot know the inner thoughts and motivations of real-life characters. In real life we can only guess at a character's motivations and thoughts from external behavior, which may conceal as much as it reveals.[25] Because literature allows us to probe a character's inward self, we can, in a sense, know literary characters more thoroughly than real-life characters. In Luke's account of the anointing of Jesus, for instance, the narrator allows us to overhear Simon the Pharisee's interior monologue: "If this man [Jesus] were a prophet, he would have known who and what kind of woman this is who is touching him—that she is a sinner" (Luke 7:39). Simon's objection allows us to see how the constraints of societal norms have shaped his understanding of Jesus.

In *telling*, which is also called *direct presentation*, the narrator intervenes to comment directly on a character—singling out a trait for us to notice or making an evaluation of a character and his or her motives and disposition. This method does not rely upon the reader's ability to infer a character's attribute from what he or she does and says. Rather, the narrator tells us about the character's traits and motivations. In Mark 6:52, for example, the narrator tells us that the disciples were undiscerning and recalcitrant, "for they did not understand about the loaves, but their hearts were hardened." Or in the Gospel of John the narrator tells us that "[Judas] was going to betray [Jesus]" (John 6:71). What the narrator tells us influences how we read the narrative. We rely upon the narrator to express the norms and values of the narrative and how we should respond to individual characters. Those who voice the

23. Abrams, *Glossary*, s.v. "Character and Characterization."

24. On interior monologues see Philip Sellew, "Interior Monologue as a Narrative Device in the Parables of Luke," *JBL* 111 (1992): 239–53; Dorrit Cohn, *Transparent Minds: Narrative Modes for Presenting Consciousness in Fiction* (Princeton: Princeton University Press, 1978). On inside views see Wayne Booth, *The Rhetoric of Fiction*, 2nd ed. (Chicago: University of Chicago Press, 1981), passim; Rhoads, Dewey, and Michie, *Mark as Story*, 40.

25. Arp, *Perrine's Story and Structure*, 77.

norms and values of the narrative receive approval while those who are opposed to these values are cast in a negative light.

What is meant by characters' *traits*? Seymour Chatman defines traits or attributes as the minimal, persistent quality of a character that enables the reader to distinguish one character from another.[26] The narrator may intrude into the narrative to tell us about a character's traits. Jesus is "greatly disturbed in spirit and deeply moved" at the weeping of Mary and others over Lazarus's death (John 11:33). The disciples are "filled with great awe" (Mark 4:41) on one occasion and their hearts are "hardened" on another (Mark 6:52). Cornelius is "a devout man who feared God," giving "alms generously" (Acts 10:2), and Elizabeth and Zechariah "were righteous before God, living blamelessly" (Luke 1:6). The Galatians are "foolish" (Gal. 3:1), and the opponents in Philippians are "dogs" (Phil. 3:2). Since the narrator tells us these traits, we need not infer them.

Other traits can only be inferred from the actions and speech of characters or what others say about them. What a character does may say more than what a character says: a woman anoints Jesus' feet out of love (Luke 7:36–50); a widow gives all she has (Mark 12:41–44); disciples abandon Jesus because of difficult words (John 6:66); Judas inverts the kiss of peace (Matt. 26:49; Luke 22:48; Mark 14:45); Jesus eats with tax collectors and sinners (Luke 15:1–2). A character's speech or what others say about a character reveals his or her traits. In Luke, the rich farmer's interior monologue reveals a self-absorbed, self-centered person: "'What should I do, for I have no place to store my crops?' Then he said, 'I will do this: I will pull down my barns and build larger ones, and there I will store all my grain and my goods. And I will say to my soul, 'Soul, you have ample goods laid up for many years; relax, eat, drink, be merry'" (Luke 12:17b–19).

Proper names are "saturated with meaning" and disclose a character's traits.[27] "Emmanuel" means "God is with us" (Matt. 1:23). Simon, the son of Jonah, is also known as "Peter," or Rock (Matt. 10:2; 16:18; Mark 3:16; Luke 6:14); James and John are surnamed "Boanerges," or "sons of thunder" (Mark 3:17); followers of Jesus are said to belong to "the Way" (Acts 9:2); and Jesus "the Christ" becomes "Jesus Christ" (Mark 1:1; Rom. 1:1; etc.). Proper names can be a way of generating authority and linking an individual with history itself.[28] Jesus is Joshua. The genealogy in Matthew links Jesus to Abraham and David (Matt. 1:1), while Luke's genealogy goes further and links Jesus to the progenitor of the human race, "Adam, son of God" (Luke 3:38). And Paul uses his

26. Chatman, *Story and Discourse*, 121.

27. Hochman, *Character in Literature*, 37. On names see also Docherty, *Reading (Absent) Character*, chapter 2.

28. Docherty, *Reading (Absent) Character*, 66.

heritage to undermine his opponents' claims: "If anyone else has reason to be confident in the flesh, I have more: circumcised on the eighth day, a member of the people of Israel, of the tribe of Benjamin, a Hebrew born of Hebrews; as to the law, a Pharisee" (Phil. 3:4b–5).

Epithets and sobriquets (nicknames) may also provide an open window into a character's traits. Take, for instance, the sobriquet "the one whom Jesus loved" in the Gospel of John (13:23). The disciple has no proper name and indeed, needs no name, for his descriptive self-designation identifies his unique relationship to Jesus. It adds an element of mystery that a proper name lacks. Who is this "beloved disciple" and why is he described in this way? His trait of privilege allows him to represent the ideal point of view of the Gospel. He "sees" what others fail to "see" (John 20:8; 21:7), and his inside point of view parallels his closeness to Jesus (literally, "while leaning on Jesus' bosom" in John 13:25).

An overfull sobriquet may describe a character that literally and figuratively fills up the narrative. Consider John's description of God in the Apocalypse as "the one who is seated on the throne" (Rev. 4:2, 3, 9; 5:1, 7, 13; 6:16; 7:10, 15; 19:4; 20:11; 21:5) or the pleonasm "who is and who was and who is to come" (Rev. 1:8). The expansive description corresponds to the overfull character of God. Similarly, in a description of Jesus the reader is hit over the head with redundancy. Just in case the reader misses his defining trait, it is repeated three times: "I am the Alpha and Omega, the first and the last, the beginning and the end" (Rev. 22:13). In a description of Satan, John of the Apocalypse uses no less than five names or epithets to impress upon the reader the dragon's character: "The *great dragon* . . . that *ancient serpent*, who is called the *Devil* and *Satan*, the *deceiver* of the whole world . . . was thrown down to the earth" (Rev. 12:9).

Anonymity may also accent a character's traits.[29] In the parable of the Rich Man and Lazarus in Luke's Gospel, the rich man is anonymous while the poor beggar is named. Naming is a way of bestowing identity and elevating the poor man from his unseen position just as he is elevated from the depths of poverty to a celebrated position in the bosom of Abraham (Luke 16:22). The anonymity of the rich man works in the opposite way. His unnamed identity parallels his loss of position. His selfishness devours everything, leaving him with nothing—not a drop of water, not even a name.

29. On anonymity in biblical literature see Adele Reinhartz, "Anonymity and Character in the Book of Samuel," *Semeia* 63 (1993): 117–41; David R. Beck, "The Narrative Function of Anonymity in Fourth Gospel Characterization," *Semeia* 63 (1993): 143–58; idem, *The Discipleship Paradigm: Readers and Anonymous Characters in the Fourth Gospel*, BIS 27 (Leiden: Brill, 1997).

Yet anonymity may also emphasize a character's marginalization. The unnamed are also unseen, as in the case of the woman who anoints Jesus' feet in Luke 7:36–50. She is nameless, whereas the host of the banquet, Simon, not only is named but is identified as a ranking member of society. He is a Pharisee. Yet the woman overcomes her nameless identity through exuberant hospitality—acts that the host oddly neglects. As she moves to the center, he is forced to the margins. As she gains an identity, he loses face. As she moves to the foreground, he recedes into the background. As she is celebrated, he is shamed.

Anonymity also allows us to identify with a character's traits, for we can inhabit the locus of the nameless character, identifying with the character's success or, in other instances, with his or her failure. But anonymity also allows for selective identification. We can pick and choose with whom we want to identify, refusing to identify with unpromising traits. Who, for instance, wants to identify with the traits of the elder son in the parable of the Prodigal Son?[30] Instead we assign those traits to the religious leaders of the day, thereby letting ourselves off the hook. Or who wants to identify with the "callous and indifferent" traits of the priest and Levite; instead we prefer the "good" traits of the anonymous Samaritan (Luke 10:30–37). Narrative criticism is interested in how the unnameable functions in a narrative; it also seeks to attenuate selective identification by showing how the narrator's point of view is expressed in both the positive and negative traits of characters. A negative trait may be a compelling critique of a self-absorbed life and a positive trait may inspire us to change.

4.5 Robert Alter's Scale of Means

Robert Alter has suggested a scale of means for analysis of characters' motives, attitudes, and moral nature in biblical literature.[31] The scale ascends from the least certain and explicit means for conveying information about a character to the most certain and explicit.

30. Henri J. M. Nouwen, *The Return of the Prodigal Son: A Story of Homecoming* (New York: Doubleday, 1992), does encourage identification with all three characters in the parable.

31. Robert Alter, *The Art of Biblical Narrative* (New York: Basic Books, 1981), 116–17. Meir Sternberg, *The Poetics of Biblical Narrative: Ideological Literature and the Drama of Reading* (Bloomington: Indiana University Press, 1985), 475–81, lists fifteen rhetorical devices that aid in the analysis of character. John Petersen, *Reading Women's Stories: Female Characters in the Hebrew Bible* (Minneapolis: Fortress, 2004), uses Sternberg's and Alter's tools for analysis of character in the Hebrew Bible.

1. At the lower end of the scale are aspects of showing, such as the actions of a character and his or her appearance. Showing is less certain, for we must infer the meaning from what a character does or what is implied by a character's costume and posture. What are we to make of Jesus' changed countenance and clothes at the transfiguration? Or what does his changing of water into wine at Cana signify? The meaning of these actions must be inferred from the narrative context.

2. More certain is a character's direct speech or what other characters say about him or her. Even here claims have to be weighed, for a person's "speech may reflect the occasion more than the speaker, may be more a drawn shutter than an open window."[32] Is the speaker reliable or unreliable? Is what others say about a character reliable or unreliable? If Jesus is said to have "gone out of his mind" (Mark 3:21) or he "has a demon" (John 10:20), we automatically consider the claims unreliable because they are made by his adversaries. But when Jewish elders approach Jesus on behalf of a centurion who wants his slave healed, they say, "He is worthy of having you do this for him, for he loves our people, and it is he who built our synagogue for us" (Luke 7:4–5). We judge their speech to be reliable. And when the centurion speaks through his friends ("I am not worthy to have you come under my roof"), we consider the claim genuine, not words of false humility. Not only the speaker but also the context of the speech must be weighed. What are we to make of Paul's discourse to the Corinthians? "We are fools for the sake of Christ, but you are wise in Christ. We are weak, but you are strong. You are held in honor, but we in disrepute" (1 Cor. 4:10). We suspect Paul is speaking ironically, but we need the context to confirm his sarcasm.

3. With characters' inward speech we enter the "realm of relative certainty about character."[33] As we overhear a character's thoughts, we apprehend his or her conscious intentions and motivations. In the interior monologue of Luke 18, for instance, the unjust judge discloses his reasons for giving up and giving in to the widow's request: "Though I have no fear of God and no respect for anyone, yet because this widow keeps bothering me, I will grant her justice, so that she may not wear me out by continually coming" (Luke 18:4–5). In this example, the explicitness of the judge's intentions allows us to see his motivations and to applaud the widow's persistence.

4. At the top of the scale are the narrator's comments on the motives, feelings, intentions, and desires of characters. If the narrator is unreliable, as may happen in modern literature, we question the narrator's assess-

32. Alter, *Art of Biblical Narrative*, 117.
33. Ibid.

ment.[34] If the narrator is reliable, as is the case with biblical literature, we accept the narrator's assessment at face value.[35] After Jesus healed a man's withered hand, the Pharisees "went out and conspired against him, how to destroy him" (Matt. 12:14; cf. Mark 3:6; Luke 6:11). After the seventh bowl is poured out in Revelation, the narrator tells us that people "cursed God for the plague of hail, so fearful was that plague" (Rev. 16:21). The narrator's comments are important for understanding the point of view of the narrative. We rely on his or her assessment to sort out the characters and their motivations, to clarify the theological or ideological perspective of the narrative, to understand customs that are foreign to us, and, in general, to shape our response to the story.

4.6 A Reading of Character in Chopin's "Story of an Hour"

A short story by Kate Chopin will illustrate how a character's speech, actions, and appearance; the narrator's comments; and the narrative setting contribute to our understanding of a narrative. The full text of "The Story of an Hour" is presented.

The Story of an Hour

Knowing that Mrs. Mallard was afflicted with a heart trouble, great care was taken to break to her as gently as possible the news of her husband's death.

It was her sister Josephine who told her, in broken sentences, veiled hints that revealed in half concealing. Her husband's friend Richards was there, too, near her. It was he who had been in the newspaper office when intelligence of the railroad disaster was received, with Brently Mallard's name leading the list of "killed." He had only taken the time to assure himself of its truth by a second telegram, and had hastened to forestall any less careful, less tender friend in bearing the sad message.

She did not hear the story as many women have heard the same, with a paralyzed inability to accept its significance. She wept at once, with sudden,

34. Booth, *Rhetoric of Fiction*, 158–59, defines a reliable narrator as one who "speaks for or acts in accordance with the norms of the work" (i.e., the norms of the implied author). An unreliable narrator, who is invented by the implied author, does not support the norms and values of the implied author.

35. Some critics argue that some biblical narrators are unreliable. For example, James M. Dawsey, *The Lukan Voice: Confusion and Irony in the Gospel of Luke* (Macon, Ga.: Mercer University Press, 1986), argues that the narrator of Luke is unreliable. But an unreliable narrator is entirely a modern invention—"the sophisticated product of an empirical and ironical age"—and is not found in ancient literature. See Scholes and Kellogg, *Nature of Narrative*, 264.

wild abandonment, in her sister's arms. When the storm of grief had spent itself she went away to her room alone. She would have no one follow her.

There stood, facing the open window, a comfortable, roomy armchair. Into this she sank, pressed down by a physical exhaustion that haunted her body and seemed to reach into her soul.

She could see in the open square before her house the tops of trees that were all aquiver with the new spring life. The delicious breath of rain was in the air. In the street below a peddler was crying his wares. The notes of a distant song which some one was singing reached her faintly, and countless sparrows were twittering in the eaves.

There were patches of blue sky showing here and there through the clouds that had met and piled one above the other in the west facing her window.

She sat with her head thrown back upon the cushion of the chair, quite motionless, except when a sob came up into her throat and shook her, as a child who has cried itself to sleep continues to sob in its dreams.

She was young, with a fair, calm face, whose lines bespoke repression and even a certain strength. But now there was a dull stare in her eyes, whose gaze was fixed away off yonder on one of those patches of blue sky. It was not a glance of reflection, but rather indicated a suspension of intelligent thought.

There was something coming to her and she was waiting for it, fearfully. What was it? She did not know; it was too subtle and elusive to name. But she felt it, creeping out of the sky, reaching toward her through the sounds, the scents, the color that filled the air.

Now her bosom rose and fell tumultuously. She was beginning to recognize this thing that was approaching to possess her, and she was striving to beat it back with her will—as powerless as her two white slender hands would have been.

When she abandoned herself a little whispered word escaped her slightly parted lips. She said it over and over under her breath: "Free, free, free!" The vacant stare and the look of terror that had followed it went from her eyes. They stayed keen and bright. Her pulses beast fast, and the coursing blood warmed and relaxed every inch of her body.

She did not stop to ask if it were not a monstrous joy that held her. A clear and exalted perception enabled her to dismiss the suggestion as trivial.

She knew that she would weep again when she saw the kind, tender hands folded in death; the face that had never looked save with love upon her, fixed and gray and dead. But she saw beyond that bitter moment a long procession of years to come that would belong to her absolutely. And she opened and spread her arms out to them in welcome.

There would be no one to live for her during those coming years; she would live for herself. There would be no powerful will bending her in that blind persistence with which men and women believe they have a right to impose a private will upon a fellow creature. A kind intention or a cruel intention made the act seem no less a crime as she looked upon it in that brief moment of illumination.

And yet she had loved him—sometimes. Often she had not. What did it matter! What could love, the unsolved mystery, count for in face of this possession of self-assertion which she suddenly recognized as the strongest impulse of her being.

"Free! Body and soul free!" she kept whispering.

Josephine was kneeling before the closed door with her lips to the keyhole, imploring for admission. "Louise, open the door! I beg; open the door—you will make yourself ill. What are you doing, Louise? For heaven's sake open the door."

"Go away. I am not making myself ill." No; she was drinking in a very elixir of life through that open window.

Her fancy was running riot along those days ahead of her. Spring days, and summer days, and all sorts of days that would be her own. She breathed a quick prayer that life might be long. It was only yesterday she had thought with a shudder that life might be long.

She arose at length and opened the door to her sister's importunities. There was a feverish triumph in her eyes, and she carried herself unwittingly like a goddess of Victory. She clasped her sister's waist, and together they descended the stairs. Richards stood waiting for them at the bottom.

Some one was opening the front door with the latchkey. It was Brently Mallard who entered, a little travel-stained, composedly carrying his gripsack and umbrella. He had been far from the scene of the accident, and did not even know there had been one. He stood amazed at Josephine's piercing cry; at Richards' quick motion to screen him from the view of his wife.

But Richards was too late.

When the doctors came they said she had died of heart disease—of joy that kills.

How does Chopin present the characters?[36] Do the characters develop? How does setting contribute to characterization? What rhetorical devices are used to enhance characterization? How does analysis of characterization develop and elaborate the point or theme of the story?

The characters include the protagonist, Louise Mallard, her husband, Brently Mallard, her sister, Josephine, and her husband's friend, Richards. The narrator uses double entendre, irony, nature setting, direct discourse, and inside views to portray the slow, gradual development of Mrs.

36. For an analysis of this story in terms of point of view, see Susan Sniader Lanser, *The Narrative Act: Point of View in Prose Fiction* (Princeton: Princeton Univerity Press, 1981), chapter 6. I acknowledge my indebtedness to her commentary on the story.

Mallard. In following the development of Mrs. Mallard's characterization, we can know the point of the story.

We learn at the beginning that Mrs. Mallard was afflicted with "heart trouble"—an ambiguous term that can mean heart disease or an emotional affliction. Both meanings are intended, for not only does she die of heart disease at the end but she is also emotionally troubled by her marriage. The double entendre heightens the irony of the story: Brently Mallard's death occasions her rebirth and his rebirth occasions her death.[37] As readers, we first look *at* Mrs. Mallard as she hears the news of her husband's death. When she goes to her room, however, we look *with* Mrs. Mallard as she experiences the sights and sounds of nature. Then we look *at* Mrs. Mallard once more as Brently Mallard appears unexpectedly in the foyer. This progressive movement from object to subject and then object parallels the progressive development of her characterization from Mrs. Mallard, wife of Brently Mallard, to Louise, a person in her own right. The names and epithets accent her awakening. Initially she is linked to her husband's identity, but as she experiences a rebirth in her private room, she is called by her given name, Louise. At the end, she is once more linked to her husband's identity ("his wife"). In other words, as she gains a new selfhood, she is no longer identified by her husband's name but is called by her Christian name. The descriptions also support her progressive development. Initially, she is like a little child who cries herself to sleep. But as she descends the stairs with her sister Josephine, she is like "a goddess of Victory." The movement from child to goddess parallels her development from a dependent wife to self-asserting subject. The metaphor of "eyes" also traces her development. Before her awakening, her eyes have "a dull stare" that indicates "a suspension of intelligent thought," but afterward her eyes have "a feverish triumph."

The only occurrences of Louise Mallard's direct discourse are in her room, where she speaks three times. Even though her speech is sparing, what she says is important. First, she repeats over and over again: "Free, free, free." The second time, she whispers repeatedly, "Free! Body and soul free." Her newfound freedom now extends to the very depth of her being—her soul as well as her body. The third and final time she speaks, she asserts herself and tells her sister to go away for she is not making herself ill. Significantly, the textual occurrences of her speech affirm her independence, which the narrator highlights. "What could love, the unsolved mystery, count for in the face of this possession of self-assertion which she suddenly recognized as the strongest impulse of her being!"

37. Noted by Lanser, *The Narrative Act*, 255.

The springtime setting in which the earth awakens to new life is the background for Louise Mallard's self-realization. As she sits in a comfortable armchair facing the open window, the sights and sounds of her environment come alive. The treetops are "all aquiver with the new spring life." A "delicious breath of rain" is in the air, and sparrows are "twittering in the eaves." Patches of blue sky appear between the broken clouds, imagery that suggests her "storm of grief" is passing. The rebirth of the earth corresponds to her rebirth; as the earth awakens to new life, she awakens to a new self. "Her fancy was running riot along those days ahead of her. Spring days, and summer days, and all sorts of days that would be her own. She breathed a quick prayer that life might be long. It was only yesterday she had thought with a shudder that life might be long."

What is the point of this story? Is, as Laurence Perrine suggests, the development of the protagonist the "surest clue" to the meaning of the story? Is the story about Mrs. Mallard? Or is the story a generalization about life, which Mrs. Mallard's experience happens to illustrate? Is the narrative about Mrs. Mallard's marriage, or is the point of the story broader than her marriage to Brently Mallard? If we trace Mrs. Mallard's development from object to subject, the story appears to be about one woman who comes to self-awareness after she learns of her husband's death. She weeps as any person would weep upon learning of a spouse's death. "She wept at once, with sudden, wild abandonment in her sister's arms." Thus her awakening is not her own doing; it is not something she willed. In fact, "this thing" overcomes her through the scents and sounds and color of her environment. And although she tried to beat it back with her will, she was powerless to resist it. Eventually, she opens her arms and welcomes this new life. "She saw beyond that bitter moment a long procession of years to come that would belong to her absolutely."

The story could be about one woman's discovery of her selfhood apart from her husband's identity. No longer is she Mrs. Mallard, but Louise. But the point of the story is broader than this, for the narrator tips her hand when she turns Mrs. Mallard's story into a generalization about marriage in particular and human relationships in general. "There would be no powerful will bending her in that blind persistence with which *men and women believe they have a right to impose a private will upon a fellow-creature*" (italics mine). At issue is the imposition of one will upon another. Often it is done in "blind persistence" by women as well as men who believe they have "a right" to impose their will upon another. It makes little difference whether the more powerful dominates the other with the best of intentions or out of cruelty. Whatever the intentions may be, the outcome is the same: it is the subjection of one will to another, the assertion of a more powerful self over another. "A kind intention or a cruel intention made the act seem no less a crime as she looked upon it in that brief moment of illumination."

4.7 Reading Biblical Characters

Biblical characters may be at the center of power and influence or at the margins of society. Character analysis prompts us to ask: How do those at society's margins overcome their marginality? What do they see that we should see? What do they do that is instructive for us? Similarly, what hinders those at the center of power and influence from seeing what the marginalized see? What keeps them from following Jesus? What is their tragic flaw? Or, if they follow Jesus, how do they overcome their attachment to the accoutrements of this world? How are they able to reverse a downward trajectory to disaster? The complexity of characterization and character development is explored in three narratives of characters at the margins of society: (1) the woman with a hemorrhage (Mark 5:25–34), (2) Mary Magdalene (John 20:1–2, 11–18), and (3) the man born blind (John 9:1–41). Two further narratives are about persons who collaborate with the structures of power and influence in the dominant culture of the first century: (1) Zacchaeus (Luke 19:1–10), and (2) Judas Iscariot in the Gospel of John.

Marginalized Characters

Biblical characters at the margins are those who are not part of the structures of power and domination in first-century society.[38] Some are at the lowest rungs of the first-century status hierarchy. They may be expendables, waifs of society, who are discarded and unseen: the blind, the lame, the maimed, and the poverty-stricken. They may be ritually unclean because of some malady or deformity or because of their husband's unclean occupation (a tanner, for instance). They may be among the shamed and degraded: sinners, tax collectors, and Gentiles. Women are of relatively low status in the Palestinian status hierarchy and thus are at the margins or outer boundaries of society.[39] Often their identity is defined by reference to male characters—as mothers, mothers-in-law,

38. See Gerhard E. Lenski, *Power and Privilege: A Theory of Social Stratification*, 2nd ed., McGraw-Hill Series in Sociology (New York: McGraw-Hill, 1984); Halvor Moxnes, *The Economy of the Kingdom: Social Conflict and Economic Relations in Luke's Gospel* (Philadelphia: Fortress, 1988).

39. Halvor Moxnes, *Putting Jesus in His Place: A Radical Vision of Household and Kingdom* (Louisville: Westminster John Knox, 2003), 99–100, argues that the women who followed Jesus were at the margins of society.

daughters, or wives (e.g., 1 Cor. 11)—or, in the case of widows, by the absence of a male in the household. Yet there are important exceptions. There are women who are not known by the males in their lives, or women who overcome their marginalized status to gain an identity apart from others. The woman with a hemorrhage is one who is not identified by the males in her life.

Woman with a Hemorrhage (Mark 5:25–34)

The woman with a hemorrhage is a character within a frame. As the term suggests, a frame character forms a parenthesis around another character, the embedded character.[40] Visually the frame character borders the text with another character or characters at the center—a rhetorical strategy that may accent the marginality of the frame character. Or the frame character may heighten the visibility of the character within the frame. A frame character may also establish a point of view that is elongated or further developed by the character at the center. Or the frame character may offer a contrast to the embedded character.

Jairus and his daughter are framing characters for the woman with a hemorrhage, an embedded character (Mark 5:22–24, 35–43; cf. also Matt. 9:18–19, 23–26; Luke 8:41–42, 49–56).[41] The hemorrhaging woman is known by her actions, by the words she speaks, by what others say about her, by Jesus' interpretation of her actions, and by the setting. She interrupts the story about Jairus and his daughter and pushes the synagogue ruler temporally to the margins of the text. The hemorrhaging woman is given—or rather she takes—center stage.[42] Frank Kermode notes several similarities between the frame and the embedded characters.[43] Both female characters—Jairus's daughter and the hemorrhaging

40. On frame characters in literature see Springer, *A Rhetoric of Literary Character*, chapter 4.

41. On the woman with a hemorrhage see Frances Taylor Gench, *Back to the Well: Women's Encounters with Jesus in the Gospels* (Louisville: Westminster John Knox, 2004); Marla J. Selvidge, "Mark 5:25–34 and Leviticus 15:19–20: A Reaction to Restrictive Purity Regulations," *JBL* 103 (1984): 619–23; Malbon, *In the Company of Jesus*, 50–51; Vernon K. Robbins, "The Woman Who Touched Jesus' Garment: Socio-rhetorical Analysis of the Synoptic Accounts," *NTS* 33 (1987): 502–15; Winsome Munro, "Women Disciples in Mark?" *CBQ* 44 (1982): 225–41; Frank Kermode, *The Genesis of Secrecy: On the Interpretation of Narrative* (Cambridge, Mass.: Harvard University Press, 1979), 131–33; James R. Edwards, "Markan Sandwiches: The Significance of Interpolations in Markan Narratives," *NovT* 31 (1989): 193–216; Tom Shepherd, "The Narrative Function of Markan Intercalation," *NTS* 41 (1995): 522–40.

42. Others see the story of the hemorrhaging woman as creating suspense (so Edwards, "Markan Sandwiches," 204) or heightening the drama of the first story (so Joel B. Green, *The Gospel of Luke*, NICNT [Grand Rapids: Eerdmans, 1997], 343).

43. Kermode, *The Genesis of Secrecy*, 132–33. Curiously, Edwards, "Markan Sandwiches," 204, notes that Jairus and the woman share only one thing in common: "victims of desper-

woman—are unclean, socially polluted. One is unclean as a result of her death (cf. Num. 19:10b–22); the other is unclean as a result of her chronic bleeding, which leaves her near death (cf. Lev. 15:19–31).[44] Both are called "daughter" (Mark 5:34, 35), and both are dead—one physically, the other socially. The twelve year old is reborn (Mark 5:35, 41–42);[45] the older woman, who has been socially impure for twelve years, is cured (Mark 5:25, 29). Both are restored to society.

But there are differences. The hemorrhaging woman touches Jesus (Mark 5:27, 28, 30, 31), whereas Jesus touches the young girl (Mark 5:41).[46] The young girl must rely on a male character to intercede, whereas the hemorrhaging woman takes the initiative to arrest her suffering. The twelve-year-old girl is passive while the woman who bled for twelve years is active. The hemorrhaging woman speaks whereas the young girl is silent.

The setting is an undifferentiated sea of humanity from which emerges a single person who takes a singular action: she touches Jesus' garment. Whereas Jairus comes face-to-face to speak with Jesus—as befits his position in society, she approaches Jesus secretly, from behind—as befits her position in society. She then returns to the safety of anonymity, blending into the faceless crowd. In Luke 5:27 she hides in the crowd. But her audacity halts Jesus from going about his business. Her action causes a chain reaction.

> *Immediately* her hemorrhage stopped. . . . *Immediately* [Jesus was] aware that power had gone forth from him.
>
> (Mark 5:29–30).

Her gain is his loss. Her change in direction causes Jesus to change direction. "Jesus turned about in the crowd and said, 'Who touched my clothes'?" (Mark 5:30). The woman stops Jesus in his tracks, and Jesus stops the woman in her pursuit of anonymity.

A second time she emerges from the crowd, this time "in fear and trembling," and falls down before Jesus to tell "the whole truth" (Mark 5:33). No longer anonymous or outside society's boundaries, she is ad-

---

ate circumstances." While technically true, Edwards has marginalized the ruler's daughter by leaving her out of the story.

44. But see Richard A. Horsley, *Hearing the Whole Story: The Politics of Plot in Mark's Gospel* (Louisville: Westminster John Knox, 2001), 208–12, who makes the case that impurity is not an issue in these stories.

45. The command *egeire* is used for awakening of the dead. See BDAG, s.v. ἐγείρω 13a.

46. Although the woman touches Jesus' garments, his clothing is identical to his selfhood. This is clarified by the disciples' restatement of Jesus' query ("Who touched *my clothes*") to "Who touched *me*?"

dressed as "daughter," as one who is welcomed back into the family. And no longer is she unnamed or unseen; she is a subject in her own right. She is spoken to, not spoken about. "*Your* faith has made *you* well; go in peace, and be healed of *your* disease" (Mark 5:34). The woman who "had been suffering from hemorrhages" (Mark 5:25) and had been suffering from a society that treated her as unclean is "made well" (*sōzō*, also "saved")[47] by *her* faith. She is at the center of this framing narrative, where she belongs.

She has several traits. An unnamed woman who is disease-ridden and probably considered unclean, she is impoverished by those unable to cure her, and she suffers due to her malady. But she is also daring, fearful, and an exemplar of faith. Her root traits are reduced to one or two: she is outside the powers of influence, and she is a model of bold faith. Although she is not a "round" character, she is a developing character who moves from being unseen to become a highly visible character in this narrative. While the crowd is merely a walk-on—part of the background setting—she emerges from anonymity to become a character in her own right, which the narrative emphasizes by the rhetorical device of repetition. The key word, "touch," is mentioned no less than four times: by the narrator, by the woman herself, by Jesus, and by the disciples. Her touching underscores her bold action of crossing boundaries.

Narrator:	She "*touched* his cloak" (5:27).
Her speech:	"If I but *touch* his clothes, I will be made well" (5:28).[48]
Jesus' speech:	"Who *touched* my clothes?" (5:30).
Disciples' speech:	"How can you say, 'Who *touched* me?'" (5:31)

Her decisive action results in a reversal of her selfhood: she is no longer unclean, unspoken to, and unseen. The crowd, the disciples, and especially Jesus notice her. What could be interpreted as a violation of the biblical purity code is interpreted as an act of faith. What could be conceived as a daring act of foolishness is seen as a commendable act of boundary-crossing. Although she intrudes into the narrative, diverts attention from the synagogue ruler, and halts Jesus from going about his business, she is not condemned for her action or for crossing boundaries. Rather she is commended for her bold action. She is declared "well" and goes "in peace," restored to wholeness—physically, religiously, and socially.

47. The spiritual sense of *sōzō* as well as the physical sense of being healed may be present here. See BDAG, s.v. σώζω 2γ.

48. Matthew 9:21 makes explicit that the woman said this to herself; in Mark it is implied.

Her development as a character parallels the development of the plot. The plot is about a woman who hemorrhaged for twelve years and was made poor and worse by the physicians who took her money. This is the downward slope of a U-shaped plot.[49] But she faces a crisis of decision—"she had heard about Jesus"—that she does not let pass by. The crisis is resolved not by speaking to him, as does Jairus, but by secretly touching him. This marks the reversal in the U-shaped plot which leads to the upward turn and a new state of equilibrium. Because of her active faith, she receives healing and wholeness from Jesus. The plot progression thus corresponds to her character development. Initially she is unseen, an anonymous person at the edges of society. Yet because of her initiative—which is later identified as faith—she is no longer invisible and unnoticed. She is healed and recognized as a person in her own right, a subject who is addressed directly. Further, she is called "daughter"—an acknowledgment that she is part of the family of God. Jesus thus completes what she initiated. She steps out from the margins to be healed, and Jesus makes her "well," reversing her physical, religious, and social marginality.

Mary Magdalene (John 20:1–2, 11–18)

In the Gospel of John, Mary Magdalene is a frame character who brackets the story of the male disciples' discovery of the empty tomb.[50] Although she is temporally pushed to the margins of the text as the two disciples take center stage (John 20:3–10), she regains her footing and takes command of the narrative after the disciples return home (John 20:11–18). Unlike the woman with a hemorrhage who is the central character within a frame, Mary is the frame character for Peter and the beloved disciple. But like the hemorrhaging woman, Mary overcomes her marginality. She is the first witness to the risen Lord and the first person—male or female—to learn a new language in this Gospel: the language of the resurrection.

49. On plot patterns see §6.3 below.

50. On Mary Magdalene see James L. Resseguie, *The Strange Gospel: Narrative Design and Point of View in John*, BIS 56 (Leiden: Brill, 2001), 145–49; Sandra M. Schneiders, "John 20:11–18: The Encounter of the Easter Jesus with Mary Magdalene—a Transformative Feminist Reading," in *"What Is John?" Readers and Readings of the Fourth Gospel*, ed. Fernando F. Segovia (Atlanta: Scholars Press, 1996), 155–68; Pheme Perkins, "'I Have Seen the Lord' (John 20:18): Women Witnesses to the Resurrection," *Int* 46 (1992): 31–41; Robert Gordon Maccini, *Her Testimony Is True: Women as Witnesses according to John*, JSNTSup 125 (Sheffield: Sheffield Academic Press, 1996), 207–33; Adeline Fehribach, *The Women in the Life of the Bridegroom: A Feminist Historical-Literary Analysis of the Female Characters in the Fourth Gospel* (Collegeville, Minn.: Liturgical Press, 1998), 150.

Mary is known by her speech, what others say about her, by the temporal and physical settings, and by the narrator's comments. How the narrator introduces a character into the narrative is important, for it sets the tone and atmosphere for apprehending the character's traits. What terms are used to describe Mary? What titles, proper names, or epithets are accented in the narrative? Does the setting illumine the character's traits? Does she develop, and if so, how can we characterize her development?

In Mary's first appearance in the Gospel, she is introduced with these words:

> Meanwhile, standing near the cross of Jesus were his mother, and his mother's sister, Mary . . . of Clopas, and Mary Magdalene. (John 19:25)

The male disciples—with the exception of the beloved disciple—have defected, leaving the women to mourn Jesus' death and, more important, to be eye-witnesses to the crucifixion. Two of the women, Jesus' mother and his mother's sister, are unnamed.[51] Their identity is tied to their relationship to Jesus. Two other women are named. Although Mary of Clopas is named, her identity is tied to her husband or some other male person in her household, such as a son or father. Mary Magdalene, on the other hand, is unique in this listing, for no male defines who she is.[52] She is Mary Magdalene or Mary of Magdala, a town near Tiberias. She is also distinguished in another way: Mary is the only female witness who is present at both the crucifixion and the empty tomb. (The beloved disciple is the only male witness to both events.) Mary's appearance at the cross and tomb thus places her on an equal footing with the "ideal witness" of the Gospel, the beloved disciple.[53]

The temporal setting—"early on the first day of the week while it was still dark"—adds mystery to a suspenseful and surprising plot (20:1). The two-step progression—"early . . . while it was still dark"—is suggestive of Mary's inner landscape, her incomprehension of the resurrection. Darkness in John may symbolize opacity or represent separation from the light. Nicodemus, for instance, comes to Jesus "by night" (John 3:2)

51. Does John 19:25 refer to two, three, or four women? Mary of Clopas could be Jesus' mother and Mary Magdalene his aunt (thus only two women are mentioned). Or Mary of Clopas could be Jesus' aunt (thus three women are mentioned). Or it could be that four women were present as the NRSV concludes. See Richard Bauckham, *Gospel Women: Studies of the Named Women in the Gospels* (Grand Rapids: Eerdmans, 2002), chapter 6, for a detailed discussion.

52. She is not known by her father, or her husband (if she had one), or her relationship to Jesus.

53. On the beloved disciple as ideal witness see Richard Bauckham, "The Beloved Disciple as Ideal Witness," *JSNT* 49 (1993): 21–44.

and mistakes rebirth for a self-improvement program.[54] Darkness is the setting for a sea crossing: "It was now dark, and Jesus had not yet come to them" (John 6:17). Separation from Jesus is a form of darkness.[55] It is also dark when the disciples go fishing and catch nothing; yet at daybreak, Jesus appears and their lack turns to abundance (John 21). Darkness may also represent alignment with the powers of darkness and rejection of the light. When Judas receives the sop from Jesus and goes out, "it was night" (John 13:30).

A character's first words are usually significant. Mary's first words are: "They have taken the Lord out of the tomb, and *we do not know* where they have laid him" (John 20:2). She is known by what she does not know, which is emphasized a total of three times. In John 20:13 she says: "I *do not know* where they have laid him." Finally, the narrator mentions her lack of understanding: "She *did not know* that it was Jesus" (John 20:14). Her speech parallels the pattern of the plot. This is a plot of discovery, an awakening to something of great importance that a person could not see beforehand. She fails to understand the resurrection and does not see Jesus. The theme of the narrative is found by asking: What does Mary discover? How does her nonrecognition turn to recognition? What is it that Mary needs to understand in order to see Jesus? And what is it that we learn from Mary's discovery? What do we need to understand differently in order to *see* Jesus?

After her discovery of the empty tomb, Mary moves to the margins of the text. She becomes a courier who delivers the troubling news to the male disciples: "So she ran and went to Simon Peter and the other disciple, the one whom Jesus loved" (20:2). With Mary at the margins of the text, Peter and the unnamed disciple take command of the narrative. They are the central characters (20:3–10), with Mary as the frame. They set out on a footrace to the tomb, but the beloved disciple runs ahead and reaches the tomb before Peter. Although he arrives first at the tomb, he is not the first to go in. Peter enters before him and sees the linen wrappings lying there with the head wrapping rolled up to the side. The beloved disciple then enters the tomb, sees, and believes, apparently apprehending the significance of the discarded grave clothes.

Peter and the beloved disciple not only race to the tomb but also race for priority of position. Who will be first? Peter is the first to enter the tomb, which the narrator accents by using his full name, "Simon Peter," instead of the shortened name. Prior to his discovery of the garments the narrator calls him "Peter" twice (20:3–4),[56] but at the moment of discov-

54. On Nicodemus see §7.2 below.

55. Resseguie, *Strange Gospel*, 100–101.

56. The normal way Peter is introduced in a narrative is as "Simon Peter." In John 20:2 he is called "Simon Peter." Then the narrator uses the abbreviated name, "Peter." When,

ery he switches to the full name, perhaps to accentuate the discovery's importance. Peter enters and sees all the physical contents of the tomb, including the head wrapping (20:6–7), whereas the beloved disciple saw only the linen wrappings from outside the tomb.

The beloved disciple is also first, although in another way. He outruns Peter and reaches the tomb first (20:4);[57] he sees the linen wrappings first, while Peter, according to the narrator, follows the beloved disciple (20:6). The beloved disciple is thus given priority in understanding the significance of the garments, and the overfull epithet appears to amplify his discovery. "Then *the other disciple, who reached the tomb first*, also went in, and he saw and believed" (20:8). Peter is first to see all the contents of the tomb; the other disciple is the first to believe. Peter is the shepherd of the sheep (John 21:15–17); the beloved disciple is the ideal disciple who interprets what is seen.

After the disciples return to their homes, Mary reenters the narrative. The setting accentuates her outside status: she is physically outside (*exō*) the tomb weeping (20:11),[58] and in other ways she is outside. While the beloved disciple sees and believes, Mary sees but concludes that Jesus is missing and someone has stolen the body. Her speech—to three different characters in the story—underscores the tension and dilemma of this recognition plot. If Jesus is missing, she must find him and bring him back to where he belongs—the tomb. If he is not missing, where is he?

To the disciples:	They have taken the Lord out of the tomb, and we do not know where they have laid him (20:2).
To the angels:	They have taken away my Lord, and I do not know where they have laid him (20:13).
To Jesus:	If you have carried him away, tell me where you have laid him, and I will take him away (20:15).

Her development as a character comes as she sees what others have not seen and speaks what others are unable to say. She looks into the tomb and sees two angels in white who, like bookends, frame the empty space where Jesus was laid. When they ask why she is weeping, she responds with loss—the only way she knows how to respond. Someone has taken her Lord away and she does not know where the corpse is hidden (20:13). She sees but does not see Jesus, and with delicious

however, the narrator resorts to the full name, he is drawing attention to an incident. See Resseguie, *Strange Gospel*, 150–55.

57. The prefix of the verb *protrechō* emphasizes his priority in the footrace.

58. Most manuscripts include "outside," but a few omit it, such as א*.

irony she assumes that he is the gardener.[59] Jesus asks her not only why she is weeping but also for whom she is looking (20:15). This question recalls Jesus' first words in the Gospel to the disciples—"What are you looking for?" (1:38). "What," however, now becomes "who." The object of the disciples' quest in chapter 1 is clarified in chapter 20. The quest is for a person. Mary restates her misunderstanding: "Sir, if you have carried him away, tell where you have laid him, and I will take him away" (20:15). The narrator then marks an important discovery with the rhetorical device of repetition. The word "turn" occurs twice, and one of the occurrences seems unnecessary. The first turning is physical; the second is spiritual.

> When she had said this, she *turned around* and saw Jesus standing there, but she did not know it was Jesus. (20:14)

> Jesus said to her, "Mary!" She *turned* and said to him in Hebrew, "Rabbouni" (which means Teacher). (20:16)

The moment of recognition occurs when Jesus calls her "Mary" (20:16); the narrator emphasizes her discovery by having her turn a second time, a spiritual turning.[60]

Mary's development from outsider to insider, from unseeing to seeing, from courier to the originator of a new language ("I have seen the Lord," 20:18), parallels the changes in names and epithets. The narrator, angels, and Jesus refer to her as follows:

Narrator: Mary Magdalene (19:25)
Narrator: Mary Magdalene (20:1)
Narrator: Mary (20:11)
Angels: Woman (20:13)
Jesus: Woman (20:15)
Jesus: Mary (20:16)
Narrator: Mary Magdalene (20:18)

At the beginning and at the end of the narrative, the narrator calls her Mary Magdalene, and at 20:11, he uses the shortened name. The use of her full name at 20:1 and 20:18 is a framing device that accents the central character of the narrative. This is Mary Magdalene's story. Similarly,

59. He is the keeper of the "new garden." See Nicolas Wyatt, "Supposing Him to Be the Gardener (John 20, 15): A Study of the Paradise Motif in John," *ZNW* 81 (1990): 21–38.

60. Schneiders, "John 20:11–18," 162.

the names and epithets others use for her are important. The angels call her "woman" and, initially, Jesus calls her "woman."[61]

But when Jesus calls her Mary, the veil of incomprehension is lifted. Her given name, previously unspoken by any character within the narrative, startles her into recognition. She, in turn, calls him "Rabbouni" or "Teacher."[62] The scene recalls the sayings of Jesus in John 10: "the one who enters by the gate is the shepherd of the sheep" and "the sheep hear his voice" (10:2–3a). The shepherd also "calls his own sheep by *name* and leads them out" (10:3b).

Naming identifies Mary as a subject in her own right. She is no longer at the margins, no longer a courier. Instead she teaches others a new language, the language of the resurrection. Prior to her recognition of the risen Jesus, Mary's language was characterized by loss: "They have taken the Lord out of the tomb" (20:2); "they have taken away my Lord" (20:13); and "Sir, if you have carried him away . . ." (20:15). A risen Jesus was not part of her vocabulary and not part of the vocabulary of others (with the possible exception of the beloved disciple). At the moment of discovery her speech changes from loss to hope ("I have seen the Lord," 20:18), which the others learn to repeat. "I have seen the Lord" is the standard credential formula of the apostles. Paul, for instance, uses it to claim apostolic status: "Have I not seen Jesus our Lord?" (1 Cor. 9:1). And the disciples use the same language in John 20:25: "We have seen the Lord." Although Simon Peter is the first to see the contents of the tomb and the beloved disciple is the first to apprehend the meaning of the discarded grave clothes, Mary is the first to see the risen Lord and to learn the new language. This privileged information moves her from the margins to the center.

Mary also moves out of the margins through the striking mode of narration. This is one of the two most memorable resurrection stories in our Gospels—the other being Luke's account of the disciples on the Emmaus road.[63] In the narration of these disciples' discovery, there is no direct speech, no display of emotion, no face-to-face encounter with the risen Jesus, no pathos, and no rebuke. Although the two validate the empty tomb, they are flat and static characters.

61. The vocative, "woman" (*gynai*), is not disrespectful, but it is certainly less personal than "Mary"—as evidenced by Mary's nonrecognition when called "woman" and recognition when called "Mary."

62. Some commentators make a distinction between *rhabbouni* and *rhabbi*, but John translates both the same (compare John 1:38 with 20:16). See E. Lohse, "ῥαββί, ῥαββουνί," *TDNT* 6:961–65 at 964.

63. This is Richard Bauckham's assessment in *Gospel Women* (pp. 283–84); most others would agree with his view.

By contrast, Mary is a round, dynamic character. The narrator uses dialogue, emotion (weeping), suspense (will she recognize Jesus?), dramatic irony (asking Jesus for his own body!), recognition, rebuke, and commissioning. Mary has several traits: she is perplexed, unseeing, and unknowing. She is disconsolate, yet persistent in her quest to find the Lord. She believes that the Jesus she sees is the Jesus she knew, and thus, she attempts to cling to the old Jesus—or at least, the earthly Jesus she thought she saw (John 20:17). But Mary develops in the narrative. Although she seeks, she is found. Although she wants to hold onto the old Jesus, she accepts the new Jesus. Although her language was filled with loss, she learns a new language of hope. Lively narration makes Mary the more memorable character in John 20:1–18.

If describing and stating the change in a character allows us to get at the point of the story, what is the point of this story? Certainly one aspect, often noted, is that Jesus knows his sheep and reveals himself to them, calling them by name. The appearance of Jesus to the individual believer is a fulfillment of his promise made in John 14:21: "The one who has my commandments and keeps them, that one loves me. And the one who loves me will be loved by my Father, and I will love him/her and I will reveal myself to him/her."[64] But another theme is more prominent. Mary's development as a character illustrates an important theological theme or ideological point of view. The dialogue, suspense, and then discovery outline a fundamental difficulty in recognizing the Jesus of the Gospels: the Jesus of our expectations is not the Jesus who finds us. The surprise is that our expectations are so hobbling, so different from the Jesus that we encounter. Mary expects to find a dead Jesus, and when she does not, she weeps. Rather than shedding tears because Jesus was present in the tomb, she weeps because he is absent. And then when she does find Jesus—or, rather, when Jesus finds her—she wants to cling to the Jesus she thought she knew, the earthly Jesus. But once again her expectations are dashed. The new Jesus is present in a new way. As Mary develops, she discards old ways of understanding how God works in this world—just as the grave clothes were discarded as useless relics of the past—and she learns new ways of the working of God.

The Man Born Blind (John 9:1–41)

The man born blind is one of the most memorable minor characters of the New Testament. He routs the religious authorities by dissembling their inflated claims and models the triumph of light over darkness. He

64. Author's translation. Bauckham, *Gospel Women*, 284, notes that the NRSV obscures the individualism of this saying by putting the pronouns into the plural rather than the singular.

is known by the setting, by his actions, and by what he says. As the narrative progresses, he develops into an engaging character, which parallels his understanding of Jesus.

Jesus is a frame character in John 9; he appears at the beginning and at the end and is absent from the central section, where the man born blind and the Pharisees verbally duel each other. The narrative structure consists of seven scenes with two characters or sets of characters in each scene:[65]

Scene 1: Jesus and disciples talk about the man (9:1–7)
Scene 2: The man and his neighbors (9:8–12)
Scene 3: The man and the authorities (9:13–17)
Scene 4: The man's parents and the authorities (9:18–23)
Scene 5: The man and the authorities (9:24–34)
Scene 6: Jesus and the man (9:35–39)
Scene 7: Jesus and the authorities (9:40–41)

The blind man is the protagonist that appears in five of the seven scenes and speaks in thirteen of the forty-one verses. Jesus appears in three scenes and speaks in eight verses while the authorities are present in four scenes and speak in nine verses. The neighbors and parents speak in three verses each, and the disciples speak only once.

It is important to pay attention to the way the narrator introduces a character. What do others say about the main character? Does the setting contribute to the understanding of a character? Is it symbolic? The narrative begins, "As [Jesus] walked along, he saw a man blind from birth. His disciples asked him, 'Rabbi, who sinned, this man or his parents, that he was born blind?'"(9:1–2). The nameless man appears as the object of a theological question. Whose sin caused his blindness, his own or his parents? The religious authorities regard him as a waif of society, born "entirely in sins" (John 9:34),[66] and thus he is at the margins of society, an object but not a subject.

65. See Resseguie, *Strange Gospel*, 140n97, for those who concur with seven scenes.

66. On John 9 see James L. Resseguie, "John 9: A Literary-Critical Analysis," in *The Gospel of John as Literature: An Anthology of Twentieth-Century Literature*, ed. Mark W. G. Stibbe (Leiden: Brill, 1993), 115–22; repr. from *Literary Interpretations of Biblical Narratives*, ed. Kenneth R. R. Gros Louis, 2 vols. (Nashville: Abingdon, 1974–1982), 2:295–303; idem, *Strange Gospel*, 139–44; J. W. Holleran, "Seeing the Light: A Narrative Reading of John 9," *ETL* 69 (1993): 5–26, 354–82; John Painter, "John 9 and the Interpretation of the Fourth Gospel," *JSNT* 28 (1986): 31–61; J. L. Staley, "Stumbling in the Dark, Reaching for the Light: Reading Character in John 5 and 9," *Semeia* 53 (1991): 55–80; Mark W. G. Stibbe, *John*, RNBC (Sheffield: JSOT Press, 1943), 103–13; Dorothy A. Lee, *The Symbolic Narratives of the Fourth Gospel: The Interplay of Form and Meaning*, JSNTSup 95 (Sheffield: JSOT Press, 1994), 164.

Scene 1 has an architectural setting, the pool of Siloam, and a simple prop, dirt. Jesus spits on the ground, makes mud with his saliva, and then anoints the man's eyes with the clay (9:6). Like the Lord God who formed Adam from the dust of the earth, Jesus makes clay and creates a new man.[67] He then tells the man to go and wash in the pool of Siloam. Narrative comments are at the top of Robert Alter's scale for analysis, for when the narrator intervenes to tell us something, we can be sure it is important. In this instance, he translates the name of the pool as "Sent" (9:7). The pool of Siloam is mentioned seldom in the Gospels—at Luke 13:4, John 9:7, and 9:11—but the word "sent" appears frequently in John's Gospel as an epithet for Jesus.[68] Examples include:

> You do not believe him whom he has sent (5:38).
> I did not come on my own, but he sent me (8:42).
> We must work the works of him who sent me (9:4).
> Whoever receives me receives him who sent me (13:20).

Jesus, who is sent by God, thus sends the man born blind to a pool that means "Sent." The physical setting of the miracle is symbolic. Just as Jesus was sent by the Father to give light/enlightenment, he sends the man to a pool that means "Sent" to gain sight/insight. The blind man obeys his command and "went and washed and came back able to see" (9:7).

The neighbors are foils that enhance his characterization. With unintended irony, they ask, "'Is this not the man who used to sit and beg?' Some were saying, 'It is he.' Others were saying, 'No, but it is someone like him.' He kept saying, 'I am the man'" (9:8b–9). Both conclusions are correct. He is the same and not the same; he is the man who used to sit and beg, yet he is a new person. His first words in the narrative suggest an emerging selfhood. Like a child learning to speak for the first time, he says, "I am the man," or simply, "I am" (*egō eimi*). The one who was merely an object of discussion is now a subject and a predicate; his self-affirmation mimics Jesus' *egō eimi*. Although he does not take on the identity of the divine, he finds his identity in an encounter with the divine.[69] It is not yet clear who he will be, but it is clear who he is not. He is no longer the beggar "who used to sit and beg."

67. Noted by Jonathan Bishop, "Encounters in the New Testament," in *Literary Interpretations of Biblical Narratives*, ed. Kenneth R. R. Gros Louis, 2 vols. (Nashville: Abingdon, 1974–1982), 2:285–94 at 2:287.

68. The narrator uses either *apostellō* or *pempō* to describe Jesus as the one sent by the Father.

69. J. Bishop, "Encounters," 288.

The narrator once again intervenes: the Pharisees are summoned because Jesus committed a double violation of the Sabbath laws.[70] He not only healed a man on the Sabbath but also kneaded clay. Like the neighbors who are divided concerning the blind man's identity, the Pharisees are divided concerning Jesus' identity. Some say he "is not from God, for he does not observe the sabbath," but others wonder how "a sinner [could] perform such signs" (9:16). The narrator once more intrudes into the story to draw attention to their division: "and they were divided"—literally, "there was a schism [*schisma*]." Two other times in the Gospel he intrudes to draw attention to a schism that erupted over Jesus. At 7:43, the crowd is divided concerning Jesus' identity: some believe he is the Messiah but others have doubts. And at 10:19–21, "the Jews" are divided over Jesus' words. Some say, "He has a demon and is out of his mind," while others say, "These are not the words of one who has a demon. Can a demon open the eyes of the blind?" In John 9, the unlearned man is ironically asked to resolve the schism. "What do you say about him? It was your eyes he opened," the authorities ask. He calls Jesus a prophet.

Like the man's neighbors, his parents are foils whose fear of the authorities contrasts with the man's boldness. Twice the parents refuse to answer the authorities' questions concerning their son: "Ask him; he is of age"; "He is of age, ask him" (9:21, 23). The narrator once again intrudes to explain the reason for their reticence: "His parents said this because they were afraid of the Jews, for the Jews had already agreed that anyone who confessed Jesus to be the Messiah would be put out of the synagogue" (9:22). J. Louis Martyn has shown that the community of the Fourth Gospel is in danger of being excommunicated from the synagogue if they should confess Jesus as the Messiah. The parents' reluctance to speak up, however, may serve a rhetorical function in the narrative. While the parents fear expulsion from the synagogue, the man actually is expelled from the synagogue (at 9:34).[71] Their fear contrasts with his fearlessness, their timidity with his boldness. While the parents remain inside, where the authorities are, the man is cast outside—where Jesus is (9:34).

The parents say their son is "of age" and "he will speak for himself" in 9:21, and indeed, he does "speak for himself" in scene 5. No longer mimicking the divine voice as in scene 2, the emboldened man gains a

70. See Raymond E. Brown, *The Gospel according to John*, 2 vols., AB 29–29A (Garden City, N.Y.: Doubleday, 1966–1970), 1:373.

71. C. K. Barrett, *The Gospel according to St. John: An Introduction with Commentary and Notes on the Greek Text*, 2nd ed. (Philadelphia: Westminster, 1978), 364; J. Louis Martyn, *History and Theology in the Fourth Gospel*, 3rd ed. (Louisville: Westminster John Knox, 2003), 45.

voice of his own that blends the serious with the sarcastic. Meanwhile, the speech patterns of the religious authorities coalesce into a single voice of opposition: "We know that this man is a sinner" (9:24). The earlier schism as to whether Jesus is "from God" or "a sinner" is now resolved. With the authoritative first person plural, they render their judgment. Yet their pronouncement opens the door for an eiron—in this case, the healed man—to enter and deflate their overconfidence. D. C. Muecke defines *alazon* as "the man who blindly assumes or asserts that something is or is not the case, or confidently expects something to happen or not to happen; he does not even remotely suspect that things might not be as he supposes them to be, or might not turn out as he expects them to."[72] The authorities are alazons in this scene, and the man born blind is the eiron who brings to light their alazony. He begins with the irrefutable—"though I was blind, now I see" (9:25)—and, when they question him again, turns the table and becomes the interrogator. He deflates their orotundity, all the time feigning innocence. "Why do you want to hear it again? Do you also want to become his disciples?" (9:27). Although they claim a privileged position as disciples of Moses, their words trip them up: "You are his disciple, but we are disciples of Moses. We know that God has spoken to Moses, but as for this man, we do not know where he comes from" (9:28–29). Their confession of the truth—that is, that they do not know the origins of "that one"[73] —is too good to resist. Using the voice of authority (the first person plural), the man then lectures them on the way God works in this world:

> Here is an astonishing thing! You do not know where he comes from, and yet he opened my eyes. *We know* that God does not listen to sinners, but he does listen to one who worships him and obeys his will. Never since the world began has it been heard that anyone opened the eyes of a person born blind. If this man were not from God, he could do nothing. (9:30–33, italics added)

Although the authorities are incensed at his claim to knowledge, they are shown to be the real philistine interpreters. Because of his daring speech they expel him from the synagogue, and once again he is at the margins. At the beginning of the narrative he was at the margins of the text and of society, and at the conclusion of the story he returns to the

72. D. C. Muecke, *The Compass of Irony* (London: Methuen, 1969), 30.

73. "That one" (*ekeinos*), which the NRSV translates as "his," is used contemptuously by the authorities. See F. Blass and A. Debrunner, *A Greek Grammar of the New Testament and Other Early Christian Literature* (trans. and ed. Robert W. Funk; Chicago: University of Chicago Press, 1961), §291; noted by Barrett, *John*, 362; Rudolf Bultmann, *The Gospel of John: A Commentary*, trans. G. R. Beasley-Murray (Philadelphia: Westminster, 1971), 336n3; Martyn, *History and Theology*, 47n43.

margins. The second time, however, marginality takes on a new and different meaning. Jesus is at the margins of the text (scenes 1, 6, 7) while the authorities are at the center of the text (scenes 3, 4, 5, 7). To be outside is to be where Jesus is; to be inside is to be where the authorities are. Thus, to be an outsider is to be inside, and to be an insider is to be outside.

In scene 6, Jesus returns to the narrative and finds the man (9:35). Just as he initiated the physical healing, he initiates the man's spiritual healing. He asks him if he believes in the Son of Man. The man confesses his faith—"Lord, I believe"—and worships Jesus (9:38).

Jesus is the frame character of the narrative, and so Jesus' speech summarizes the point of view that is developed and elaborated by the characters at the center. A crisis of judgment or decision occurs when Jesus is around.

> As long as I am in the world, I am the light of the world. (9:5)
>
> I came into this world for judgment[74] so that those who do not see may see, and those who do see may become blind. (9:39)

The surest clue to the point of a story is seen in the development of the protagonist and in the predictability of the flat characters, the authorities. As the light of the world, Jesus brings about a crisis of decision; this accounts for the narrator's repeated emphasis on schisms concerning Jesus' identity. The narrative models the triumph of light over darkness. Darkness in this narrative comes in the form of physical blindness and spiritual darkness—a darkness that can be cured. Darkness can also be a kind of seeing that refuses to see. This darkness cannot be cured.

The blind man and the authorities represent two different responses to this crisis. As light separates night from day, Jesus' presence separates the darkness from the light (9:5), the unseeing from the seeing, the unknowing from the knowing. The blind man is a round, dynamic character who, from the beginning of the narrative to the end, develops from an object to a character in his own right. His traits are opposite pairs, reflecting his characterization before and after his encounter with Jesus. In column A are his traits before and in column B are his traits after.

A	B
unseeing	seeing
unknowing	knowing
unbelieving	believing

74. The word is *krima*, "the judicial decision which consists in the separation of those who are willing to believe fr. those who are unwilling to do so." So BDAG, s.v. κρίμα 6.

object	subject
unseen	seen
colorless	colorful
static	dynamic

The narrator shows us the blind man's development through his speech, his actions, and what the others say about him. His first act is obedience and his last act is worship; obedience and worship are thus the framing activities for his speech. He obeys Jesus' command to go and wash in the pool of Siloam (9:7), which he reiterates twice—once to his neighbors (9:11) and then to the authorities (9:15)—while his final action is to worship Jesus (9:38). More than his actions, his evolving speech patterns show us the development of his character. As his speech matures from childlike utterances to the nuanced discourse of an adult, his statements concerning his healer expand from a primitive understanding to a full confession of faith. As his understanding of Jesus increases, he develops as a person. In the first scene he is mute—talked about but not talked to (except for Jesus, who commands him to go to the pool), and when he speaks, his speech is simple and childlike. Like a child who says "Mom! Mom! Mom!" he repeatedly cries, "I am the man," "I am the man," "I am the man."[75] Just as his discourse is basic, his recognition of Jesus is primitive. He is "the *man* called Jesus" (9:11). As he rehearses the details of his healing in the third scene, his understanding of Jesus expands: "He is *a prophet*" (9:17). In the fifth scene (9:24–34), he finds his own voice, speaking in six of the eleven verses and lecturing the authorities with wit, irony, and sarcasm. He even resolves the argument as to whether Jesus is "from God" or "a sinner," although the authorities are unwilling to accept his conclusion: "If this man were not from God, he could do nothing" (9:33). As he develops, his understanding of Jesus develops, and as his understanding of Jesus develops, he develops. Enlightenment works in two ways: understanding of Jesus increases self-understanding; and self-understanding increases understanding of Jesus. His final words in the narrative reflect his completed development, "*Lord,* I believe."[76]

By contrast, the religious authorities are flat characters who see yet are unseeing, and know yet are unknowing. They illustrate the tragedy of the sighted blind, and their tragic flaw is that they assume they know how God works in this world. Jesus does not fit their categories: how can one heal on the Sabbath and still be from God? The more they insist on the clarity of their vision, the further they descend into spiritual darkness.

75. The imperfect tense, *elegen*, is translated by the NRSV as "kept saying."

76. *Kyrie* can be a polite address ("sir"), but the man's action of worshiping Jesus clarifies the meaning intended.

Unlike the blind man, who surprises us, they are static and predictable. There are no surprises in their characterization. Initially they hold out the promise of an impartial debate with their schism over Jesus' identity: some believe he is from God, while others believe he is a sinner. But authoritative pronouncements characterize their speech later (9:24), and their discourse becomes increasingly ironical, although the irony is unintended. They are victims of the narrator's irony, saying more than they mean but not less than the narrator intends.[77] For instance, when they say, "We know that God has spoken to Moses, but as for this man, we do not know where he comes from," their speech exhibits unintentional irony.[78] The authorities' final words are filled with tragic irony: "Surely we are not blind, are we?" (9:40).[79] Blindness can be cured; sightless seeing, on the other hand, is incurable: "If you were blind, you would not have sin. But now that you say, 'We see,' your sin remains" (9:41).

Dominant Characters

Dominant characters are part of the structures of power and domination in the first century. They include the rich and powerful, the highly visible, rulers, members of the governing class, patrons, priests, and religious leaders, among others.[80] Dominant characters are at the opposite end of the status hierarchy from the marginalized: the expendables, unclean, degraded, peasants, poor, widows, Gentiles, and children. If marginalized characters are off-center, at the edges of society, dominant characters are at-center, at the political, economic, and cultural centers of society.

Zacchaeus (Luke 19:1–10)

Zacchaeus is an in-between character. He is part of the structures of power and domination, yet his own people relegate him to the margins of society.[81] His traits are conflicting. He is a "ruler"[82] in the Greco-Roman

77. On the irony in John 9 see Paul Duke, *Irony in the Fourth Gospel* (Atlanta: John Knox Press, 1985), 117–26.

78. To know "where" (*pothen*) Jesus comes from is to know who Jesus is. "A principal difference between Jesus and his enemies in John is that he knows where he is from and where he is going and they do not (see 8:14)." See Sandra M. Schneiders, "John 20:11–18," 155–68. The quoted sentence is on p. 157.

79. The negative *mē* expects the answer, "No." They expect Jesus to say that they are not blind. He agrees that they are not blind, which is what makes them culpable.

80. On the structures of power and domination in an agarian society see Lenski, *Power and Privilege*, 189–296.

81. His name is Jewish. See Joseph A. Fitzmyer, *The Gospel according to Luke*, 2 vols., AB 28–28A (Garden City, N.Y.: Doubleday, 1981–1985), 2:1223.

82. He is called an *architelōnēs*, which is usually translated as "chief tax collector." The prefix *archi-* generally refers to a ruler, as in *archisynagōgos*, a "ruler of a synagogue"

world, yet he is low in social status among Jews. He is a toll collector[83] who works for a foreign government, yet he is a child of Abraham. He is a wealthy entrepreneur, yet socially impoverished. Zacchaeus is an enigma; he is neither here nor there, caught in-between. His is the story of modern men and women who climb the ladder of social and economic success only to be alienated from their social and religious roots.

The narrator tells us about Zacchaeus and his traits and also shows us what he does. Unlike the rich ruler in Luke 18:18–25, Zacchaeus is a named character, but his negative attributes sully his name. Not only is he a toll collector; he is a "chief toll collector," a district supervisor perhaps responsible for several toll collectors.[84] To an expanding list of negative traits the narrator adds, "he was rich." In the Gospel of Luke, the rich are routinely portrayed in a negative light, for they have already received their consolation (6:24). A rich farmer secures his life with wealth yet loses it that very night (12:16–21), and a wealthy man feasts sumptuously in this life yet lives in torment in the next (16:19–31).

The setting magnifies Zacchaeus's marginality. The crowd—walk-ons who are part of the background setting—voice a damaging trait that characterizes his marginality: he is "a sinner" (19:7). The narrator and the crowd are in agreement that Zacchaeus is among the despised and marginalized of society, even though his position as chief toll collector accords him relative power and privilege in the Greco-Roman world. Along with widows, the blind, the lame, and children, he joins the ranks of society's lowliest.[85] The crowd also creates a barrier to the tax collector's quest. His diminutive stature makes it impossible to see or find Jesus because the crowd blocks him (19:3).[86]

Zacchaeus's negative traits outline the downward turn of a U-shaped plot. He is alienated from his religious and social roots, a lost or misplaced person within Israel. Just as the coin was lost and the sheep was missing in Luke 15, Zacchaeus is a missing person who needs to be found. The reversal at the bottom of the U-shaped plot is prefigured in Zacchaeus's surprising action of climbing the sycamore tree. In the Magnificat, Mary proclaims that the Lord "has brought down the powerful from their thrones, and lifted up the lowly" (Luke 1:52). Zacchaeus climbs the syca-

(8:49; 13:14); by analogy, Zacchaeus would be a ruler or leader among toll collectors. But the translation of the Greek is uncertain because it occurs only here in the New Testament. See BDAG, s.v. ἀρχιτελώνης. Green, *Luke*, 668, argues that he is a ruler.

83. On toll collectors see Otto Michel, "τελώνης," *TDNT* 8:88–105; John R. Donahue, "Tax Collectors and Sinners: An Attempt at Identification," *CBQ* 33 (1971): 39–61.

84. See John Gillman, *Possessions and the Life of Faith: A Reading of Luke-Acts*, ZSNT (Collegeville, Minn.: Liturgical Press, 1991), 89, for the suggestion that he is a district manager.

85. Green, *Luke*, 670.

86. *Hēlikia* appears to refer to bodily stature rather than his age. See BDAG, s.v. ἡλικία 3.

more tree—the lowly and despised seeking to go high—only to find out that he must come down to receive what he wants—the lofty or wealthy being brought low.[87]

Who speaks first in the narrative and what does he say? All the characters have speaking parts—the crowd (actually part of the setting), Zacchaeus, and Jesus—but Jesus is the first and last to speak. His words frame the narrative.

> Zacchaeus, hurry and come down; for I must stay at your house today. (19:5)
>
> Today salvation has come to this house, because he too is a son of Abraham. (19:9)

Unlike the anonymous rich ruler whose only identifying features are his wealth and status in society (Luke 18:18–23), Zacchaeus is called by name, recognized as a subject in his own right. Jesus emphasizes that his own quest cannot be delayed. He uses the strong words of divine necessity: "I must stay at your house."[88] The addition of "today," a verbal thread, contributes a note of eschatological urgency to his quest. Several times in the Gospel "today" punctuates a momentous and transitional event:

> To you is born *this day* [i.e., *today*] in the city of David a Savior. (2:11)
>
> *Today* this scripture has been fulfilled in your hearing. (4:21)
>
> *Today* salvation has come to this house. (19:9)

Jesus' initiative and Zacchaeus's response signal the upward turn of the U-shaped plot. Zacchaeus descends the tree and stands before Jesus. In Luke, standing is more than simply assuming an upright position; it also implies standing with a purposeful resolve.[89] Zacchaeus's first words in the narrative express this resolve: "Look, half of my possessions, Lord, I will give to the poor; and if I have defrauded anyone of anything, I will pay back four times as much" (19:8). Some scholars translate the present tense as a customary present, rather than the more common rendering as a futuristic present. If translated in the present, Zacchaeus says, "I *give as is my custom* to the poor and I *customarily make reparations* to anyone I have extorted." In other words, he is not stating a future resolve;

87. Resseguie, *Spiritual Landscape*, 108–9.

88. *Dei*, "it is necessary." See Charles H. Cosgrove, "The Divine δεῖ in Luke-Acts: Investigations into the Lukan Understanding of God's Providence," *NovT* 26 (1984): 168–90.

89. See D. A. S. Ravens, "Zacchaeus: The Final Part of a Lucan Triptych?" *JSNT* 41 (1991): 26. He cites Luke 11:18 as an example of standing firm and Acts 26:16 as an example of standing ready for a purpose.

on the contrary, he is defending himself and emphasizing his normal, everyday practice of generosity. Joseph Fitzmyer suggests that Zacchaeus "bristles" at what the crowd says about him and offers a defense of his actions. "He may be a 'sinner,' but he gives half of his possessions to the poor and makes reparation in generous fashion for any extortion in which he may have been involved."[90] Dennis Hamm, however, has shown that Zacchaeus is not speaking about a normal practice of generosity; rather, he states his future resolve to make right his wrongs.[91] From now on he will he give to the poor and will make fourfold restitution to anyone he has defrauded.

The last words of the narrative belong to Jesus. The one on a quest discovers that Jesus has been on a quest for him all along: "Today salvation has come to this house, because he too is a son of Abraham. For the Son of Man came to seek out and to save the lost" (19:9). This is the top of the U, a new stable condition. The mutual quests are successful, for Jesus has found the lost, and Zacchaeus has found salvation.

The point or the theme of the story is found in the development of Zacchaeus's character. He is lost yet found, and this theme frames the entire story. Zacchaeus and Jesus are on mutual quests. Zacchaeus is on a quest to see Jesus and Jesus is on a quest to find the lost. Twice the verbal thread "to seek" is repeated.

> [Zacchaeus] *was trying* [i.e., *seeking*] to see who Jesus was (19:3).
> For the Son of Man came *to seek out* and to save the lost (19:10).

But another theme is found in the repetitions of a different word, the verb "to see." This story is also about seeing differently. Jesus initiates the new way of seeing, and Zacchaeus's development as a character elaborates this new way. The crowd represents the old way of seeing. The following words for "see" appear in six of the ten verses of the narrative.

> *Look,*[92] a man was there named Zacchaeus (19:2).
> He was *trying to see* who Jesus was (19:3).

90. Fitzmyer, *Luke*, 2:1221. Others who interpret the verbs as customary presents include Ravens, "Zacchaeus," 19–32; Alan C. Mitchell, "Zacchaeus Revisited: Luke 19,8 as a Defense," *Bib* 71 (1990): 153–76; Richard C. White, "Vindication for Zacchaeus?" *ExpT* 91 (1979): 21; Green, *Luke*, 671–72.

91. Dennis Hamm, "Luke 19:8 Once More: Does Zacchaeus Defend or Resolve? *JBL* 107 (1988): 431–37; idem, "Zacchaeus Revisited Once More: A Story of Vindication or Conversion?" *Bib* 72 (1991): 249–52; cf. also David A. Neale, *None but the Sinners: Religious Categories in the Gospel of Luke*, JSNTSup 58 (Sheffield: JSOT Press, 1991), 187; Robert C. Tannehill, "The Story of Zacchaeus as Rhetoric: Luke 19:1–10," *Semeia* 64 (1993): 201–11.

92. The NRSV does not translate "look" (*idou*).

So he ran ahead and climbed a sycamore tree *to see* him (19:4).
When Jesus came to the place, he *looked up* (19:5).
All who *saw* it began to grumble (19:7).
Look, half of my possessions, Lord, I will give (19:8).

The narrative is about adopting a new point of view, a new way of seeing. Jesus initiates the whole process when Zacchaeus, who seeks to see him, is first seen by Jesus: "When Jesus came to the place, he looked up" (19:5). The crowd, however, sees in the conventional way, grumbling that Jesus accepts hospitality from an outcast, a sinner and a tax collector. Zacchaeus's encounter with the divine, on the other hand, enables him to see in a new way. Unlike the rich ruler—a foil who illuminates Zacchaeus's response to the divine—the tax collector gives half of his possessions to the poor and repairs any wrongs he has committed.[93] By distributing his wealth to outsiders, Zacchaeus abandons the old way of seeing or doing business. "Negative reciprocity" attempts to get something for nothing. Wealth is gained through fraud and exploitation, which characterizes Zacchaeus's modus operandi. His new point of view, however, is characterized by "generalized reciprocity" in which those who are unable to repay are given alms. In other words, the poor and disenfranchised are treated like family, one's own kin, in this new way of seeing. They are no longer outsiders.[94]

Zacchaeus is more round than flat. He is a dynamic or developing character with conflicting traits that are capable of surprising the reader. E. M. Forster defines a round character as unpredictable and surprising. Zacchaeus's action of climbing a sycamore tree surprises and delights, but more surprising is his response of dispossession and restitution. The point of the story is his development to a person who embraces kingdom values and is restored to the people of God. Zacchaeus is raised up from his lowly status as an outcast by his encounter with the divine; but the divine encounter also brings him down from the lofty heights of the rich.

Judas Iscariot, Scene 1 (John 6:64, 70–71)

In the Gospel of John, Judas appears or is mentioned in four scenes.[95] (A fifth passage in John 17:12 refers to Judas as "the one destined to

93. Green, *Luke*, 671n208, notes that "fourfold restitution is by almost any reckoning excessive."

94. See Moxnes, *Economy of the Kingdom*, 34–35, for a definition of these terms.

95. On Judas in the Gospel of John see Kim Paffenroth, *Judas: Images of the Lost Disciple* (Louisville: Westminster John Knox, 2001), 33–36; William Klassen, *Judas: Betrayer or Friend of Jesus?* (Minneapolis: Fortress, 1996), 137–59; idem, "Judas Iscariot," *ABD* 3:1091–96; J. S. Billings, "Judas Iscariot in the Fourth Gospel," *ExpT* 51 (1939): 156–58;

be lost.") Judas is known by what he does rather than by what he says, although the one time he speaks in the Gospel is telling. He is also known by the narrator's comments and what Jesus says about him. He is a flat character who does not develop, yet he plays a crucial role in the development of the plot. Judas appears late in the Gospel of John, which is not unusual for this writer; for the beloved disciple does not make a formal appearance until John 13. Judas first appears in 6:64 and 6:70–71:

> "But among you there are some who do not believe." For Jesus knew from the first who were the ones that did not believe, and who was the one that would betray him. (6:64)

> "Did I not choose you, the twelve? Yet one of you is a devil." He was speaking of Judas son of Simon Iscariot, for he, though one of the twelve, was going to betray him. (6:70–71)

Judas neither speaks nor acts. Rather Jesus mentions Judas while the omniscient narrator interprets what he meant. What is striking is that he is one of the "twelve," which is mentioned once by Jesus and a second time by the narrator, and he is a betrayer or the one who hands Jesus over to the authorities.[96] Another epithet is harsher: he is called "a devil." Judas's conflicting traits reflect his conflicting loyalties. He is "chosen," yet he is among those who do not believe. He is "one of the twelve," yet he is a "devil." He is part of the inner circle, yet he hands Jesus over to outsiders, the authorities. By portending the struggle between light and darkness, Judas is more a function of the plot than a character in his own right. The cosmic struggle between light and darkness, God and Satan, is played out on the human level in the character of Judas.[97] In scene 2, Judas's first and only speech of the Gospel enlarges and deepens his characterization.

Eric F. F. Bishop, "'He That Eateth Bread with Me. . .'" *ExpT* 70 (1959): 331–33; K. Hein, "Judas Iscariot: Key to the Last-Supper Narratives?" *NTS* 17 (1970/1971): 227–32; Steven M. Sheeley, "Judas Iscariot," *EDB* 748–49; F. W. Gingrich, "Judas," *IDB* 2:1006–8; Raymond E. Brown, *The Death of the Messiah: From Gethsemane to the Grave*, 2 vols. (New York: Doubleday, 1994), 2:1394–1418; R. Alan Culpepper, *Anatomy of the Fourth Gospel: A Study in Literary Design* (Philadelphia: Fortress, 1983), 166–68; Resseguie, *Strange Gospel*, 164–67; Craig R. Koester, *Symbolism in the Fourth Gospel: Meaning, Mystery, Community*, 2nd ed. (Minneapolis: Fortress, 2003), 150–51, 206–8; Kermode, *Genesis of Secrecy*, 91–94.

96. Despite the negative connotations of betrayal, the word actually means "hand over" and not an act of treachery. See BDAG, s.v. παραδίδωμι 1b. Luke 6:16, however, labels Judas's "handing over" as an act of betrayal (*prodotēs* = "traitor, betrayer").

97. Culpepper, *Anatomy*, 124.

Judas Iscariot, Scene 2 (John 12:1–8)

> Six days before the Passover Jesus came to Bethany, the home of Lazarus, whom he had raised from the dead. There they gave a dinner for him. Martha served, and Lazarus was one of those at the table with him. Mary took a pound of costly perfume made of pure nard, anointed Jesus' feet, and wiped them with her hair. The house was filled with the fragrance of the perfume. But Judas Iscariot, one of his disciples (the one who was about to betray him), said, "Why was this perfume not sold for three hundred denarii and the money given to the poor?" (He said this not because he cared about the poor, but because he was a thief; he kept the common purse and used to steal what was put into it.) Jesus said, "Leave her alone. She bought it so that she might keep it for the day of my burial. You always have the poor with you, but you do not always have me." (John 12:1–8)

Only John's Gospel records that Judas objected to the anointing of Jesus. In Mark, "some" (Mark 14:4) objected, and in Matthew, "the disciples" protested the "waste" (Matt 26:8). But in John, Judas expresses dissatisfaction. John also is the only Gospel that mentions that Judas was "a thief," which has led some scholars to question the historicity of John's account. In *Judas: Betrayer or Friend of Jesus?* William Klassen claims that John's account demonizes Judas. He accuses John of "bearing false witness, slander, and calumny"[98] and of sullying Judas's reputation.

> In view of the severe condemnation that sin carries and the destruction it can bring to people's reputations, indeed the harm it has done to the person of Judas in history, it may be time to come to terms with it and bury once and for all the belief that Judas was a thief or was motivated by demonic forces. Not for a moment does it seem credible that the Johannine portrait of Judas could be authentic.[99]

Whatever the historical authenticity of John's account, the narrator is reliable (i.e., he is in agreement with the implied author's norms and values). What, then, is the narrative function of this portrait of Judas in the Gospel? Both Jesus and the narrator have commented on Judas; now the narrator allows Judas to speak in his own voice. What does his speech add to his characterization? How does the setting amplify Judas's characterization? What does the narrative aside add to our understanding of the disciple?

The setting is Mary's anointing of Jesus in Lazarus's house. She pours a costly perfume on Jesus' feet and wipes them with her hair, a symbolic act that prefigures Jesus' preparation for death and burial. Judas, however,

98. Klassen, *Judas*, 146.
99. Ibid.

misses the symbolism and sees only waste: "Why was this perfume not sold for three hundred denarii and the money given to the poor?" Since a character's first words in a narrative are usually important, a comparison of Judas's first speech with the first words of the other disciples is instructive for our understanding of Judas's characterization:

Two of John's disciples:	"Rabbi . . . where are you staying?" (1:38).
Andrew:	"We have found the Messiah" (1:41).
Philip:	"We have found him about whom Moses in the law and also the prophets wrote, Jesus son of Joseph from Nazareth" (1:45).
Nathanael:	"Can anything good come out of Nazareth?" (1:46); "You are the Son of God . . . the King of Israel" (1:49).
Peter:	"We have come to believe and know that you are the Holy One of God" (6:69).
Thomas:	"Let us also go, that we may die with him" (11:16).

The first words of the other disciples are lofty confessions of faith, or a willingness to die with Jesus in Judea (Thomas), or a desire to abide (i.e., stay or remain) with Jesus (the "two disciples"). By contrast, Judas is indignant that an expensive perfume—worth a year's wages—has been wasted on Jesus rather than lavished on the poor. While the other disciples anoint Jesus with extravagant titles and confessions of faith, Judas's response is niggardly. No title or confession of faith flows from his lips, only a complaint that the anointing is a waste.

The theme of John 12:1–8 is giving: Mary gives extravagantly, Jesus gives himself completely (12:7–8), and Judas desires to give to the poor. Two acts of giving are genuine expressions of self-sacrifice; the other act is deceptive. The narrator's aside explains Judas's po-faced deceit: "He said this not because he cared about the poor, but because he was a thief; he kept the common purse and used to steal what was put into it" (12:6). Judas's growing list of negative traits is now supplemented with thievery, which a double entendre elaborates. *Ebastazen* literally means "he used to carry" what was put into the purse, but it can also mean, as the NRSV translation indicates, "he used to carry away" or "lift" (i.e., "steal").[100] In other words, Judas is the treasurer of the group (he "carries" what was put into the purse) but also steals from the purse (he "lifts" from the purse). Despite this negative characterization, Judas is still part of the intimate group, "one of [Jesus'] disciples" (12:4). Although he is inside, with the light, his speech implies that his loyalties lie with darkness.

100. BDAG, s.v. βαστάζω 3b.

He is part of the inner group, but he stands apart, as his self-revelation shows. In scene 3, Judas's defection is complete.

Judas Iscariot, Scene 3 (John 13:2, 10–11, 18–19, 21, 26–30)

The devil had already put it into the heart of Judas son of Simon Iscariot to betray him. (13:2)

Jesus said to [Peter], "One who has bathed does not need to wash, except for the feet, but is entirely clean. And you [pl.] are clean, though not all of you." For he knew who was to betray him; for this reason he said, "Not all of you are clean." (13:10–11)

I am not speaking of all of you; I know whom I have chosen. But it is to fulfill the scripture, "The one who ate my bread has lifted his heel against me." I tell you this now, before it occurs, so that when it does occur, you may believe that I am he. (13:18–19)

Very truly, I tell you, one of you will betray me. (13:21)

Jesus answered, "It is the one to whom I give this piece of bread when I have dipped it in the dish." So when he had dipped the piece of bread, he gave it to Judas son of Simon Iscariot. After he received the piece of bread, Satan entered into him. Jesus said to him, "Do quickly what you are going to do." Now no one at the table knew why he said this to him. Some thought that, because Judas had the common purse, Jesus was telling him, "Buy what we need for the festival"; or, that he should give something to the poor. So, after receiving the piece of bread, he immediately went out. And it was night. (13:26–30)

Judas joins the other disciples for the washing of feet and the Last Supper. This is not only the climactic event in the Gospel but also the turning point in the development of Judas's characterization in John. The religious setting is prior to the festival of the Passover, when Jesus "knew that his hour had come to depart from this world and go to the Father." The narrator sets the tone for what is about to happen: "The devil had already put it into the heart of Judas son of Simon Iscariot to betray/hand over" Jesus (13:1–2, author's translation). The devil's move is countered by Jesus' move: he washes the disciples' feet, including Judas's, but this remarkable display of love—a symbolic prelude to the ultimate act of self-giving on the cross—still leaves one person unclean. "And you are clean, though not all of you," which the narrator explains: "for he knew who was to betray him" (13:10–11). Judas is spoken about but not identified. He is anonymous—unseen by the others but seen by Jesus and the narrator for who he is. His elusive, dark portrayal fits his characterization as one who goes out into the night.

The extent of Jesus' love is seen in his act of giving. The one who is the bread of life does not withhold bread from the one who turns against him. Judas does not *take* bread; Jesus *gives* it (13:26). Twice the narrator mentions that Judas received bread from Jesus, a framing device that places the act of conspiracy within the act of giving.

> After he received the piece of bread, Satan entered into him. (13:27)

> So, after receiving the piece of bread, he [lit. "that one"] immediately went out. (13:30)

Yet, like the washing of feet, the gift of bread has little effect upon Judas. His response to Jesus' gift is to lift his heel against him, to reject Jesus' overture of hospitality: "The one who ate my bread has lifted his heel against me" (13:18; cf. Ps. 41:9).[101] Upon his receiving the bread, Satan enters the defector, and Judas becomes a passive agent in the drama—little more than a pawn in a cosmic struggle between God and Satan, good and evil, light and darkness. The stronger one, however, is in control of the ensuing battle. Judas leaves only when he is told to: "Do quickly what you are going to do" (13:27). As Koester notes, "The Son of God was stronger than Satan's emissary, for Judas left the table only at Jesus' bidding."[102] "He immediately went out. And it was night" (13:30). The temporal setting strikes a note of finality: Judas, who is now called emphatically "that one," leaves the light for the darkness.

Judas Iscariot, Scene 4 (John 18:1–8)

> After Jesus had spoken these words, he went out with his disciples across the Kidron valley to a place where there was a garden, which he and his disciples entered. Now Judas, who betrayed him, also knew the place, because Jesus often met there with his disciples. So Judas brought a detachment of soldiers together with police from the chief priests and the Pharisees, and they came there with lanterns and torches and weapons. Then Jesus, knowing all that was to happen to him, came forward and asked them, "Whom are you looking for?" They answered, "Jesus of Nazareth." Jesus replied, "I am he." Judas, who betrayed him, was standing with them. When Jesus said to them, "I am he," they stepped back and fell to the ground. Again he asked them, "Whom are you looking for?" And they

101. Bishop, "'He That Eateth Bread with Me . . .,'" 331–33; Klassen, *Judas*, 147–48. V. H. Koov, "Heel, Lifted," *IDB* 2:577, says that "The NT phrase means 'acted treacherously,' and applies to deeds. But the emphasis would seem to be that one, with whom one was bound by a covenant of peace, who partook of one's bread, had violated the laws of hospitality, and had turned on his host."

102. Craig R. Koester, *Symbolism in the Fourth Gospel: Meaning, Mystery, Community* (Minneapolis: Fortress, 1995), 207.

> said, "Jesus of Nazareth." Jesus answered, "I told you that I am he. So if you are looking for me, let these men go."

In Judas's final appearance in the Gospel, he is little more than a "walk-on," a part of the background setting.[103] Judas and Jesus have nothing to do with each other, for the separation between the realm of light and darkness is complete.[104] Judas neither speaks, as in Matt. 26:49 and Mark 14:45, nor gives Jesus a kiss, as in the other three Gospels. Judas's act of betrayal is the framing device.

> Now Judas, who betrayed him, also knew the place. (18:2)

> Judas, who betrayed him, was standing with them. (18:5b)

Judas brings a large detachment of soldiers—a cohort, which is normally six hundred men—to the place where he knew Jesus would be—a faint reference to his earlier status as one of Jesus' disciples. Despite the large contingent of soldiers and police, Jesus slays all with his self-revelatory "I am" (*egō eimi*; NRSV translates "I am he"). At his divine disclosure, they step back and fall down, presumably Judas also (18:6).[105] The darkness cannot overcome the light. Jesus then tells the arresting posse what to do, affirming his sovereignty over the events that will take place.

The narrator's final mention of Judas in the Gospel is instructive, especially in comparison with his first appearance in the Gospel. In John 6:70, Judas is referred to as one of the Twelve; here he is identified as "standing with them," that is, with the arresting party. His defection is complete; no longer part of the Twelve, he has joined the dominant culture in their rebellion against the light.

The inverted U-shaped plot, a tragic plot, parallels the characterization of Judas. He is part of the Twelve, an insider, yet the inverted U turns to disaster as Judas reveals his disaffection by speech and actions. Judas is a flat character, a function of the plot and a representative character type.[106] His characterization is consistent throughout the Gospel of John, although, as Steven Sheeley notes, his characterization would be easier to accept if he were an outsider.[107] Jesus, the narrator, and even Judas's own speech merge to portray a person who, though an insider, becomes

103. So Klassen, *Judas*, 154.

104. Ibid.

105. On the garden scene in John see Resseguie, *Strange Gospel*, 67–69.

106. Kermode, *Genesis of Secrecy*, 85, says that Judas is "a character being possessed by his narrative role." The narrative plot calls for betrayal and so "betrayal becomes Judas."

107. Sheeley, "Judas Iscariot," 749.

an outsider. He starts out as "one of the twelve," but ends up "with them," that part of the dominant culture that rejects Jesus. He represents in human form the cosmic struggle between good and evil, between God and Satan. He also represents the individual soul torn between following Jesus and departing from his presence, between abiding in the light and going out into darkness. It is difficult to say to what extent Judas is a willing participant in this drama.[108] We have Judas's own speech in John 12, which, in contrast to the other disciples' first words, is characterized by disaffection. We also have Jesus' act of love in the washing of Judas's feet along with those of the others; yet it seemed to have had little affect on him. Judas is an insider who goes outside; he abandons light for darkness; he is a type of the "antichrists" mentioned in the First Epistle of John who, though part of the fellowship, went out from the community of believers (1 John 2:18–19).

108. Theologians debate this issue. See the helpful summary of theological responses to Judas in Klassen, *Judas*, chapter 10.

5

Point of View

5.1 Definition

Point of view "signifies the way a story gets told."[1] The actions of the characters, their dialogue, their rhetoric, and the setting are presented through the narrator's perspective. The influence of point of view is seen in the events a narrator selects for the story, what the characters say or do, what settings are elaborated, what comments and evaluations are made, and so forth. In apprehending narrative point of view, the reader discovers the norms, values, beliefs, and general worldview that the narrator wants the reader to adopt or to reject. In what follows, point of view is defined, developed, and elaborated with a short story by Kate Chopin, illustrated with examples from the New Testament, and applied to an extended narrative, the parable of the Good Samaritan (Luke 10:29–37).

An ambiguous term, "point of view" can refer to (1) the "angle of vision" from which the narrator tells the story, or (2) the conceptual worldview of the narrator. In the first instance, the "angle of vision,"—what Susan Sniader Lanser calls the "objective" point of view[2]—designates a relationship between the narrator and the narrative. For instance: What is the position from which the narrator views the narrative? Is the

1. M. H. Abrams, *A Glossary of Literary Terms*, 7th ed. (Fort Worth: Harcourt Brace College Publishers, 1999), s.v. "Point of View."

2. Susan Sniader Lanser, *The Narrative Act: Point of View in Prose Fiction* (Princeton: Princeton University Press, 1981), 16; see also James L. Resseguie, *The Strange Gospel: Narrative Design and Point of View in John* (Leiden: Brill, 2001), 2–4.

narrator outside the story or a character within the story? If the narrator is outside, does she or he have privileged access to the characters' thoughts, motivations, and feelings? A third-person omniscient narrator tells the story from outside and refers to the characters by name or by "he," "she," or "they." Similar to a moving camera and montage, this narrator is free to roam from character to character, provide close-ups of some characters, glances at others, and move at will from one event to another. The gospel writers are third-person omniscient narrators who roam from character to character, event to event, delving into the thoughts of some characters, elaborating the motivations of others, commenting on characters, and so forth.

But not all narrators are third-person narrators, nor are they all omniscient. A first-person narrator speaks as "I" and is to some degree a participant in the story. The narrator may tell his or her own story ("I" as the protagonist) or someone else's story ("I" as witness).[3] In this mode of narration, the narrator's freedom to look inside other characters is limited. As with any outside observer, this narrator infers knowledge concerning characters' motivations and thoughts from what they do and say. The narrator of the book of Revelation is a participant in the story and uses the first person to tell us what he sees in heaven: "After this *I* looked, and there in heaven a door stood open," or "*I* saw a mighty angel" (Rev. 4:1; 5:2). His stance as a participant in the story lends authority to what he says. The narrator of the Acts of the Apostles uses the first person plural in four sections of the book (Acts 16:10–17; 20:5–15; 21:1–18; 27:1–28:16). The sudden appearance of the "we sections" in a narrative that is predominately third-person is puzzling. One explanation is that the narrator is a participant within the story, or he may be relying on another's itinerary notes, or using a stylistic convention.[4] In 16:10, a first-person perspective suddenly appears: "When [Paul] had seen the vision, *we* immediately tried to cross over to Macedonia, being convinced that God had called *us* to proclaim the good news to them." The prologues of the Gospels of Luke and John also rely on first-person narration. "And the Word became flesh and lived among *us*, and *we* have seen his glory, the glory as of a father's only son, full of grace and truth" (John 1:14). First-person narration lends authority to what is written since the narrator is presumably a witness to the events. Use of

3. Wallace Martin, *Recent Theories of Narrative* (Ithaca and New York: Cornell University Press, 1986), 135.

4. Other possible reasons for the narrator switching to the first plural are summarized by David E. Aune in *The Westminster Dictionary of New Testament and Early Christian Literature and Rhetoric* (Louisville: Westminster John Knox, 2003), s.v. "'We'-passages" (481–82).

the first person plural can also be a stylistic device to lend authority to one's pronouncements.[5]

By far the most important aspect for biblical narrative critics is the second meaning of point of view: the conceptual framework or worldview of the narrator, also called the ideological point of view. Whereas "angle of vision" refers to the narrator's stance toward the narrative in terms of space, time, and voice, the conceptual or ideological point of view refers to the narrator's attitude toward or evaluation of the action, dialogue, characters, setting, and events. Lanser calls this aspect of point of view the "subjective" point of view.[6] It is the way the person on the street understands point of view. When someone wants to know your point of view on global warming, for example, she or he is asking for your evaluation or your attitude toward it. Literary critics refer to this aspect as ideological[7] or conceptual[8] point of view. Some narrative critics prefer the term "standards of judgment" for this aspect of point of view.[9] For example, Rhoads, Dewey, and Michie define standards of judgment as "a system of beliefs and values implicit in the point of view from which the narrator judges and evaluates the characters in the story."[10] All characters within the Gospels are judged from the point of view of the narrator, which also coincides with Jesus' point of view.

5.2 Four Planes of Point of View

Boris Uspensky identifies four planes on which point of view is expressed: phraseological (what words and phrases are used in the narrative?); spatial-temporal (where and when are events narrated?); psychological (what are the characters' thoughts and behaviors?); and ideological (what are the narrator's norms, values, and worldview?).[11] Ideological point of view in a narrative is expressed through phraseological, psy-

5. See Aune, *Literature and Rhetoric*, s.v. "First-person plural" (184–85).

6. Lanser, *Narrative Act*, 16.

7. Boris Uspensky, *A Poetics of Composition: The Structure of the Artistic Text and Typology of a Compositional Form*, trans. V. Zavarin and S. Wittig (Berkeley: University of California Press, 1973); Lanser, *Narrative Act*.

8. Seymour Chatman, *Story and Discourse: Narrative Structure in Fiction and Film* (Ithaca: Cornell University Press, 1978), 152.

9. David Rhoads, Joanna Dewey, and Donald Michie, *Mark as Story: An Introduction to the Narrative of a Gospel*, 2nd ed. (Minneapolis: Fortress, 1999), 44–45; also David Rhoads, *Reading Mark, Engaging the Gospel* (Minneapolis: Fortress, 2004), chapter 3; Powell, *What Is Narrative Criticism?* 24. Powell also uses the term "evaluative" for point of view.

10. Rhoads, Dewey, and Michie, *Mark as Story*, 44.

11. Uspensky, *Poetics of Composition*; Lanser, *The Narrative Act*, 184–225, develops and elaborates Uspensky's planes on which point of view operates.

chological, and spatial-temporal planes. Ideological and psychological points of view correspond to the subjective point of view or the narrator's attitude toward his or her material. The spatial-temporal points of view (and to a certain extent the phraseological plane) corresponds to the objective point of view. These are not hard-and-fast categories, for a phraseological point of view may also reveal a narrator's attitude to his or her subject matter. The point is that the norms, values, beliefs, and worldview of the author are important for the narrative critic's analysis of individual narratives. What is the implied author's point of view, and how is that expressed in the narrative? [12]

Phraseological Point of View

Phraseological point of view focuses on the narrator's discourse as well as the way the speech of the characters is presented. The choice of words and expressions by both characters and narrator represents a point of view; thus, speech is an open window into a character's or narrator's point of view. Some questions that help to identify phraseological point of view are: What names, titles, and epithets are used for a character by the narrator or by other characters? What tone is expressed in their speech? Is it affirming or disparaging? What are a character's

12. See Mieke Bal, *Narratology: Introduction to the Theory of Narrative*, trans. Christine van Boheemen (Toronto: University of Toronto Press, 1985), 100–114; Shlomith Rimmon-Kenan, *Narrative Fiction: Contemporary Poetics* (Routledge: London and New York, 1983), chapter 6. Some literary critics prefer the term "focalization" rather than "point of view" to describe the relationship between the narrator and his or her subject matter. Focalization asks: "Who sees?" and "Who speaks?" The one who sees the events and happenings of the story need not be the one who speaks in the narrative, although usually the narrator is the focalizer. Events are seen through his or her perspective and told in his or her own voice. Yet that is not always the case. The narrator may relate the events through the perspective of a character. In this case, the character is the focalizer while the narrator is the one who speaks. This distinction is useful for some narratives—especially in modern literature—but not especially helpful in biblical literature, where the focalizer and narrative voice are often the same. In Revelation, for instance, the focalizer and narrator is John. He sees what happens and tells his readers about it. At other times in the New Testament, the focalizer is a character or characters within the narrative. Notice in the following example how the events are related through the perspective of the disciples on the Sea of Galilee: "They saw Jesus walking on the sea and coming near the boat, and they were terrified" (John 6:19). The disciples are the focalizer; what they see and feel is related through their eyes. But the distinction of "who sees" and "who speaks" is of limited value in New Testament narrative analysis, for the perception of the disciples—as this instance illustrates—is mediated through the narrator and his voice. Focalization is a useful concept in modern literature that uses the "free indirect style" of narration where a narrative represents a character's thoughts and feelings without the usage of quotation marks. See H. Porter Abbott, *The Cambridge Introduction to Narrative* (Cambridge: Cambridge University Press, 2002), 190–91.

first words? Does a character's speech change in a narrative or remain the same? Does the narrator comment on a character or evaluate an action? Does the narrator offer asides such as explanations or parenthetical comments? Does the narrator provide an interpretation or evaluation of characters or events?

Spatial-Temporal Point of View

As the term implies, spatial-temporal point of view has two dimensions. Spatial point of view refers to the narrator's relationship to the narrative in terms of space. From what vantage point does the narrator view the actions? Does a narrator see events from one character's perspective, moving with that character throughout the narration? Or is the narrator an invisible, roving presence similar to a moving camera and montage? The roving narrator has the advantage of moving freely from character to character, stopping long enough to focus on certain details and then moving on to another character or series of events. This technique, found in the Gospels, has the distinct advantage of presenting differing and conflicting points of view with remarkable ease. In Mark, the narrator moves seamlessly from Jesus' trial before the chief priests and the council to Peter's "trial" in the courtyard below that culminates in his denial of Jesus. The narrator is not limited by one spatial perspective but views Jesus and Peter simultaneously. The roving perspective thus allows the reader to compare and contrast Jesus' trial with Peter's "trial." In Revelation, the narrator alternates between an "above" point of view and a "below" perspective. This enables events on earth to be interpreted from an "above" point of view or, alternatively, events in heaven to be interpreted in terms of what happens "below."

Temporal point of view refers to the pace of the narration or the temporal distance between the time of narration and time of the story.[13] Does the narration take place prior to the events? Prophecy, for instance, recounts events prior to the time they take place. Or does the narration take place simultaneously with the events as they unfold? Or have the events of the narrative already taken place? The Gospel writers record events that have already taken place from a postresurrection perspective that influences their ideological point of view. For example, in John 2:22, after Jesus refers to the destruction of the temple of his body, the narrator reveals his temporal point of view: "After he was raised from the dead, his disciples remembered that he had said this; and they believed the scripture and the word that Jesus had spoken." The narrator's temporal stance not only provides a reason for the disciples' lack of percep-

13. Lanser, *Narrative Act*, 198.

tion—how could they know that Jesus was referring to the temple of his body?—but also provides a testimony to the significance of the events ("his disciples remembered" and "they believed the scripture").

Temporal point of view may also refer to the pace of the narration. A narrator may accent an ideological point of view by slowing down the narration or, conversely, may attenuate the importance of an event by glossing over it rapidly. In Revelation, the narrative pace lurches ahead, slows down, and then speeds up again. It lingers over some events and then speeds past others at a whirlwind pace. When the narrative slows down, the reader is to take special notice.

Psychological Point of View

The inner disposition, thoughts, and emotions of characters are the focus of psychological point of view. Some narrative critics refer to this aspect of point of view as *inside views*.[14] The omniscient narrator of Mark, for instance, reveals that the scribes were "*questioning in their hearts*, 'Why does this fellow speak in this way? It is blasphemy! Who can forgive sins but God alone?'" (Mark 2:6–7). Their interior monologue[15] voices a commonplace point of view—namely, that God alone forgives sins—which is the basis for their accusation of blasphemy. Jesus assumes the divine prerogative in pardoning sin. By providing an inward plunge into the scribes' thinking, the narrative heightens the clash of perspectives. Inside views reveal the conceptual world of the opponents and others, and develop and elaborate the extent and nature of the polarization between Jesus and the authorities. Through this conflict, a new, strange point of view emerges.

Ideological Point of View

Ideological point of view refers to the norms, values, beliefs, and general worldview of the narrator. The ideological perspective may be made explicit in the narrative, but often it is determined by looking at other aspects of point of view. The narrator's asides or inside views, or

14. E.g., Steven M. Sheeley, *Narrative Asides in Luke-Acts*, JSNTSup 72 (Sheffield: JSOT Press, 1992), 114–15; Robert M. Fowler, *Let the Reader Understand: Reader-Response Criticism and the Gospel of Mark* (Minneapolis: Fortress, 1991), 120–26; Wayne Booth also uses the term "inside views" in *The Rhetoric of Fiction*, 2nd ed. (Chicago: University of Chicago Press, 1983), 12–13, 163–65.

15. On interior monologues as a narrative device see Dorrit Cohn, *Transparent Minds: Narrative Modes for Presenting Consciousness in Fiction* (Princeton: Princeton University Press, 1978), chapter 2; Philip Sellew, "Interior Monologue as a Narrative Device in the Parables of Luke," *JBL* 111 (1992): 239–53.

the way characters are described, or the words and actions of characters help to determine ideological perspective. Some of the questions to consider are: What ideological point of view does the narrator want the reader to adopt? Why is one point of view acceptable and another defective? How is the reader to view reality differently after reading a narrative? How are points of view that are at odds with the narrator's ideological perspective made to seem strange? How does the narrator's ideological point of view illuminate the theme of a narrative, the plot development, and other aspects of narrative analysis?

5.3 A Reading of Point of View in Chopin's "Ripe Figs"

A short story by Kate Chopin, "Ripe Figs", illustrates the importance of point of view for narrative analysis. How can we know what her point of view is, and how does it contribute to the theme or main point of the story? Kate Chopin's story is cited in full with an accompanying commentary on point of view.

Ripe Figs

Maman-Nainaine said that when the figs were ripe Babette might go to visit her cousins down on the Bayou-Lafourche where the sugar cane grows. Not that the ripening of figs had the least thing to do with it, but that is the way Maman-Nainaine was.

It seemed to Babette a very long time to wait; for the leaves upon the trees were tender yet, and the figs were like little hard, green marbles.

But warm rains came along and plenty of strong sunshine, and though Maman-Nainaine was as patient as the statue of la Madone, and Babette as restless as a humming-bird, the first thing they both knew it was hot summertime. Every day Babette danced out to where the fig-trees were in a long line against the fence. She walked slowly beneath them, carefully peering between the gnarled, spreading branches. But each time she came disconsolate away again. What she saw there finally was something that made her sing and dance the whole long day.

When Maman-Nainaine sat down in her stately way to breakfast, the following morning, her muslin cap standing like an aureole about her white, placid face, Babette approached. She bore a dainty porcelain platter, which she set down before her godmother. It contained a dozen purple figs, fringed around with their rich, green leaves.

"Ah," said Maman-Nainaine arching her eyebrows, "how early the figs have ripened this year!"

"Oh," said Babette, "I think they have ripened very late."

> "Babette," continued Maman-Nainaine, as she peeled the very plumpest figs with her pointed silver fruit-knife, "you will carry my love to them all down on Bayou-Lafourche. And tell your Tante Frosine I shall look for her at Touissant—when the chrysanthemums are in bloom."

What is the point of view of this brief story? How does characterization contribute to point of view? What does the setting add to point of view? Does the rhetoric or narrator's style elaborate a point of view? And how does point of view develop and elaborate the theme of the story?

A third-person narrator who knows the thoughts and feelings of the characters tells the story. The narrator is outside—not within—the narrative, and she is omniscient; that is, she is able to determine the moods and feelings of the characters. She presents the characters through a combination of showing and telling, although showing is the primary mode of characterization. The point of view of the story is expressed in the usual ways: through a spatial stance to the narrative, a temporal perspective, words and phrases, thoughts and feelings, and through an ideological perspective.

The theme of this brief story is that growing up seems to take an interminably long time for the young whereas it happens far too quickly for the old. And like the development of succulent fruit and the blooming of beautiful flowers, aging—whether it is the young growing up or the mature getting old—is a beautiful process. Babette represents one point of view while Maman-Nainaine represents the opposite. But what is the ideological point of view of the narrator, and how can we determine it? Does the narrator agree with Babette's perspective, or does the narrative favor another point of view?

The narrative point of view is that youth's impatience with growing up needs to be tempered by the perspective of an older person. What seems to take a very long time—that is, maturation—occurs very quickly, and youth's perspective, although natural, needs to be counterbalanced by the perspective of the old. The narrator builds sympathy for both Babette and Maman-Nainaine. But Maman-Nainaine is the stable presence in the narrative and her point of view is given greater weight through her characterization. What textual features privilege Maman-Nainaine's point of view? How can we know that the narrator agrees with the godmother's perspective and that her perspective offsets Babette's? How do the various aspects of point of view support the ideological perspective?

The *spatial point of view* looks *at* the characters and their actions, not *with* them. First, we look at Maman-Nainaine, who says that Babette may visit her cousins when the figs ripen. Then we look at Babette's reaction to the development of the figs and her presentation of the platter of figs to her godmother. Only at this point do the characters speak in their own voice; they become subjects who express an opinion or a point of view. Finally, the narrative closes with the godmother's words; she says that she will visit Tante Frosine when the autumn flowers bloom. Spatially, Maman-Nainaine's point of view frames Babette's and provides a perspective from which to evaluate Babette's actions and speech. Babette's actions, however, make up the central portion of the narrative and the bulk of the narrative space. This suggests what is important: Babette's development as a character.

One of the most accessible aspects of point of view is the *phraseological plane,* or the point of view expressed in the words and phrases that the narrator selects for the characters as well as the narrator's own voice. What titles or epithets (i.e., descriptive phrases) does she use to develop characterization? When do the characters speak and what do they say?

The phraseological point of view develops two divergent points of view. The story begins in the narrator's own voice and develops the nature setting for Maman-Nainaine's and Babette's direct discourse. The narrator's voice emerges at two significant places in the narrative. (1) When Babette is told that she could see her cousins when the figs ripen, the narrator comments: "Not that the ripening of figs had the least thing to do with it, but that is the way Maman-Nainaine was." The disclaimer draws attention to itself and suggests that there is indeed a relationship between the ripening of figs and Babette's characterization. (2) The narrator also says, "It *seemed* to Babette a very long time to wait" (italics mine). The verb is significant, for what appears to be a long time for Babette may not actually be that long.

Significantly, the characters' direct discourse is delayed until after the exposition of the setting and their responses to the ripening of figs. In this climactic position of the narrative, Babette speaks eight words and her godmother speaks thirty-nine words. The economy of words suggests that what they do say is important for the narrative point of view. Both begin with one-syllable exclamations that summarize diverse points of view toward the ripening of figs. Maman-Nainaine says, "Ah," which expresses her surprise that the figs have ripened so early, while Babette says, "Oh," which expresses her disappointment that they are so late. The "how early" and "very late," the "ah" and "oh," establish the contours of the "debate," the two differing points of view.

The phraseological point of view is reinforced by the narrator's choice of words to describe the setting. As the title suggests, the setting is about the ripening of figs, and Chopin takes great care in her word-choice to describe the ripening process. In the springtime, the leaves of the trees are "tender yet," while in late summer they mature and develop "rich, green leaves." The figs are like "little hard, green marbles" that become "purple," plump fruit at maturity. The ripening of figs parallels Babette's "ripening." She is a "tender" young girl who develops into a "rich" or mature adolescent.

The *temporal point of view*, which refers to the pace of narration or the perspective in time of the narrated events, supports the ideological stance of the story. It is difficult to argue that the narrative pace either speeds up or slows down; the story is too brief to make a claim one way or the other. It is over almost before it begins. But even that is significant. In terms of the ideological point of view, aging or maturation occurs far more rapidly than the young can imagine. In a sense, it seems to be over almost before it begins. Thus a story that is this brief reinforces the rapidness of the maturation process.

The temporal framework of the narrative is the passage of seasons of the year. Spring rains yield to the hot days of summertime, and autumn, when the chrysanthemums are in bloom, rapidly approaches. The passage of seasons is a common metaphor in film and literature for aging. The major portion of the story focuses on the passage of time from spring to summer, when the young figs turn to plump, succulent fruit. This suggests what is important. It is not the passage of time from summer to fall, which is mentioned only briefly at the end, but the slow, seemingly long process (from Babette's perspective) of the ripening of figs.

The *psychological point of view* also supports the ideological perspective. Babette grows from a young, impatient girl to one who is more mature. The narrator's characterization focuses on the progressive changes in her moods, which range from disconsolation to dancing out to where the fig trees grow. When she finds mature figs, she sings and dances "the whole long day." Similar to her shifting moods, Babette develops from an impatient youngster who is "restless as a humming-bird" to a girl who bears a "dainty platter" of twelve plump, purple figs to her godmother. The grammar is suggestive of her development to comparative maturity, for she did not simply carry the platter of figs to Maman-Nainaine. Instead, "she *bore* a dainty porcelain platter" (italics mine).

By contrast, the psychological point of view of Maman-Nainaine is a portrait in patience. She is "as patient as the statue of la Madone," and sits down in "her stately way" at breakfast. The godmother wears a cap that stands—not sits, as we might expect—on her head like a halo ("aureole") around a venerated figure. There are no inside views of Maman-Nainaine's perspective; no inner thoughts or feelings are revealed. Yet the narrator's descriptive terms for her characterization (part of the phraseological point of view) provide a glimpse into her stable presence in the narrative. For instance, her face is described as "white, placid," like a statue, and she is as patient as a statue of the Virgin Mary. Her stately demeanor contrasts with Babette's impatience. Maturation occurs in its own time and is a process to be enjoyed—a point that is reinforced by Maman-Nainaine's enjoyment of the plump, purple figs.

5.4 Point of View in the New Testament

How is point of view expressed in a New Testament narrative? What is the ideological view that the narrator wants the reader to adopt? And how can we be certain that we are not reading our own perspectives into the text? One way—but certainly not the only way—is to examine the various planes on which point of view is expressed, and to ask how the narrator's perspective twists common, everyday points of view in such a way as to make them appear strange.

Phraseological Point of View

Phraseological point of view surfaces in names, titles, sobriquets (nicknames), epithets (descriptions), as well as in the speech of the narrator or a character. When and where characters speak and what they say is important. In John 6:42, for instance, the crowd asks this question: "Is not this Jesus, the son of Joseph, whose father and mother we know? How can he now[16] say, 'I have come down from heaven'?" A close reading of the question not only suggests a disparaging view toward Jesus but also reveals their inadequate view of revelation in general. The negative implies no indecisiveness on their part, for the rhetorical question expects an affirmative answer. Further, the usage of the pronoun, "this," creates distance and conveys disparagement.[17] Just as the elder son in Luke's parable of the Prodigal Son uses a disparaging "this" ("*this* son of yours") to establish a superior stance, the crowd uses "this" to underscore their superior stance. They also give authoritative expression to their point of view with the first person plural. "Is not *this* Jesus, the son of Joseph, whose parents *we know*?" The first person plural rules out any uncertainty on their part that Jesus' origins may be from above. Then they add a temporal marker, "now," to heighten the discrepancy between Jesus' claim and what they know. Thus their question implies the following tone and point of view: "How can *this* Jesus, whose origins *we are certain of, now* claim that he comes down from heaven?" Jesus' family comes from Nazareth; how can he be from above? Their disap-

16. Some manuscripts have "how then" instead of "how now."

17. Cf. Raymond E. Brown, *The Gospel according to John*, 2 vols., AB 29–29A (Garden City, N.Y.: Doubleday, 1966–1970), 1:270: "There is an element of disparagement in this pronoun."

proval, however, reveals a deeper ideological perspective: How is it possible for the divine to be revealed in the ordinary, the everyday, and the familiar? The point of view of the Johannine narrator is not only that the divine *is* revealed in the everyday but that the divine is *only* made known in the everyday. The prologue clarifies this viewpoint: "And the word became flesh and lived among us, and we have seen his glory, the glory as of a father's only son, full of grace and truth" (John 1:14). The divine glory is in the flesh.

The religious authorities of John 9 rely on the first person plural and the disparaging "this" to assert that Jesus is "a sinner" and not "from God."

> *We know* that *this man* is a sinner. (9:24)
>
> *We know* that God has spoken to Moses, but as for *this man, we do not know* where he comes from. (9:29)

Their point of view expresses at the level of words and phrases a deeper, more profound ideological perspective. They contend that human judgment, human criteria, and a human point of view are adequate and accurate lenses through which to judge the workings of God in this world. The Gospel sets out to demolish this deficient perspective. In John 7:24 and 8:15, Jesus voices the correct ideological point of view of the Gospel:

> Do not judge by appearances, but judge with right judgment. (7:24)
>
> You judge by human standards;[18] I judge no one. (8:15)

The plot conflict surfaces in the two points of view expressed here. On the one hand, appearance judgment, or evaluation according to human standards, is a form of exegesis that sees at a surface level and misses the deeper meaning of Jesus' words and actions. This view resorts to first plurals, disparaging pronouns, as well as other rhetorical forms to signal overconfidence in human judgment. Appearance judgment assumes that it knows more than it does. But it is unknowing in its insistence on knowing. It is unable to see the paradox of the incarnation. Rather than seeing divine glory in the flesh, appearance judgment sees only flesh. Judgment according to the flesh concludes that Jesus is a man from Nazareth but is not a man from above. This surface view is not the province of a single group in the Gospel. All—disciples, crowds, and religious authorities—are capable of falling victim to appearance judgment.

18. *Kata tēn sarka* (according to the flesh).

The ideological point of view of Mark's Gospel also appears in a saying of Jesus.[19] When Jesus asks the disciples who people say that he is, Peter confesses that he is the Messiah. After making that bold confession, however, he rebukes Jesus for suggesting that he must suffer and die. Jesus, in turn, rebukes Peter with words that summarize the ideological point of view of the Gospel: "Get behind me Satan! For you think not the things of God but [you think] in human terms" (Mark 8:33, author's translation). Similarly to the Fourth Gospel's two ways of judging—appearance judgment and right judgment—the Markan characters either "think the things of God" or "think in human terms," or in the case of the disciples, they waver between the two points of view, sometimes thinking rightly while at other times thinking in human terms.[20]

Antithetical and paradoxical sayings of Jesus express the two ways of thinking. Gentile rulers, for instance, think in human terms. They "lord it over" others and "their great ones are tyrants over them" (Mark 10:42). Jesus' way of thinking turns this commonplace point of view upside down. "Whoever wishes to become great among you [the disciples] must be your servant, and whoever wishes to be first among you must be slave of all" (Mark 10:43–44). Other antithetical sayings heighten the contrast between thinking in human terms and thinking in divine terms. The first are last, the last first; the exalted are humbled, the humble exalted; saving life means losing life; losing life results in saving life.

Characters—often at opposite ends of the status hierarchy—represent the two ways of thinking. The scribes love to walk around in long robes and to be greeted with respect in the marketplaces. They seek places of honor at banquets and the best seats in the synagogues. Their desire for respect and honor from others is a human way of thinking. The Pharisees resort to human ways of thinking when they nullify God's command to honor their mother and father by depriving their aging parents of needed support (Mark 7:9–13). The poor widow, on the other hand, represents God's way of thinking. While others donate to the treasury out of a poverty of abundance, she gives out of her abundance of poverty. Similarly, the Syrophoenician woman is unwavering in her belief that Jesus can heal her demon-possessed daughter. She thinks the things of God. A woman who prepares Jesus for burial by anointing him with a costly ointment of nard thinks in divine terms. Those who object, on the other hand, see only waste. They think in human terms. The centurion who recognizes God at work in the cross thinks the things of God. The

19. Norman R. Petersen, "'Point of View' in Mark's Narrative," *Semeia* 12 (1978): 97–121. Petersen's findings are widely accepted among narrative critics. See, for example, Rhoads, Dewey, and Michie, *Mark as Story*, 44–45; Rhoads, *Reading Mark*, chapter 3. The authors of *Mark as Story* also call the ideological point of view "standards of judgment."

20. Rhoads, Dewey, and Michie, *Mark as Story*, 45, 101.

passersby, chief priests, and scribes mock Jesus and see only failure. They think in human terms.

The disciples, however, vacillate between thinking in human terms and thinking in divine terms. Peter represents correct thinking when he says that he has left everything to follow Jesus, but then slips back into a human way of thinking when he rejects the notion of a suffering Messiah. On the way to Jerusalem the disciples argue who is the greatest, and James and John request the places of honor next to Jesus when he enters into his glory. They think in human terms.

Phraseological point of view is found in the narrator's and characters' use of names, titles, epithets, and sobriquets. Changes in names generally signal an awakening or a new perspective. When Mary Magdalene does not recognize Jesus, she is called "woman." But at the moment of recognition her name becomes "Mary" (John 20:15, 16). When Peter falls asleep in the garden of Gethsemane, he is called by his prediscipleship name. To the narrator he is "Peter," but to Jesus he is only "Simon" (Mark 14:33, 37). The prediscipleship name corresponds to the ideological perspective of the narrative: "the spirit indeed is willing, but the flesh is weak" (Mark 14:38). Similarly, Jesus resorts to Peter's prediscipleship name in John 21. The patronymic recalls their first meeting when Jesus called him "Simon son of John" (John 1:42). Peter begins all over again as a disciple. In his initial call he proved to be overzealous and self-willed: following Jesus on his own terms (John 13:36–38), severing Malchus's right ear (18:10), and denying Jesus (18:15–18, 25–27). In his second "call," the raw, self-determined Peter is ready to be a disciple and follow Jesus (21:15–17).

Overfull names also signal a distinctive ideological perspective. In Revelation, God is not simply called God; rather, overfull, pleonastic descriptions accentuate God's full nature or expansive character. For John of the Apocalypse, God's reach is limitless and thus names and descriptions that accentuate God's unlimited nature are used: "The one seated on the throne," or the one "who is and who was and who is to come," or "the Alpha and Omega," or "the Lord God the Almighty."

A narrator establishes an ideological perspective by the names or titles that characters apply to Jesus. In Mark, for instance, everyone calls Jesus "teacher"—disciples, suppliants, and religious authorities.[21] But the narrator of Matthew restricts who calls Jesus "teacher." Scribes, Pharisees, Sadducees, and the rich young man, among others, call him teacher, but the disciples, potential disciples, and suppliants call him "Lord." In the stilling of the storm, the disciples call Jesus "teacher" in Mark,

21. The following examples are taken from Luke Timothy Johnson, *The Writings of the New Testament: An Interpretation* (rev. ed., Minneapolis: Fortress, 1999), 195.

but in Matthew he is called "Lord."[22] In Mark's transfiguration, Peter calls Jesus "Rabbi," but in Matthew he calls him "Lord." The suppliants who come to Jesus in faith—a leper, a centurion, the blind, a Canaanite woman, and a father whose son is an epileptic—call him "Lord," which is a form of address that is restricted to those who follow, or desire to follow, or exhibit faith in Jesus.[23] For others, Jesus is simply one among many teachers, a respected rabbi but not "Lord." An exception proves the rule, for one disciple never calls Jesus "Lord."[24] At the Last Supper Jesus predicts that one of them will betray him, and all "began to say to him one after another, 'Surely not I, Lord?'" Judas, however, says "Surely not I, Rabbi?" (Matt. 26:22, 25). In the garden, Judas's greeting is "Rabbi!" (Matt. 26:49).

Epithets develop and elaborate an ideological perspective. In Mark's account of the stilling of the storm, Jesus rebukes the disciples with a two-step question: "Why are you afraid? Have you still no faith?" (Mark 4:40). But in Matt. 8:26 the question becomes "why are you afraid, you of little faith?" When the winds blow and the sea billows, Peter is a "[man] of little faith" (Matt. 14:31). And when the disciples become anxious about what they will wear or what they will eat or drink, they are people of "little faith" (Matt. 6:25–34). For the narrator of Matthew, the disciples can have "little faith"—a faith that needs to be strengthened in times of distress or an inadequate faith that needs release from crippling doubt—but they are not without faith.[25]

The narrator of Revelation uses two points of view to forge a new point of view. What is heard reinterprets what is seen, and vice versa. "What is heard, the 'voice,' represents the inner reality, the spirit; what is seen, the 'appearance,' represents the outward, the flesh."[26] A celebrated example of hearing and seeing is the poignant scene in the heavenly throne room when the slaughtered yet risen Lamb appears. A voice announces the traditional messianic expectation: "See, the Lion of the tribe of Judah, the root of David, has conquered, so that he can open the scroll and its seven seals" (Rev. 5:5). This is what is heard. Yet John does not see a

22. The vocative, *kyrie*, is used in the examples cited here. Günther Bornkamm, "The Stilling of the Storm," in *Tradition and Interpretation in Matthew*, ed. Günther Bornkamm et al. (Philadelphia: Westminster, 1963), 52–57 at 55, has shown that the vocative is "a divine predicate of majesty" in this context.

23. Johnson, *Writings*, 195.

24. Ibid.

25. Cf. Jack Dean Kingsbury, *Matthew as Story*, 2nd ed. (Minneapolis: Fortress, 1988), 134–35.

26. John Sweet, *Revelation*, TPINTC (Philadelphia: Trinity Press International, 1990), 125. On hearing and seeing in Revelation see Sweet, *Revelation*, 125–27; Caird, *Revelation*, 73; James L. Resseguie, *Revelation Unsealed: A Narrative Critical Approach to John's Apocalypse*, BIS 32 (Leiden: Brill, 1998), 33–37.

lion; rather he sees a slaughtered yet risen Lamb (5:6). The seeing interprets the hearing. The familiar expectation of a conquering Messiah is defamiliarized: God's victory is achieved through the death and resurrection of Jesus. What is seen not only interprets the hearing; the hearing reinterprets what is seen. After the presentation of the Lamb (what is seen), the four living creatures and the twenty-four elders sing a new song (what is heard): "You are worthy to take the scroll and to open its seals, for you were slaughtered and by your blood you ransomed for God saints from every tribe and language and people and nation; you have made them to be a kingdom and priests serving our God, and they will reign on earth" (Rev 5:9–10). At the level of words and phrases, hearing and seeing forge a new, unjaded ideological perspective.

A phraseological point of view may look at the same event from two different angles. In Rev. 7, for example, the narrator *hears* the number of those who were sealed—the symbolic number 144,000. But when he *looks,* he sees a "great multitude that no one could count, from every nation, from all tribes and peoples and languages, standing before the throne" (7:9). These are not two separate groups as some contend,[27] but the same group presented from two different angles. The 144,000 is the inner reality—the true Israel of God—whereas the countless multitude is the outward reality. All of God's people—both Jew and Gentile—make up the new Israel.

In some instances, the outer reality is deceptive and requires the hearing to reveal the inner reality. The beast from the land, for example, appears with two horns like a lamb. The hearing, however, clarifies its true nature: "It spoke like a dragon" (Rev. 13:11). In Rev. 17 John is "greatly amazed" at the beguiling appearance of the whore of Babylon. Seeing alone is inadequate, so the angel tells him about the mystery of the woman. In both examples, the phraseological point of view reveals a deeper ideological perspective. Evil appears good; outward appearance may mask inward reality.

Narrative commentary is another way the narrator persuades the reader to adopt his or her point of view. In the New Testament, the narrator's annotations are found in asides to the reader, comments by the narrator that explain customs, clarify events, or provide other commentary on the story. This information is addressed to the reader and is not available to some or all of the characters in the story.[28] A break in the syntax (an *anacoluthon,* for instance), an explanatory clause (introduced by "for"), an apostrophe (a direct address to an absent person),

27. For example, Robert H. Mounce, *The Book of Revelation*, NICNT, rev. ed. (Grand Rapids: Eerdmans, 1998), 161–62.

28. Rhoads, Dewey, and Michie, *Mark as Story*, 41.

a gloss on a character's disposition, and an annotation on a narrative event are kinds of asides.

Matthew's narrator uses asides to place the disciples in a more favorable light than in Mark. In a discussion of the yeast of the Pharisees, the Markan narrator does not say that the disciples understood Jesus' teaching. Instead, the narrative ends with a query: "Do you not yet understand?" (Mark 8:21). In Matthew, however, an aside places the disciples in a more favorable light. "Then they understood that he had not told them to beware of the yeast of bread, but of the teaching of the Pharisees and Sadducees" (Matt. 16:12). At the conclusion of the walking on the water, Matthew adds a comment not found in Mark: "And those in the boat worshiped him, saying, 'Truly you are the Son of God.'" (Matt. 14:33). Mark, on the other hand, provides an explanatory aside: "for they did not understand about the loaves, but their hearts were hardened" (Mark 6:52). When Peter fails at Gethsemane in Mark, he is called by his prediscipleship name, "Simon." In Matthew, however, his prediscipleship name is omitted (Matt. 26:40).

A narrator's parenthetical comment may summarize a perspective that deforms a routine, formulaic point of view. When Jesus declares that what goes inside from the outside cannot defile a person, the Markan narrator breaks the narrative syntax with an anacoluthon: "Thus he declared all foods clean" (Mark 7:19). The aside accents a countercultural point of view that clashes with a commonplace perspective among the religious elite, whose point of view is also explained by a narrative aside. "For the Pharisees, and all the Jews, do not eat unless they thoroughly wash their hands, thus observing the tradition of the elders; and they do not eat anything from the market unless they wash it; and there are also many other traditions that they observe, the washing of cups, pots, and bronze kettles" (Mark 7:3). The two parenthetical asides italicize two divergent points of view. One point of view is made strange while the other is made more familiar.

A narrative aside may draw attention to an event of unprecedented importance. In Mark 13:14, the narrator interrupts what Jesus says about the "desolating sacrilege" with an apostrophe: "let the reader understand." Just as Jesus underlines his *words* with markers such as "listen" (Mark 4:3), or "let anyone with ears to hear listen" (4:9), or "listen to me, all of you, and understand" (7:14), the Markan narrator underlines an *event* that is out of the ordinary. The reader is not simply to be aware of an imminent crisis but is to "understand" its underlying significance in the same way that the disciples are to listen with understanding. The aside jolts the reader out of the nullity of the routine.

What the narrator includes or omits establishes on a phraseological plane an ideological perspective. The narrator of Matt. 1–2 argues that everything—the good and the bad—is part of God's overall design for the characters. Nothing is happenstance. All is by design. Events take place because they fulfill Scripture, or because an angel directs the characters, or because a supernatural event, such as a star or a dream, guides the characters. Joseph plans to divorce Mary, but an angel intervenes and tells him to take her as his wife. The child to be born fulfills Scripture: "Look, the virgin shall conceive and bear a son, and they shall name him Emmanuel" (Matt. 1:23). A star guides the wise men from the East (2:2). Scripture foretells the birthplace of the Messiah (2:5–6). A dream directs the wise men not to return to Herod (2:12). Joseph is told in a dream to flee from Bethlehem to Egypt (2:13), which also fulfills another scripture (2:15). The massacre of children in the region of Bethlehem fulfills a prophecy spoken by Jeremiah (2:18). An angel directs Joseph to return to Israel upon Herod's death (2:19). Joseph is warned in a dream not to go to Judea (2:22). Instead, he settles in Nazareth, which completes yet another scripture (2:23). The string of predicted and guided events accentuates the narrative's ideological point of view. Nothing unexpected and nothing by human design can possibly thwart God's plan of salvation.

Spatial Point of View

In Luke's parable of the Tax Collector and the Pharisee, the spatial positioning of characters parallels two contrasting ideological perspectives. We look at both characters and overhear their speech. The Pharisee stands "by himself"[29] in the temple while the tax collector stands "far off." The physical posture of the tax collector parallels his inner, spiritual state. He "would not even look up to heaven" but instead beat his breast (Luke 18:13). Similarly, the physical posture of the Pharisee corresponds to his spiritual state. He stands by himself, distancing himself from everyone else, including God. The characters' speech also corresponds to their physical demeanor. The Pharisee fills his prayer with first person singulars with the self as the subject of his prayer. "God, *I* thank you that *I* am not like other people: thieves, rogues, adulterers, or even like this tax collector. *I* fast twice a week: *I* give a tenth of all *my* income" (18:11–12). The tax collector, on the other hand, places God at the center of his prayer. "God, be merciful to me, a sinner" (18:13). The one who stands far off, presuming nothing, goes home justified; the one who stands by himself, presuming everything, receives nothing. Their

29. It is possible to read the Greek as "standing, he prayed these things *to himself*." This is less likely in view of the parallel with the tax collector who is "standing *far off*." See Green, *Luke*, 648.

respective spatial stances are reversed. The exalted are humbled and the humbled exalted (18:14).

A shifting spatial stance may catch the reader by surprise—a type of entrapment that forces the reader to slow down and ponder what is being said. In Luke 17:7–10, the reader initially adopts the perspective of a slave-owner and then suddenly learns that he or she is the slave. Jesus asks the apostles "who among *you* would say to *your* slave" who has worked all day in the fields to come and sit at table as the master serves the slave? The normal social script requires the slave to prepare the supper for the master—not the other way around.[30] Further, the slave is not commended for working the entire day in the fields and afterward preparing the evening meal. The spatial stance compels the reader to identify with the perspective of a slave-owner and to conclude that it is risible to expect the master to serve the slave or for the master to thank the slave for doing only what is expected. Once the reader's identification with the master is certain, the parable switches perspective. "So *you* also, when *you* have done all that you were ordered to do, say, 'We are worthless slaves; we have done only what we ought to have done!'" (Luke 17:10).

A progressive narrowing of the spatial stance focuses attention on what is at the center. In the raising of Lazarus, the spatial stance progressively narrows from Judea (John 11:1–16), to Bethany (11:17–37), to the tomb (11:38–44). The tomb is the focal center for a defamiliarized point of view. Similarly, the temple is the focal and ideological center for a new point of view in John 2:11–22. The spatial stance once again progressively narrows from Galilee to Judea to Jerusalem to the temple, where Jesus redefines the temple as person, not place.

In Revelation, the narrator alternates between an *above* perspective and a *below* perspective. The differing spatial stances provide two angles from which to view the same event. A war between Michael and his angels and the great dragon "called the Devil and Satan" and his angels is described from an above point of view (Rev. 12:7–9). The devil is defeated and thrown down to earth to make war upon the woman and her offspring. The below point of view, however, offers another interpretation of this battle. Satan's defeat is by "the blood of the Lamb and by the word of [the saints'] testimony" (Rev. 12:10–12). Christ's death on the cross conquers Satan and thus the below point of view reinterprets the above perspective. But the above point of view also reinterprets the below perspective. Jesus' death on the cross is a cosmic battle waged between God and Satan. The spatial point of view portrays the paradoxical point

30. In one parable in Luke the normal social script is violated. In Luke 12:35–38, the master does serve the faithful slaves.

of view of Revelation: the great cosmic battle of evil's defeat occurs in Christ's death on the cross.

The spatial center of a narrative can correspond to the ideological or theological center. In Rev. 4 and 5 concentric circles underline the sublime unity and balanced harmony of a universe that recognizes God as the center of all things. The circles widen as the entire universe is caught up in song and adoration to the one who sits on the throne. On each side of the throne are four living creatures who sing without pause, "holy, holy, holy" (Rev. 4:8). The circle expands to include the twenty-four elders, who add an act of obeisance—casting their crowns—to the hymns of praise (Rev. 4:10–11). The circle widens further to include myriads and myriads and thousands and thousands of angels who sing "with full voice" (Rev. 5:11–12). Finally, the circle expands to include "every creature in heaven and on earth and under the earth and in the sea" who praise the one seated on the throne and the Lamb (Rev. 5:13). The spatial point of view accents the ideological perspective. God brings order and harmony to a creation whose natural and spontaneous response to the numinous is to worship.[31]

Temporal Point of View

A temporal point of view defines the relationship between the narrator and the text in terms of time and the pace of the narration.

Paul's temporal point of view shapes his narrative theology or ideological point of view. The crucifixion and resurrection, death and life, provide the structure for a theology of antitheses and paradoxes: then and now, old creation and new creation, flesh and spirit, already and not yet, appearance and reality (e.g., weak yet strong).[32] The temporal perspective of two ages enlarges the antithetical point of view. The old self dies (crucifixion) and the new self rises (resurrection); the old creation passes away (crucifixion) and the new creation is born (resurrection). The following passages illustrate the tension between this age and the new age:

> Live by the Spirit, I say,
> and do not gratify the desires of the flesh.
>
> (Gal. 5:16)

31. Richard Bauckham, *The Theology of the Book of Revelation*, NTT (Cambridge: Cambridge University Press, 1993), 32–33.

32. I owe this insight to Leonard L. Thompson, *Introducing Biblical Literature: A More Fantastic Country* (Englewood Cliffs, N.J.: Prentice-Hall, 1978), 285.

We have been buried with him by baptism into death, so that,
just as Christ was raised from the dead by the glory of the Father, so
we too might walk in newness of life.

(Rom. 6:4)

You . . . were slaves of sin.
But now . . . you have been freed from sin.

(Rom. 6:20, 22)

Even when we were dead through our trespasses,
[God] made us alive together with Christ.

(Eph. 2:5)

Similarly, Luke's temporal point of view of "now" and "then" is the structural outline for his theology of reversals. Those who fare well now will fare ill in the eschaton, while those who are oppressed now will receive their reward in the kingdom of God. Matthew's beatitudes (Matt. 5:3–12) are not neatly paired with woes, but Luke's beatitudes have corresponding woes—a pairing that is both temporal and ideological. The temporal perspective is seen in the refrain, "now" and "will be." The ideological perspective is expressed in the reversal of present status and future status in the kingdom.

Blessed are you who are poor, for yours is the kingdom of God.
But woe to you who are rich, for you *have received* your consolation.
Blessed are you who are hungry *now*, for you *will be filled*.
Woe to you who are full *now*, for you *will be hungry*."
Blessed are you who weep *now*, for you *will laugh*.
Woe to you who are laughing *now*, for you *will mourn and weep*.
Blessed are you when people hate you.
Woe to you when all speak well of you.

(Luke 6: 20–26)

The hearer/reader's current status is reversed in the future. The staid, familiar perspective is that the rich and the full are better off—more blessed—than those who are poor and are hungry (cf. Deut. 28). Yet this natural point of view is turned on its head, and contrary to expectations, the poor and hungry are blessed while the well-off are cursed. Joel Green describes the defamiliarizing effect of Luke's beatitudes: "An unconventionalized understanding of the world . . . is designed to jolt [Jesus'] audience into new perceptions of God's redemptive aim."[33] A similar point of view surfaces in Mary's song (Luke 1:46–55).

33. Green, *Luke*, 265–66.

He has shown strength with his arm;
he has scattered the proud in the thoughts of their hearts.
He has brought down the powerful from their thrones,
and lifted up the lowly;
he has filled the hungry with good things,
and sent the rich away empty.

(1:51–53)

The proud, the powerful, and the rich are brought down and left empty while the lowly and hungry are lifted up and sated. So certain is the reversal of status that the verbs are placed in a past tense, the aorist.[34] Even more dramatic is the temporal perspective in the parable of the Rich Man and Lazarus (16:19–31). The contrasts in this life are reversed in the next life. The rich man is clothed in purple and fine linen while Lazarus is clothed with sores; he feasts while Lazarus starves; he receives good things while Lazarus receives evil things. Lazarus is poor while the rich man has no material needs. But the temporal and spatial perspectives are reversed, underscoring the ideological perspective. Angels carry Lazarus away to Abraham's bosom while the rich man descends to Hades. Lazarus is comforted; the rich man is in agony. Lazarus receives his consolation in the next life; the rich man has already received his consolation. This "topos of reversal" is Luke's way of "replacing common representations of the world with a new one."[35]

In the Gospel of John, the temporal pacing comes to an abrupt halt at the passion, death, and resurrection to focus the reader's complete attention on an ideological perspective: the "lifting up" of Jesus. Alan Culpepper notes that "the 'speed' of the narrative reduces steadily . . . until it virtually grinds to a halt at the climactic day."[36] Whereas the first twelve chapters of John span approximately two and a half years or two Passovers (2:13; 6:4), John 12–20 covers a two-week period. Chapters 13–19 focus even more narrowly upon a mere twenty-four hours.[37] As the narrative pace grinds to a halt, the all-important "hour," which is anticipated in 2:4, 7:30, and 8:20, is enlarged in this section: "Now before the festival of the Passover, Jesus knew that his *hour* had come to depart from this world and go to the Father" (John 13:1). Spatial and temporal points of view merge to develop the narrator's ideological view that Jesus' death also constitutes his exaltation. The spatial perspective is amplified by a double entendre involving the verb "to lift up" (*hypsoō*; 3:14, 8:28, 12:32). Jesus is lifted up on a stake, i.e., the cross. This is

34. See Green, *Luke*, 98–101.

35. "Topos of reversal" is Green's term. See *Luke*, 264–67 at 265.

36. R. Alan Culpepper, *Anatomy of the Fourth Gospel: A Study in Literary Design* (Philadelphia: Fortress, 1983), 72.

37. Ibid.

one meaning of "lift up." But the other meaning of "lift up"—"exaltation"—is also intended (cf. 7:39; 11:4). The degradation on the cross is paradoxically Jesus' enthronement as "King of the Jews." The temporal and spatial points of view merge for a proper understanding of the cross in John. Gail O'Day explains the narrative point of view: "The lifting up is incomplete without the accompanying exaltation, but similarly, and perhaps most importantly, there is no exaltation unless there is the physical lifting up on the cross."[38]

In Matt. 27:52–53 the temporal point of view causes considerable consternation for readers of Matthew and commentators alike:[39] "The tombs also were opened, and many bodies of the saints who had fallen asleep were raised. After his resurrection they came out of the tombs and entered the holy city and appeared to many." Is this an event that happens at Jesus' resurrection? Is it a future, apocalyptic event? Is it fiction—theology in the guise of history? Kenneth Waters argues that the raising of the saints does not refer to an event in Matthew's past but to the general resurrection at the end of time. The "holy city" is not the literal Jerusalem but the figurative Jerusalem of Hebrews and Rev. 21, and the resurrected persons are analogous to the 144,000 in Rev. 7. Although the events are future, they are described in Matthew in a past tense—a historicized future. "The historic past [is] an envelope for the apocalyptic future."[40] In this instance, a proper understanding of temporal point of view may help resolve the ambiguities of a puzzling passage.

In Revelation the temporal point of view and narrative pacing reflect the "soon but not yet" ideological point of view of the writer.[41] The Apocalypse prepares the reader for "what must soon take place" (Rev. 1:1). Events on earth lurch forward at a breathless, unrelenting pace: seven seals unfold, seven trumpets blow, and seven bowls are poured out on the earth. Yet, even as events get into full swing with a cadence of disaster, time slows down. The souls under the altar ask "how long" before they are vindicated, and just as everything seems to be wrapping up, they are jolted into reality and told "to rest a little longer" (Rev. 6:10–11). Events speed ahead and then slow down and then speed ahead again. Although "soon" seems to be just around the corner, it is delayed with repeated calls to "hold fast" (Rev. 2:25, 3:11) or with warnings to remain clothed and stay awake (Rev. 16:15).

38. Gail O'Day, *Revelation in the Fourth Gospel: Narrative Mode and Theological Claim* (Philadelphia: Fortress, 1986), 111.

39. See Kenneth L. Waters Sr., "Matthew 27:52–53 as Apocalyptic Apostrophe: Temporal-Spatial Collapse in the Gospel of Matthew," *JBL* 122 (2003): 489–515.

40. Ibid., 505.

41. For these observations I rely upon Harry O. Maier, *Apocalypse Recalled: The Book of Revelation after Christendom* (Minneapolis: Fortress, 2002), chapter 5.

The narrative pacing reflects this frantic tempo. Some events are glossed over, barely mentioned, while other events are lengthened and thickened with repetitive details. The retardation of the narrative pace calls attention to the most important events.[42] It is not the locusts or the two hundred million that are important; the narrative speeds over these events without a second thought. Rather, the narrative slows down to linger on the close-ups of the throne-room scene in chapters 4 and 5, the 144,000 in chapter 7, the judgment of the whore of Babylon in chapters 17–18, and the new Jerusalem in chapters 21–22, among others. These are the events worthy of notice—not the gloom-and-doom passages that are narrated with breathless alacrity.

Psychological Point of View

Psychological point of view looks at the inner disposition, thoughts, and emotions of a character—also called *inside views* by narrative critics. In the Gospels, the omniscient narrator knows the thoughts and views of characters that are hidden from others. Only Jesus, like the narrator, knows what others think and feel.

Inside views enable the reader to understand the motivations and intentions of the antagonists in the Gospels. In Mark 2:5–8 Jesus perceives "in his spirit" that the scribes are questioning "in their hearts" why Jesus blasphemously declares the paralytic forgiven of his sins. The psychological point of view sharpens the divergent perspectives and makes strange the point of view of the religious leaders. Without the scribes' inside view the healing miracle stands naked: a healing without understanding. There are three parts to the deformation of the scribes' commonplace point of view: (1) The old perspective is voiced as an interior objection to something Jesus does. The scribes question in their hearts why Jesus claims a divine prerogative by forgiving the paralytic of his sins. (2) Jesus reframes the question. "Which is easier, to say to the paralytic, 'Your sins are forgiven,' or to say, 'Stand up and take your mat and walk'?" (Mark 2:9). (3) A new point of view emerges that questions the religious assumptions of a conformist culture. A prerogative claimed only in heaven is now present here on earth. The Son of Man has the "authority" to forgive sins on earth.

In Luke 7:36–50, an interior monologue brings to the forefront an everyday, yet deficient, point of view. When a woman "in the city, who was a sinner," washes and anoints Jesus' feet, Simon the Pharisee voices within himself a commonplace perspective of the dominant culture: "If this man were a prophet, he would have known who and what kind of

42. Ibid., 157.

woman this is who is touching him—that she is a sinner" (Luke 7:39). Jesus responds with a parable that deforms everyday perspectives. A creditor cancels the debts of one debtor who owes five hundred denarii and another debtor who owes fifty. "Which of them," Jesus asks, "will love him more?" Simon responds with the obvious: the one whose debt was greater has the greater love. Whereas Simon saw only the violation of cultural norms and the diminished authority of Jesus, Jesus saw a woman who was grateful that her sins were forgiven. Without this inside view, the narrative stands naked: an action without perspective. With the inside view an old point of view is made strange and a new view is made to seem obvious.

In the raising of Lazarus (John 11), the psychological point of view brings pathos to a narrative that begins dispassionately with Jesus' initial delay to save his friend. Jesus was "glad" that he was not there when Lazarus died. Yet, as he approaches the tomb, the pathos increases with an unprecedented display of inside views. At the weeping of Mary and others Jesus "was greatly disturbed in spirit and deeply moved" (11:33), and upon arriving at the tomb he "began to weep" (11:35). Again Jesus is "greatly disturbed in himself" before he raises Lazarus (11:38, author's translation). In a Gospel that does not readily display Jesus' inner state, the interior views heighten the conflict between a redoubtable opponent—death—and Jesus. The inward progression to Jesus' inner self parallels his outward advance on the tomb. As the tomb looms large and the enemy's grasp on his friend is certain, Jesus' anger intensifies—perhaps at the lack of faith by the mourners,[43] or the destructive power of Satan and death.[44] Even his own impending death may be the occasion for his disturbed state.[45] Whatever may be the explanation for Jesus' distress, the psychological point of view amplifies the ideological confrontation between Jesus and the enemy, death.

In Mark 3:5, the inward plunge into Jesus' emotions heightens the ideological crisis. Not only does he feel "anger"; he is "grieved at [the Pharisees'] hardness of heart." Their hard heart is a perceptible lack of insight—a point of view that blinds them to another, strange point of view. "Hardness of heart," however, is not a psychological point of view

43. So Rudolf Schnackenburg, *The Gospel according to St. John*, 3 vols. (New York; Crossroad, 1980–1990), 2:335–36; Rudolf Bultmann, *The Gospel of John: A Commentary*, trans. G. R. Beasley-Murray (Philadelphia: Westminster, 1971), 406; R. H. Lightfoot, *St. John's Gospel: A Commentary* (Oxford: Clarendon, 1956), 229; Thomas L. Brodie, *The Gospel according to John: A Literary and Theological Commentary* (New York: Oxford University Press, 1993), 395.

44. Brown, *John*, 1:435.

45. So Dorothy A. Lee, *The Symbolic Narratives of the Fourth Gospel: The Interplay of Form and Meaning* (Sheffield: JSOT Press, 1994), 211–12; Culpepper, *Anatomy*, 111; Barnabas Lindars, *The Gospel of John*, NBC (London: Oliphants, 1972), 398.

limited to the religious leaders. In Mark, the disciples reveal their own hard heart—a dulled, narcotized perspective that blinds them to the significance of the feeding of the five thousand (6:52; also 8:17).

In Mark 5:27–30 the entire narrative turns on a succession of inside views that elaborate a stigmatized woman's thoughts and develop Jesus' inner consciousness. The first half of the narrative is surreptitious until what happens is publicly revealed. Initially an interior monologue establishes the hemorrhaging woman's confidence that Jesus can make her well: "If I but touch his clothes, I will be made well" (Mark 5:28).[46] An inside view then confirms that she was healed: "She felt in her body that she was healed of her disease" (5:29). Finally, an inside view reveals what happened to Jesus. "Immediately [he was] aware that power had gone forth from him" (5:30). The woman knows something that Jesus does not know (she was healed). Jesus knows something the woman does not know (power went out from him). And the disciples and crowd know nothing of what happened. What is achieved in this series of inside views? The psychological point of view confirms the healing in ways that the onlookers could not possibly know. More important, an ideological point of view emerges—for it is not her bold act of touching his cloak that healed her. Rather it is her faith that made her well: "Daughter, your faith has made you well; go in peace and be healed of your disease" (5:34). The psychological point of view confirms a healing; the ideological point of view confirms the cause of the healing.

5.5 A Reading of Point of View in Luke 10:25–37

A close reading of the parable of the Good Samaritan will highlight the value of all four planes of point of view for narrative analysis. The *spatial point of view* in Luke's parable shifts from one character to another. First we look at the wounded man, then at the priest and Levite, and finally at the Samaritan. The glance at the Samaritan, however, lingers for a long time, and the spatial stance shifts from looking *at* the Samaritan to looking *with* him. He is the only one in the parable who speaks, and thus the only one who emerges as a subject in his own right. The others remain objects that are either given aid or, in the case of the priest and Levite, refuse to give aid.[47] Ironically, the ones with a voice in Israelite society—the first two travelers—are speechless in the parable while

46. Matthew 9:21 makes explicit that the woman said this "to herself."

47. Charles Hedrick, *Parables as Poetic Fictions: The Creative Voice of Jesus* (Peabody, Mass.: Hendrickson, 1994), 111, argues incorrectly that "the auditor/reader sees the story and experiences it alongside the injured man." The injured man, like the priest and Levite, is an object in the parable—unlike the Samaritan.

the one who lacks a voice in Israelite society—the Samaritan—speaks. Speech and silence in the parable are similar to van Gogh's rendition of the priest and Levite as small, insignificant persons in contrast to the Samaritan, who is painted bigger than life. The Samaritan's first words, spoken to the innkeeper, broaden the cycle of care and concern to involve others in the injured man's recovery: "Take care of him" (10:35a). But the Samaritan expects neither the innkeeper nor the rescued man to repay the cost of care. Instead he offers to pay for the debt in full—whatever the cost: "And when I come back, I will repay you whatever more you spend" (10:35b). Speech and actions blend seamlessly to define what it means to be a neighbor.

The *temporal point of view* accents the spatial perspective; the narrative pacing slows down when the Samaritan appears on the scene. A narrator can accent what is important by slowing down the temporal pace of the narrative or can gloss over narrative events by speeding up the pace. A summary statement, for instance, passes over an event quickly, while a detailed description of the same event slows down the pacing, forcing the reader to pay attention to the details. In Luke's parable, the temporal point of view focuses attention on the actions of the Samaritan by slowing down the narration. The responses of the priest and Levite are described in summary form with a series of similar verbs: "was going down," "came," "saw," and "passed by."

> Now by chance a priest *was going down* that road;
> and when he *saw* him,
> he *passed by* on the other side.
> So likewise a Levite, when *he came* to the place
> and *saw* him,
> *passed by* on the other side.
>
> (Luke 10:31–32)

A cadence is established: go/come, see, and pass by. But when the Samaritan comes, the narrative pace slows down. Twice as much space is given over to the Samaritan as to the priest and Levite. Sixty words in the United Bible Societies' *Greek New Testament* (4th ed.) highlight the Samaritan's behavior, while the priest and Levite together receive just twenty-six words. Similar to van Gogh's spatial point of view in *The Good Samaritan*, which has the priest and Levite fade into the distant background while the Samaritan fills the foreground, the Lukan narrator slows down the narrative pace to describe carefully and with great detail the Samaritan's compassionate, overabundant response to the injured man.

The *psychological point of view* reinforces the spatial and temporal perspective of the narrative. Of the four characters in the parable—the man in the ditch, the priest, the Levite, and the Samaritan—only the motivation of the Samaritan is noted. There are no inside views of the priest's and Levite's motivations. Although both saw the man lying in the road, they passed by on the opposite side. Were they afraid that the robbers were still lurking nearby and might rob them if they stopped? Did they fear corpse-defilement that would prevent them from performing temple duties (cf. Lev. 21:1–2; Num. 5:2; 19:11–13)?[48] It is pointless to conjecture about their motivations, for the narrative—perhaps intentionally—is silent.[49] The stark reality is that they did not respond to a fellow traveler in need. On the other hand, an inside view provides a clear motivation for the Samaritan's response: "he was moved with pity" (10:33). The word for compassion (*splanchnizomai*) is the focal point of the narrative unit (10:25–37).[50] This is the peripety, or reversal, in the U-shaped plot.[51] The onslaught of the robbers and the egregious passivity of the priest and Levite mark the downward trajectory, whereas the Samaritan's compassion reverses the downward spiral in the man's fortunes.[52]

The *phraseological point of view* develops and elaborates the perspectives established by the other planes. In Luke 10:33, *Samaritēs* (Samaritan) is in the emphatic position—the first word in the sentence—and draws attention to a change in perspective. "But a Samaritan . . . came near him." A break in the cadence of the verbs also marks a change in direction. The three verbs—"came," "saw," and "passed by"—are repeated with the exception of the final verb, breaking the cycle of indifference.

> But a Samaritan while traveling *came near* him;
> and when he *saw* him,
> he *was moved with pity*.
>
> (Luke 10:33)

48. Bernard Brandon Scott, *Hear Then the Parable: A Commentary on the Parables of Jesus* (Minneapolis: Fortress, 1989), 195–96, shows that concerns for defilement could not be invoked as a reason to refuse aid. Green, *Luke*, 430, also finds the concern for defilement implausible.

49. Scott, *Hear Then the Parable*, 197; cf. also John Nolland, *Luke*, 3 vols., WBC 35A–C (Dallas: Word, 1993), 2:593.

50. M. J. J. Menken, "The Position of σπλαγχνίζεσθαι and σπλάγχνα in the Gospel of Luke," *NovT* 30 (1988): 107–14, notes that "compassion" is at the center of the entire narrative unit (10:25–37) in the Nestle-Aland 26th edition: There are sixty-eight words of Jesus preceding and sixty-seven following.

51. On plot see §6.3 below.

52. Green, *Luke*, 431.

Instead of "passing by," the Samaritan is "moved with pity." Another series of verbs—again part of the phraseological point of view—reverses the cycle of uncaring. The Samaritan "*went to*" the man, "*bandaged* his wounds," and "*poured* oil and wine on them." Then he "*put* him on his own animal," and "*brought* him to the inn," and "*took care* of him." Finally, he gave the innkeeper the equivalent of two day's wages (cf. Matt. 20:9–13), instructed him to look after him, and offered to repay any additional expenses upon his return (10:34–35). Caring and compassion replace uncaring and indifference. The narrator's description of the wounded man makes him anyone or everyone. He is "a certain man" who is stripped of his clothes and left half dead; he cannot, therefore, be identified as either friend or foe,[53] or by "race, religion, region or trade."[54] He is simply a neighbor in need. On the other hand, the other travelers on the road are identified by their status in the social hierarchy of the day. The priest and Levite are high in the hierarchy, while the Samaritan is a "socio-religious outcast."[55]

The phraseological point of view underscores the distance between the anonymous man and the two passersby. The priest and Levite do not merely "pass by" the man in the ditch; they "pass by on the other side"—a verb used only here in the New Testament (10:31–32). Opposition is built into the verb with its *anti*-prefix (*antiparerchomai*). Whereas the Levite came "up to the place"[56] where the man was lying and passed to the other side, the Samaritan closes the gaping hole of indifference. He comes "near" the man—not "the place"—and goes "to him" (10:33–34). Nearness is built into this verb with its *pros*-prefix (*proserchomai*). Similar to van Gogh's painting, in which the priest and Levite move away from us while the Samaritan moves toward us, *anti* ("opposite") summarizes the actions of priest and Levite while *pros* ("toward") characterizes the Samaritan's response.

The question of who is a neighbor frames the narrative and expresses two divergent *ideological points of view* (10:29, 36). When Jesus asks the lawyer which of the three was "a neighbor to the man who fell into the hands of the robbers," he replies with a description that confirms the inside view: "the one who showed him mercy" (10:37). A shift on the phraseological plane represents a shift on the ideological plane. Initially the lawyer asks Jesus, "who is my neighbor?" (10:29), and rather than debate the unanswerable, Jesus rephrases the question. The one who is a neighbor is the one who acts as a neighbor to one in need—that is,

53. Ibid., 429.

54. R. Alan Culpepper, "The Gospel of Luke," *The New Interpreter's Bible*, ed. Leander E. Keck, 12 vols. (Nashville: Abingdon, 1994–), 9:3–490 at 229.

55. Green, *Luke*, 431.

56. BDAG, s.v. κατά B1b.

"one who show[s] . . . mercy." The phraseological perspective elaborates and develops two views: one is commonplace within that society, and perhaps within any society; the other is a marked departure from the familiar point of view. The lawyer's question seeks to define not only who is the neighbor but also who is not the neighbor.[57] What are the boundaries that separate a neighbor from the person who does not qualify as neighbor? Is a neighbor a fellow Israelite or a proselyte? Is a neighbor a Roman soldier or an oppressive tyrant? Is a neighbor a Samaritan? How large does the circle have to be?[58] But Jesus turns this point of view on its head and redefines neighbor as one who shows compassion and mercy to others. A neighbor knows no boundaries: "Social position—race, religion, or region—count for nothing."[59] Rather a neighbor is one who acts—who *does*, which Jesus' final words accent: "Go and *do* likewise" (10:37).

57. Richard Bauckham, "The Scrupulous Priest and the Good Samaritan: Jesus' Parabolic Interpretation of the Law of Moses," *NTS* 44 (1998): 475–89. Bauckham interprets the question to mean: "who is the neighbour whom the commandment obliges me to love?" (475).

58. Arland J. Hultgren, *The Parables of Jesus: A Commentary* (Grand Rapids: Eerdmans, 2000), 94.

59. Culpepper, "Luke," 229.

6

Plot

6.1 Definition

"Plot" is an elusive term and any definition is likely to be incomplete. Nevertheless, an understanding of plot is important to determine structure, unity, and direction of a narrative. It is the designing principle that contributes to our understanding of the meaning of a narrative.[1] More concretely, the plot is the sequence of events or incidents that make up a narrative. Events include actions (or acts) that bring about changes of state in the characters. Or the action of characters may bring about changes of state in the narrative events.[2] A character's acts are his or her physical actions, speech, thoughts, feelings, and perceptions. When we ask, "What do characters think, feel, or do, and how does this change the characters themselves?" we are asking a question about plot. Or when we ask, "What do characters think, feel, or do, and how does this bring about a change in narrative events?" we are once again exploring plot. By and large, a character is the *subject* of acts; she or he initiates acts that bring about changes in the plot.

1. William Harmon and C. Hugh Holman, *A Handbook to Literature*, 8th ed. (Upper Saddle River, N.J.: Prentice Hall, 1999), 393–94. On plot in the New Testament see Frank J. Matera, "The Plot of Matthew's Gospel," *CBQ* 49 (1987): 233–53; Mark Allan Powell, "The Plots and Subplots of Matthew's Gospel," *NTS* 32 (1992): 187–204; Warren Carter, "Kernels and Narrative Blocks: The Structure of Matthew's Gospel," *CBQ* 54 (1992): 463–81; Jack D. Kingsbury, "The Plot of Matthew's Story," *Int* 46 (1992): 347–56.

2. Seymour Chatman, *Story and Discourse: Narrative Structure in Fiction and Film* (Ithaca: Cornell University Press, 1978), 44–45.

But a plot does not consist solely of acts. A plot also consists of *happenings*. As the term suggests, happenings are things that happen to a character. Happenings are also events that occur in a setting. In happenings, the character is the object, not the subject, of actions; the affected, not the effector.[3] When we ask, "What happens to a character and why?" we are asking a question related to plot. Or when we ask, "What happens in a setting such as the stilling of a storm on the sea, and how does that event change the disciples' perception of Jesus?" we are developing the notion of plot. Plot and character are thus inseparable in a narrative. Henry James has said, "What is character but the determination of incident? What is incident but the illustration of character?"[4]

In what follows, (1) the elements of a plot are developed (unity, causation, conflict, suspense, and surprise); (2) the types of plots and plot patterns are elaborated (masterplots, U-shaped plots, and inverted U-shaped plots); (3) the rhetorical and artistic influence of the order of events in a narrative are explained; and (4) a close reading of plot in John's Apocalypse is given.

6.2 Elements of a Plot

Unity of Action

A plot generally has unity of action: a beginning, middle, and end. Aristotle defined a plot (*mythos* in Greek) as a continuous sequence of events or actions with a beginning, middle, and end. "A beginning is that which does not itself follow necessarily from something else, but after which a further event or process naturally occurs. An end, by contrast, is that which itself naturally occurs, whether necessarily or usually, after a preceding event, but need not be followed by anything else. A middle is that which both follows a preceding event, and has further consequences."[5] In other words, "in the beginning anything is possible; in the middle things become probable; in the ending everything is necessary."[6]

Aristotle also defined a plot as a unified whole. It "should be so structured that if any [part] is displaced or removed, the sense of the whole is

3. Ibid., 45.

4. Henry James, "The Art of Fiction," in *The Art of Fiction and Other Essays by Henry James*, ed. Morris Roberts (New York: Oxford University Press, 1948, orig. publ. 1884), 3–23 at 13.

5. Aristotle, *Poetics* 7 (1450^{b} 27–31; trans. Halliwell, LCL).

6. Paul Goodman, *The Structure of Literature* (Chicago: University of Chicago Press, 1954), 14.

disturbed and dislocated."[7] Aristotle's definition is helpful as long as we recognize that some plots begin *in medias res* (Latin for "in the middle of things") or begin at the end and then loop back to the beginning. Lawrence Sterne, for instance, plays with plot when he delays the preface to *Tristram Shandy* (1759–1767) to chapter 20 of volume 3 and also places chapters 18 and 19 of volume 9 *after* chapter 25.[8] And the movie thriller *Memento* (2001) is a playful rearrangement of plot; it begins at the end and works backward to the beginning.

Causation

A story is different from a plot. Although both are sequences of events, a plot is linked by cause and effect. A story merely requires us to ask, "*What* happens next?" whereas a plot requires us to ask, "*Why* do things happen as they do?" E. M. Forster's oft-cited example illustrates the difference between a story and a plot:

> A: The king died and then the queen died.
> B: The king died, and then the queen died of grief.[9]

In the first instance (A) the events are strung together with no causal connection between the two. The queen could have died from an accident—falling down the stairs, for instance—or from health problems such as heart disease. But there is nothing in this brief story to suggest that the queen's death is directly related to the king's death. The only link between the two events is the suggestive but inconclusive "and then." In the second instance (B) the same story is told with two additional words that suggest a relationship between the events. B answers the question "why?" "The queen died of grief" turns the story into a plot.[10] Biblical plots, in particular, rely on cause and effect to answer some of life's most important questions: questions of origin, destiny, and purpose.

Although causation is a necessary element in plots, it can also lead to some treacherous interpretations because some mistake mere cor-

7. Aristotle, *Poetics* 8 (1451[a] 32–34; trans. Halliwell, LCL).

8. See Victor Shklovsky, "Sterne's *Tristram Shandy:* Stylistic Commentary," in *Russian Formalist Criticism: Four Essays*, trans. Lee T. Lemon and Marion J. Reis (Lincoln: University of Nebraska Press, 1965), 25–57.

9. E. M. Forster, *Aspects of the Novel* (New York: Harcourt, Brace, 1927), 86.

10. Seymour Chatman argues that even A qualifies as a plot because readers will intuitively fill in the gap and assume a connection between the king's death and the queen's. "Unless otherwise instructed, readers will tend to assume that even 'The king died and the queen died' presents a causal link, that the king's death has something to do with the queen's." See Chatman, *Story and Discourse*, 45–46.

relation—events linked together—for causation. In E. M. Forster's example—"the king died and then the queen died"—there is a correlation between the queen's death and the king's death, which is indicated by two words, "and then." Yet correlation is not cause. Only when Forster adds the phrase "of grief" is it evident that the king's death is the cause of the queen's.

In Rev. 12:7–9 a fierce battle takes place in heaven between Michael and his angels, on the one hand, and Satan and his angels, on the other. Satan is defeated and thrown down to earth. There is a correlation between the war in heaven and Satan's expulsion from the heavenly realm.

> And war broke out in heaven; Michael and his angels fought against the dragon. The dragon and his angels fought back, but they were defeated, and there was no longer any place for them in heaven. The great dragon was thrown down, that ancient serpent, who is called the Devil and Satan, the deceiver of the whole world—he was thrown down to the earth, and his angels were thrown down with him.

But correlation is not the same as cause. Michael did not cause Satan's fall from heaven. In fact, Revelation offers an entirely different cause-and-effect sequence in verses 10–12.

> Then I heard a loud voice in heaven, proclaiming,
> "Now have come the salvation
> and the power
> and the kingdom of our God
> and the authority of his Messiah,
> for the accuser of our comrades
> has been thrown down,
> who accuses them day and night
> before our God.
> But they have conquered him by
> the blood of the Lamb
> and by the word of their testimony,
> for they did not cling to life even in the face of death."

The victory is won by Christ's victory on the cross, not by Michael's triumph in heaven. Michael's battle is the *above* perspective on what happens *below* on earth. G. B. Caird uses the imagery of a staff officer (Michael) and the field officer (Christ) to explain the heavenly battle. Michael is the "staff officer" in the heavenly throne room who removes

"Satan's flag from the heavenly map because the real victory has been won on Calvary."[11]

Conflict

Almost all plots involve some clash of actions, ideas, points of views, desires, values, or norms. The conflict may be physical, mental, emotional, spiritual, or moral. It may add suspense or surprise to a narrative. Or it may develop and elaborate values, beliefs, and norms that may be at conflict with society or with the reader. The Greek word for conflict is *agōn*, which occurs in our word for hero or heroine, a protagonist, and for his or her opponent, an antagonist. Plots frequently involve conflicts or contests between protagonist and antagonist, or groups of good characters and bad characters. Conflicts may be external or internal. Examples of external conflicts include:

- Conflicts with other characters, whether villains (evil characters) or adversaries (characters whose values, goals, or norms differ from those of the protagonist). Jesus' conflict with religious authorities involves a clash of values, norms, and beliefs (e.g., Matt. 9:14–17; Mark 2:18–22; Luke 5:33–39).
- Conflicts with nature, such as the quelling of the tempest on the sea (Matt. 8:23–27; Mark 4:35–41; Luke 8:22–25).
- Conflicts with the supernatural, such as healing a demoniac (Matt. 8:28–34; Mark 5:1–20; Luke 8:26–39).
- Conflicts with society, such as Jesus' conflicts with norms and values of the dominant culture of his day (Mark 7:1–23).

Conflicts may also be internal—within the protagonist or a group of characters:

- Conflicts within the desires and values of the protagonist, such as Jesus' desire in the garden to have the cup of suffering taken away from him (Matt. 26:36–46; Mark 14:32–42; Luke 22:39–46).
- Conflicts of decision. The protagonist may encounter a *dilemma* that involves two choices or actions, both of which are undesirable. The decision may determine success with a prosperous ending or failure with a tragic ending. The Rich Young Man faces a conflict of decision (Matt. 19:16–22; Mark 10:17–22; Luke 18:18–23).

11. G. B. Caird, *A Commentary on the Revelation of St. John the Divine*, HNTC (New York: Harper & Row, 1966), 154.

- Conflict between the protagonist and the protagonist's own goals. In the parable of the Rich Farmer (Luke 12:13–21), the protagonist sets a goal—building bigger barns—that conflicts with another more compelling reality—his impending death.

Suspense and Surprise

"All successful narratives of any length are chains of suspense and surprise that keep us in a fluctuating state of impatience, wonderment, and partial gratification."[12] Suspense derives from incomplete knowledge about a crisis, conflict, or some unknown in a plot. It causes us to ask, "What will happen next?" or "How will this turn out?" Alfred Hitchcock, a master of suspense, keeps viewers on the edge of their seats by prolonging the plot with twists and turns until a surprise gratification at the end. Few biblical narratives offer the suspenseful satisfactions of mysteries, but biblical narratives can use suspense to create interest, to dramatize events, or to drive home an ideological or moral point of view. The parable of the Laborers in the Vineyard, for instance, uses suspense to dramatize the difference between God's justice and humankind's notion of justice (Matt. 20:1–16). A landowner hires workers early in the morning, at nine o'clock, at noon, and then at the end of the day, five o'clock. At the end of the day, the laborers are paid in reverse order: the last-hired are paid first and the first-hired are paid last. The last-hired are paid a full days' wage even though they worked only one hour. This rhetorical maneuver creates suspense. Will the first-hired receive a bonus for working longer and in the heat of the day? Will they be paid twice as much? As it turns out, they are paid the same as those who work only one hour. The suspense created by the delay drives home the point that the landowner is not only generous but also exceedingly fair, which turns on its head our everyday norms of justice or fairness.

Closely related to suspense is surprise. Suspense causes us to ask, "What will happen next?" Surprises occur when we find out what happens next. The surprise is proportional to the clash between suspense and our expectations: the greater the clash, the greater the surprise. In the parable of the Laborers in the Vineyard, it is a surprise that the last-hired are paid the exact same wage as the first-hired. If employers today paid workers who put in just one hour of work the same as those who worked eight hours, there would be an avalanche of complaints because this conflicts with our notions of fairness. Those who worked all day would naturally say, "This is not fair." By setting up a scene that

12. H. Porter Abbott, *The Cambridge Introduction to Narrative* (Cambridge: Cambridge University Press, 2002), 53.

all workers (then or today) can relate to and then shattering normal expectations, the narrator conveys the difference between God's ways and our ways. The surprise twist in the parable's ending is essential to explain God's notion of justice.

6.3 Plot Types and Plot Patterns

Masterplots

Masterplots are "recurrent skeletal stories, belonging to cultures and individuals that play a powerful role in questions of identity, values, and the understanding of life."[13] Masterplots deal with universal stories such as the quest for meaning in life (where are we going?), questions of origins (where did we come from?), the quest for identity (who are we?), the quest to find our way home (alienation and reconciliation), and questions of free will and determinism (is our destiny determined or are we free agents?). Since many of the New Testament narratives deal with basic questions of identity, values, and our understanding of life, it is important to think in terms of masterplots.

An example of a masterplot is the Oedipus narrative, which elaborates the conflict between one's free will and fate. Can we escape the constraints of life whatever they may be—our heredity, looks, status, societal values, and so forth—to find our destiny apart from those constraints? Or is the outcome unavoidable because the constraints of life cannot be changed? Oedipus learned from the Oracle at Delphi that he is fated to kill his father Laius, the king of Thebes, and marry his mother, Jocasta. He determines to avoid his dilemma by never returning to Corinth, which he mistakenly believes to be his place of origin. One day he meets a traveler who happens to be his father, Laius. Oedipus, having been sent away at a young age, does not recognize him. When Laius refuses to move out of Oedipus's way, the son kills him. He goes on to Thebes, where Jocasta, his mother, lives as a widow. A Sphinx—a terrible creature part human, part animal—is terrorizing the city, devouring anyone who fails to answer her riddle: What walks on four legs in the morning, two legs at noon, and three legs in the afternoon and has one voice? Creon, the brother of Jocasta, proclaims that whoever answers the riddle and frees the city of the influence of the Sphinx will be made king. Oedipus successfully answers the riddle: as infants, humans walk on four legs, as adults on two legs, and as elders with the use of a cane on three legs. The Sphinx throws herself to death from

13. Abbott, *Cambridge Introduction to Narrative*, 192.

the walls of Thebes, and Oedipus is given in marriage to Jocasta. The gripping tale of Oedipus's struggle to avoid his fate exemplifies the masterplot of determinism and free will. In attempting to flee his fate, he ironically fulfills his fate.

Another example of a masterplot is humankind's desire to be independent and free; yet the drive for independence can lead to disaster and a longing for home. In the parable of the Prodigal Son the younger son sets out on a quest for freedom; disaster ensues, resulting in his desire to return home (Luke 15:11–24). *The Wizard of Oz* and *E.T.: The Extra-Terrestrial* also draw upon the universal plot of longing to return home.

Plot Patterns

The choice of plot pattern depends on the emotional or artistic effects that the writer wants to achieve. "Some plots are designed to achieve tragic effects, and others to achieve the effects of comedy, romance, satire, or of some other *genre*. Each of these types in turn exhibits diverse plot-patterns."[14] A recognition plot, for instance, posits characters that are initially unseeing and unknowing but eventually awaken to an important discovery. Recognition plots in the New Testament include the rich young man (Matt. 19:16–22; Mark 10:17–22; Luke 18:18–23), the journey to Emmaus (Luke 24:13–35), Jesus at the Sea of Tiberias (John 21:1–14), the miraculous draught of fish (Luke 5:1–11), the stilling the storm (Matt. 8:23–27; Mark 4:35–41; Luke 8:22–25), the woman with ointment (Matt. 26:6–13; Mark 14:3–9; Luke 7:36–50; John 12:1–8), and Mary Magdalene (John 20:1–2, 11–18).

Two common plot patterns in the New Testament are comedy (a U-shaped plot) and tragedy (an inverted U-shaped plot). Northrop Frye argues that the shape of the Bible is a series of U-shaped and inverted U-shaped plots, a series of disasters and restorations that begins in Genesis with the loss of the tree and water of life and ends in Revelation with the tree and water of life restored.[15] The series of ups and downs, rises and falls, misfortunes and restorations, not only is the plot of the entire Bible but is also the plot of individual biblical narratives. Generally speaking, it is also the plot of our own personal lives, which makes plot analysis more than an academic exercise.

14. M. H. Abrams, *A Glossary of Literary Terms*, 7th ed. (Fort Worth: Harcourt Brace College Publishers, 1999), s.v. "Plot."

15. Northrop Frye, *The Great Code: The Bible and Literature* (New York: Harcourt Brace Jovanovich, 1981), 169–71.

U-shaped Plot (Comic Plot)

A U-shaped plot begins at the top of the U with a state of equilibrium, a period of prosperity or happiness, which is disrupted by disequilibrium or disaster. Adversity, misunderstanding, or rebellion propels the plot downward to disaster or bondage. At the bottom of the U the direction is reversed by a fortunate twist, divine deliverance, an awakening of the character to his or her tragic circumstances, or some other action or event that results in an upward turn. Aristotle referred to the reverse in fortunes as a *peripety* (from the Greek for "reversal").[16] The reversal depends frequently on a recognition or discovery, which Aristotle called an *anagnōrisis*—a change in the protagonist from "ignorance to knowledge" involving "matters which bear on prosperity or adversity."[17] The protagonist recognizes something of great importance that was previously hidden or unrecognized. The change in direction marks the beginning of the *dénouement* (French for "unraveling") or resolution of the plot. An action is taken that ends in success, or the misunderstanding is solved, or rebellion ceases. The upward turn represents movement toward a new state of equilibrium—a return home, reconciliation, new life. The final state is characterized by happiness and prosperity or, in biblical terms, peace, salvation, and wholeness.

The Parable of the Prodigal Son (a U-shaped plot)

The parable of the Prodigal Son is a classic example of a U-shaped plot or comedy (Luke 15:11–24). It is a masterplot of homeleaving and homecoming. The parable opens with an *initiating action* that begins the downward turn. The younger son asks his father for his share of the property and sets out for a "distant country" or a "far away place" (15:13). The setting of "a distant country" spatially suggests a story of alienation and rebellion, or at the very least a desire for freedom and independence. The father does not refuse his son's wish. Disaster, however, strikes; freedom is replaced by captivity and bondage. The choice of verbs reinforces the *falling action*: the son "squandered his property in dissolute living" and "spent everything" (15:13–14a). Disaster of the land replicates and intensifies personal disaster: "a severe famine took place throughout that country" (15:14b), and the son "began to be in need" (15:14c). The prodigal's resolution of the crisis is to look for work with one of the citizens of "that country," who sends him to feed pigs. But this only increases disaster. His hunger reduces him to an animal-like state:

16. Aristotle, *Poetics*, 11.
17. Ibid.

if he could, he would even eat pigs' food. The stark summary of his lack expresses the depth of his despair: "no one gave him anything" (15:16). The *dénouement,* or resolution of the crisis, begins with a recognition and a reversal that turns the falling action into a *rising action*. "When he came to himself," he makes an important and previously unrecognized discovery. "How many of my father's hired hands have bread enough to spare, but here I am dying of hunger! I will get up and go to my father, and I will say to him, 'Father, I have sinned against heaven and before you; I am no longer worthy to be called your son; treat me like one of your hired hands'" (15:17). He recognizes that he would be better off in his father's house as a hired hand who has food than enslaved and starving in an alien land. His recognition is a desire for survival, and "so he set off and went to his father" (15:20). In the upward turn the narrative shifts from the actions of the son to the actions of the father. While the son is "still far off" (15:20b) the father runs, puts his arms around him, and kisses him. The surprise is that he is received back as a son, not as a hired hand. The clothing (best robe, sandals, and ring) and the feast represent the top of the U, a new state of equilibrium, which the father summarizes in terms reminiscent of death and resurrection, homelessness and homecoming: "this son of mine was dead and is alive again; he was lost and is found" (15:24).

Other U-shaped plots in the New Testament include the healing of Bartimaeus (Mark 10:46–52), Zacchaeus (Luke 19:1–10); the Syrophoenician woman (Matt. 15:21–28); the parable of the Unjust Judge (Luke 18:1–8); the parable of the Unjust Steward (Luke 16:1–9), the book of Revelation, and the Gospels,[18] to name a few.

Inverted U-shaped Plot (Tragic Plot)

An inverted U-shaped plot is the shape of a tragedy.[19] The introduction of a conflict initiates the *rising action*, the beginning of the upward turn.

18. Some apply the plot pattern of tragedy (an inverted U) to Mark, including Stephen H. Smith, *A Lion with Wings: A Narrative-Critical Approach to Mark's Gospel*, BS 38 (Sheffield: Sheffield Academic Press, 1996), 82–123, and Gilbert G. Bilezikian, *The Liberated Gospel: A Comparison of the Gospel of Mark and Greek Tragedy* (Grand Rapids: Baker, 1977). The plot pattern of tragedy has also been applied to John. See Jo-Ann A. Brant, *Dialogue and Drama: Elements of Greek Tragedy in the Fourth Gospel* (Peabody, Mass.: Hendrickson, 2004).

19. The inverted U is similar to Gustav Freytag's Pyramid (1863), which depicts a plot as an inverted V with an *exposition* that introduces characters, setting, and other facts necessary for understanding the plot; the introduction of *conflict*; a *rising action* that includes the *complication* and development of the conflict; a *climax* or turn of action from rising to falling; a *dénouement,* or resolution of the conflict, that includes a *reversal* and *falling action*. See Jean Louis Ska, *"Our Fathers Have Told Us": Introduction to the Analysis of Hebrew Narratives* (Rome: Pontificio Istituto Biblico, 1990), 20–30, who applies Freytag's

The conflict is developed and complicated until the rising action reaches the *climax* of the protagonist's fortunes. This is the top of the inverted U. A *crisis* or turning point marks the reversal of the protagonist's fortunes and begins the descent or *falling action* to disaster. As in comedy, the *dénouement* (also called *catastrophe* in tragedies) involves a reversal in the character's fortune and sometimes a recognition scene where the protagonist recognizes something of great importance that was previously unrecognized. The final state is disaster, adversity, and unhappiness. An example of an inverted U is the parable of the Ten Bridesmaids.

The Parable of the Ten Bridesmaids

The story of the foolish bridesmaids in Matt. 25:1–13 takes the shape of an inverted U-shaped plot. Ten maidens are to meet the bridegroom and light the path to the marriage feast. The exposition introduces the setting (a marriage feast) and the characters (five wise bridesmaids who took extra flasks of oil and five foolish ones who brought no additional oil). The conflict is introduced early on: "the bridegroom was delayed" (Matt. 25:5a). The rising action describes the response of both the wise and foolish to the bridegroom's delay: "all of them became drowsy and slept" (Matt. 25:5b). At midnight the bridegroom arrives, which initiates a crisis that marks the turning point in the fortunes of the five foolish bridesmaids. Since the foolish have not brought sufficient oil for their lamps, the falling action develops and elaborates the bridesmaids' efforts to reverse the downward turn. They ask the wise for oil, but the wise decline. They rush to the market to buy more oil. Despite their last-minute efforts to avoid catastrophe, the bridegroom arrives before they return, "and those who were ready went in with him to the wedding banquet" (Matt. 25:10). When the foolish arrive at the wedding, they find that the door is already shut. The recognition scene comes at the end of the parable when the foolish plead with the bridegroom to open the door. His response certainly comes as a surprise, "Truly I tell you, I do not know you" (Matt. 25:12). The bridesmaids' nonrecognition of their responsibilities is greeted by the bridegroom's nonrecognition of them, an even exchange that restores the imbalance. The foolish failed to recognize the need to bring extra oil perhaps because of hubris (Greek for "pride")—i.e., self-confidence grounded in their misguided assumption that the bridegroom would arrive on time. The foolish discover too late that their lack of preparation for a crisis excludes them from the very

---

Pyramid to Hebrew narrative. On comic and tragic plots in the parables see Dan O. Via, *The Parables: Their Literary and Existential Dimension* (Philadelphia: Fortress, 1967).

feast they anticipated, and nothing they do makes up for their lack of preparation.

This last example illustrates the importance of plot analysis for understanding a narrative. The reversal and recognition scenes provide important information for the interpretation of comic and tragic plots. Although the foolish maidens make their discovery too late to avert disaster, the reader benefits from their folly. The reader can ask: "What should the foolish bridesmaids have recognized that they failed to recognize?" "How could they have averted disaster?" "What is the tragic flaw or *hamartia* (Greek for "error of judgment") that causes their downfall?" "What did the five wise bridesmaids recognize that the foolish missed?" Questions such as these allow us to enter the narrative world and understand the narrative in ways traditional methods of interpretation do not allow.

Other inverted U-shaped plots in the New Testament include the parable of the Talents or Pounds (Matt. 25:14–30; Luke 19:11–27), parable of the Sheep and the Goats (Matt 25:31–46), parable of the Rich Man and Lazarus (Luke 16:19–31), parable of the Rich Fool (Luke 12:16–21), parable of the Unforgiving Servant (Matt. 18:23–35), parable of the Wicked Tenants (Matt. 21:33–46; Mark 12:1–12; Luke 20:9–19), and the Rich Young Man (Matt. 19:16–22; Mark 10:17–22; Luke 18:18–23).

6.4 Order of Narration

The arrangement of events in a plot can be ordered to achieve rhetorical, emotional, or artistic effects. A plot can be ordered to convince the reader of a new point of view, or to persuade the reader to adopt a different set of values, beliefs, or norms, or to catch the reader by surprise, creating delight or frustration. Ordering alone is not the only way to achieve these effects, but it is a common and forceful way to convince, persuade, or move the reader to a particular end. Two concepts are helpful for understanding the order of narration in a plot: (1) *fabula* (story) and *sjužet* (plot) and (2) primacy and recency effect.

Fabula *(Story) and* Sjužet *(Plot)*

The Russian Formalists made an important distinction between the basic story stuff or raw materials—the chronological or logical sequence of events—that is called the *fabula* or story, and the events as they actually appear in a narrative, called the *sjužet* or plot. The *fabula* is the raw materials for the construction of a narrative; the *sjužet* is the final product. The basic story stuff, or *fabula,* may consist of three events: 1,

2, 3. But the *sjužet* can be molded into any of six combinations: 1, 2, 3; 1, 3, 2; 2, 1, 3; 2, 3, 1; 3, 2, 1; 3, 1, 2.[20] A plot may begin *in medias res*, so that the narrative opens at the middle and then supplies information about the beginning of the action, or it may begin at the end and work backwards to the beginning. In other words, plots do not need to follow the chronological and logical order of a story, and the deformation of a plot creates interesting effects. A writer may withhold important information that logically occurs earlier in the story (*fabula*), but in the plot (*sjužet*) it is delayed to drive home a point or in some other way to influence a character and/or reader. This happens in Jesus' encounter with the woman at the home of Simon the Pharisee (Luke 7:36–50). The chronological sequence of events in the story is as follows:

1. A Pharisee invites Jesus to dinner.
2. The host omits customary amenities for his guest.
3. A sinful woman enters, washes Jesus' feet with her hair, and anoints his feet.
4. Simon objects.
5. Jesus confronts Simon.
6. Jesus pronounces the woman forgiven.

But the story stuff is not the plot recorded by Luke. Number 2 in the above diagram—Simon's feckless behavior—is delayed until number 5, and thus the plot sequence is 1, 3, 4, 5, 2, and 6. The rhetorical power of Jesus' confrontation with the religious leader is increased by this delay. Simon's omission of customary acts of hospitality is postponed until the contrast between his wan reception of Jesus and the woman's effusive behavior can be fully developed.

Primacy and Recency Effects

The material that occurs first in a plot and affects the reader initially is known as the primacy effect, while the material that follows later is known as the recency effect. The order of the material in a plot creates expectations in the reader—a primacy effect—that is fulfilled, modified, or even shattered by what comes later in the narrative—the recency effect.[21]

20. See Meir Sternberg, *Expositional Modes and Temporal Ordering in Fiction* (Baltimore: Johns Hopkins University Press, 1978), 9; James L. Resseguie, "Defamiliarization in the Gospels," *Mosaic: A Journal for the Interdisciplinary Study of Literature* 21 (1988): 25–35 at 32.

21. See Menakhem Perry, "Literary Dynamics: How the Order of a Text Creates Its Meanings," *Poetics Today* 1 (1979): 35–64.

Three types of primacy/recency effects have practical and theoretical implications for the reading of New Testament literature:[22] (1) A primacy effect can be developed, elongated, and reinforced by the recency effect. (2) A recency effect can undermine, demolish, shatter, or in some other way subvert the primacy effect. (3) A recency effect can modify, exploit, or revise the primacy effect.

In the first instance, a primacy effect is developed, sustained, and elongated as the plot unfolds. Nothing that occurs later in the narrative can withstand or perceptively modify the powerful rhetorical effect of the primacy. The reader is lured into making a deep emotional commitment, into accepting the norms of the narrator, and into forming a solid opinion that is driven home by the recency effect. An example of this type of primacy and recency effect is found in the Gospel of John, which establishes an overwhelming positive effect in chapters 1–4 that cannot be undermined by subsequent chapters. Jesus' point of view is reinforced throughout the first four chapters so that the appearance of antagonists and a contrary point of view in John 5 cannot destabilize the powerful primacy. By establishing the superiority of Jesus' countercultural point of view at the beginning of the plot, the traditional and conformist point of view of the dominant culture—that is, the point of view of the religious leaders of the day—appears wrongheaded, shortsighted, and contrary to the will of God.[23]

A different primacy and recency effect is achieved when the primacy develops commitments on the part of the reader and then overthrows, undermines, or deconstructs these firmly held commitments in the recency. The primacy invites stock responses from the readers that initially encourage them to lean the wrong way until they are unexpectedly trapped by the recency effect and forced to modify their assumptions and commitments. Caught by surprise, the reader must modify his or her prior commitments. A brief saying of Jesus (Mark 10:29–32) and a scene from Rev. 5 will illustrate this type of plot effect.

Mark 10:29–30

The disciples have just heard Jesus declare that it is easier for a camel to go through the eye of a needle than for a rich man to enter the kingdom of God (Mark 10:25), causing them to wonder, "Who can be saved?" Jesus replies that what is impossible for humankind is possible for God. Peter then announces that they have already sacrificed all to follow Jesus:

22. See Sternberg, *Expositional Modes*, 90–158, for further development of these types of primacy/recency effects.

23. See James L. Resseguie, *The Strange Gospel: Narrative Design and Point of View in John*, BIS 56 (Leiden: Brill, 2001), chapter 4, for full discussion.

"Look, we have left everything and followed you" (Mark 10:28). Jesus' reassurance, however, is both confirming and surprising:

> Truly I tell you, there is no one who has left house
> or brothers or sisters or mother or father or children or fields,
> for my sake
> and for the sake of the good news,
> who will not receive a hundredfold
> now in this age—
> houses, brothers and sisters, mothers and children, and fields
> with persecutions—
> and in the age to come eternal life.

Initially the saying confirms their decision—for loss is gain and what is left behind will be multiplied many times over.[24] Jesus reinforces this expectation by listing the family members and possessions that have been left behind, which creates what E. H. Gombrich calls the "etc. principle." "The assumption we tend to make is that to see a few members of a series is to see them all."[25] The "etc. principle" is reinforced by repeating the series—this time with the plural throughout. Further the decisive "and" replaces the indecisive "or" in the second series. The disciple who has left "house *or* brothers *or* sisters *or* mother *or* father *or* children *or* fields" will in turn receive "houses *and* brothers *and* sisters *and* mothers *and* children *and* lands" (author's translation). The primacy is intensified with a "hundredfold" reward and a temporal annotation—"now in this age." The recency effect, however, is jarring. "With persecutions" is an unexpected addendum that awakens the disciples and readers to reality. It shatters their expectation of a blissful life of material abundance and derails any false expectation of "cheap grace." The positive primacy effect has little chance of withstanding a recency effect created by these two surprising words. Only by glossing over the glaring insertion or by eliminating them entirely can the primacy of a blissful, uneventful state be sustained. Matthew and Luke, who were likely dependent on Mark's Gospel at this point, were perhaps unsettled by this troublesome phrase—for they chose to eliminate the offending words from their parallel accounts (cf. Matt. 19:29; Luke 18:29b–30).

24. See Tannehill, *The Sword of His Mouth: Forceful and Imaginative Language in Synoptic Sayings*, Semeia Supplements 1 (Philadelphia: Fortress, 1975), 147–53, for an excellent discussion of this passage.

25. E. H. Gombrich, *Art and Illusion: A Study in the Psychology of Pictorial Representation*, 2nd ed., Bollingen Series 35 (Princeton: Princeton University Press, 1961), 220.

Revelation 5:5–6

The primacy/recency effect of Rev. 5:5–6 is a brilliant maneuver by the implied author to alter one's perspective of how God works in this world. In the Apocalypse, John alternates scenes that elaborate what he *hears* with what he *sees*. Hearing interprets seeing; seeing reinterprets hearing. J. P. M. Sweet refers to John's technique as a juxtaposition of outer appearance with inner reality. "What is heard, the 'voice,' represents the inner reality, the spirit; what is seen, the 'appearance,' represents the outward, the flesh."[26] John hears the voice of an elder announce the appearance of a lion who will open the scroll and reveal its contents: "Then one of the elders said to me, 'Do not weep. See, the Lion of the tribe of Judah, the Root of David, has conquered, so that he can open the scroll and its seven seals" (5:5). The primacy effect raises conventional expectations that a fierce animal of conquest (cf. Prov. 30:30) will appear on the scene from the tribe of Judah (Gen. 49:9) and the Root of David (cf. Isa. 11:10). This imagery elicits stock responses from both Jewish and Christian audiences that a messianic deliverer will appear to overcome Israel's enemies by conquest and righteous judgment. Yet what John sees inverts the demotic expectation: "Then I saw between the throne and the four living creatures and among the elders a Lamb standing as if it had been slaughtered, having seven horns and seven eyes, which are the seven spirits of God sent out into all the earth" (5:6).

The recency effect shatters conventional expectations while ironically fulfilling them. A lamb is neither powerful nor an animal of conquest; rather it is an animal of sacrifice. Thus the juxtaposition of lion and lamb, hearing and seeing, redefines the way God conquers in this world—not by conventional conquest and righteous judgment but by the death and resurrection of Christ. God's Messiah does not come as a conquering lion but as a suffering lamb. While the recency redefines the primacy, the primacy also fulfills the recency. Jesus is indeed the lion of the tribe of Judah, the messianic deliverer, although his conquest comes not through the subjugation of enemies but through his death and resurrection.

A third type of primacy effect is neither reinforced without qualification nor overturned or surprisingly fulfilled. Rather it is qualified or modified from the beginning. The recency effect develops the modifications to the primacy. Meir Sternberg refers to this as "the rhetoric of anticipatory caution" in which "the primacy effect itself . . . is perceptively qualified from

26. J. P. M. Sweet, *Revelation*, TPINTC (Philadelphia: Trinity Press International, 1990), 125. Cf. also James L. Resseguie, *Revelation Unsealed: A Narrative Critical Approach to John's Apocalypse*, BIS 32 (Leiden: Brill, 1998), 33–37, for other examples of the relationship between seeing and hearing.

the beginning."[27] This third type of primacy/recency effect occurs in the book of Revelation. The book establishes a stable condition in chapter 1 with the appearance of one like the Son of Man who is sovereign and a stable presence in a chaotic world. Chapters 2 and 3, however, suggest danger and instability that qualifies and modifies the stable condition, and although chapters 4 and 5 reinforce the stable conditions of chapter 1, the remainder of the book goes on to qualify the primacy and develop the threats to stability on earth. The book's end, chapters 21–22, establishes a new stable condition. The remainder of this chapter provides a close reading of the U-shaped plot of the book of Revelation.

6.5 A Reading of Plot in the Book of Revelation

The book of Revelation is a U-shaped plot that takes the form of a journey and involves a recognition or discovery of something of great importance that was previously unseen or unrecognized by the characters in the book (thus the need for revelation). Characters move from ignorance to knowledge, from imperceptibility to an awakening. What is it that the characters in the book of Revelation discover? How do they see reality differently? What obstacles or trials must they overcome? Who are the helping characters on this journey and who hinders? Is there a recognition scene in which they discover something that was previously hidden from their view?

A journey setting is common among both U-shaped and inverted U-shaped plots. A protagonist goes on a journey, faces numerous trials and obstacles, makes crucial decisions, and arrives at a different, often better land. Or sometimes the character arrives at a bleak, dark land, as in Joseph Conrad's *Heart of Darkness*. During the journey the main character comes to an awakening of the direction she or he is taking in life, or adopts a new perspective, or awakens to some other important discovery. In L. Frank Baum's *The Wonderful Wizard of Oz*, for instance, Dorothy's symbolic and spiritual journey takes her through various trials and tribulations on her way to the Emerald City. She awakens to her inner desires and dreams as she travels to a new land. In the film version of Baum's novel, Dorothy is swept away to an oneiric land of Munchkins, witches, talking scarecrows, and flying monkeys. She follows the yellow brick road from Munchkinland to the Emerald City, encountering along the way dangerous and menacing characters: an animated apple tree pelts her with apples, a deadly poppy field lulls her to sleep, and flying monkeys harass her. Dorothy meets fellow pilgrims on her journey, help-

27. Sternberg, *Expositional Modes*, 129.

ing characters that give her strength to continue the difficult journey to the Emerald City. At the end, however, Dorothy makes a discovery that "there's no place like home."[28]

Masterplot and Theme

Like *The Wizard of Oz*, the Apocalypse tells a story of discovery in which Christians awaken to the dangers of compromise with the dominant culture, the allurements of the earthly city Babylon, and the role of the church in God's plan for history. The masterplot is a quest for identity (who are we?) and destiny (where are we going?). The plot pattern is U-shaped. On an exodus from oppression in this world to the harmonious peace of a new promised land (the new Jerusalem), the pilgrims discover where their loyalties lie and what is important in this life. All Christians in all times and in all places travel this exodus. The Israelites' freedom from oppression and slavery under Pharaoh and Egypt and the subsequent trials in the wilderness are metaphors for the Christian's journey in Revelation.

The Apocalypse opens with a reference to Exod. 19:1–6, where God bore the Israelites on eagles' wings into the wilderness and made them into "a priestly kingdom and a holy nation" (Exod. 19:6). John links Israel's formative experience in the desert to the Christian community, which is a new "priestly kingdom" on a new exodus from slavery and oppression to freedom in a new promised land. Just as the Israelites were freed from Egyptian bondage, Christians are released from bondage to sin through the blood of Christ and made "to be a kingdom, priests serving [Jesus'] God and Father" (Rev. 1:5b–6). They travel through a wilderness of danger, face minatory trials, and experience temptations to idolatry and tests of resolve. There is a new pharaoh on this exodus, a seven-headed dragon (Satan) whose earthly incarnations, the beasts from the sea and from the land, pursue and persecute the pilgrim church.[29] The goal is to arrive at a new promised land, the new Jerusalem. On the way they are faced with a crisis of decision: Will they follow the Lamb to the new promised land, or will they be sidetracked by the lure of Babylon and set down roots in the city of this world?[30]

28. J. Scott Cochrane, "The *Wizard of Oz* and Other Mythic Rites of Passage," in *Image and Likeness: Religious Visions in American Film Classics*, ed. John R. May (New York: Paulist Press, 1992), 79–86.

29. Others who argue for an exodus pattern in Revelation include: Håkan Ulfgard, *Feast and Future: Revelation 7:9–17 and the Feast of Tabernacles*, ConBNT 22 (Lund: Almqvist, 1989), 35–41; Caird, *Revelation*, passim.

30. Barbara R. Rossing, *The Choice between Two Cities: Whore, Bride, and Empire in the Apocalypse*, HTS 48 (Harrisburg, Pa.: Trinity Press International, 1999), argues a

Laodicea and the U-shaped Plot

The church at Laodicea models the U-shaped plot of the entire book. There is the falling action of the downward U followed by a crisis of decision with a recognition scene that is intended to reverse the downward movement to adversity. The upward movement comes with reliance upon Christ. The new state of equilibrium occurs when they receive their reward—a place on Christ's throne in the new city. The recognition scene is elaborated in this confrontation.

> For you say, "I am rich, I have prospered, and I need nothing." You do not realize that you are wretched, pitiable, poor, blind, and naked. Therefore I counsel you to buy from me gold refined by fire so that you may be rich, and white robes to clothe you and to keep the shame of your nakedness from being seen; and salve to anoint your eyes so that you may see. (3:17–18)

They believe they are rich, but are spiritually impoverished; they need nothing yet are stark naked. Their polluted gold needs refinement by fire so that they become spiritually wealthy. They lack white robes to cover the shame of their spiritual poverty (3:18). "You say . . . [yet] you do not realize you are" (3:17) summarizes the recognition or discovery that the Laodiceans must make.[31] This is a church that cannot see things as they appear. They are self-deceived and, therefore, are in need of revelation—not of the future, but of the present. They believe Christ dwells in their church, yet, ironically, he stands like a stranger at the door of the church knocking. He is an outsider in his own church, waiting for the Laodiceans to invite him in for fellowship (3:20). They are blind to their spiritual dwelling place and, therefore, need to purchase salve from Christ to anoint their eyes (3:18). This is the language of awakening or discovery. The upward movement of the U begins with the recognition

---

similar point: "In the book of Revelation, John . . . present[s] Jerusalem and Babylon as opposing figures in the most thorough economic, political, religious, and ethical appeal of his time, calling believers to come out of the whorish city and to take part in the glory of a bridal vision" (1).

31. Harry O. Maier, *Apocalypse Recalled: The Book of Revelation after Christendom* (Minneapolis: Fortress, 2002), argues that we need to read Revelation as contemporary Laodiceans. He writes: "For where is a first-world white male of privilege to find himself described in the Apocalypse if not in this seventh message—rich, not needing anything, neither hot nor cold, but lukewarm—the typical citizen of a reigning order that keeps the majority of the planet's inhabitants in servitude to furnish me with my comforts? Who if not me needs persuasion that I am naked, blind, pitiable, and wretched, I who walk down golden-lit streets in my expensive clothing with the jingle-jangle of money in my pocket, window shopping as recreation beneath jewel-colored neon lights urging me to buy? . . . Who if not I needs salve for my eyes and to be rescued at last 'from single vision and Newton's sleep'?" (38).

Figure 2. Luca Signorelli (1441–1523), *The Sermon and Deeds of the Antichrist*, 1500–1503. Fresco, postrestoration. Duomo, Orvieto, Italy.

of their self-deception and spiritual poverty. If they conquer, they are given a place with Christ on his throne in the new Jerusalem—a new state of equilibrium at the top of the U.

Helping and Hindering Characters in the Apocalypse

Helping characters in the Apocalypse guide pilgrims through times of distress and trial as they journey to Jerusalem, while destructive characters hinder their progress to journey's end. John is taken on a fantastic odyssey through heaven and earth where he sees the helping characters (e.g., one seated on a throne, and a slaughtered yet risen lamb with seven horns and seven eyes) and menacing characters of destruction (e.g., a seven-headed dragon, a beast from the sea with seven heads, and a beast with two horns that arises from the earth). A recognition scene occurs when the deceptive nature of evil is revealed: evil characters that appear to be good and worthy of worship are shown to be beastly and destructive. Ordinary people of this world (John calls them "the inhabitants of the earth") are in thrall with the destructive characters and seem completely unaware of their perverse, evil nature.

A striking portrayal of evil's deceptive guise is Luca Signorelli's fresco, *The Sermon and Deeds of the Antichrist* (see figure 2). Satan whispers into the ear of a Christlike character, so that at first glance this could be a painting of Christ's temptation by Satan. But a second, closer look uncovers disturbing anomalies in the portrayal of *this* Christ. The eyes of Christ are menacing and harsh, and two tuffs of hair protrude from his head, giving the eerie appearance of horns. There are six points to his beard, barely noticeable. This Christ wears a lavish purple garment, the colors of the whore of Babylon. What appears to be his left arm actually belongs to Satan, who has slipped his arm through the robe of Christ—this Christ is merely a puppet of the devil. There is no cross in the painting; rather the fraudulent Christ is a conquering hero on a marble pedestal for the world to admire. At the foot of the pedestal are the spoils of war, offerings placed at his feet as a testimony to his conquering might. Signorelli paints the antichrist in the guise of Christ (or at least, in the style of popular renditions of Christ) because evil's deceptive nature appears noble and good. This painting summarizes the dilemma the Christians and others encounter in their journey to the new Jerusalem: evil looks almost identical to good. How is it possible to see through this deceptive façade?

Albrecht Dürer's woodcut on Revelation 13, *The Beast with Two Horns Like a Lamb* (see figure 3), is also a feast of details that captures the curious irony of ordinary people worshiping evil as if it is good. In the left hand corner of the woodcut, kings and rulers, men and women, clerics and others kneel with folded hands before the seven-headed beast, unaware of the hideous, terrifying appearance of the very characters they worship in utter amazement. They follow the beast seemingly unaware of their disastrous choice. Although the hindering characters appear good and worthy of worship, Dürer has drawn them very literally as the grotesque, beastly creatures from the deep they really are.

How can the deceptive nature of the beasts be known? The plot unmasks evil's deceptive nature by offering an above point of view that contrasts with what is seen on earth. While the below point of view is visible to all, the above point of view, a heavenly perspective, remains hidden, for recognition comes only through revelation. Dürer accents and separates the two points of view with a layer of clouds. The lower half shows the beasts ruling the earth while the upper half has God directing events on earth from a heavenly throne. Dürer also renders the paradox of the way God defeats evil in the right-hand corner of the woodcut. An angel bears a cross on his back and wields a sword in his right hand. The sword and cross are symbolic of the way God defeats enemies. The cross *is* the sword that God uses to defeat the villains of this narrative. The dragon and beasts are defeated "by the blood of the Lamb and by the word of [the saints'] testimony" (12:11).

Figure 3. Albrecht Dürer (1471–1528), *The Beast with Two Horns Like a Lamb*, from *The Apocalypse of St. John* (1496–1498).

The Top of the U (a Stable Condition)

To offset the below point of view—which is the only view we can see unless an above point of view is revealed—John establishes a positive primacy effect of order and symmetry (Rev. 1–5) that counterbalances the recency effect of chaos and destruction that the hindering characters unleash (Rev. 11–18). The opening vision (1:12–20) establishes a powerful primacy effect of a Christ who is continually present and in control of his church. This is the stable condition at the top of the U. With a dazzling array of metaphors and similes, John accents Christ's otherness and sovereignty. The one like a Son of Man is clothed with a long robe and his head and hair are white *as* snow, his eyes are *like* a flame of fire, his feet are *like* burnished bronze, and his voice is *like* the sound of many waters. Out of his mouth comes a sharp two-edged sword, and his face is *like* the sun shining with full force. Albrecht Dürer's *The Seven Candlesticks* (see figure 4) portrays a transcendent Christ with seven stars in his right hand and seven candlesticks arranged symmetrically around him. The seven stars are the angels of the seven churches, which are held in the right hand to symbolize his sovereignty over the churches. The seven lampstands, which are the seven churches (seven is a symbolic number representing the church universal),[32] are clustered around its source of light. A two-edged sword comes out of his mouth and represents the way in which he conquers: by word and deed.[33] Whereas the beast slays his opponents in a traditional manner (he is a bloodthirsty red in 17:3), Christ conquers with the powerful testimony of his death and resurrection.

The stable condition is reinforced in the descriptions of Christ in chapters 2 and 3. He is the ever-present Christ at Ephesus, the one "who holds the seven stars in his right hand, who walks among the seven golden lampstands" (2:1). At Pergamum he wields the sharp two-edged sword of his testimony (2:12). At Thyatira his searing eyes penetrate the pretenses of this world (2:18). The stable condition, however, is modified by the rhetoric of anticipatory caution—the language of spiritual pollution or spiritual fornication. The positive primacy effect is qualified by trouble in the churches, which face a crisis of decision. A major conflict in the plot is introduced. Two cities, Thyatira and Pergamum, tolerate spiritual pollution: "You tolerate that woman Jezebel, who calls herself a prophet and is teaching and beguiling my servants to practice fornication and to eat food sacrificed to idols" (Rev. 2:20). Jezebel was the pagan queen of

32. On the numerals in Revelation see Resseguie, *Revelation Unsealed*, 52–54.

33. David L. Barr, *Tales of the End: A Narrative Commentary on the Book of Revelation* (Santa Rosa, Calif.: Polebridge Press, 1998), 40. Barr notes that "Jesus' testimony is itself two-edged, both what he said and what he did, which in Revelation focuses on his death."

Israel who lured the Israelites into worshiping the pagan god Baal (cf. 1 Kings 18–22, 2 Kings 9:22). John's Jezebel, the whore at Thyatira, is a type of the whore of Babylon. Both trade in spiritual harlotry and religious fornication—i.e., infidelity to God. In other words, John's Jezebel

Photograph courtesy of Wetmore Print Collection, Connecticut College.

Figure 4. Albrecht Dürer (1471–1528), *The Seven Candlesticks*, from *The Apocalypse of St. John* (1496–1498).

lures Christians into assimilating their faith with the dominant culture, blending Christian norms and values with the values and norms of Babylon. Thyatira faces the crisis of decision of how to live in this world—a crisis all Christians face. Pergamum also is guilty of spiritual pollution: "You have some there who hold to the teaching of Balaam, who taught Balak to put a stumbling block before the people of Israel" (Rev. 2:14). Balaam lives there along with the Nicolaitans (2:15). In the Old Testament, Balaam, a pagan prophet, was hired by King Balak of Moab to place a curse on Israel. But God prevented him from cursing Israel and the prophet issued a blessing on the nation instead (Num. 22:5–24:25). Nevertheless, Balaam is credited with corrupting Israel by devising a plan to lead the Israelite men astray by having sexual relations with Moabite women (Num. 31:16). The Israelites fell into idolatry and worshiped the god Baal (Num. 25:1–3), and thus Balaam became synonymous in Jewish tradition with cultural accommodation. John's Balaam is similar to the beast from the land in Rev. 13. Both are false prophets (cf. Rev. 16:13; 19:20; 20:10) that lead others into religious harlotry by offering the special privileges of economic, social, and political security. This security is achieved by abandoning faithfulness to God. The crisis of chapters 2 and 3 is worked out in more detail in chapters 12 and 13.

Other imagery in the letters hints at how widespread spiritual pollution is among the churches. Some at Sardis have soiled their clothes (3:4) and are in need of white robes. Others at Pergamum hold to the polluting teaching of the Nicolaitans (2:15), whose name suggests that they conquer people (*nikaō* = conquer; *laos* = people) with their false teachings and practices. The Jezebels, Balaams, and Nicolaitans symbolize the nature of the conflict that lies ahead on this journey. The church must choose, as Barbara Rossing argues, which city it will live in—Babylon or Jerusalem.[34] Will the church accommodate itself to the successes of the dominant, contemporary culture and put down roots in Babylon? Or will it reject spiritual fornication with Babylon in order to enter the heavenly city as spiritual "virgins" (cf. 14:4)?

The rhetoric of anticipatory caution, however, does not mean that the church will go astray on its exodus to the new promised land. It anticipates, rather, the difficulties that lie ahead and the danger of idolatry on the journey. Each of the seven letters ends on a positive note—a promise that the church will share in the new Jerusalem—if the church conquers (*nikaō* in 2:7; 2:11; 2:17; 2:26; 3:5, 12, 21). Conquering is a metaphor for faithfulness to God on this exodus. Ephesus will eat from the tree of life in the paradise of God (2:7; cf. 22:2). Smyrna escapes the second

34. Rossing, *Choice between Two Cities*, passim.

death, a spiritual death (2:11; cf. 20:6, 14). The saints at Pergamum will receive a white stone with a new name on it (2:17), their admission ticket to the new Jerusalem. They will also eat the "hidden manna," an exodus allusion that is applied to the messianic banquet. The church at Thyatira will receive the morning star (2:28; cf. 22:16), which is Christ himself. Those at Sardis will be given clean white robes, the required attire of those who dwell in the heavenly city (3:5; cf. 7:9, 13–14; 22:14). The church at Philadelphia will be made a pillar in the temple of God and will receive the name of the city of God, the new Jerusalem (3:12; cf. 21:2, 10), while the Laodiceans will be given a place with Christ on his throne (3:21; 22:1, 3). These promises are the reward for those who persevere on this journey, a new state of equilibrium at the end of the book.

If chapter 1 establishes the primacy of Christ's authority over the church, chapters 4 and 5 establish the primacy of God's harmonious, orderly rule over the creation. The stable condition in chapter 1 is reinforced in chapters 4 and 5. John looks through an open door in heaven and sees a creation in perfect harmony with its Creator. Albrecht Dürer's *John and the Twenty-four Elders* (see figure 5) portrays the balanced harmony of a theocentric universe by drawing expanding, concentric circles. The one seated on the throne is the focal point with more and more of the creation joining the ranks of those who acknowledge God as worthy of worship until unrestrained adoration wafts throughout the cosmos.[35] The innermost circle consists of four mysterious creatures, hybrids combining characteristics of the world above and this world. They represent the unity of the created order with its Creator. With eyes in front and behind and six wings full of eyes, they have characteristics of another world, the world above. Yet they also share characteristics with this world: one is like a lion, a second like an ox, a third has a face like a human face, and the fourth is like a flying eagle (4:7). The four hybrids—four is a symbolic number representing the earth—are emblematic of the balanced harmony and unity between the world above and this world. Each creature is at the apex of its respective domain: the lion, the king of the beasts; the ox, chief among the domesticated animals; the eagle, premier among the winged animals; and man, preeminent over all creation. What John sees is the way the creation is meant to be ordered—not at enmity with its Creator but in peaceful harmony, worshiping day and night. The

35. Stephen D. Moore, "The Beatific Vision as a Posing Exhibition: Revelation's Hypermasculine Deity," *JSNT* 60 (1995): 27–55, and idem, *God's Gym: Divine Male Bodies of the Bible* (New York: Routledge, 1996), passim, suggests that the vision is similar to a modern-day gym with mirrors to reflect the bodybuilder's physique. In Rev. 4 the creation reflects back on God's character.

circle expands to include the twenty-four elders, kings of heaven who cast their most prized possession before the throne—their crowns—in an act of submission and homage to the One greater than they are.

Photograph courtesy of Wetmore Print Collection, Connecticut College.

Figure 5. Albrecht Dürer (1471–1528), *John and the Twenty-four Elders*, from *The Apocalypse of St. John* (1496–1498).

This heightens the primacy effect of God's harmonious rule, for unlike the kings of the earth who worship the beast (18:3, 9), the kings of heaven acknowledge the only Ruler who is worthy of allegiance and worship.

In chapter 5 myriads of myriads and thousands of thousands of angels surround the throne singing a sevenfold acclamation in "full voice." The circle widens to include more and more of the creation, until "every creature *in heaven* and *on earth* and *under the earth* and *in the sea*" (5:13)—again fourfold—join in song. The rhetorical uses of sevens (5:12), a perfect number; fours (5:13), the number of the earth; and threes (4:8), the number of God, accentuate the unity between heaven and earth. The ever-widening concentric circles establish the primacy that God orders the universe perfectly and, therefore, God alone is worthy of worship. The recency effect of disorder and destruction brought by the beast cannot overturn the primacy of a creation at joyous harmony with its Creator.

Suspense and Surprise

The reader and John, who is both narrator and a character in the story, learn something new at this juncture in the plot, namely, the way God conquers in this world. Suspense is heightened when a "mighty angel" asks, "Who is worthy to open the scroll and break its seals" (5:2). A search of the heavens, earth, and under earth turns up no one, and John responds with despair—for an unopened book means history is at a standstill. He weeps bitterly. Surprise follows suspense. One of the elders consoles John with words of hope, leading him to expect to see a lion: "Do not weep. See, the Lion of the tribe of Judah, the root of David, has conquered, so that he can open the scroll and its seven seals" (5:5). Yet this is not what the prophet sees. "Then I saw between the throne and the four living creatures . . . a Lamb standing as if it had been slaughtered, having seven horns and seven eyes . . ." (5:6). The Lion of Judah (what John hears) is a traditional messianic image of deliverance through military might. Yet this common expectation is not what John sees. "Rather than the lion who tears his prey (Ps. 17:12), Jesus is the torn lamb."[36] The traditional imagery of a lion is important: God provides a messianic deliverer. But the surprise is that the deliverer conquers by his sacrificial death on the cross.

36. Barr, *Tales of the End*, 70; cf. also idem, "The Apocalypse as a Symbolic Transformation of the World: A Literary Analysis," *Int* 38 (1984): 39–50.

The Downward Turn (Falling Action)

A crisis of recognition occurs for ordinary people. Will they awaken from their own spiritual darkness? Will the peoples of the earth recognize God's ways and shun their idolatrous practices?

The first five trumpet plagues of Rev. 8:7–9:21 are modeled on the plagues of Egypt, which hardened Pharaoh's heart and demonstrated God's unlimited power (Exod. 4:21; 7:5; 9:16; 10:1–2).[37]

hail (Rev. 8:7)	hail (Exod. 9:23)
blood (Rev. 8:9)	blood (Exod. 7:20)
poisoned water (Rev. 8:11)	poisoned water (Exod. 7:24)
darkness (Rev. 8:12)	darkness (Exod. 10:22)
locusts (Rev. 9:3)	locusts (Exod. 10:13)

The cataclysmic disruption in the cosmos (earthquakes; poisoned water; moon, sun, and stars darkened) is the earth mourning the spiritual sclerosis of ordinary people. Physical disruption of the earth parallels spiritual and moral darkness in the lives of disoriented persons (see Hos. 4:1–3). A third of the earth, a third of the trees, and a third of the green grass is burned up, and yet the rest of humankind that is spared "did not repent of the works of their hands" (9:20). A fiery mountain is thrown into the sea, and a third of the sea turns to blood and a third of the creatures in the sea die and a third of the ships are destroyed. Still the unrepentant "did not . . . give up worshiping demons" (9:20). And a third of the rivers and springs become bitter, like wormwood, and peoples' thirst is slaked by poisonous water, yet the surviving remnant "did not give up worshiping . . . idols of gold and silver" (9:20). A third of the luminaries—the sun, moon, and stars—are darkened and still the inhabitants of the earth continue to worship "idols of bronze and stone and wood" (9:20). If the heavens above are unable to soften the hearts of the inhabitants, perhaps the earth below can be more persuasive, and thus creatures from the deep are given permission to unleash a hellish nightmare on the land. The abyss is opened and locusts—hybrids that have characteristics of the world below ("tails like scorpions, with stingers") and this world ("faces like human faces")—torture those who do not have the seal of God on their foreheads. Even so the rest of humankind insists on worshiping idols "which cannot see or hear or walk" (9:20). Certainly 200 million troops of cavalry can persuade those left behind

37. See G. K. Beale, *The Book of Revelation: A Commentary on the Greek Text*, NIGTC (Grand Rapids: Eerdmans, 1999), 465.

to repent? Nevertheless, "they did not repent of their murders or their sorceries or their fornication or their thefts" (9:21).

The plot is temporally frustrated, for ordinary people are, without exception, anesthetized to the disruptions in the cosmos. There appears to be no recognition scene for the inhabitants of the earth. Even though the darkening of the luminaries is a cosmic commentary on their own spiritual darkness, they refuse to see. And although polluted water is a sign of their own spiritual pollution, they tenaciously cling to their foul ways of living. The disruption of the order of the earth is an annotation on the ethical, political, and economic disorientation in their own lives, yet they remain hardened to their ways. What happens in the created world seems to make little difference to them because they have created a world with their own hands. The creature has become the goal of creation. The appeal of idolatry is strong because it is something we make with our own hands and embodies our aspirations, hopes, and desires. An idol is at our beck and call, a god that we can touch and control.[38] The Israelites, for example, worshiped the golden calf on their wilderness journey (Exod. 32) because they wanted a god that was tangible, enabling them to deal with the complexities of life, not a God that seemed absent.

Will ordinary people awaken to their self-destructive ways? The dismal effect of the trumpet plagues seems to suggest no, but the plot holds out the possibility that a suffering and persecuted church can do what cosmic signs alone were unable to achieve (see Rev. 11).

A Recognition Scene

Revelation 11 is a *crux interpretum* for the plot, and since the numerous symbols are ambiguous, it is easy to miss the importance of this chapter in the overall narrative. This chapter is a recognition scene for the Christian community. They discover their essential role in God's plan of salvation as a witnessing and persecuted church. John is given a measuring rod and told to measure the temple of God and altar and the worshipers, but he is not to measure the court outside the temple. Instead he leaves the court unmeasured because the nations will trample the "holy city" for forty-two months (11:1–2). Measuring establishes boundaries, while not measuring leaves boundaries undetermined. In Zech. 2:1–2 Jerusalem is measured, and in Ezek. 40–48 the temple is measured. In Rev. 21:15 an angel measures the new Jerusalem. The juxtaposition of measured temple and unmeasured courtyard sets up a contrast between boundaries determined and boundaries left unmarked.

38. Christopher Rowland, *Revelation*, EpCom (London: Epworth, 1993), 117.

But what does this mean? It is an action similar to sealing (see Rev. 7:2–8, where the 144,000, i.e., all Christians, are sealed). Sealing determines ownership while not sealing leaves ownership in question; those who are sealed are protected spiritually while those not sealed are left spiritually unprotected. In this instance, the temple is protected or preserved but the outer courtyard is left unprotected. The measured temple and unmeasured courtyard are two different ways of looking at the same reality, the church universal. The inward reality (the measured temple and altar) is a church protected and secure, like the seven stars in Christ's right hand of chapter 1; but the outward reality (the unmeasured courtyard) is a vulnerable and persecuted church. The tension is developed in the story of two witnesses, who appear unstoppable, yet they are stopped in their tracks; unbeatable, yet they are annihilated; powerful, yet they are defeated (11:3–13). The imagery overwhelms, providing a feast of details that elaborate the church's secure yet vulnerable position in the world. The two witnesses are also referred to as two olive trees (11:4), two lampstands (11:4), and two prophets (11:10). Lampstands are an image of the church (1:20). John mentions two—not seven—because two is the number of witnesses required by the Law (Deut. 19:15) to validate a testimony. John underscores the churches' role as witnesses.

The witnesses are also called prophets—in contrast to the beast from the land which is the false prophet (16:13; 19:20; 20:10)—because the church fulfills the role of a true prophetic voice in the world. The nature of the church's prophetic role is represented by the clothing the prophets wear and by a comparison with two Old Testament figures: Elijah and Moses. They are clothed in sackcloth (11:3), the garb of repentance. Jonah (Jonah 3:6, 8) wears sackcloth as does Jeremiah (Jer 4:8), and in Matt. 11:21 Jesus links sackcloth and ashes with repentance. Like Elijah, the witnesses have power to shut up the sky so that rain may not fall during their days of prophesying (1 Kings 17). But unlike Elijah who called down fire from heaven on his adversaries (2 Kings 1:10–16), the witnesses' fire comes out of their mouths (11:5). Their testimony is their words and deeds, including the powerful testimony of their deaths. Like Moses, the witnesses have the power to turn water into blood and to send plagues upon the earth (11:6; cf. Exod. 7:17–21).

Where they testify is a puzzle. No fewer than four places are mentioned: "the great city"; "Sodom"; "Egypt"; and where the "Lord was crucified" (11:8). Is this Babylon, Jerusalem, or some other city? Or are all four descriptions figurative representations of the same place, the city of this world? "The great city" is used consistently in this book to refer to Babylon (16:19; 17:18; 18:10, 16, 18, 19, 21). It is called Sodom because of Sodom's wickedness and spiritual degradation, and Egypt because the biblical Egypt was a place of captivity and oppression. "Where the

Lord was crucified" suggests Jerusalem but this allusion is also figurative. A place that crucifies Christ is a place that dethrones him and enthrones the beast. Like Sodom and Egypt, Jerusalem is symbolic of Babylon. Thus the two witnesses lie in Babylon, a place of wickedness and captivity where the beast reigns. Many commentators conclude that "the great city," Babylon, is ancient Rome, but there is no compelling reason to limit Babylon to the Roman Empire.[39] Rather, Babylon is the "other" city in this book—the alternative to the heavenly city. It is the city of this world that seeks to build its own empire, a tower of Babel that rises to the heavens. It is the city that seeks to be godlike and thus dethrones Christ. Martin Kiddle describes Babylon as Bunyan's Vanity Fair: "It is the city of this world order, the Earthly City, which included all peoples and tribes and tongues and nations. It is, so to say, the city of civilization, utterly alien to the will of God."[40]

The church's prophetic witness of calling the world to repentance extends for 1260 days (11:3), which is the same as 42 months, the period of the beast's autarchy (13:5) and the time given over to the nations to trample the holy city (11:2). The timeframe is also the same as "time, times, and half a time," or three and a half years, a broken seven. A broken seven is John's way of providing an above and below perspective, a spiritual rather than chronological period of time. Although evil (the beast's reign) appears to run rampant throughout the earth, it is counterbalanced by the powerful testimony of the church. And although the below perspective appears interminable, it is only part of the story. The broken seven shows that the beast's reign and the persecution of the church are limited. Although it is an intense period that tests the Christian community's forbearance on this exodus, it is not unlimited, not a "complete" time, which the perfect number seven would convey.

It is a time of spiritual testing as well as witness. Will the church remain loyal to God during its passion, as Christ remained faithful in his? The words to Smyrna are worth recalling: "Do not fear what you are about to suffer. Beware, the devil is about to throw some of you into prison so that you may be tested, and for ten days you will have affliction. Be faithful until death" (Rev. 2:10). The devil's representative, the beast that comes up from the bottomless pit, makes war on the witnesses, conquers them, and kills them (11:7). This is the first mention of that

39. Among those who argue for Rome are Robert M. Royalty Jr., *The Streets of Heaven: The Ideology of Wealth in the Apocalypse of John* (Macon, Ga.: Mercer University Press, 1998), 65, 69, 71, 188, 207; Barr, *Tales of the End*; 129, 132, 136, 163; Maier, *Apocalypse Recalled*; 179–80; Caird, *Revelation*; 138, 209, 214, 216, 227; R. H. Mounce, *The Book of Revelation*, NICNT (Grand Rapids: Eerdmans, 1998) 220–21, 311.

40. Martin Kiddle, *The Revelation of St. John*, MNTC (New York: Harper and Brothers, 1940), 184–85.

destructive character, the beast from the sea (13:1–10), who persecutes faithful Christians and denies them the dignity of burial (11:9). Their bodies lie in the streets of Babylon for three and a half days, another symbolic number similar to three and a half years, 1260 days, and 42 months. The church's persecution is identical with its period of witness. During the symbolic three and a half days, the inhabitants of the earth gloat, celebrate, and exchange gifts because their source of torment has been defeated. All this is the language of good versus evil. Evil is irritated, annoyed by good's testimony, and the seeming defeat of good brings relief and joy. However, this is another aspect of the plot of discovery. God uses defeat and persecution of the Christian community for good ends.

After three and a half days the two witnesses are resurrected, the "breath of life from God entered them" (11:11), and the people are terrified. The next scene shows that the church's passion—like Christ's passion—is God's way of converting a recalcitrant world: "At that moment there was a great earthquake, and a tenth of the city fell; seven thousand people were killed in the earthquake, and the rest were terrified and gave glory to the God of heaven" (11:13). In this symbolic city of seventy thousand, a tenth of the city fell and seven thousand, or a tithe, were killed. The remnant of nine-tenths is spared and "gave glory to God." This is a complete inversion of Old Testament judgments in which nine-tenths are destroyed and a tithe is spared (cf. Isa. 6:13; Amos 5:3). In 1 Kings 19:14–18—an account from Elijah's ministry—the seven thousand, the faithful minority who refused the seductions of Jezebel to worship Baal, are spared. In Revelation, the exact opposite happens: the majority, nine-tenths, are spared and give glory to God. Whereas the plagues in Rev. 9 resulted only in hardening the hearts of those who are spared (9:20), the testimony of the church accomplishes what the threat of judgment by itself could not do.[41]

The Bottom of the U: A Crisis of Decision

Conflict creates a crisis of decision. The wilderness or desert is a place of trial and divine succor, where two different types of conflicts are resolved. The Israelites, for instance, faced an external conflict with Pharaoh and the Egyptians. They were held in captivity and pursued by Pharaoh to the edges of the Red Sea. The wilderness was a place of divine sanctuary where the Israelites received sustenance (manna; Exod. 16:31–35) and guidance (a cloud during the day and a pillar of fire at

41. See Richard Bauckham, *The Theology of the Book of Revelation* (Cambridge: Cambridge University Press, 1993), 87; Resseguie, *Revelation Unsealed*, 151; Craig R. Koester, *Revelation and the End of All Things* (Grand Rapids: Eerdmans, 2001), 110–11.

night; Exod. 13:20–22; 14:24). It is in-between space, neither here nor there, neither captivity in Egypt nor new life in the promised land.

The Israelites also dealt with inner conflict in the desert, where the loyalties of their heart were tested. The inner conflict can be expressed as a dilemma: Should they follow God on an uncertain journey to an end they cannot see? Or should they follow other gods on a journey to an end that they can determine? Their decision was to turn back to Egypt "in their hearts" and to make a golden calf (Acts 7:38–42; cf. also 1 Cor. 10:1–13; Heb. 3:7–4:7). Captivity in a known place was preferable to freedom in an uncertain place. Revelation 12 develops the external conflict with the dragon and divine deliverance in the wilderness; chapter 13 develops the inner conflict of decision.

Albrecht Dürer's *The Woman Clothed with the Sun* (see figure 6) places conflict with the dragon side by side with divine deliverance of the woman. The source of external conflict is a fierce, terrifying dragon with seven heads and ten horns and seven diadems on his head (an impossible feat to portray literally). The dragon's tail sweeps down a third of the stars out of the heavens, demonstrating his fierce power and his ability to bring chaos to the cosmos. He appears intent upon disrupting the cosmos, bringing disorder wherever there is order, and darkening the universe, which is symbolic of the spiritual darkening he brings to God's creation. Out of one mouth of the dragon, Dürer draws a river of destruction that attempts to sweep away the woman. The seven crowns symbolize the dragon's desire to rule the world, although he must contend with Christ, who has innumerable crowns (Rev. 19:12).

The woman and her offspring stand in the way of the dragon's success, and so he attempts to devour the pregnant woman's newborn child (12:4–5) and make war on the rest of her children (12:17). The woman cries out in pain at the agony of giving birth (12:2)—not the labor of childbirth but spiritual and physical anguish brought on by the pharaoh of this narrative, the dragon, also called "that ancient serpent," "the Devil and Satan, the deceiver of the whole world" (12:9). In the Old Testament, Pharaoh and Egypt are portrayed as the sea dragons, Rahab and Leviathan, which are defeated by God at the exodus deliverance (cf. Ps. 74:13–14; 89:10; Isa. 30:7; 51:9–10). Ezekiel also refers to "Pharaoh king of Egypt" as "the great dragon" (Ezek. 29:3; 32:2–3). The dragon of the Apocalypse, however, is foiled when God provides sanctuary for the woman in the wilderness, "where she has a place prepared by God, so that there she can be nourished for one thousand two hundred sixty days" (12:6). Just as the Israelites received manna in the wilderness, the woman is nourished during this period of anguish that lasts for a symbolic three and a half years or 1,260 days. The woman is an image of the messianic community that encounters trials and tribulations on its pilgrimage to the new promised land (cf. Rev. 12:17, where the identification with the church is clear).

Other exodus imagery is found in Rev. 12:13–17. The woman is given "two wings of the great eagle," which Dürer literally gives her, so that

Photograph courtesy of Wetmore Print Collection, Connecticut College.

Figure 6. Albrecht Dürer (1471–1528), *The Woman Clothed with the Sun*, from *The Apocalypse of St. John* (1496–1498).

she can escape to the desert for "a time, and times, and half a time," or three and a half years, once again a symbolic period of persecution and protection. This is a reference to the exodus deliverance in which God bore the Israelites on eagles' wings to a place of refuge in the desert (Exod. 19:4). The Israelites also were delivered from Pharaoh at the Red Sea when God divided the sea and "broke the heads of the dragons in the waters," crushing the sea monster Leviathan (Ps. 74:13–14). The Red Sea is thus a threatening barrier that blocks the Israelites from safety in the desert, but God removes the threat and turns it into a passageway for deliverance. The Red Sea deliverance is reenacted in Revelation: the dragon spews out of his mouth a torrential flood to drown the woman, but the earth comes to her rescue and opens its mouth to swallow the river (12:16), similar to the earth swallowing the waters of the Red Sea with Moses's separation of the sea (Exod. 15:12). Even the time the woman is in the wilderness—three and a half years, or forty-two months—may be a reference to the forty-two encampments of Israel in the wilderness (Num. 33:5–49).[42]

The plot develops the external conflict with the introduction of two new characters of destruction: the beast from the sea or the abyss (13:1–10; cf. 11:7) and the beast from the land (13:11–17). The inner conflict is implied in John's "call for endurance and faith of the saints" (13:10). The same language is used later when Babylon falls and those who worship the beast drink the wine of God's wrath (14:8–12): "Here is a call for the endurance of the saints, those who keep the commandments of God and hold fast to the faith of Jesus." The inner conflict is a test of loyalty. Not only do the saints have to withstand the onslaught of the beast; they also have to resist the temptation to join the ranks of those who have settled down in Babylon, that is, the temptation of idolatry. "Endurance and faith" recall Christ's language of endurance and steadfastness in chapters 2 and 3. Jesus encourages Ephesus because they "are enduring patiently and bearing up for the sake of [his] name" (2:3), and Pergamum has held fast to Christ's name even though they live where Satan's throne is (2:13). Smyrna is warned, "the devil is about to throw some of you into prison so that you may be tested, and for ten days you will have affliction." They are to remain faithful until death (2:10). Ten, like multiples of ten such as one thousand (the millennium), represents a complete period. Thus ten is similar to the symbolic three and a half days or three and a half years of persecution the church endures. Thyatira is told to endure patiently, to "hold fast to what [they] have" until Jesus comes (2:25). Philadelphia has kept Jesus' word of "patient endurance" and thus will be kept "from the hour of trial that is coming on the whole world to test

42. Beale, *Revelation*, 565–68.

the inhabitants of the earth" (3:10). But they are also warned, "Hold fast to what you have, so that no one may seize your crown" (3:11). This is a test of loyalty.

Both external and inner conflicts create a dilemma for pilgrims on this exodus. The inner conflict concerns whom they will follow. Will they remain faithful to God and follow the Lamb to "springs of the water of life" (7:17), or will they follow the counterfeit god, Satan, and his minions, the beast from the sea and the beast from the land? If they remain faithful to God, they face certain persecution, even death, from the beast. If they follow the beast, they will avoid persecution but will perish in the desert (Babylon is turned into a desert in 18:2) and remain outside the promised land. To the churches that conquer—that is, all Christians who endure faithfully—Jesus promises a share in the new Jerusalem.[43]

The Conflict Further Defined

Satan, who has been thrown out of heaven (12:10–12) and has pursued the woman, now makes war on her offspring, the Christian community (12:18). He stands on the sands of the seashore and calls for reinforcements, and two evil emissaries wage a fierce war on earth. Because of evil's deceptive nature, it is easy to mistake the beasts for good, helping characters, rather than evil, destructive characters. The first beast arises from the sea, the realm of chaos, and has seven heads and ten horns with ten diadems on its horns (13:1; cf. 17:3). The color of this beast, scarlet (17:3), is the color of the dragon (12:3), whose bloodlike appearance accents his destructive nature. Just as Christ is God incarnate, the beast is Satan incarnate. Like Christ, the beast has a mortal wound that has been healed (13:3, 12). This striking mimicry causes the whole earth to follow the beast in amazement and to worship the dragon and the beast (13:3–4). The beast was allowed to exercise authority for forty-two months, the time, according to some accounts, Israel wandered in the wilderness (Num. 33:5–49).[44] In addition to its deceptive character the beast utters blasphemies against God. On its heads are blasphemous names (13:1); it speaks "haughty and blasphemous words" (13:5); and it utters "blasphemies against God, blaspheming his name and his dwelling, that is, those who dwell in heaven" (13:6). The redundancy of the term "blasphemy" underscores the beast's singular vocation to be Godlike: it assaults heaven and its reputation, and in doing so elevates itself as God. The earth's inhabitants are convinced or wooed by the beast's

43. See above, p. 222
44. See Beale, *Revelation*, 647.

demonstration of power and hubris and worship the beast. The saints, who refuse to identify with the beast or receive its mark of ownership, are victims of its violent rage and are conquered (13:7).

John adds mystery by giving the beast a number: "This calls for wisdom: let anyone with understanding calculate the number of the beast, for it is the number of a person. Its number is six hundred sixty-six" (13:18).[45] Attempted identifications of this person have ranged from the emperor Nero to medieval popes to tyrants like Hitler to an eschatological, future antichrist.[46] None of these suggestions is entirely satisfactory. The NRSV translates the Greek (*arithmos anthrōpou*), "the number of a person," as if this number refers to a specific person. But it could also be translated as a collective noun: "humanity's number," or "a human number," or "the number of humankind."[47] The number six falls short of the number of perfection, seven. It is the penultimate, striving for ultimacy. The sixth seal, trumpet, or bowl, for example, looks like the end has appeared, but it is somewhat deceptive. The end only occurs at the seventh bowl. John's call for wisdom is part of the recognition scene of the plot. The mystery to be solved is to recognize that the beast is not an individual antichrist figure (in fact, the term "antichrist" is never used in this narrative) but is a collective reference for humankind in its strivings to be Godlike. Beale is correct: "One way to portray humanity when it perverts God's order is through the depiction of a beast."[48] Whenever humankind attempts to build a world at odds with God's interests, whenever humankind seeks good that becomes a perversion of good, whenever humankind uses power to promote its own interests and goals to the detriment of God's goals and interests, then it becomes the beast. The allure of the beast is that its goals, interests, and strivings seem good or, at the very least, a neutral enterprise devoid of self-interest. It offers ordinary people normal and acceptable goals—economic security, social and political stability—but when these goals become ends

45. The number 666 applies to the beast from the sea described in 13:1–8, not to the beast from the land described in 13:11–17. "15:2 (cf. 20:4) clearly shows that the number is that of the first beast, who is described in 13:1–8, not of the second beast, described in vv. 11–16"; so Beale, *Revelation*, 718.

46. The popular series by Tim LaHaye and Jerry B. Jenkins, *Left Behind: A Novel of the Earth's Last Days* (Wheaton: Tyndale, 1995), 413–15, 426, 435–36, portrays a future antichrist, Nicolae Carpathia.

47. Paul Minear, *I Saw a New Earth: An Introduction to the Visions of the Apocalypse* (Washington: Corpus Books, 1968), 258; Richard Bauckham, *The Climax of Prophecy: Studies on the Book of Revelation* (Edinburgh: T. & T. Clark, 1993), 398–400.

48. Beale, *Revelation*, 723. Also Resseguie, *Revelation Unsealed*, 126: "John is reflecting on the human enterprise of which Rome is a part. The seven-headed beast is humankind's attempt at self-deification—not just Rome's attempt to displace God."

in themselves, they become structures of domination and tyranny that blaspheme God.

The role of the second beast, the beast from the land, is to convince the inhabitants of the earth that the strivings of the beast are for the betterment of society. This beast causes anyone who opposes the first beast and its acts of self-aggrandizement to be repudiated and subjugated. The plot, however, unmasks the deceptive nature of evil and society's call for Christians to conform to its aims. Christians have a different calling on their pilgrimage to the new promised land: "endurance and faith" (13:10).

Reversal and the Upward Turn of the U (Rising Action)

In Rev. 15:2–4 John recalls Israel's deliverance at the Red Sea: "And I saw what appeared to be a sea of glass mixed with fire, and those who had conquered the beast and its image and the number of its name, standing beside the sea of glass with harps of God in their hands" (15:2). The triumph over the beast is likened to the Israelites' escape from captivity in Egypt. The Red Sea appeared to trap the people as Pharaoh's army approached, and thus it represented a threat and a barrier that God turned into a passageway to freedom. The Red Sea was a threshold experience, representing release from captivity in Egypt to freedom in the desert, from oppression to liberation.

A "sea of glass mixed with fire" is a red sea and thus represents a threshold experience from captivity by the beast to freedom in the wilderness.[49] The new Israel conquers the beast by "endurance and faith" (13:10; 14:12) and by fleeing the tyranny of Babylon (18:4). When the Israelites reached the other side of the sea, they sang a song of deliverance, the song of Moses (Exod. 15). Similarly, those who pass through this sea—variously called the 144,000 who have been redeemed (14:3); spiritual "virgins" who follow the Lamb (14:4); the sealed (7:1–8); and the Conquerors (2:7, 11, 17, 26; 3:5, 12, 21)—sing the song of Moses and the song of the Lamb (15:3), a song of deliverance praising divine justice and God's ways.

The **Dénouement**

The *dénouement* describes the upward movement of the U-shaped plot to a new stable condition. It comes in two stages: (1) the destruction and judgment of Babylon and the defeat of the destructive characters of the narrative and (2) the arrival of the pilgrims at the new Jerusalem.

49. Whatever other symbolism John intends by a "sea of glass mingled with fire," he certainly sees this as a description of the Red Sea. For other symbolism, see Beale, *Revelation*, 789–92.

The plot concludes with one last opportunity for ordinary people to awaken to the passing away of the city of this world and to join others on the exodus to the new promised land. The seven bowls are poured out on those who follow the beast—their last opportunity for repentance (cf. 16:9, 11). The sixth angel pours his bowl on the river Euphrates, the river of Babylon, and its waters are dried up so that the kings of the earth can cross and the demonic spirits from the dragon, the beast from the sea, and the beast from the land can battle God at Armageddon or Harmagedon (NRSV). Armageddon is a spiritual battle that takes place at a spiritual locale, Mount Megiddo (*har* is Hebrew for mountain), where evil is routed by good. A mountain is the earth reaching to the heavens and is a natural place for God and humankind to meet (cf. Mount Zion, 14:1). Megiddo is a well-known site where battles took place (cf. Judg. 5:19), and, therefore, the decisive battle between God and Satan, Christ and antichrist takes place on a symbolic mountain called Harmagedon.

The *dénouement,* or resolution of the conflict, reveals the identity of the whore of Babylon and presents the call for the saints to flee this city (Rev. 18:4). In the Old Testament, Babylon is a symbolic city of exile and alienation, of captivity and oppression (Ps. 137; cf. 1 Pet. 5:13). It is a symbol of homelessness for the people of God. Whereas the 144,000—all God's people—enter the new Jerusalem as "virgins" (14:4) because they have resisted illicit collaboration or spiritual fornication with Babylon, the kings of the earth and ordinary people commit fornication and get drunk on Babylon's wine. Dürer's powerful drawing *Harlot of Babylon* (see figure 7) portrays a wealthy woman raising an ornate cup to the heavens in celebration of her many victories. In her cup are "abominations and the impurities of her fornication" (17:4), which have intoxicated the inhabitants of the earth. The woman also is drunk with the blood of the saints (17:6). Both Babylon and her fornicators are numb to the destructiveness of their ways. She sits astride a monstrous seven-headed beast, enthroned on her evil accomplices that give her power and worldwide dominance. The woman and the beast represent the two faces of evil: alluring yet monstrous, pleasurable yet destructive, beguiling yet horrifying. In the left hand corner of the woodcut, one person kneels with folded hands worshiping the counterfeit gods of wealth and power. Kings, merchants, and sailors discuss among themselves their illicit collaboration with the whore, while a mighty angel clutches a millstone overhead, an ominous sign of impending judgment. Yet the kings and others who benefit from this illicit affair conduct business as usual completely unaware of the imminent destruction of their source of power and pleasure.

Babylon is seated on seven hills or mountains, which many commentators understand as a reference to Rome, a city built on seven hills. But

Figure 7. Albrecht Dürer (1471–1528), *Harlot of Babylon*, from *The Apocalypse of St. John* (1496–1498).

more may be at work here than mere identification of the ancient city of Rome. Elsewhere in the book *oros* is translated as "mountain," not "hill" (e.g., 14:1; 21:10) and should be translated as "mountain" in 17:9 (as the NRSV does). The mountain is physically the earth reaching to the heavens where God and humankind meet: the 144,000 gather on Mount Zion (14:1) and the new Jerusalem comes down from heaven and sits on a "great, high mountain" (21:10). But the mountain can also represent the earth reaching to the heavens, striving to displace God. Going up the mountain is associated with human pride, lofty ambition, haughtiness, and self-exaltation in the Old Testament.[50] The artificial mountain, the tower of Babel, for instance, represents the peoples' desire to make a "name" for themselves (Gen. 11:4). It is an affront to God, who responds by coming down and scattering the people. Ascending the mountain is also a way of mocking God's authority. In Isa. 37:24 Sennacherib, king of Assyria, takes chariots up "the heights of the mountains" in order to mock God.

Babylon, perched on seven mountains, is the satanic parody of God's mountain (Mount Zion, new Jerusalem). It represents the earth reaching toward the heavens in a defiant act of self-aggrandizement. Seven reinforces this interpretation since it is a symbolic number in the Apocalypse representing completeness. Babylon, seated on seven mountains, is the whole earth reaching heavenward, just as the tower of Babel lurched toward the heavens to be like God. The whore represents this world-city—not just Rome—a home for those who labor to be Godlike, a counterfeit city that offers the securities of this world but never measures up to God's city, the new Jerusalem.

The city of this world is inherently unstable. Unlike the heavenly city that is built to last, on twelve foundations (21:14), this city sits on water (17:1, 15), a sign of its ephemeral existence. The waters are the world—peoples and multitudes and nations and languages (four = number of creation)—a further indication that Babylon is the city of this world. In the end, evil turns against itself: "The beast will hate the whore . . . will make her desolate and naked . . . and will devour her flesh and burn her up with fire" (17:16). Nakedness, a state of abysmal shame and poverty, reveals the spiritual impoverishment of Babylon.

Christians are urged to flee Babylon. In Rev. 18:4 a voice from heaven cries out,

> Come out of her, my people,
> so that you do not take part in
> her sins,
> and so that you do not share
> in her plagues.

Babylon is destined for destruction, and Christians are to keep their distance from the city and her idolatrous practices. John offers no sug-

50. Robert L. Cohn, *The Shape of Sacred Space: Four Biblical Studies* (Chico, Calif.: Scholars Press, 1981), 33. Some of the examples listed here are drawn from Cohn's study.

gestion as to how the Christian should do this except to resist the lure of wealth and success and participation in the structures of domination and tyranny. This is perhaps why he uses the metaphor of fornication and the image of a whore for Babylon. In the Old Testament Israel is depicted as an unfaithful wife that has broken her marriage covenant to pursue foreign gods (Hos. 2:2). Israel gains wealth and security from this illicit relationship since her lovers give her bread and water, wool and flax, oil and drink (Hos. 2:5). In Rev. 2:20 the lovers of Jezebel benefit by compromise with the dominant culture, and in 2:14 the followers of Balaam practice religious fornication. The appeal of Babylon's grandeur is irresistible for some, for she offers economic security and wealth, political stability, and social acceptance for those willing to bear the mark of the beast. Like the Israelites who made idols in the desert, the pilgrims on this exodus are tempted to settle down in Babylon and benefit from her wealth and power, but only virgins (14:4), not fornicators (21:8), will enter the promised land. Therefore, those on the exodus are urged again to flee Babylon and not take part in her sins.

The Top of the U (a New Stable Condition)

Closure of the story requires resolution of the external and internal conflicts.[51] The plot moves toward the top of the U, a new state of equilibrium. The sources of external conflict—Babylon and the beasts—are destroyed (18:1–24; 19:20), and the pilgrims' perseverance is rewarded with a reign for a symbolic period of a thousand years (20:4–10). The last threats, Satan, Death, and Hades, are thrown into the lake of fire, a second death (20:10, 14). Nothing "accursed" enters the new creation (22:3), and the twelve gates of the city are swung wide open in celebration of the removal of all threats to peace and harmony.

The pilgrims on the journey have resolved the internal tension of whether they will follow the Lamb "to springs of the water of life" (7:17) and remain faithful to God or settle down in Babylon. They have heeded the call to endure patiently (2:3; 3:10; 13:10; 14:12), to be faithful unto death (2:10), to "hold fast" (2:25; 3:11; 14:12), to "wake up" (3:3), and to "repent" (2:5, 16, 21; 3:3, 19). They have ears that listen to what the Spirit says (2:7, 11, 17, 29; 3:6, 13, 22). The cry to flee Babylon has been obeyed (18:4).

51. Closure, of course, could be frustrated or unfulfilled, but that is more common in modern-day narratives than in biblical narratives, although Mark 16:8 is a prominent case of unfulfilled closure in the New Testament. The reader's drive for closure accounts for the existence of textual emendations to Mark 16.

John uses negative language to describe what it is like to be in the new promised land, for no one since Adam and Eve has experienced a place like this before. Death is no more; suffering and mourning and crying no longer exist (21:4). There is no sea of chaos and the monsters from the deep are destroyed (21:1). Darkness is banned in this city of light. No sun or artificial light is needed, for God is the perpetual source of light for the city (22:5), and for the first time people will be able to look upon the face of God and not die (22:4). There is no temple; God and the Lamb are their sanctuary (21:22). Because God's rule is life-sustaining, the river of the water of life flows from the throne of God and of the Lamb. The tree of life with its twelve kinds of fruit—one for each month—symbolizes the banishment of hunger. This city sustains life forever. The pilgrims of this exodus have arrived at the land of milk and honey.

7

Applying Narrative Criticism

7.1 Approaching Texts

Like a complex and intriguing puzzle, narrative analysis enlivens the imagination and offers new ways of looking at the familiar. Rhetoric and setting provide clues to a narrative's organization and structure, and the characters provide texture and depth to the narrative puzzle. The plot adds surprise and suspense. Point of view is the conceptual framework or theme of the puzzle. Just as a puzzle cannot be visualized until it is assembled, the point of a narrative is not realized until the parts are put together.

Narrative criticism looks at a narrative as an organic whole and pays close attention to its nuances. It examines New Testament literature as literature—not as history or dogma, or as social or political criticism. For some, this is a limitation of narrative criticism. But even those who prefer to look at the New Testament through another lens—feminist or postcolonial criticism, for example—would also acknowledge that biblical literature should be examined on its own terms, that is, as literature. An understanding of the literariness of the New Testament and its literary qualities is an important first step for other forms of criticism.

Listed below are several questions that this narrative critic asks of texts. The questions are then applied to a sample narrative—the story of Nicodemus—to show how the puzzle fits together.

Rhetoric

1. Is there repetition of key words, phrases, themes, patterns, situations, or actions?
2. Do verbal threads suggest a theme?
3. What do figures of speech—parallelisms, antitheses, inclusions, chiasms, rhetorical questions—contribute to the narrative?
4. What is the structure of the passage? Do inclusions, changes in setting, changes in characters or actions, or some other change demarcate scenes?
5. How does the narrative begin? How does it end?
6. What images, symbols, paradoxes, similes, or metaphors are present in the text? Do they suggest a theme? How do they contribute to characterization and plot?
7. If a misunderstanding is present, how does it contribute to the narrative theme?
8. Is verbal or dramatic irony used? How does it express a point of view?
9. Do the rhetorical devices "make strange" commonplace or everyday points of view?

Setting

1. What geographical, topographical, or architectural settings are present? Are they symbolic? Do the settings recall important events within Israel's history?
2. Are social, cultural, religious, or political settings present?
3. Are props or MacGuffins used? How do they serve to advance the plot, develop characterization, or elaborate a point of view?
4. What temporal settings are present? What are their symbolic values in the narrative?

Characterization

1. What do the characters say? What are their first words? Is a tone or attitude implied in their speech?
2. What are the characters' actions?
3. How do the settings influence our understanding of characters?
4. What do others say about a character? What titles and descriptive phrases do they use?
5. What traits does a character exhibit? Is the character round or flat? Does a character develop (a dynamic character) or does she

or he remain the same at the end as at the beginning (a static character)? If the character develops, what contributes to his or her development? How is the character different at the end?

6. Does a change in character provide a clue to the plot or the point of the narrative?
7. Is a character a foil that illumines or "makes strange" another character's traits?
8. What does the narrator say about a character? What comments and annotations does the narrator make? Does the narrator provide inside views of what a character thinks, feels, or believes? Is a character's worldview made known? Does it confirm or clash with the overall narrative worldview?

Point of View

1. What is the evaluative or ideological point of view of the narrative?
2. Does the narrator provide asides that reveal a character's point of view? How does the character's point of view confirm or clash with the narrative point of view or with other characters' point of view?
3. What inside views of a character's thoughts, feelings, and motivations are offered (psychological point of view)?
4. Is a point of view expressed in what a character says or does? How does this point of view compare with the overall ideological perspective of the narrative?
5. How does the narrative point of view defamiliarize or "make strange" a character's perspective?

Plot

1. What conflicts are present in the narrative? Are there conflicts with nature, with the supernatural, or with society? Does the character have internal conflicts?
2. Does a character face a dilemma? How does the character solve it?
3. If the plot is U-shaped (comic plot), what is the initiating action or crisis that begins the downward turn? What is the reversal that turns the falling action into a rising action? Is there a recognition scene? What is the *dénouement* or resolution of the crisis?

4. If the plot is an inverted U (tragic plot), what is the character's fatal flaw (*hamartia*) that contributes to the downward turn? Or what circumstances contribute to disaster? Is there a recognition scene? If not, what important factor should the character have seen but failed to see?
5. If the plot pattern is a recognition plot, what important discovery does the character make? In what ways does this discovery change the character's point of view? How is reality viewed differently?
6. What is the point of the narrative? Does it present a new point of view, a change in behavior, or a discovery of something important that could not be seen before?

Reader

1. What expectations are developed in the (implied) reader, and how are they fulfilled or frustrated as the narrative proceeds?
2. What new, defamilarized point of view results from the fulfilling or overturning of expectations?
3. What is the new point of view the narrator wants the reader to adopt? How is the reader to view reality differently?

7.2 A Reading of the Story of Nicodemus

The story of Nicodemus in the Gospel of John is examined in terms of structure, rhetoric, setting, character, point of view, and plot.[1] Part 1 of the following analysis is an overview of the narrative features, while part 2 is a close reading. It is recommended that the student list or identify rhetorical devices, settings, aspects of characterization and plot, and so forth in summary form before proceeding with a close reading of the entire narrative. The overview allows the student to identify the parts that contribute to the whole. The close reading should follow the narrative progression, commenting on the rhetoric and other aspects of the narrative while noting how they contribute to the whole.

1. On Nicodemus see Jouette M. Bassler, "Mixed Signals: Nicodemus in the Fourth Gospel," *JBL* 108 (1989): 635–46; Wayne A. Meeks, "The Man from Heaven in Johannine Sectarianism," *JBL* 91 (1972): 44–72; Dennis Sylva, "Nicodemus and His Spices (John 19:39)," *NTS* 34 (1988): 148–51; James L. Resseguie, *The Strange Gospel: Narrative Design and Point of View in John*, BIS 56 (Leiden: Brill, 2001), 120–27; Craig R. Koester, *Symbolism in the Fourth Gospel: Meaning, Mystery, Community*, 2nd ed. (Minneapolis: Fortress, 2003), 45–47; R. Alan Culpepper, *Anatomy of the Fourth Gospel: A Study in Literary Design* (Philadelphia: Fortress, 1993), 134–36.

Part One: An Overview

Nicodemus appears three times in the Gospel of John: one lengthy appearance at 3:1–21 and two cameo appearances at 7:50–52 and 19:39. The *structure* of John 3 can be divided into three sections that are based on Nicodemus's three speeches in 3:2, 4, 9 and Jesus' responses. The structure is thus: (1) verses 1–3; (2) verses 4–8; and (3) verses 9–21.[2] The entire section is held together by an *inclusion* that signals one of Nicodemus's defining traits:

> 3:2 [Nicodemus] came to Jesus *by night*.
> 3:19 And this is the judgment, that the light has come into the world, and people loved *darkness*.

Other *rhetorical devices* of the Nicodemus narrative include: two double entendres (3:3, 7; 3:8), a misunderstanding that builds on the first double entendre (3:3–21), a simile (3:8), rhetorical questions (3:10; 7:51), and Old Testament imagery (3:14). The narrator uses repetition and verbal threads: "come" (3:2; 7:50; 19:39), "by night" (3:2; 19:39), "how" (3:4, 9), "to be able" (3:2, 4, 9), and "again/above" (3:3, 7). One verbal thread not only signals the beginning of Jesus' discourses but also marks a new point of view: "very truly, I tell you" (3:3, 5, 11).

The primary *setting* of John 3 is temporal ("by night"). In Nicodemus's second appearance the setting is religious ("festival of Booths" or "Tabernacles," 7:2), and in the third, the setting is social (the burial of Jesus). A geographical setting at 7:52 ("Galilee") is symbolic. In the third vignette, a prop or MacGuffin (prodigious burial spices) teases the reader's imagination (19:39).

Two *ideological points of view* surface at the level of words and phrases in John 3. Nicodemus's point of view is made to seem strange, and Jesus' point of view undermines the naturalized or everyday point of view. The narrator's point of view and Jesus' point of view merge as one in John 3. In fact, translators have difficulty determining when Jesus speaks and when the narrator speaks in his own voice. The NRSV and NIV, for example, use quotation marks to indicate that Jesus speaks in 3:16–21, while the RSV and TNIV attribute the same words to the narrator. An ideological point of view is also expressed in Nicodemus's defense of Jesus at 7:51, and in the lavish amount of burial spices that he brings in 19:39.

The narrator's *characterization* of Nicodemus relies on both showing and telling. Nicodemus's speech, discourse patterns, and actions and what Jesus says to him are the primary methods of showing his characteriza-

2. Raymond E. Brown, *The Gospel according to John,* 2 vols. (New York: Doubleday, 1966–1970), 1:136–37.

tion. The narrator's descriptive comments and annotations serve to tell. If John 3 were the only narrative about Nicodemus, he would remain a flat, static character, but the subsequent cameos suggest a dynamic or developing character who adopts a new point of view in his encounter with the divine.

The narrator develops a typical *U-shaped plot*: Nicodemus descends into darkness at the beginning, but his encounter with the light marks a reversal (a peripety) that is realized in his later appearances. The primary conflict is within himself: what should he do? His dilemma is whether to abandon the relative safety of darkness so that the light may reveal his deeds, or retreat into darkness. The point of the Nicodemus narrative is found in his characterization and the progression of the plot.

Part Two: A Close Reading

Nicodemus, Scene 1 (John 3:1–21)

Nicodemus progressively develops as a character in each of his three appearances. Initially, the narrator tells us about Nicodemus, using a string of epithets that places him within Israel's dominant culture: "Now there was a Pharisee named Nicodemus, a leader of the Jews" (3:1). He is identified as a man ("now there was a *man*," not translated in NRSV), then a Pharisee, and finally a "leader of the Jews." He is also named, and in 3:10, Jesus confirms his prominent status by calling him a "teacher of Israel." Whether he is a member of the Jewish Sanhedrin, the highest governing body of the Jewish people,[3] is uncertain, but as C. K. Barrett notes, the narrator "seems to be collecting titles in order to portray Nicodemus as a representative Jew."[4] He is certainly a representative of the elite within Israel, although it may be going too far to say that he is a "representative Jew."

The temporal setting of John 3 is symbolic. Nicodemus comes to Jesus "by night," which accents one of the Pharisee's defining traits: his lack of understanding. Just as Jesus and "light" are mutually defining terms in this Gospel, Nicodemus and "night" are complimentary terms. A repetition of the temporal setting underscores this connection, for in John 19:39, the narrator once again mentions that Nicodemus, "who had at first come to Jesus *by night*," brings a hundred pounds of burial spices. Light and darkness are opposing points of view in John. The light shines and the darkness cowers. Darkness can neither overcome

3. Ibid., 1:130.
4. C. K. Barrett, *The Gospel according to John: An Introduction with Commentary and Notes on the Greek Text*, 2nd ed. (Philadelphia: Westminster, 1978), 204.

nor comprehend the light (John 1:5).[5] Light, in fact, reveals the dark side of humanity.

> And this is the judgment, that *the light* has come into the world, and people loved *darkness* rather than *light* because their deeds were evil. For all who do evil hate *the light* and do not come to *the light*, so that their deeds may not be exposed. But those who do what is true come to *the light*, so that it may be clearly seen that their deeds have been done in God. (John 3:19–21)

When Nicodemus comes to Jesus "by night," he comes uncomprehending and unseeing.

Yet his nocturnal appearance is balanced by a positive action: "he *came* to Jesus" (3:2). Just as Nicodemus and "night" are mutually defining terms, Nicodemus and "coming to Jesus" are also complementary terms. In John 1, coming to Jesus is an important first step in becoming a follower. Two disciples ask him where he is staying; he says, "*Come* and see," and they "*came* and saw where he was staying" (1:39). And when Nathanael asks Philip whether anything good can come out of Nazareth, Philip says, "*Come* and see" (1:46).[6] When Nicodemus defends Jesus before the other Pharisees in John 7:50, the narrator once again notes that he came to Jesus: "Nicodemus, who *had gone* [or *had come*] to Jesus before."[7]

Thus far Nicodemus's characterization is ambiguous. He approaches Jesus at night, yet he comes. He comes in darkness, yet he seeks the light. Will he return to the darkness because his deeds are evil and because he hates the light? Or will he remain in the light so that it may be clearly seen that his deeds have been done in God? The narrative introduction makes Nicodemus an in-between figure, straddling two separate worlds or points of view. He has one foot in the dominant religious culture which is uncomprehending, even hostile to Jesus' point of view. On the other hand, he comes to the light.

The narrator uses Nicodemus's speech patterns to show us his development as a character. In his first speech, he takes the initiative to seek out Jesus, and his discourse is marked by self-confidence, even overconfidence: "Rabbi, we know that you are a teacher who has come from God; for no one can do these signs that you do apart from the presence of God" (3:2). It may be that Nicodemus uses the first person plural, "we know," because he is speaking as a representative

5. The word *katalambanō* is a double entendre that means both "understand" and "overcome." See §2.5 above.

6. Noted by Bassler, "Mixed Signals," 637.

7. The verb, *erchomai*, is the same as in 3:2. One manuscript (א*) omits the phrase "who had gone."

of a group who have believed because of Jesus' miraculous "signs" (cf. 2:23). In favor of this interpretation is Jesus' own speech pattern. In 3:7, he lectures Nicodemus in the second person singular ("do not be astonished that I said to you [s.]") but switches to the plural to conclude his lecture ("You [pl.] must be born from above"). The second person plural suggests that he is addressing a wider audience. Yet Nicodemus's use of the first person plural could be a way of adding a note of authority to his voice and accentuating his self-importance. Just as the blind man of John 9 bolsters his voice with the first person plural (cf. 9:31), Nicodemus calls attention to what he knows: because Jesus performs signs, he comes from God. In favor of this interpretation is Jesus' usage of the first person plural in 3:11, which parodies Nicodemus's speech: "Very truly, I tell you, *we speak* of what *we know* and [*we*] *testify* to what *we have seen*." Whether the Pharisee is speaking as an individual or as a representative of a group, he is speaking as one who knows or thinks he knows where Jesus comes from. But his knowing is undermined and his speech collapses into stunned amazement in his encounter with Jesus. As the narrative progresses, his speech becomes more halting and his lack of understanding more apparent.

Jesus uncovers Nicodemus's lack of understanding with a double entendre that is part of a Johannine misunderstanding. First, Jesus' pronouncement is ambiguous: "Very truly, I tell you, no one can see the kingdom of God without being born *from above* [or *again*]" (3:3). The narrator intends both meanings of *anōthen*. One must be born "from above," that is, a spiritual birth, and a person must be "born again," that is, a second birth.[8] Second, Nicodemus takes a wrong turn and provides an amusingly literal interpretation. He assumes that being "born again" is a physical rebirth: "How can anyone be born after having grown old? Can one enter a second time into the mother's womb and be born?" (3:4). According to Nicodemus's point of view, rebirth or salvation is a human enterprise, and therefore, his response to Jesus is uncomprehending. The misunderstanding is an intentional Johannine rhetorical device, which Rudolf Bultmann elaborates:

> For the Evangelist chooses this grotesque way of making it abundantly clear that rebirth is in no sense a natural process, an event which can be set in motion by man himself. In the human sphere it is impossible for there to be anything like a rebirth. For rebirth means—and this is precisely the point made by Nicodemus' misunderstanding—something more than an

8. See §2.5 above.

> improvement in man; it means that man receives a new *origin*, and this is manifestly something which he cannot give himself.[9]

Nicodemus's speech patterns parallel his increasing misunderstanding. Whereas he begins with bold confidence and speaks twenty-four words in the UBS Greek text in 3:2, his discourse shrinks to eighteen words in 3:4. Further, he abandons the assurance of the declarative for the tentativeness of the interrogative. He goes from a confident "we know" to an incredulous "how," from self-confidence to amazement, from assertion to stumbling.

Third, Jesus clarifies the misunderstanding in 3:9–21. But, if Nicodemus's final speech pattern is any indication of his level of understanding, it is apparent that he retreats back into darkness. His dialogue ends with a query of deflated consternation, a mere four words in Greek: "How can these things be?" (3:9).[10] Jesus' rhetorical question underscores his lack of understanding, rendering him speechless: "Are you a teacher of Israel, yet you do not understand these things?" (3:10).

While Nicodemus's speech is bewildered ("How can?" in 3:4a and 9, "can one?" in 3:4b), Jesus' speech is marked by solemn assertions: "Very truly, I tell you" (3:3, 5, 11). And while Nicodemus's speech progressively withers, Jesus' discourse progressively expands. He speaks sixteen words in the UBS Greek text in 3:3; seventy words in 3:5–8; and over two hundred words in 3:9–21. While Nicodemus fades into the background, Jesus moves to the foreground. In scene 1, the characterization of Nicodemus and the symbolism of darkness develop the downward turn of a U-shaped plot. As Jouette Bassler notes, "Jesus' response to Nicodemus suggests that the negative symbolism of the darkness dominates the narrative here. Indeed, if this were the only scene with Nicodemus, one would have to place him on the side of those whose intentions are good but who are ultimately left in the dark."[11] Will the downward slope of the U-shaped plot be reversed, or will the plot continue on to disaster?

Nicodemus, Scene 2 (John 7:50–52)

As Bassler notes, if John 3 were the only appearance of Nicodemus in the Gospel, we would have to conclude that he remains in darkness, perplexed by Jesus' point of view and still wondering what he needs to do to be born again/from above. He is an inquirer but not a follower; a

9. Rudolf Bultmann, *The Gospel of John: A Commentary*, trans. G. R. Beasley-Murray (Philadelphia: Westminster, 1971), 136–37.

10. Although five words in English, it is four words in Greek.

11. Bassler, "Mixed Signals," 638.

seeker but not a disciple. Fortunately, Nicodemus reappears in John 7 and we can learn more of his characterization.

The religious setting of Nicodemus's second appearance is the Jewish festival of Booths (John 7:2), where Jesus announces on the last day of the festival that anyone who comes to him and believes in him will receive thirst-quenching water: "As the scripture has said, 'Out of his belly[12] shall flow rivers of living water'" (7:38, author's translation). His pronouncement on the "great day" of the festival causes a rift among those present. Some believe he is the Messiah, but others argue that the Messiah does not come from Galilee. The chief priests and Pharisees wonder why the temple police do not arrest Jesus. Then they say: "Has any one of the authorities or of the Pharisees believed in him?" (7:48). Their question expects a resounding no: none of the authorities or of the Pharisees, including Nicodemus, has believed in Jesus. But is this an instance of Johannine irony?[13] Do the Pharisees say more than they know? Does one of the Pharisees, Nicodemus, believe in him? This is one interpretation of their question. The only way to decide is to examine Nicodemus's characterization more closely.

The narrator first *tells* us about Nicodemus and then *shows* us what he says:

> Nicodemus, who had gone to him [i.e. Jesus] before, and who was one of them, asked, "Our law does not judge people without first giving them a hearing to find out what they are doing, does it?" (John 7:50–51)

The narrator tells us that he is "one of them," that is, one of the Pharisees, who accuse the temple police of being deceived by Jesus (7:47). Nicodemus speaks up and questions the propriety of arresting Jesus without first giving him a fair hearing. His objection recalls Jesus' ideological point of view in 7:24: "Do not judge by appearances, but judge with right judgment."[14] Nicodemus calls for right judgment rather than appearance judgment. Although he is "one of them," he stands apart from them by speaking up and offering a different point of view from that of the other Pharisees. His implicit defense of Jesus causes the other Pharisees to wonder if he also comes from Galilee: "Surely you are not also from Galilee, are you?" (7:52). Their question cannot be taken literally, for in scene 1 Nicodemus is from Jerusalem. It must be taken figuratively, as a type of slur against Nicodemus. But in what sense is Nicodemus

12. What is the antecedent of "his," the believer or Jesus? The NRSV translates it as "out of the believer's heart" shall flow living waters.

13. Paul Duke, *Irony in the Fourth Gospel* (Atlanta: John Knox, 1985), 80–81, and Culpepper, *Anatomy*, 135–36, understand the question ironically.

14. Bassler, "Mixed Signals," 639–40.

a "Galilean?" Jouette Bassler has shown that in the Fourth Gospel a Galilean "is tantamount . . . to . . . [a] believer."[15] Their accusation is perhaps ironical: "Surely you are not also a believer, are you?" But the reader is left wondering if they say more than they know or if their words are merely sarcastic, labeling him a Galilean but knowing full well that he is "one of them." Their question recalls Nathanael's suspicion that nothing good can come out of Galilee. But unlike Nathanael, they do not come and see.

The characterization of Nicodemus in John 7 places the Pharisee in an in-between position, neither among the adversaries of Jesus nor among his supporters. The narrator's comments reinforce his in-between status. He is "one of them," but he is also one "who had come to Jesus before"—a positive endorsement that parallels the disciples' "coming to" Jesus (cf. 1:39, 47). He is not yet a believer, for he has neither made a confession of faith nor has he actually sided with Jesus. Yet his legal query implies that he is adopting a new point of view that is not captive to appearance judgment but is determined by right judgment. His in-between status—neither here nor there—places him in the company of the authorities mentioned in John 12:42–43.

> Nevertheless many, even of the authorities, believed in him. But because of the Pharisees they did not confess it, for fear that they would be put out of the synagogue; for they loved human glory more than the glory that comes from God.

At best, Nicodemus, like Joseph of Arimathea (19:38), is a "secret disciple," which means that he is still in the dark.

Nicodemus, Scene 3 (John 19:39)

Will Nicodemus move beyond his in-between status? Will he take the final step and become a follower of Jesus and be cast out of the synagogue as one who confesses that Jesus is the Messiah (cf. 9:22)? In Nicodemus's final vignette, the narrator shows us what he does, without a clarifying commentary on his actions:

> Nicodemus, who had at first come to Jesus by night, also came, bringing a mixture of myrrh and aloes, weighing about a hundred pounds. (19:39)

The setting is the anointing of Jesus' body for burial after Joseph of Arimathea, "who was a disciple of Jesus, though a secret one because

15. Ibid., 640; idem, "The Galileans: A Neglected Factor in Johannine Community Research," *CBQ* 43 (1981): 243–57.

of his fear of the Jews" (19:38), asks Pilate for the body of Jesus. The narrator's description of Joseph is positive and negative at the same time. Although he is a disciple of Jesus, the concessive phrase "though a secret one because of his fear of the Jews" casts him in a negative light. Secret disciples avoid open commitment because they fear the Jewish leadership, which has agreed to expel from the synagogue anyone who confesses Jesus as the Messiah (9:22). Secret disciples love "human glory [honor]" more than "the glory [honor] that comes from God" (12:43). Secret disciples are noncommittal, saying both yes and no, wanting to be disciples but avoiding a public stance that leads to excommunication from the synagogue. Secret disciples "allow the decision of faith to be affected by a desire for personal security."[16] Yet what the narrator shows us concerning Joseph's actions attenuates what he tells us. He publicly requests the body of Jesus from Pilate, which is tantamount to an open confession of his intention to be a disciple of Jesus. His actions ameliorate the narrator's description. Although he was a secret disciple, he is one no longer.

Nicodemus enters the scene bearing a sumptuous amount of embalming spices, nearly a hundred pounds of myrrh and aloes. The burial spices are a MacGuffin, a puzzling prop that is key to the plot, or at least to our understanding of Nicodemus. Is the staggering amount of spices a confirmation of his personal awakening, a public demonstration of his resolve to follow Jesus? Or does it prove that the Pharisee is more confused than ever: he hopes to preserve a dead Jesus from corruption by lavishly anointing his body. Wayne Meeks, for instance, regards the large amount of burial spices as a "ludicrous" expression that shows that Nicodemus "has not understood the 'lifting up' of the Son of Man."[17] David Rensberger concurs: "Nicodemus shows himself capable only of burying Jesus, ponderously and with a kind of absurd finality, so loading him down with burial as to make it clear that Nicodemus does not expect a resurrection any more than he expects a second birth."[18]

Meeks and Rensberger illustrate the difficulty of drawing firm conclusions solely based on what a narrator shows us. Robert Alter argues that a character's actions and appearance are at the lower end of the scale of explicitness and certainty for conveying information about his or her motives, attitudes, and moral nature.[19] Thus a "character revealed through actions or appearance—leaves us substantially in the realm

16. Barrett, *John*, 433.

17. Meeks, "The Man from Heaven," 55. Cf. also Sylva, "Nicodemus and His Spices (John 19:39)," 148–51.

18. David Rensberger, *Johannine Faith and Liberating Community* (Philadelphia: Westminster, 1988), 40.

19. Alter, *Art of Biblical Narrative*, 116–17.

of inference."[20] If what the narrator shows us about Nicodemus leaves us in the arena of inference, does what he tells us clarify Nicodemus's intentions? The narrator tells us that Nicodemus "had at first come to Jesus by night." Coming to Jesus, as we have already seen, is a positive endorsement in this Gospel; it represents a first step toward discipleship. The nighttime reference is also important. Nicodemus came to Jesus secretly ("by night") on the first occasion, but this time he comes before nightfall, publicly, on the day of Preparation (19:31, 42). No longer does he come under the cloak of darkness, imperceptive and unresponsive to the light of revelation; rather he comes during the day, accompanied by "a disciple of Jesus," who makes his own daring confession of faith by asking for the body of Jesus. Nicodemus's public appearance is tantamount to making a confession of faith, and the staggering amount of spices and oils for burial is a convincing display of homage. The MacGuffin demonstrates that he understood who Jesus is—for he provides a burial fit for a king.[21] His "gift [is] so extravagant that it would have been suitable only for a king."[22] Jesus said earlier in the Gospel that "when I am lifted up from the earth, [I] will draw all people to myself" (12:32). "Lifted up" (*hypsōthēnai*) is a double entendre in John (cf. 3:14; 8:28; 12:32–33).[23] One meaning of *hypsōthēnai* describes the way Jesus is to die by being lifted up on a stake, while another meaning refers to his death as his glorification (cf. 7:39; 11:4).[24] In this narrative we see the effects of Jesus being lifted up. Joseph of Arimathea is drawn out of secrecy, while Nicodemus is drawn out of darkness.

Nicodemus is a complex, round character with conflicting traits. He is a Pharisee, a leader of the Jews, a teacher of Israel, a member of the ruling class. He has a voice both in the dominant culture and in the narrative, unlike, for instance, the woman who anoints Jesus in Luke 7, who has a voice neither in the culture nor in the narrative. He comes to Jesus at night, a significant detail in this Gospel, which plays continuously on the symbolism of light and darkness. He represents the uncomprehending nature of darkness: he does not understand what it means to be born again (3:4–9). He believes a second birth is something that humans can accomplish, and thus he is like modern men and women who seize upon

20. Ibid., 117.

21. Those who see Nicodemus's enormous amount of burial spices as a positive testimonial include: Brown, *John*, 2:959–60; idem, *The Death of the Messiah: From Gethsemane to the Grave*, 2 vols. (New York: Doubleday, 1994), 2:1261; Francis J. Moloney, *Glory Not Dishonor: Reading John 13–21* (Minneapolis: Fortress, 1998), 149; Mark W. G. Stibbe, *John*, RNBC (Sheffield: JSOT Press, 1993), 197.

22. Koester, *Symbolism*, 228.

23. See Resseguie, *Strange Gospel*, 55.

24. See BDAG, s.v. ὑψόω.

self-help and self-improvement programs as a way to wholeness and happiness. Although he is part of the religious establishment that has opposed Jesus—another layer of darkness in John's Gospel—he *comes* to Jesus. He comes to the light. He is an inquirer and a seeker—not unlike many who seek and inquire about Jesus today.

"How can anyone be born again after having grown old" has many facets to it, both individually and corporately. How can an institution be rejuvenated when it has become senescent? How can a way of thinking, a point of view be enlivened when it has become jaded? How can the old become new? The answer is found in Nicodemus's characterization.

Nicodemus moves from speech in scenes 1 and 2 to actions in scene 3. He does not speak at all in scene 3, nor does he need to speak. His actions speak for him. His development as a character is subtle, which makes him more lifelike. The narrator does not hit us over the head with the obvious or tell us the point of the story, like a moralizing preacher. Instead, we discover Nicodemus's complexity, and in that discovery we learn something about ourselves. The downward slope of the U-shaped plot makes a sharp turn or peripety in this scene. Nicodemus steps forward with a public display of affection that shows he has understood what it means to be born from above/again. The point of view of the narrator is that it is possible for one who has grown old to be born anew; that the light overcomes the darkness; and that a human way of thinking can be transformed.

7.3 Conclusion

Narrative criticism breathes new life into a familiar passage such as the Nicodemus narrative. Its holistic approach to biblical literature, with its painstaking analysis of the nuances of the text, makes narratives that seem staid and commonplace appear fresh and new. It enlivens the imagination and strips away the "film of familiarity"[25] that clouds our apprehension of biblical narratives. Narrative criticism looks at narratives as works of art in which every piece fits together to form the whole, and the whole accents the splendor of every piece.

25. Robert Scholes, *Structuralism in Literature: An Introduction* (New Haven: Yale University Press, 1974), 174. Scholes is quoting Coleridge.

Bibliography

1. Introduction

Narrative Criticism of the Bible

Aichele, George, et.al., eds. *The Postmodern Bible.* New Haven: Yale University Press, 1995.

Alter, Robert. *The Art of Biblical Narrative.* New York: Basic Books, 1981.

Aune, David E. "Narrative Criticism." Pages 315–17 in *The Westminster Dictionary of New Testament and Early Christian Literature and Rhetoric.* Louisville: Westminster John Knox, 2003.

Brooke, G. J., and J.-D. Kaestli. *Narrativity in Biblical and Related Texts.* Bibliotheca Ephemeridum Theologicarum Lovaniensium 149. Leuven: Leuven University Press, 2000.

Culpepper, R. Alan. *Anatomy of the Fourth Gospel: A Study in Literary Design.* Philadelphia: Fortress, 1983.

Fishbane, Michael. *Text and Texture: Close Readings of Selected Biblical Texts.* New York: Schocken Books, 1979.

Gros Louis, Kenneth R. R., ed. *Literary Interpretations of Biblical Narratives.* 2 vols. Abingdon: Nashville, 1974–1982.

Kort, Wesley A. *Story, Text, and Scripture: Literary Interests in Biblical Narrative.* University Park, Pa.: Pennsylvania State University Press, 1988.

Malbon, Elizabeth Struthers. "Narrative Criticism: How Does the Story Mean?" Pages 23–49 in *Mark and Method: New Approaches in Biblical Studies*. Edited by Janice Capel Anderson and Stephen D. Moore. Minneapolis: Fortress, 1992.

Marguerat, Daniel, and Yvan Bourquin. *How to Read Bible Stories: An Introduction to Narrative Criticism*. London: SCM, 1999.

McKnight, Edgar V., and Elizabeth Struthers Malbon, eds. *The New Literary Criticism and the New Testament*. Valley Forge: Trinity Press International, 1994.

Merenlahti, Petri. *Poetics for the Gospels? Rethinking Narrative Criticism*. Study of the New Testament and Its World. London: T. & T. Clark, 2002.

Powell, Mark Allan. *What Is Narrative Criticism?* Minneapolis: Fortress, 1990.

Rhoads, David. "Narrative Criticism and the Gospel of Mark." *Journal of the American Academy of Religion* 50 (1982): 411–34.

———. *Reading Mark, Engaging the Gospel*. Minneapolis: Fortress, 2004.

———. "The Syrophoenician Woman in Mark: A Narrative-Critical Study." *Journal of the American Academy of Religion* 62 (1992): 342–75.

Rhoads, David, Joanna Dewey, and Donald Michie. *Mark as Story: An Introduction to the Narrative of a Gospel*. 2nd ed. Minneapolis: Fortress, 1999.

Narrative Theory

Abbott, H. Porter. *The Cambridge Introduction to Narrative*. Cambridge: Cambridge University Press, 2002.

Bal, Mieke. *Narratology: Introduction to the Theory of Narrative*. Translated by Christine van Boheeman. Toronto: University of Toronto, 1985.

Booth, Wayne C. *The Rhetoric of Fiction*. 2nd ed. Chicago: University of Chicago Press, 1983.

Chatman, Seymour. *Story and Discourse: Narrative Structure in Fiction and Film*. Ithaca: Cornell University Press, 1978.

Eagleton, Terry. *Literary Theory: An Introduction*. Minneapolis: University of Minnesota, Press, 1983

Genette, Gérard. *Narrative Discourse: An Essay in Method*. Translated by Jane L. Lewin. Ithaca: Cornell University Press, 1980.

Graff, Gerald. *Literature against Itself: Literary Ideas in Modern Society*. Chicago: University of Chicago Press, 1979.

Kermode, Frank. *The Genesis of Secrecy: On the Interpretation of Narrative*. Cambridge: Harvard University Press, 1979.

Lentricchia, Frank. *After the New Criticism*. Chicago: University of Chicago Press, 1980.

Martin, Wallace. *Recent Theories of Narrative*. Ithaca: Cornell University Press, 1986.

Phelan, James. *Reading People, Reading Plots: Character, Progression, and the Interpretation of Narrative*. Chicago: University of Chicago Press, 1989.

Rimmon-Kenan, Shlomith. *Narrative Fiction: Contemporary Poetics*. London: Routledge, 1983.

Robey, David. "Anglo-American New Criticism." Pages 65–83 in *Modern Literary Theory: A Comparative Theory*. Edited by Ann Jefferson and David Robey. Totowa, N.J.: Barnes & Noble, 1982.

Scholes, Robert, and Robert Kellogg. *The Nature of Narrative*. New York: Oxford University Press, 1966.

Sternberg, Meir. *Expositional Modes and Temporal Ordering in Fiction*. Baltimore: Johns Hopkins University Press, 1978.

———. *The Poetics of Biblical Narrative: Ideological Literature and the Drama of Reading*. Indiana Literary Biblical Series. Bloomington: Indiana University Press, 1985.

Reader-Response Criticism

Aichele, George, et al., eds. *The Postmodern Bible*. New Haven: Yale University Press, 1995.

Carter, Warren. *Matthew: Storyteller, Interpreter, Evangelist*. Rev. ed. Peabody, Mass.: Hendrickson, 2004.

Fowler, Robert M. "Reader-Response Criticism: Figuring Mark's Reader." Pages 50–83 in *Mark and Method: New Approaches in Biblical Studies*. Edited by Janice Capel Anderson and Stephen D. Moore. Minneapolis: Fortress, 1992.

Holub, Robert C. *Reception Theory: A Critical Introduction*. New Accents. London: Methuen, 1984.

Iser, Wolfgang. "Indeterminacy and the Reader's Response in Prose Fiction." Pages 1–45 in *Aspects of Narrative*. Edited by J. Hillis Miller. New York: Columbia University Press, 1971.

———. *The Implied Reader: Patterns of Communication in Prose Fiction from Bunyan to Beckett*. Baltimore: Johns Hopkins University Press, 1974.

———. *The Act of Reading: A Theory of Aesthetic Response*. Baltimore: Johns Hopkins University Press, 1978.

Mailloux, Steven. "Learning to Read: Interpretation and Reader-Response Criticism." *Studies in the Literary Imagination* 12 (1979): 93–108.

———. *Interpretive Conventions: The Reader in the Study of American Fiction*. Ithaca: Cornell University Press, 1982.

Moore, Stephen D. *Literary Criticism and the Gospels: The Theoretical Challenge*. New Haven: Yale University Press, 1989.

Powell, Mark Allan. *Chasing the Eastern Star: Adventures in Biblical Reader-Response Criticism*. Louisville: Westminster John Knox, 2001.

Rabinowitz, Peter J. *Before Reading: Narrative Conventions and the Politics of Interpretation*. Ithaca: Cornell University Press, 1987.

Resseguie, James L. "Reader-Response Criticism and the Synoptic Gospels." *Journal of the American Academy of Religion* 52 (1984): 307–24.

Suleiman, Susan R., and Inge Crosman, eds. *The Reader in the Text: Essays on Audience and Interpretation*. Princeton: Princeton University Press, 1980.

Tompkins, Jane P., ed. *Reader-Response Criticism: From Formalism to Post-Structuralism*. Baltimore: Johns Hopkins University Press, 1980.

Defamiliarization

Erlich, Victor. *Russian Formalism: History-Doctrine*. 3rd ed. New Haven: Yale University Press, 1981.

Jefferson, Ann. "Russian Formalism." Pages 16–37 in *Modern Literary Theory: A Comparative Introduction*. Edited by Ann Jefferson and David Robey. Totowa, N.J.: Barnes & Noble, 1982.

Resseguie, James L. "Automatization and Defamiliarization in Luke 7:36–50." *Literature and Theology: An Interdisciplinary Journal of Theory and Criticism* 5 (1991): 137–50.

———. "Defamiliarization and the Gospels." *Biblical Theology Bulletin* 20 (1990): 147–53.

———. "Defamiliariztion in the Gospels." *Mosaic: A Journal for the Interdisciplinary Study of Literature* 21 (1988): 25–35

———. *The Strange Gospel: Narrative Design and Point of View in John*. Biblical Interpretation Series 56. Brill: Leiden, 2001.

Martin, Wallace. *Recent Theories of Narrative*. Ithaca: Cornell University Press, 1986.

Shklovsky, Victor. "Art as Technique." Pages 3–24 in *Russian Formalist Criticism: Four Essays*. Translated by Lee T. Lemon and Marion J. Reis. Lincoln, Neb.: University of Nebraska Press, 1965.

2. Rhetoric

Handbooks of Literary Terms

Abrams, M. H. *A Glossary of Literary Terms*. 7th ed. Fort Worth: Harcourt Brace College Publishers, 1999.

Aune, David E. *The Westminster Dictionary of New Testament and Early Christian Literature and Rhetoric*. Louisville: Westminster John Knox, 2003.

Bailey, James L., and Lyle D. Vander Broek. *Literary Forms in the New Testament: A Handbook*. Louisville: Westminster John Knox, 1992.

Fowler, Roger, ed. *A Dictionary of Modern Critical Terms*. Rev. and enl. ed. London: Routledge & Kegan Paul, 1987.

Harmon, William and C. Hugh Holman. *A Handbook to Literature*. 8th ed. Upper Saddle River, N.J.: Prentice Hall, 1999.

Lausberg, Heinrich. *Handbook of Literary Rhetoric: A Foundation for Literary Study*. Edited by David E. Orton and R. Dean Anderson. Translated by Matthew T. Bliss et al. Leiden: Brill, 1998.

Repetition

Anderson, Janice Capel. *Matthew's Narrative Web: Over, and Over, and Over Again*. Journal for the Study of the New Testament: Supplement Series 91. Sheffield: Sheffield Academic Press, 1994.

Merenlahti, Petri. *Poetics for the Gospels? Rethinking Narrative Criticism*. London: T. & T. Clark, 2002.

Neirynck, Frans. *Duality in Mark: Contributions to the Study of Markan Redaction*. Rev. ed. Bibliotheca Ephemeridum Theologicarum Lovaniensium 31. Louvain: Louvain University Press, 1988.

Resseguie, James L. *Revelation Unsealed: A Narrative Critical Approach to John's Apocalypse*. Biblical Interpretation Series 32. Leiden: Brill, 1998.

Witherup, Ronald D. "Cornelius Over and Over and Over Again: 'Functional Redundancy' in the Acts of the Apostles." *Journal for the Study of the New Testament* 49 (1993): 45–66.

Type Scenes

Alter, Robert C. *The Art of Biblical Narrative*. New York: Basic Books, 1981.

Brant, Jo-Ann A. “Husband Hunting: Characterization and Narrative Art in the Gospel of John.” *Biblical Interpretation* 4 (1996): 205–23.

Eslinger, L. “The Wooing of the Woman at the Well: Jesus, the Reader, and Reader-Response Criticism.” *Literature and Theology: An Interdisciplinary Journal of Theory and Criticism* 1 (1987): 167–83.

Petersen, John. *Reading Women's Stories: Female Characters in the Hebrew Bible.* Minneapolis: Fortress, 2004.

Rhoads, David. *Reading Mark: Engaging the Gospel.* Minneapolis: Fortress, 2004.

Framing Narratives

Edwards, James R. “Markan Sandwiches: The Significance of Interpolations in Markan Narratives.” *Novum Testamentum* 31 (1989): 193–216.

Kermode, Frank. *The Genesis of Secrecy: On the Interpretation of Narrative.* Cambridge: Harvard University Press, 1979.

Shepherd, Tom. “The Narrative Function of Markan Intercalation.” *New Testament Studies* 41 (1995): 522–40.

Chiasm

Aune, David E. *The Westminster Dictionary of New Testament and Early Christian Literature and Rhetoric.* Louisville: Westminster John Knox, 2003.

Breck, John. “Biblical Chiasmus: Exploring Structure for Meaning.” *Biblical Theology Bulletin* 17 (1987): 70–74.

Dart, John. *Decoding Mark.* Harrisburg, Pa.: Trinity Press International, 2003.

Dewey, Joanna. *Markan Public Debate: Literary Technique, Concentric Structure, and Theology in Mark 2:1–3:6.* Society of Biblical Literature Dissertation Series 48. Chico, Calif.: Scholars Press, 1980.

Heil, John Paul. “The Chiastic Structure and Meaning of Paul's Letter to Philemon.” *Biblica* 82 (2001): 178–206.

Luter, A. Boyd. and Michelle V. Lee. “Philippians as Chiasmus: Key to the Structure, Unity, and Theme Questions.” *New Testament Studies* 41 (1995): 89–101.

Resseguie, James L. “New Testament as Literature.” Pages 815–17 in *Eerdmans Dictionary of the Bible*. Edited by D. N. Freedman. Grand Rapids: Eerdmans, 2000.

Stock, Augustine. "Chiastic Awareness and Education in Antiquity." *Biblical Theology Bulletin* 14 (1984): 23–27.

Thomson, Jan H. *Chiasmus in the Pauline Letters.* Journal for the Study of the New Testament: Supplement Series 111. Sheffield: Sheffield Academic Press, 1995.

Simile and Metaphor

Caird, G. B. *The Language and Imagery of the Bible.* Philadelphia: Westminster, 1980.

Richards, I. A. *The Philosophy of Rhetoric.* New York: Oxford University Press, 1936.

Double Entendre and Misunderstanding

Bultmann, Rudolf. *The Gospel of John: A Commentary.* Translated by G. R. Beasley-Murray, R. W. N. Hoare, and J. K. Riches. Philadelphia: Westminster, 1971.

Culpepper, R. Alan. *Anatomy of the Fourth Gospel: A Study in Literary Design.* Philadelphia: Fortress, 1983.

Resseguie, James L. *The Strange Gospel: Narrative Design and Point of View in John.* Biblical Interpretation Series 56. Leiden: Brill, 2001.

Irony

Abrams, M. H. *A Glossary of Literary Terms.* 7th ed. New York: Harcourt Brace College Publishers, 1999.

Booth, Wayne C. *A Rhetoric of Irony.* Chicago: University of Chicago Press, 1974.

Camery-Hoggatt, Jerry. *Irony in Mark's Gospel: Text and Subtext.* Society for New Testament Studies Monograph Series 72. Cambridge: Cambridge University Press, 1992.

Duke, Paul D. *Irony in the Fourth Gospel.* Atlanta: John Knox, 1985.

Fowler, Robert M. *Let the Reader Understand: Reader-Response Criticism and the Gospel of Mark.* Minneapolis: Fortress, 1991.

Fowler, Roger, ed. *A Dictionary of Modern Critical Terms.* Rev. and enl. ed. London: Routledge & Kegan Paul, 1987.

Muecke, D. C. *The Compass of Irony.* London: Methuen, 1969.

O'Day, Gail R. *Revelation in the Fourth Gospel: Narrative Mode and Theological Claim.* Philadelphia: Fortress, 1986.

Resseguie, James L. *The Strange Gospel: Narrative Design and Point of View in John.* Biblical Interpretation Series 56. Leiden: Brill, 2001.

Smith, Stephen H. *A Lion with Wings: A Narrative-Critical Approach to Mark's Gospel.* The Biblical Seminar 38. Sheffield: Sheffield Academic Press, 1996.

Carnivalesque

Bakhtin, Mikhail. *Problems of Dostoevsky's Poetics.* Edited and translated by Caryl Emerson. Theory and History of Literature 8. Minneapolis: University of Minnesota Press, 1984.

———. *Rabelais and His World.* Translated by Hèléne Iswolsky. Bloomington: Indiana University Press, 1984.

Brawley, Robert L. *Text to Text Pours Forth Speech: Voices of Scripture in Luke-Acts.* Indiana Studies in Biblical Literature. Bloomington: Indiana University Press, 1995.

Craig, Kenneth M. *Reading Esther: A Case for the Literary Carnivalesque.* Literary Currents in Biblical Interpretation. Louisville: Westminster John Knox, 1995.

3. Setting

Desert

Cohn, Robert L. *The Shape of Sacred Space: Four Biblical Studies.* American Academy of Religion Studies in Religion 23. Chico, Calif.: Scholars Press, 1981.

Kittel, Gerhard. "ἔρημος κτλ." Pages 657–60 in vol. 2 of *Theological Dictionary of the New Testament.* Edited and translated by Geoffrey W. Bromiley. 10 vols. Grand Rapids: Eerdmans, 1964–1976.

Lane, Belden C. *The Solace of Fierce Landscapes: Exploring Desert and Mountain Spirituality.* New York: Oxford, 1998.

Mauser, Ulrich W. *Christ in the Wilderness: The Wilderness Theme in the Second Gospel and Its Basis in the Biblical Tradition.* Studies in Biblical Theology 39. Naperville, Ill.: Allenson, 1963.

Malbon, Elizabeth Struthers. *Narrative Space and Mythic Meaning in Mark.* New Voices in Biblical Studies Series. San Francisco: Harper & Row, 1986.

Radl, Walter. "ἔρημος." Pages 51–52 in vol. 2 of *Exegetical Dictionary of the New Testament*. Edited by Horst Balz and Gerhard Schneider. 3 vols. Grand Rapids: Eerdmans, 1990–1993.

Resseguie, James L. *Spiritual Landscape: Images of the Spiritual Life in the Gospel of Luke*. Peabody, Mass.: Hendrickson, 2004.

———. *Revelation Unsealed: A Narrative Critical Approach to John's Apocalypse*. Biblical Interpretation Series 32. Leiden: Brill, 1998.

Sea

Heil, John Paul. *Jesus Walking on the Sea: Meaning and Gospel Functions of Matthew 14:22–33, Mark 6:45–52, and John 6:15b–21*. Analecta biblica 87. Rome: Biblical Institute Press, 1981.

Kratz, Reinhard. "θάλασσα." Pages 127–28 in vol. 2 of *Exegetical Dictionary of the New Testament*. Edited by Horst Balz and Gerhard Schneider. 3 vols. Grand Rapids: Eerdmans, 1990–1993.

Malbon, Elizabeth Struthers. "The Jesus of Mark and the Sea of Galilee." *Journal of Biblical Literature* 103 (1984): 363–77.

———. *Narrative Space and Mythic Meaning in Mark*. San Francisco: Harper & Row, 1986.

Mountain

Cohn, Robert L. *The Shape of Sacred Space: Four Biblical Studies*. American Academy of Religion Studies in Religion 23. Chico, Calif.: Scholars Press, 1981.

Donaldson, Terence L. *Jesus on the Mountain: A Study in Matthean Theology*. Journal for the Study of the New Testament: Supplement Series 8. Sheffield: Journal for the Study of the Old Testament Press, 1985.

Foerster, Werner. "ὄρος." Pages 475–87 in vol. 5 of *Theological Dictionary of the New Testament*. Edited and translated by Geoffrey W. Bromiley. 10 vols. Grand Rapids: Eerdmans, 1964–1976.

Malbon, Elizabeth Struthers. *Narrative Space and Mythic Meaning in Mark*. New Voices in Biblical Studies. San Francisco: Harper & Row, 1986.

Swartley, Willard M. *Israel's Scripture Traditions and the Synoptic Gospels: Story Shaping Story*. Peabody, Mass.: Hendrickson, 1994.

Way

Best, Ernest. *Following Jesus: Discipleship in the Gospel of Mark*. Journal for the Study of the New Testament: Supplement Series 4. Sheffield: Journal for the Study of the Old Testament Press, 1981.

Donahue, John R. *The Theology and Setting of Discipleship in the Gospel of Mark*. Milwaukee: Marquette University Press, 1983.

Michaelis, Wilhelm. "ὁδός." Pages 65–91 in vol. 5 of *Theological Dictionary of the New Testament*. Edited and translated by Geoffrey W. Bromiley. 10 vols. Grand Rapids: Eerdmans, 1964–1976.

Resseguie, James L. *Spiritual Landscape: Images of the Spiritual Life in the Gospel of Luke*. Peabody, Mass.: Hendrickson, 2004.

Architectural

Bal, Mieke. *Narratology: Introduction to the Theory of Narrative*. Translated by Christine van Boheemen. Toronto: University of Toronto Press, 1985.

Malbon, Elizabeth Struthers. *Narrative Space and Mythic Meaning in Mark*. New Voices in Biblical Studies. San Francisco: Harper & Row, 1986.

Michel, O. "ναός." Pages 880–89 in vol. 4 of *Theological Dictionary of the New Testament*. Edited and translated by Geoffrey W. Bromiley. 10 vols. Grand Rapids: Eerdmans, 1964–1976.

Resseguie, James L. *The Strange Gospel: Narrative Design and Point of View in John*. Biblical Interpretation Series 56. Leiden: Brill, 2001.

Shrenk, Gottlob. "ἱερός, κτλ." Pages 221–47 in vol. 3 of *Theological Dictionary of the New Testament*. Edited and translated by Geoffrey W. Bromiley. 10 vols. Grand Rapids: Eerdmans, 1964–1976.

Stibbe, M. W. G. *John as Storyteller: Narrative Criticism and the Fourth Gospel*. Cambridge: Cambridge University Press, 1992.

Props

Hamel, Gildas. *Poverty and Charity in Roman Palestine, First Three Centuries C.E.* Berkeley: University of California Press, 1990.

Resseguie, James L. *Spiritual Landscape: Images of the Spiritual Life in the Gospel of Luke*. Peabody, Mass.: Hendrickson, 2004.

———. *Revelation Unsealed: A Narrative Critical Approach to John's Apocalypse*. Biblical Interpretation Series 32. Leiden: Brill, 1998.

Temporal

Powell, Mark Allan. *What Is Narrative Criticism?* Minneapolis: Fortress: 1990.

Social

Lenski, Gerhard E. *Power and Privilege: A Theory of Social Stratification.* McGraw-Hill Series in Sociology. New York: McGraw-Hill, 1966.

Moxnes, Halvor. *The Economy of the Kingdom: Social Conflict and Economic Relations in Luke's Gospel.* Philadelphia: Fortress, 1988.

Resseguie, James L. *Spiritual Landscape: Images of the Spiritual Life in the Gospel of Luke.* Peabody, Mass.: Hendrickson, 2004.

Rhoads, David. "Social Criticism: Crossing Boundaries." Pages 135–61 in *Mark and Method: New Approaches in Biblical Studies*. Edited by Janice Capel Anderson and Stephen D. Moore. Minneapolis: Fortress, 1992.

———. *Reading Mark, Engaging the Gospel.* Minneapolis: Fortress, 2004.

Smith, Dennis E. *From Symposium to Eucharist: The Banquet in the Early Christian World.* Minneapolis: Fortress, 2003.

Political

Derrett, J. Duncan M. "Contributions to the Study of the Gerasene Demoniac." *Journal for the Study of the New Testament* 3 (1979): 2–17.

Dormandy, Richard. "The Expulsion of Legion: A Political Reading of Mark 5:1–20." *Expository Times* 111 (2000): 335–37.

Myers, Ched. *Binding the Strong Man: A Political Reading of Mark's Story of Jesus.* Maryknoll, N.Y.: Orbis Books, 1988.

Horsley, Richard A. *Hearing the Whole Story: The Politics of Plot in Mark's Gospel.* Louisville: Westminster John Knox, 2001.

4. Character

Characterization in Literature

Chatman, Seymour. *Story and Discourse: Narrative Structure in Fiction and Film.* Ithaca: Cornell University Press, 1978.

Docherty, Thomas. *Reading (Absent) Character: Towards a Theory of Characterization in Fiction.* Oxford: Clarendon, 1983.

Harvey, Walter J. *Character and the Novel.* Ithaca: Cornell University Press, 1965.

Hochman, Baruch. *Character in Literature.* Ithaca: Cornell University Press, 1985.

Springer, Mary Doyle. *A Rhetoric of Literary Character: Some Women of Henry James.* Chicago: University of Chicago Press, 1978.

Characterization in Biblical Literature

Culpepper, R. Alan. *Anatomy of the Fourth Gospel: A Study in Literary Design.* Philadelphia: Fortress, 1983.

Darr, John A. *On Character Building: The Reader and the Rhetoric of Characterization in Luke-Acts.* Louisville: Westminster John Knox, 1992.

Koester, Craig R. *Symbolism in the Fourth Gospel: Meaning, Mystery, Community.* 2nd ed. Minneapolis: Fortress, 2003.

Kort, Wesley A. *Story, Text, and Scripture: Literary Interests in Biblical Narrative.* University Park, Pa.: Pennsylvania State University Press, 1988.

Malbon, Elizabeth Struthers. *In the Company of Jesus: Characters in Mark's Gospel.* Louisville: Westminster John Knox, 2000.

Malbon, Elizabeth Struthers, and Adele Berlin, eds. *Characterization in Biblical Literature*. *Semeia* 63 (1993).

Marguerat, Daniel, and Yvan Bourquin. *How to Read Bible Stories: An Introduction to Narrative Criticism.* Translated by John Bowden. London: SCM, 1999.

Powell, Mark Allan. *What Is Narrative Criticism?* Minneapolis: Fortress, 1990.

Resseguie, James L. *Spiritual Landscape: Images of the Spiritual Life in the Gospel of Luke.* Peabody, Mass.: Hendrickson, 2004.

———. *Strange Gospel: Narrative Design and Point of View in John*. Biblical Interpretation Series 56. Leiden: Brill, 2001.

Rhoads, David, Joanna Dewey, and Donald Michie. *Mark as Story: An Introduction to the Narrative of a Gospel.* 2nd ed. Minneapolis: Fortress, 1999.

Rhoads, David and Kari Syreeni, eds. *Characterization in the Gospels: Reconceiving Narrative Criticism.* Journal for the Study of the New Testament: Supplement Series 184. Sheffield: Sheffield Academic Press, 1999.

Character Types

Abrams, M. H. *A Glossary of Literary Terms*. 7th ed. Fort Worth: Harcourt Brace College Publishers, 1999.

Forster, E. M. *Aspects of the Novel.* New York: Harcourt Brace Jovanovich, 1927.

Harmon, William, and C. Hugh Holman. *A Handbook to Literature*. 8th ed. Upper Saddle River, N.J.: Prentice Hall, 1999.

Dynamic and Static Characters

Arp, Thomas R. *Perrine's Story and Structure.* 9th ed. Fort Worth: Harcourt Brace College Publishers, 1998.

Docherty, Thomas. *Reading (Absent) Character: Towards a Theory of Characterization in Fiction.* Oxford: Clarendon Press, 1983.

Interior Monologues and Inside Views

Booth, Wayne C. *The Rhetoric of Fiction.* 2nd ed. Chicago: University of Chicago Press, 1983.

Cohn, Dorrit. *Transparent Minds: Narrative Modes for Presenting Consciousness in Fiction.* Princeton: Princeton University Press, 1978.

Rhoads, David, Joanna Dewey, and Donald Michie. *Mark as Story: An Introduction to the Narrative of a Gospel.* 2nd ed. Minneapolis: Fortress, 1999.

Sellew, Philip. "Interior Monologue as a Narrative Device in the Parables of Luke." *Journal of Biblical Literature* 111 (1992): 239–53.

Showing and Telling

Abrams, M. H. *A Glossary of Literary Terms*. 7th ed. Fort Worth: Harcourt Brace College Publishers, 1999.

Alter, Robert. *The Art of Biblical Narrative.* New York: Basic Books, 1981.

Harmon, William, and C. Hugh Holman. *A Handbook to Literature*. 8th ed. Upper Saddle River, N.J.: Prentice Hall, 1999.

Petersen, John. *Reading Women's Stories: Female Characters in the Hebrew Bible.* Minneapolis: Fortress, 2004.

Sternberg, Meir. *The Poetics of Biblical Narrative: Ideological Literature and the Drama of Reading.* Bloomington: Indiana University Press, 1985.

5. Point of View

Booth, Wayne C. *The Rhetoric of Fiction.* 2nd ed. Chicago: University of Chicago Press, 1983.

Chatman, Seymour. *Story and Discourse: Narrative Structure in Fiction and Film.* Ithaca: Cornell University Press, 1978.

Culpepper, R. Alan. *Anatomy of the Fourth Gospel: A Study in Literary Design.* Philadelphia: Fortress, 1983.

Kingsbury, Jack Dean. *Matthew as Story.* 2nd ed. Minneapolis: Fortress, 1988.

Lanser, Susan Sniader. *The Narrative Act: Point of View in Prose Fiction.* Princeton: Princeton University Press, 1981.

Lotman, J. M. "Point of View in a Text." *New Literary History* 6 (1975): 339–52.

Powell, Mark Allan. *What Is Narrative Criticism?* Minneapolis: Fortress, 1990.

Petersen, Norman R. "'Point of View' in Mark's Narrative." *Semeia* 12 (1978): 97–121.

Stanzel, Franz K. *A Theory of Narrative.* Translated by Charlotte Goedsche. Cambridge: Cambridge University Press, 1984.

Focalization

Bal, Mieke. *Narratology: Introduction to the Theory of Narrative*. Translated by Christine van Boheemen. Toronto: University of Toronto Press, 1985.

Rimmon-Kenan, Shlomith. *Narrative Fiction: Contemporary Poetics.* London: Routledge, 1983.

Standards of Judgment

Rhoads, David. *Reading Mark: Engaging the Gospel.* Minneapolis: Fortress, 2004.

Rhoads, David, Joanna Dewey, and Donald Michie. *Mark as Story: An Introduction to the Narrative of a Gospel.* 2nd ed. Minneapolis: Fortress, 1999.

Four Planes of Point of View

Lanser, Susan Sniader. *The Narrative Act: Point of View in Prose Fiction.* Princeton: Princeton University Press, 1981.

Resseguie, James L. *The Strange Gospel: Narrative Design and Point of View in John.* Biblical Interpretation Series 56. Leiden: Brill, 2001.

Uspensky, Boris. *A Poetics of Composition: The Structure of the Artistic Text and Typology of a Compositional Form.* Translated by V. Zavarin and S. Wittig. Berkeley: University of California Press, 1973.

Inside View and Asides

Cohn, Dorrit. *Transparent Minds: Narrative Modes for Presenting Consciousness in Fiction.* Princeton: Princeton University Press, 1978.

Sellew, Philip. "Interior Monologue as a Narrative Device in the Parables of Luke." *Journal of Biblical Literature* 111 (1992): 239–53.

Sheeley, Steven M. *Narrative Asides in Luke-Acts.* Journal for the Study of the New Testament: Supplement Series 72. Sheffield: Journal for the Study of the Old Testament Press, 1992.

6. Plot

Plot in the New Testament

Carter, Warren. "Kernels and Narrative Blocks: The Structure of Matthew's Gospel." *Catholic Biblical Quarterly* 54 (1992): 463–81.

Culpepper, R. Alan. *Anatomy of the Fourth Gospel: A Study in Literary Design.* Philadelphia: Fortress, 1983.

Kingsbury, Jack Dean. "The Plot of Matthew's Story." *Interpretation* 46 (1992): 347–56.

Matera, Frank J. "The Plot of Matthew's Gospel." *Catholic Biblical Quarterly* 49 (1987): 233–53.

Powell, Mark Allan. "The Plots and Subplots of Matthew's Gospel." *New Testament Studies* 38 (1992): 187–204.

Plot Theory

Aristotle. *Poetics*. Edited and translated by Stephen Halliwell. Loeb Classical Library. Vol. 23 of *Aristotle*. Cambridge: Harvard University Press, 1995.

Chatman, Seymour. *Story and Discourse: Narrative Structure in Fiction and Film*. Ithaca: Cornell University Press, 1978.

Crane, R. W. "The Concept of Plot." Pages 233–43 in *Approaches to the Novel: Materials for a Poetics*. Edited by Robert Scholes. Rev. ed. San Francisco: Chandler, 1966.

Forster, E. M. *Aspects of the Novel*. New York: Harcourt, Brace, 1927.

———. "The Plot." Pages 218–32 in *Approaches to the Novel: Materials for a Poetics*. Edited by Robert Scholes. Rev. ed.. San Francisco: Chandler, 1966.

Goodman, Paul. *The Structure of Literature*. Chicago: University of Chicago Press, 1954.

Masterplots

Abbott, H. Porter. *The Cambridge Introduction to Narrative*. Cambridge: Cambridge University Press, 2002.

Plot Patterns

Abrams, M. H. *A Glossary of Literary Terms*. 7th ed. Fort Worth: Harcourt Brace College Publishers, 1999.

Bilezikian, Gilbert G. *The Liberated Gospel: A Comparison of the Gospel of Mark and Greek Tragedy*. Grand Rapids: Baker, 1977.

Brant, Jo-Ann A. *Dialogue and Drama: Elements of Greek Tragedy in the Fourth Gospel*. Peabody, Mass.: Hendrickson, 2004.

Frye, Northrop. *The Great Code: The Bible and Literature*. New York: Harcourt Brace Jovanovich, 1982.

Ska, Jean Louis. *"Our Fathers Have Told Us": Introduction to the Analysis of Hebrew Narratives*. Rome: Pontificio Istituto Biblico, 1990.

Smith, Stephen H. *A Lion with Wings: A Narrative-Critical Approach to Mark's Gospel*. The Biblical Seminar 38. Sheffield: Sheffield Academic Press, 1996.

Via, Dan O. *The Parables: Their Literary and Existential Dimension*. Philadelphia: Fortress, 1967.

Fabula *and* Sjužet

Martin, Wallace. *Recent Theories of Narrative.* Ithaca: Cornell University Press, 1986.

Resseguie, James L. "Defamiliarization in the Gospels." *Mosaic: A Journal for the Interdisciplinary Study of Literature* 21 (1988): 25–35.

Shklovsky, Victor. "On the Connection between Devices of *Syuzhet* Construction and General Stylistic Devices." Pages 48–72 in *Russian Formalism*. Edited by S. Bann and J. E. Bowlt. New York: Barnes & Noble, 1973.

Sternberg, Meir. *Expositional Modes and Temporal Ordering in Fiction.* Baltimore: Johns Hopkins University Press, 1978.

Primacy and Recency Effects

Gombrich, E. H. *Art and Illusion: A Study in the Psychology of Pictoral Representation.* Princeton: Princeton University Press, 1969.

Martin, Wallace. *Recent Theories of Narrative.* Ithaca: Cornell University Press, 1986.

Perry, Menakhem. "Literary Dynamics: How the Order of a Text Creates Its Meanings." *Poetics Today* 1 (1979): 35–64, 311–61.

Subject Index

Index of Modern Authors

Scripture Index

Malachi

Matthew

Mark

John

Acts

Romans

1 Corinthians

2 Corinthians

Galatians

Ephesians

Philippians

Colossians

2 Thessalonians

1 Timothy

Hebrews

1 Peter

1 John

Revelation